Quality
Information
Systems

Fatemeh Zahedi
University of Wisconsin – Milwaukee

boyd & fraser publishing company

I(T)P   An International Thomson Publishing Company

Danvers • Albany • Bonn • Boston • Cincinnati • Detroit • London • Madrid • Melbourne
Mexico City • New York • Paris • San Francisco • Singapore • Tokyo • Toronto • Washington

To my daughter Lara, and to Love, that give
my life quality, peace, and beauty.

Executive Editor: James H. Edwards
Editorial Assistant: Beth A. Sweet
Production Editor: Barbara J. Worth
Marketing Coordinator: Daphne J. Meyers
Manufacturing Coordinator: Tracy Megison
Production Services, Composition,
and Interior Design: Integre Technical Publishing Co., Inc.
Cover Design: Diana Coe
Cover Photo: Kevin C. Beebe/Tony Stone Worldwide

I(T)P   The ITP™ logo is a trademark under license.

Printed in the United States of America

This book is printed on recycled, acid-free paper that meets Environmental Protection
Agency standards.

For more information, contact boyd & fraser publishing company:

boyd & fraser publishing company
One Corporate Place Ferncroft Village
Danvers, Massachusetts 01923, USA

International Thomson Publishing Europe
Berkshire House 168-173
High Holborn
London, WC1V 7AA, England

Thomas Nelson Australia
102 Dodds Street
South Melbourne 3205
Victoria, Australia

Nelson Canada
1120 Birchmont Road
Scarborough, Ontario
Canada M1K 5G4

International Thomson Editores
Campose Eliseos 385, Piso 7
Col. Polanco
11560 Mexico D.F. Mexico

International Thomson Publishing GmbH
Konigswinterer Strasse 418
53227 Bonn, Germany

International Thomson Publishing Asia
221 Henderson Road
#05-10 Henderson Building
Singapore 0315

International Thomson Publishing Japan
Hirakawacho Kyowa Building, 3F
2-2-1 Hirakawacho
Chiyoda-ku, Tokyo 102, Japan

1 2 3 4 5 6 7 8 9 10   MT   8 7 6 5 4

Library of Congress Cataloging-in-Publication Data

Zahedi, Fatemeh, 1945–
   Quality information systems / Fatemeh Zahedi.
     p. cm.
   Includes index.
   ISBN 0-7895-0061-2
   1. Management information systems. 2. Total quality management.
3. System design. I. Title.
T58.6.Z32 1995
658.4'038—dc20   94-37172
                                           CIP

Contents

Preface ◆ vii

1 **Introduction** ◆ 1

1.1 Total Quality Management 3
1.2 Quality Awards and Standards 12
1.3 Quality vs. Traditional Information Systems 16

2 **IS Leadership with Vision and Empowerment** ◆ 31

2.1 Vision 32
2.2 Creating Vision 38
2.3 Employee Empowerment and Involvement 48

3 **Continuously Improving Information Systems** ◆ 73

3.1 Paradigms for Improvement in Information Systems 74
3.2 Policy Deployment in Information Systems 83
3.3 Continuous Improvement in Information Systems 90
3.4 Tools for Problem Identification 99

4 **Benchmarking for Information Systems** ◆ 111

4.1 The Importance of Benchmarking 112
4.2 Benchmark Planning for Information Systems 117
4.3 Collecting Benchmarking Information 122
4.4 Analysis of Benchmarking Information 129
4.5 Using the Benchmarking Results 141

5 **Quality Management in Requirements Analysis** ◆ 155

5.1 Requirements Analysis in Information Systems 156
5.2 Customer Focus in Quality Information Systems 159
5.3 Requirements Analysis Methods 163
5.4 Requirements and Technical Analysis Using Quality
Function Deployment (QFD) 166

5.5   Weight Assignments via Analytic Hierarchy Process (AHP)   177
5.6   Software Requirements Analysis   183

6   Quality Management in the Design of IS   ◆   193

6.1   Designing Value into IS Through Reengineering   195
6.2   Designing Utility in IS by Applying QFD   207
6.3   Engineering Usability into IS   212
6.4   Reducing Cost by Applying Taguchi Methods   216

7   Quality in Manufacturing and Delivery of IS Services   ◆   237

7.1   Breakthrough Service in Information Systems   238
7.2   Structural Changes in Information Systems   248
7.3   Just-in-Time Information Systems   259
7.4   Information Systems in Learning Organizations   268
7.5   Supplier Relationship   272
7.6   Information-Systems Recovery   274

8   Quality Metrics in Information Systems   ◆   281

8.1   Information-Systems Quality Metrics   283
8.2   Implementation and Operation Metrics for Information Systems   289
8.3   Team-Management Quality Metrics for Information Systems (Optional)   301
8.4   Organizational Aspects of Quality Metrics   310

9   Quality Metrics for Design, Reliability, and Project Management   ◆   321

9.1   Information-Systems Design Metrics   322
9.2   Project-Management Quality Metrics for Information Systems   343
9.3   Information-Systems Reliability Metrics (Optional)   357

10   Analysis of Quality Metrics   ◆   373

10.1   Statistical Quality Control (SQC)   376
10.2   Control Charts for Quality Metrics   387
10.3   Quality Tools   395
10.4   Software Products for Quality Methods   402
10.5   The Implementation of Quality Metrics   405

Index   ◆   411

Preface

Information systems are playing an increasingly critical role within organizations. Information systems' success and innovation in meeting the needs of systems' customers are among the critical success factors in many business undertakings. It is, therefore, only natural to expect quality in the design and implementation of information systems, as well as in the delivery of systems services. This book provides a framework for information systems in which quality is the overriding concern, hence the term quality information systems.

The quality information systems framework is built on the synthesis of quality management concepts with the existing concepts and practices of information systems. The quality information systems framework does not replace what has already been developed and is working in the field of information systems. Rather, it takes the existing successes of traditional information systems and adds to them what we have learned from quality management, combining the human and technical aspects of systems within one framework.

The overriding premise of quality information systems is that quality should be built into a system from its inception. This begins with the organization's information-systems vision and leadership, gradually taking shape as concrete requirements, technical needs, systems design and implementation, and quality measurements and analysis.

This book is designed to take the reader on a journey to create quality information systems from the inception, marking areas where quality concepts could enhance the existing working knowledge about information-systems development. This book does not cover the existing knowledge about systems analysis and design. Instead, it identifies the ways quality concepts can be applied to information systems in order to create quality information systems.

This book has a number of unique features in that it:

- Applies quality concepts to information systems;
- Provides a unifying framework for synthesizing the technical and behavioral aspects of information systems;
- Features a case, ACCU-INFO, that runs through all ten chapters, providing relevance, context, and examples for conceptual discussions;
- Offers 20 real-world cases that provide examples for the applicability of the concepts;

- Synthesizes quality concepts, using quality as the single goal for all discussions and topics. This approach brings together in one volume all major quality concepts developed by different schools of thought;
- Integrates various quality topics, such as continuous improvement, benchmarking, quality function deployment, Taguchi's approach, reengineering, concurrent engineering, just-in-time, and quality metrics, into one unified approach for application to information systems;
- Exposes the reader to quality tools and methods, as needed, within the context of information systems;
- Discusses the available software products for quality tools and methods;
- Presents quality metrics as a new area in information systems, which has the potential to put the performance measurement of information systems on par with that of other products and services;
- Introduces quality-control concepts and control charts for information systems;
- Presents many questions and problems at the end of each chapter that encourage the thinking about and practice of the concepts discussed in the chapter.

◆ Structure of the Book

The book has ten chapters, most of which are self-contained. It begins with the general, organizational, and behavioral dimensions of quality information systems and moves to more specific and technical dimensions. The chapters roughly follow the life-cycle stages in developing and implementing information systems.

Chapter 1 defines the concept of total quality management, traces its theoretical origins, and introduces the main contributors to the field. It shows how industries and governments have focused on the importance of quality through awards and standards. This chapter defines the major dimensions of quality information systems by comparing and contrasting them with those of traditional information systems.

Chapter 2 discusses the importance of vision and leadership in developing the right information systems in the proper way. It also introduces some quality tools, such as brainstorming, mental mapping, and affinity diagrams, which can help in the creation of organizational and information-systems vision. This chapter shows the relevance of employee empowerment and involvement to the vision for information systems, and the role of cross-functional teamwork in quality information systems.

Chapter 3 presents a new paradigm for system maintenance and enhancement—a continuously improving information system. This chapter demonstrates the link between strategic planning and the theory of constraints with systems that continually go through the Shewhart-Deming cycle for improvement. It compares and contrasts the approaches of continuous improvement and reengineering, and identifies their roles in the system life cycle. A number of quality tools, such as the cause and effect diagram, Pareto charts, and tree and hierarchy diagrams are presented as useful tools for the improvement teams and processes.

Chapter 4 brings the benchmarking approach to information systems. Benchmarking, as a precursor to the analysis stage of the systems life cycle, identifies the best practices. This external perspective for what is possible provides an overall view as well

"Information through Innovation"

as specific ideas on the best business practices and the type of information systems that make them possible.

Chapter 5 discusses the ways quality management concepts can contribute to the requirements analysis in information systems. It uses quality function deployment (QFD) and the analytic hierarchy process (AHP) as the methods for formalizing the stages of information-systems requirements analysis.

Chapter 6 incorporates the quality dimension into the design of information systems. This chapter discusses reengineering, process design, concurrent engineering, and parallel design. It shows how one can use QFD to move from requirements analysis to the technical design of the information-systems components. This chapter discusses usability concepts and Taguchi's methods for creating usable and robust designs.

Chapter 7 presents quality ideas for the implementation of information systems and the delivery of services. The concepts of meta-information systems and just-in-time systems provide an alternative perspective for dealing with the increasing heterogeneity and diversity in information systems. The chapter argues that the implementation and successful delivery of information-systems services can be enhanced by the learning-organization culture, focusing on the quality of relationships with information-systems suppliers, and planning for information-systems recovery.

Chapters 8 and 9 develop quality metrics for information systems. The metrics are developed based on the premise that quality should be measurable. The objective of these two chapters is to quantify the quality of different aspects of information systems, such as design, implementation, operation, teamwork, project management, and systems reliability. The organizational issues in using metrics, possible abuses, and ways to prevent these abuses are also covered.

Since these two chapters quantify various aspects of information systems, they are the most quantitative chapters in the book. These two chapters are optional reading for those who are not interested in the details of information-systems quality metrics, and for undergraduate students who do not have adequate background in statistics and quantitative methods.

Chapter 10 discusses the methods that we can use for tracking information-systems quality metrics. This chapter introduces statistical quality control as the paradigm that allows us to keep track of system quality. It reviews various types of control charts and their underlying assumptions. The chapter briefly reviews the remaining quality tools that were not discussed in the previous chapters, and some of the existing software products used to apply quality tools and methods. The chapter ends with a discussion of the implementation issues of quality metrics, such as how and when to use them, how much, and how often.

With this book I hope to tease and excite the imagination of the reader about the new ways we can look at information systems and the ways we design them, develop them, use them, measure them, and improve them.

◆ Instructional Materials

The practice materials for this book are divided into questions and problems. End-of-chapter questions are designed as a review of the materials discussed in the chapter. Problems are designed to promote discussion and to provoke alternative thinking about possible solutions and approaches. The book has an instructor's manual that provides answers to end-of-chapter questions and problems.

◆ Acknowledgments

In writing this book, I have received support and encouragement from many. Frank Ruggirello, my signing editor (now at McGraw-Hill), encouraged me to start this project. Peter Keen (ICIT Research) was the enthusiastic reviewer of the book proposal who provided me with a number of helpful pointers. Kathy Shields and Tamara Huggins (Wadsworth), and Beth Sweet and Barbara Worth (boyd & fraser) gave their unqualified support. I am thankful for all their support.

Various parts of this book were reviewed by a number of reviewers. I would like to thank them all, including Professors Charles R. Shatzer (Solano College), Joan E. Hoopes (Marist College), Marvin Rothstein (University of Connecticut), Mike Cummins (University of Miami), Michael J. Ginsberg (Case Western Reserve University), Richard Wang (Massachusetts Institute of Technology), James A. Stoner (Fordham University), and Ruth King (University of Pittsburgh). I appreciate their helpful comments and encouragement. My special thanks to my colleague Ehsan S. Soofi (University of Wisconsin Milwaukee), who read the last three chapters and made helpful suggestions.

I am grateful to my editors, Linda Kincaid and Robert Brockman, who carefully read the book, and cheerfully went along with my often impossible deadlines. I acknowledge my appreciation for their professional dedication and warm friendship in this project and over the years.

No acknowledgement is complete without expressing my unbounded love and gratitude for my mother, Rafat, whose love and faith have given me the courage to cherish what life has to offer.

Fatemeh (Mariam) Zahedi
September 1994

At long last, one day,
I will escape from the magic eye of doubt,
My scent will be of dreams' colorful flowers,
I will crawl into the ringlets of the night breeze,
And ride to the shores of the sun.

Persian Poet Forough Faroukhzad, *"The Wall"*

Quality
Information
Systems

Far away there in the sunshine are my highest aspirations. I may not reach them, but I can look up and see their beauty, believe in them and try to follow where they lead.

— Louisa May Alcott

There is nothing more difficult to take in hand, more perilous to conduct, or more uncertain in success, than to take the lead in the introduction of a new order of things.

— Niccolo Machiavelli, *The Prince*

America is the land of opportunity if you're a businessman in Japan.

— Lawrence J. Peter

Even if you're on the right track, you'll get run over if you just sit there.

— Will Rogers

◆ Chapter Objectives

The objectives of this chapter are:
- ◆ To introduce the concept of total quality management
- ◆ To trace the theoretical origins of total quality management
- ◆ To introduce quality gurus
- ◆ To introduce the major points raised by quality gurus
- ◆ To review quality awards and standards
- ◆ To introduce quality information systems by contrasting them with traditional information systems

◆ Key Words

Total quality management, quality gurus, Deming, Juran, Crosby, Feigenbaum, Taguchi, Deming Prize, Malcolm Baldrige Award, European Quality Award, ISO 9000, Q90, quality information systems, traditional information systems

Introduction

1.1 Total Quality Management
    1.1.1 Definition
    1.1.2 Theoretical Origins
    1.1.3 Quality Gurus

1.2 Quality Awards and Standards
    1.2.1 The Deming Prize
    1.2.2 The Malcolm Baldrige Award
    1.2.3 The European Quality Award
    1.2.4 ISO 9000 and Q90 Standards

1.3 Quality vs. Traditional Information Systems
    1.3.1 People
    1.3.2 Organization
    1.3.3 Approach
    1.3.4 Process
    1.3.5 Techniques
    1.3.6 Information Systems as Quality Tools

◆ Introduction

There are two paradigms in the field of information systems: behavioral and technical. The main emphasis in the behavioral approach is on the political, organizational, and human elements that impact information systems. This paradigm argues that what seems rational and technically correct may not work in an organization due to the existing barriers created by human and behavioral elements within the organization. For example, if a user deems the system threatening, he or she may enter the wrong data or complain about non-existent inadequacies of the system. The technical paradigm begins with the assumption that people behave rationally and focuses on creating systems with the best technical capabilities.

Reliance on either of the two approaches can cause major handicaps in information systems. Information systems are created for use in organizations and by people. As Figure 1 shows, reliance on either approach may lead to dealing with the wrong problems in the right way (pure technical) or dealing with the right problems in the wrong way (pure behavioral). Ideally, we wish to have a framework that provides synergy between the two approaches, so that we deal with the right problems in the right way (lower quadrant in Figure 1.1).

Therefore, it is the behavioral approach that should define what is needed and the type of problems to be addressed. The technical approach decides the way the needs should be met and the problems to be solved. In other words, the behavioral approach chooses *what* and the technical approach decides *how*. The two approaches must be synthesized for an information system to be of any use.

In this book, we argue that quality provides this badly needed framework. Quality information systems create a synthesis between the human and technical aspects of information systems, while enhancing both in many directions. The quality information systems framework does not replace what is already developed and working in the field

Behavioral

Technical	Wrong	Right
Wrong	Dealing with the wrong problems the wrong way (no knowledge)	Dealing with the right problems the wrong way (purely behavioral)
Right	Dealing with the wrong problems the right way (purely technical)	Dealing with the right problems the right way (synthesis)

Figure 1.1   Technical-Behavioral Grid in Information Systems

of information systems (we call it traditional from here onward). Rather, it takes the existing successes of traditional information systems and adds to them what we have learned from quality management by combining the human and technical aspects of systems within one framework.

Total quality management (TQM) is not a new idea; it is built on almost a century of scientific and humanistic developments in management. In this introductory chapter, we briefly trace the conceptual history of total quality management (TQM).

Prior to the global attention to quality, a number of pioneers with foresight devoted their professional lives to the promotion of the role of quality. This chapter provides an introduction to quality gurus and their main points of view. Later chapters draw on their views in more detail.

Global promotion of quality has led to establishing quality awards and setting quality standards. We briefly review quality awards and standards in this chapter.

The concept of quality information systems has been created by applying quality ideas, concepts, and techniques to the field of information systems. In this chapter, we define the quality information systems framework by contrasting it with that of traditional information systems.

1.1 ◆ Total Quality Management

Tichy and Devanna [1986] in their discussion of transitional leaders (those who bring and institutionalize organizational change) state: "We are susceptible to snake oil claims because we live in a culture that seeks easy answers to fundamental problems." Unfortunately, like most new concepts, total quality management has been at times preached like a new religion and is regarded by some as an immediate fix for a great many chronic industrial ills. Total quality management is anything but a quick fix or easy answer. It combines known technical and behavioral knowledge into a roadmap for an arduous journey of changing and learning the way a productive system works in the new global economic order.

Total quality management as a framework is a collection of ideas, concepts, and tools, all designed to promote quality throughout an organization in all of its functions and aspects. The word *total* underlies the all-encompassing nature of quality, and the word *management* removes quality from its purely technical scope and generalizes it to include organizational and behavioral components of the organization as well.

1.1.1 Definition

There is no universal definition of quality, but quality gurus have provided us with various definitions of quality.

Feigenbaum [1991] defines quality as:

The total composite of product and service characteristics of marketing, engineering, manufacture, and maintenance through which the product and service in use will meet the expectations of the customer.

Crosby [1984] defines quality as "conformance to requirements." Juran [1992] uses the phrase "fitness for use." However, he emphasizes product features that meet the customer's needs and have the fewest deficiencies.

Hunt [1992] summarizes the major ingredients of quality by dividing them into facts and perception. The factual aspects of quality are that the product or service should:

- Be the right thing
- Function the right way
- Function right the first time
- Be delivered on time

The quality perception is that the customer must believe that the product or service:

- Is the right one
- Satisfies his or her needs
- Meets his or her expectations
- Is delivered with integrity, courtesy, and respect

Juran [1992] lists a number of dimensions in quality:

- Features
- Performance
- Competitiveness
- Promptness
- Courtesy
- Process capability
- Freedom from errors
- Conformance to specifications, standards, and procedures
- User-friendliness
- Safety for employees, customers, and environment
- Reliability
- Maintainability, including the availability of spare parts
- Durability
- Esthetic appeal
- Process yield
- Cost of poor quality
- Cycle time
- Price
- Costs
- Employee satisfaction
- Social responsibilities to employees and the public

These elements vary in their importance as a commonly accepted dimension of quality. However, as we will see in this book, they form, in one way or another, the foundation of the total quality management approach.

1.1.2 Theoretical Origins

Total quality management comes on the heels of numerous breakthroughs in the technical and behavioral dimensions of management theory. In this section, we briefly review a number of major advances that form the conceptual background of quality management.

Scientific Management Theory.   Prior to the industrial revolution, production was based on craftsmanship. A craftsman went through a relatively extensive period of apprenticeship, was identified by his or her craft, and took pride in the quality of the product. Thus, quality was personalized in the craftsman. With the industrial revolution, the mass entry of workers with little experience onto the assembly line, and the disconnection of workers from the output, the question of quality and productivity became a pressing issue.

In 1911, Frederick Winslow Taylor was the first to apply scientific methods to managing the work process in organizations [Taylor 1947, originally 1911]. His approach was to consider the organization as a closed system and design work processes to maximize efficiency. Taylor's work started the scientific and technical approach in management.

Human Behavior Movement.   In line with Taylor's approach, in the period from 1924 to 1933, a number of studies, mostly at Western Electric's Hawthorne plant (near Chicago), were carried out to relate various work place conditions with industrial productivity. Starting with studying workplace lighting and its relationship to productivity, the researchers divided a selected group of workers into a test group and a control group. The effects of changing the intensity of lighting were ambiguous, but the productivity in both groups was increased. The subsequent studies on other factors had similar outcomes.

When Fritz Roethlisberger, Elton Mayo, and William Dickson later participated in these studies, they observed a pattern in the outcomes. They concluded that the increase in productivity of workers who participated in the studies was caused by the special attention the workers received from top management. This attention fostered group pride and was reinforced by the supervisors' favorable treatment. This was called the *Hawthorne* effect. This observation launched the behavioral approach in management [Roethlisberger and Dickson 1939].

Control Charts.   Modern statistical theory owes its prominence to Sir Ronald A. Fisher, a British statistician at the turn of century. His work in developing test statistics and discriminant analysis developed statistics into a modern tool.

As the industrial revolution took hold, controlling the quality of products emerged as a major industrial issue. Walter A. Shewhart, a physicist at AT&T Bell Laboratories, used Fisher's work in developing control charts in the early 1920s for controlling manufacturing quality of phones at Western Electric, a subsidiary of AT&T. In doing so, Shewhart created the discipline of statistical quality control. He later was the mentor for W. Edwards and Joseph. M. Juran, who became quality gurus after World War II.

Statistics in Economics and Business.   Although Makprang, a Danish economist, was first to apply statistical estimation and regression analysis to business and economic data in his doctoral dissertation in 1890, Ian Tinbergen and Ragnar Frisch, (the first Nobel Prize winners in economics), were the main founders of the field of econometrics. In the years between the two world wars (1919-1939), Tinbergen and Frisch expanded the theoretical and empirical applications of statistics in business and economics. Their work increased the relevancy of statistical techniques to scientific management.

Mathematics as Decision Tools.   World War II (1940-1945) brought quantitative techniques to the forefront of the decision-making process. In this period, the use of quantitative techniques in decision making became an acceptable practice. Leonid Kantorovich, a Russian mathematician and a Nobel Prize winner in economics, developed the linear programming method in 1939. George Dantzig was the U.S. counterpart of Kantorovich, who with the help of pioneers like Russell Ackoff, popularized and expanded optimization methods in the U.S. during World War II and later in the post-war business world. Large companies accepted the use of statistics and operations research (later called management science) as technical tools in their major decision processes.

Taguchi Methods.   In the 1950s, based on Fisher's and Deming's work, Genichi Taguchi developed novel ideas in design experiments and the concept of loss function, which later became known as Taguchi methods and are a cornerstone for quality design in TQM. (The term *Taguchi Methods*^{TM} is a trademark of the American Supplier Institute, Inc., Dearborn, Michigan.)

Change Model.   Kurt Lewin, in 1947, discussed the forces *driving* and *restraining* change within an organization. He suggested a three-step sequential model for accomplishing change in an organization [Lewin 1951]:

- Unfreezing: making the necessity for change obvious to all
- Changing: identifying the change values, attributes, and behavior and internalizing them within the organization
- Refreezing: reinforcing the new behavior and values by support and reinforcement

Quality Movement.   After World War II, Deming and Juran contributed extensively to the revival of Japan's economy by advising Japanese industry on the total quality approach, and initiated the global quality movement. (The main approaches of the quality gurus are discussed in the next section.)

Cost of Quality.   Armand Feigenbaum (one of the TQM gurus) was the first to introduce the concept of the cost of quality in 1956. This concept refutes the assertion that higher quality products or services require higher cost. Low quality output means unsatisfactory resource utilization, which means waste of material, labor, equipment time, rework, and maintenance, leading to loss of customers or markets [Feigenbaum 1991]. Feigenbaum suggests the definition of measures and collection of data on quality costs.

General Systems Theory.   After World War II, the idea of a general systems theory took hold. This theory posits that one can model physical, biological, or social (including computer-based) structures within the context of a general systems approach, abstracting from their peculiar properties [Boulding 1956, Miller 1972]. Applied to business organizations, an organization is modeled as a system consisting of input, process, output, and feedback components. This concept was later expanded to complex systems—in which the components are structured in a hierarchy of subcomponents with feedback—by the Nobel Prize winner Herbert Simon and his colleagues [see, for example, Simon and Newell 1956; and Simon 1981 (1961)].

Quality Circles.   Kaoru Ishikawa, a professor at Tokyo University, started the quality control circle in Japan in 1962. A quality circle consists of a small team of voluntary workers who develop and monitor quality control activities in their unit as part of company-wide quality control activities [Ishikawa 1989]. It later became all the rage in some U.S. companies. In many cases, the concept of quality circles did not go far in the U.S., partly because of the lack of a total quality control plan. Quality circles are the forerunners of the quality team concept in TQM.

Open Systems Theory.   In the open systems theory, the environment in which a business operates takes on a special importance. Katz and Kahn brought the idea of open systems to the forefront by emphasizing that:

> Traditional organization theorists have tended to view the human organization as a closed system. This tendency has led to a disregard of differing organization environments and the nature of organizational dependency on environment [Katz and Kahn, 1966].

The open systems theory formalized the importance of environment as a major factor in business decisions. This is a major point of emphasis in TQM, which requires the organization to have a close interaction with and awareness of the external environment, including its customers, suppliers, public, competitors, and other organizations in the global market.

Benchmarking.   The idea of benchmarking is to design processes and set up targets based on the best in business.

The origin of benchmarking is too old to be known. Camp [1989] reports that it originated in China 2500 years ago, when Sun Tzu, a Chinese general wrote, "If you know your enemy and know yourself, you need not fear the result of a hundred battles." Applied in Japan as *Dantotsu*, it means the best of the best, which is the essence of benchmarking. The major benchmarking process in the U.S. was initiated by Xerox's competitive benchmarking in 1979.

Organizational Culture.   In the 1980s, the concept of organizational culture was formalized. Edgar Schein [1984] defines the organizational culture as:

> *the pattern of basic assumptions that a given group has invented, discovered, or developed in learning to cope with its problems of external adaptation and internal integration, and that worked well enough to be considered valid, and, therefore, to be taught to new members as the correct way to perceive, think, and feel in relation to those problems.*

Schein [1983, 1985] discussed the role of the leader in changing the organizational culture, and the reaction of the organization to change and innovation.

> *Organizations that have reached a stage of maturity or decline resulting from mature markets and products or from excessive internal stability and comfort that prevents innovation may need to change parts of their culture, provided they can obtain the necessary self-insight [Schein 1984].*

> *Organizational cultures are created by leaders, and one of the most decisive functions of leadership may well be the creation, management, and—if and when they become necessary—the destruction of culture. In fact, there is a possibility that the only thing of real importance that leaders do is to create and manage culture and that the unique talent of leaders is their ability to work with the culture.*

Transformational Leaders.   Tichy and Ulrich [1986] studied a new brand of leaders, *transformational leaders* (as opposed to the old *transactional leaders*), with the ability to

> *Help the organizations develop a vision of what can be, to mobilize the organization to accept and work toward achieving a new vision, and to institutionalize the changes that must last over time. [Tichy and Ulrich 1984].*

Tichy and Devanna [1986] studied transformational leaders in a dozen large U.S. companies (such as Motorola, GM, Burger King, Chase Manhattan and others). They looked at the tasks of these leaders in the technical, political, and cultural dimensions, and the process by which the cocoon of organizational culture is broken and the process of change is institutionalized within the organization.

In sum, we can venture to observe that it took the first half of the twentieth century to develop the major technical breakthroughs in the theory of management, whereas the major conceptual formulations that underlie the behavioral components of TQM are more recent and have taken place in the last three decades.

1.1.3   Quality Gurus

A number of individuals have disproportionately contributed to the popularity of TQM. Their unabashed, life-long zeal for quality has made them quality gurus, of whom Deming, Juran, Feigenbaum, Crosby, and Taguchi are the most well-known.

Deming. W. Edward Deming, a physicist and mathematician, was working at the Department of Agriculture when he met and became Shewhart's disciple at Western Electric. With his one-year study with Ronald Fisher, Deming became the expert in the field and popularized statistical quality control and sampling methods outside AT&T in various government services, including the Department of Agriculture and the Census Bureau. During World War II, he proposed the idea of a short course followed by a long course to train engineers, inspectors, and industry workers to improve the quality of war-time production. These courses covered control charts and Shewhart's cycle (plan-do-check-act). An estimated 10,000 engineers were trained in statistical process control, many by Deming. Deming's followers created a group that eventually evolved into the American Society for Quality Control (ASQC) in 1946 [Gabor 1990].

After the war, Deming left the government and set up his own consulting firm. One of his clients, the State Department, sent him to Japan in 1947 to help the devastated country in a national census. He was invited back by the Japanese government to help in their quality efforts through statistical process control. His contributions led to the creation of the Deming Prize by the Japanese Union of Scientists and Engineers (JUSE). Deming received Japan's Second Order Medal of the Sacred Treasure from the emperor, an honor rarely bestowed on a foreigner.

Deming emphasized the behavioral aspects in managing quality and identified Seven Deadly Diseases in the U.S. quality crisis as:

1. Lack of constancy of purpose
2. Emphasis on short-term profits
3. Evaluations of people by rating and annual reviews; thus destroying teamwork and creating rivalry and fear
4. Management mobility, leading to inadequate understanding of how the organization works and lack of incentive for long-range planning
5. Managing the organization by visible numbers only
6. Excessive employee health-care costs
7. Excessive warranty costs, encouraged by lawyers

To counter these problems, Deming proposed a fourteen-point solution:

1. Create constancy of purpose toward improvement of product and service, with the aim to become competitive and to stay in business, and to provide jobs
2. Adopt the new philosophy—quality and customer orientation
3. Cease dependence on inspection to achieve quality
4. End the practice of awarding business on the basis of price tag
5. Improve constantly and forever the system of production and service, to improve quality and productivity, and constantly decrease costs
6. Institute training
7. Institute leadership
8. Drive out fear, so that everyone may work effectively for the company

9. Break down barriers between departments
10. Eliminate slogans, exhortations, and arbitrary numerical goals and targets for the workforce which urge the workers to achieve new levels of productivity and quality
11. Eliminate numerical quotas
12. Remove barriers that rob employees of their pride of workmanship
13. Institute a vigorous program of education and self-improvement
14. Take action to accomplish the transformation

We will refer to these points as various topics of quality information systems are discussed in the chapters that follow.

Juran.   Joseph M. Juran was another AT&T engineer involved with the quality control team at Western Electric's telephone manufacturing in the 1920s and 1930s. In 1951, Juran published *Quality Control Handbook*, which caught the attention of the managing director of the Japanese Union of Scientists and Engineers (JUSE), who had the book translated into Japanese and invited Juran to Japan to lecture and consult on quality. Juran gave his first series of lectures in 1954. JUSE planned for followup courses and a number of coordinators, including Kaoru Ishikawa and a number of other coordinators, who later became a leading quality force in Japan [Juran 1991].

Juran advocates managing quality in three parts [Juran 1992]:

- Quality planning
- Quality control
- Quality improvement

Juran recommends a seven-step breakthrough sequence:

1. Breakthrough attitude
2. Identify the few vital projects
3. Organize for breakthrough in knowledge
4. Conduct analysis
5. Determine how to overcome resistance to change
6. Institute the change
7. Institute controls

Crosby.   Philip Crosby was once an assembly line inspector, who became the vice president for quality at ITT Corporation. After the publication of his book: *Quality Is Free*, Crosby quit ITT and started Philip Crosby Associates in 1979. This firm had a more educational tilt than the traditional consulting firms. He developed two-and-a-half day seminars for senior executives, called the Executive College. Later, a series of such seminars was developed for various managerial levels and employees. In 1989 Crosby sold the institute and retired in January 1991. The institute has its own quality award called "the Quality Fanatic Award," for those companies that make significant quality improvements as defined by Crosby. Crosby's approach has been criticized as over-commercialized and uniform, disregarding the special needs of a firm or industry [Byrne 1991].

Crosby offers a fourteen-step program as:

1. Management commitment
2. Quality improvement team
3. Quality measurement
4. Cost of quality evaluation
5. Quality awareness
6. Corrective action
7. Zero-defects planning
8. Supervisory training
9. Zero-defects day (the day the new philosophy is declared)
10. Goal setting
11. Error cause removal
12. Recognition
13. Quality council
14. Do it all over again

Feigenbaum. Armand Feigenbaum first coined the term *total quality control* in the title of the first edition of his landmark book in 1951. Armand Feigenbaum founded General Systems Co., a consulting firm, and takes an engineering approach to managing quality. He sees four stages for quality-control activities [Feigenbaum 1991]:

- New-design control
- Incoming-material control
- Product control
- Special process studies

Feigenbaum identifies ten benchmarks for total quality control in the 1990s [Feigenbaum 1991]:

1. Quality is a company-wide process
2. Quality is what the customer says it is
3. Quality and cost are a sum, not a difference
4. Quality requires both individual and team zealotry
5. Quality is a way of managing
6. Quality and innovation are mutually dependent
7. Quality is an ethic
8. Quality requires continuous improvement

9. Quality is the most cost-effective, least capital-intensive route to productivity
10. Quality is implemented with a total system connected with customers and suppliers

Taguchi.   In the post war Japan of 1950, General Douglas MacArthur set up the Electrical Communication Laboratories to deal with Japan's communication problems. Dr. Genichi Taguchi was recruited to deal with the R&D productivity and quality improvement. He developed the concept of loss function, a measure that includes all subsequent losses to the system and society due to poor quality. His technical contribution was the development of a novel fractional factorial design method for designing products that can withstand unfavorable external environments.

Taguchi developed the quality philosophy as [Taguchi 1989]:

- Quality must be designed into the products, not inspected after production
- Quality means minimizing deviation and variability in the product
- Products must have a robust design so that the product will be sensitive to unfavorable external environments
- Cost of quality must be measured as deviation from standard
- Loss due to low quality must be measured system-wide

To create a robust design, Taguchi suggested a three-stage process:

- System design
- Parameter design
- Tolerance design

The Taguchi methods as applied to information systems will be discussed in detail in Chapter 4.

1.2   ◆   Quality Awards and Standards

After the stunning success of Japanese companies in their quest for quality, business communities and governments across the world have become increasingly aware of the significance of quality management in the global competitive market.

To increase the awareness of companies across the world, various agencies have taken the initiative to create awards, standards, and certificates for incorporating quality in production processes of goods and services. These efforts include:

- The Deming Prize
- The Malcolm Baldrige Award
- The European Quality Award
- ISO 9000 and Q90 Standards

1.2.1   The Deming Prize

In 1951, the Japanese Union of Scientists and Engineers (JUSE) created the Deming Prize for companies wishing to improve quality in their products. Later, JUSE revised its Deming Prize guidelines to require that quality efforts be organization-wide.

In 1989, Florida Power & Light became the first non-Japanese Deming Prize winner. The award was criticized as extremely bureaucratic and demoralizing. The Deming Prize efforts at Florida Power & Light ended with CEO John J. Hudiberg, the driving force behind the award, being pushed aside, and the quality-improvement department dismantled.

Critics point out that the Deming Prize:

- Requires an application of up to 1,000 pages
- Requires many years of work with consultants from the Union of Japanese Scientists and Engineers
- Is too bureaucratic
- Does not provide flexibility for designing unique quality approaches

On the other hand, many believe that the detailed self-study process that the Deming Prize requires and the prestige and recognition generated by winning the award make the award an effective quality incentive.

1.2.2   The Malcolm Baldrige Award

Named after the Reagan Administration Commerce Secretary in 1987, the Malcolm Baldrige National Quality Award was instituted to raise U.S. industry's awareness of the significance of quality in global competition. The award application has a limit of 75 pages. Each year, the U.S. Department of Commerce issues the award criteria. The award is administered by the American Society for Quality Control (ASQC). The first Baldrige Award was given in 1988.

The critics of the award state that it:

- Does not include productivity
- Chooses companies with little reputation for quality
- Some winners do not produce world-class quality products

The proponents of the award defend it on the basis that the award brings the important issue of quality to the forefront and poses a collective challenge to U.S. companies to make quality one of the major components of their business strategies.

1.2.3   The European Quality Award

In 1988, 14 top European companies formed the European Foundation for Quality Management. The charge of this organization is to promote TQM techniques and hand out the European Quality Award, a European equivalent of the Baldrige Award. By 1991, more than 50 European universities had altered their management curricula to include quality training.

1.2.4   ISO 9000 and Q90 Standards

The U.S. airforce in World War II recognized the necessity of quality standards for manufacturing and initiated quality assurance programs, which led to the development of the military quality assurance standard MIL-Q-9858 in 1959. This standard was revised as MIL-Q-9858A in 1963. The U.S. military standard was adopted by NATO as AQAP-1 in 1968, and the European version of the NATO standard was developed as DEF STAN 05-21 in 1970. Based on these standards, Britain developed quality assurance standards as BS 5750 in 1979.

The European Committee for Standardization, Europe's standard-setting body, commissioned the International Standards Organization (ISO), a private organization, to develop quality assurance standards. These standards were called ISO 9000 and were adopted by The European Committee for Standardization in 1987 as the norms for quality assurance. ISO 9000 series utilized the previously developed U.S. and NATO standards.

In the same year, Britain revised its BS 5750 standards to conform with ISO 9000, and the U.S. adopted the ISO 9000 series with minor language modifications as Q90 series.

The ISO 9000 series consists of the following:

- ISO 9000 outlines the general guidelines
- ISO 9001 provides quality assurance guidelines for companies engaged in the design, development, production, installation, and servicing functions
- ISO 9002 provides guidelines for companies engaged in production and installation functions only
- ISO 9003 provides guidelines for companies engaged in final inspection and testing functions
- ISO 9004 describes the elements of quality management system

ISO is presently in the process of developing standards specifically designed for service and banking industries.

Q90, Q91, Q92, Q93, and Q94 are the U.S. equivalent of ISO 9000–ISO 9004. The difference is that the ISO 9000 series is used for certification purposes, whereas the Q90 series in the U.S. is a voluntary standard of quality assurance.

Starting in 1993, companies dealing with the European Common Market (EC) countries need to have ISO 9000 certification. Companies outside the European market also consider the certificate as evidence of commitment to quality. Ford Motor Company has developed a quality certificate of its own for its suppliers, called Q1, and requires its suppliers to conform to the Q1 standard in order to be a Ford supplier.

Quality certification is gaining in popularity in the global market. However, some experts express concern that the certification process does not deal with inefficiencies of processes and customer-related issues.

◆ CASE: Information Systems for Japan's Bullet Train

At 20 minutes past midnight, in a cavernous control room 10 stories above Tokyo Station, Toshinori Takahashi punches two keys at a computer terminal. Ten minutes later, a flashing light signals the end of his work for the evening. With one touch, Takahashi has given marching orders to a gargantuan railway-control system, activating a day's worth of train and staff schedules in a massive mainframe. On peak days, the system serves 500,000 passengers riding 1,000 *Shinkansen* "bullet trains" over 730 miles of track between Tokyo and distant Hakata, in Kyushu. The stretch includes the Tokyo-Osaka commuter link, the most heavily traveled rail corridor in the world.

Developed by Japanese computer giant Hitachi Ltd., the traffic system has been up since 1972 without a glitch serious enough to dock even one train. That's because its software is practically error-free. "Programming errors per year are down to virtually zero," says information systems director Takashi Kawakami at Central Japan Railway Co. It's all in a day's work for Hitachi, which has made a crusade for raising quality standards in complex software systems in which a single bug could cause a catastrophe.

It's an edge that pays. Hitachi's largest software subsidiary, Hitachi Software Engineering Co., has achieved compound annual earnings growth of 17.7% over the past decade. Sales this year are expected to soar 20%, to $640 million. Rivals have been quick to notice. "Managers from other Japanese software firms cited Hitachi with having the stringent quality-control procedures and probably the fewest defects in the industry," writes Professor Michael Cusumano of the Massachusetts Institute of Technology in his recently published study, *Japan's Software Factories*.

Hitachi does not get everything right. It's an also-ran in consumer electronics and has never launched a successful PC product. But in software, its progress has been remarkable.

Its Omika Works computer factory is a case in point. Back in 1972, when it began developing programs for the bullet train, software was created by brute force, using a form of programming that requires a detailed understanding of how computers work. Then, in 1976, Hitachi engineers developed a breakthrough programming language called SPL, similar to the Ada language developed by the U.S. military. "In the past, you had to design a program, then run it, then test it," explains Kunio Yamanaka, Hitachi's general manager of systems engineering. But with the new language, all that could be done concurrently— which, he says, meant earlier bug detection and an immediate 40% reduction in defects.

Hitachi is at the forefront of world-class software development because it started pushing for quality earlier than almost everyone else. Indeed, in 1969, the company created the world's first "software factory." Such places are marked by rows of heavily monitored programmers working side by side. While they don't always use the latest in computer-aided software engineering technology, they try to reuse tested programs as often as possible. And they take rigorous process control regimens from Japanese manufacturing plants and apply them to writing software. Now, this approach is gaining currency all over the world.

The techniques perfected in Hitachi's early factories have been applied to all of its software operations. Hitachi Software Engineering has maintained a "distinctively higher level of quality than its competitors," says Steve Myers, an analyst with Jardine Fleming Securities Ltd. in Tokyo. An indication of Hitachi's prowess is its success even in demanding U.S. market. Its Sacramento (Calif.) subsidiary has sold geographic mapping software to local utilities, airlines, and a Bell operating company. And its DNA sequencing software is used at Stanford University and Johns Hopkins University,

Such exotic ventures are a long way from the thoughts of dispatchers in the control room at Central Japan Railway. It's 1 a.m. as Takahashi relaxes at his desk, studying the 62-foot control map at the front of the room. Typhoons can cause delays on the Tokai line, he says. So can earthquakes or a flood. But software glitches? Takahashi says he's never even given it a thought. If the past 19 years are any clue, there's no need to start now.

Source: "Rails That Run On Software," Neil Gross, *Business Week*, October 25, 1991, p. 84, reprinted from October 25, 1991 issue of *Business Week* by special permission, copyright (c) 1991 by McGraw-Hill, Inc.

1.3 ◆ Quality vs. Traditional Information Systems

Information systems have the ingredients that make them one of the most appropriate functional areas for the application of quality. The quality approach enhances these ingredients and provides a framework for putting together what has long been percolating in the field. The best way to describe the quality information system is to contrast it with what has been the norm in the traditional approach to information systems. In this analysis, the word *traditional* is used to refer to the existing practices in information systems and is not intended to belittle the advances made in the field. It is important to note that quality information systems has the underlying assumption that the organization has made a commitment to total quality.

We can compare quality and traditional information systems from a number of perspectives that are listed and briefly discussed in this section. The comparison serves also as an introduction to the major topics discussed in this book.

- People
- Organization
- Approach
- Process
- Technique
- Information Systems as Quality Tools

1.3.1   People

The behavioral approach in information systems has always put a premium on the human resources from a number of perspectives. The quality information systems approach takes the same ingredients and enhances them into an all-encompassing framework. In what follows, we contrast traditional and quality information systems from the people perspectives:

- Focus: Users vs. Customers
- Leadership: Micro vs. Macro
- Commitment: Project-based vs. Vision-based
- Communication: One-way vs. Two-way
- Involvement: Special vs. General
- Recognition: Sporadic vs. Systematic
- Training: Users Only vs. Universal
- Teamwork: Project-based vs. Broad-based

Focus: Users vs. Customers.   Traditional information systems have their focus on their immediate users, mainly those who directly access the system. Quality information systems have their focus on customers, internal and external. This is a more encompassing focus, in that it recognizes that those who develop, maintain, and indirectly use the system are as much the customer as the direct users. Indirect users are those who are otherwise impacted by the system, such as suppliers or CEOs. The customer focus is an underlying theme of almost all discussions on quality.

Leadership: Micro vs. Macro.   Traditional information systems call for leadership in project management and technical excellence. Their scope could be called a *micro* approach to leadership. The quality information system requires leadership with a vision. In this respect, the quality information system has a *macro* leadership requirement. As we will see in Chapter 2, the difference between a leader and a manager is that the leader has vision that is shared by employees, and uses it as a guiding light in all actions and decisions.

Commitment: Project-based vs. Vision-based.   Traditional information systems have long recognized that without the commitment from CEOs, an information-system project will never survive. In other words, they require a *project-based* commitment by the CEO. Quality information systems go one step further, and require that leaders be passionately committed to the quality vision in general, and the quality vision of information systems in particular. Quality information systems require *vision-based* commitment. This type of commitment reduces the project-by-project fight for the CEO's attention, and facilitates the project selection process.

Communication: One-way vs. Two-way.   Traditional information systems call for continuous communication with the top managers. Although they require that the system's developers be informed of the company's major strategical issues, the main focus of this communication is aimed at informing the CEOs what the system does and convincing them that the system's work is important. The communication is mostly, but not always, *one-way* from the IS department or project to the CEO and others.

Quality information systems call for a *two-way*, or what the Japanese call a *catch ball*, approach to communication. In this approach, the leader gets involved in collecting and synthesizing ideas from employees regarding information systems to form a unifying policy, and in creating a consensus for implementing the policy. The communication is a constant dialogue on what we can do to improve information systems and do the job better.

Involvement: Special vs. General.   Involvement has been another key word in traditional information systems. The focus of involvement is the user. In this sense, the involvement is *special* because it is mainly limited to the involvement of immediate users of the system in systems development.

Quality information systems operate in an environment of *general* involvement. The involvement has a quality-focus, in that it asks what every employee can do to improve processes with the goal of moving toward achieving the shared vision. Applied to information systems, the general involvement requires that all IS employee types— clerical, technical, and managerial—take ownership of the system and contribute to its quality improvement.

Recognition: Sporadic vs. Systematic.   Information systems have a large proportion of highly professional workers who take pride in their professional accomplishments. Traditional information systems have paid little attention to the power of non-monetary recognition in creating a culture of pride in quality and excellence. In this sense, one can say that recognition has been *sporadic* at best in traditional information systems.

Quality information systems, with their almost obsessive attention to quality, recognize the power of professional pride, and recommend a *systematic* approach to recognition and reward. They require establishing quality performance norms and regular acknowledgement of quality performance through recognitions and awards.

Training: Users Only vs. Universal.   Another hallmark of traditional information systems is the emphasis on training, but mainly training users for understanding and using the system. Hence, training programs are for *users only*, developed at the implementation phase of an information system.

Quality information systems require extensive employee training in quality as well as in technical and functional areas. The human factor is recognized as the most precious resource in an organization. Investment in training is considered an investment in upgrading this resource.

Teamwork: Project-based vs. Broad-based.   Teamwork in TQM became essential with the idea of quality circles, in which cross-functional employees would get together to discuss ways to improve their work processes. Thus, teamwork, especially cross-functional teamwork, became an essential ingredient in any quality effort.

Traditional information systems have always had cross-functional teams for design and implementation of systems. However, the basis of these teams in traditional information systems is the project. Once a system is created, the project team disappears. In quality information systems, cross-functional teams continue to exist for the purpose of process improvement, a never-ending activity. Therefore, team building and quality team participation are of great importance in removing departmental barriers in quality information systems.

1.3.2 Organization

Since quality information systems can survive only in organizations with a commitment to quality, quality systems' organizational features differ from those of traditional information systems in the following ways:

- Management: Order and Control vs. Coach and Support
- Control: By Others vs. By Self
- Structure: Hierarchy vs. Flat
- Unit: Single vs. Multiple

Management: Order and Control vs. Coach and Support.   The style of management in traditional information systems is mostly a top-down flow of orders and control, in that managers determine what should be done and then make sure that what they have ordered is indeed carried out. In quality information systems, managers act as mentors and coach workers by advising them how to solve their problems and by providing them support and facilities for doing their jobs.

Control: By Others vs. By Self.   In traditional information systems, organizational control as well as technical quality controls are partly carried out by others—managers and quality inspectors. In general, little attention is paid to measuring the reliability of information systems.

In quality information systems, reliability of information systems is of great importance. To ensure quality and reliability in the components of an information system, control is shifted to the employee himself or herself. In other words, the employee is responsible for producing an error-free product or service.

Structure: Hierarchy vs. Flat.   Control constitutes the main function of middle managers in the organizational hierarchy. Since control is shifted to employees themselves and cross-functional teamwork is encouraged, the number and levels of middle managers shrink in quality information systems. The organizational hierarchy in quality information systems is flat.

Unit: Single vs. Multiple.   A traditional information system mostly works within the boundaries of one organization, mainly as a closed system. A quality information system works as an open system, strongly interacting with the external environment of the organization. A quality information system has strong ties to outside suppliers and outside customers, hence creating a multiple-organization unit. Many cross-functional teams of quality information systems have to integrate external suppliers and customers so strongly in cross-functional teams that a *virtual* or *meta organization* is created. A virtual organization includes units from external customers and suppliers.

1.3.3   Approach

Traditional and quality information systems differ in their approach in a number of ways:

- Static vs. Dynamic
- Subjective vs. Fact-based
- Supply Push vs. Demand Pull
- Good-Enough Reliability vs. Zero Error
- Direct Cost vs. Cost of Ownership

Static vs. Dynamic.   A traditional information system works in a relatively static manner in that once the system has gone through its life cycle, i.e., is designed and implemented, it will remain unchanged until the problems mount to the point of requiring another round of life-cycle iteration. Maintenance takes place in the form of trying to fix the bugs that are discovered while the system is operating.

A quality information system has a dynamic nature, in that continuous improvement is already a formal component of the system. That is, change is internalized in quality information systems. Thus, the quality information systems framework accomplishes what the system life cycle was originally intended for—a continuous and uninterrupted process of change and improvement.

Subjective vs. Fact-based.   Traditional information systems have few processes in place for the constant collection of data on the performance of systems in operation. Therefore, any judgment regarding systems and their environments is mostly based on subjective judgments and opinions. This makes an information system subject to power struggles, political maneuvers, and personality clashes.

The quality information systems framework emphasizes defining measurements and collection of data and facts that show the true value and performance of systems. Collecting data on how an operational information system works is an integral part of systems design and deployment. Thus, analysis in such systems relies more heavily on factual information than that of traditional information systems.

Supply Push vs. Demand Pull.   In traditional information systems, the creation and provision of information services are mostly pushed by the supplier, in that hardware, software, and systems suppliers are the ones who push to create a system. Once created, it is the availability of the system that dictates when the service could be provided to its customers. This has been particularly true in the earlier developmental stage of the field in general, and in technology-driven systems at present in particular.

Quality information systems, with their focus on customers, has a demand-pull nature both in the creation as well as in the service provision of information systems. In other words, the needs of customers determine what systems are needed and what technology must be pursued to satisfy these needs. This gives a long-range and proactive nature to the creation of information systems, in that rather than reacting to the technology that becomes available in the market, the field of information systems can take a leading role in demanding what must be developed to satisfy the needs, present and future, of information systems customers.

Furthermore, the demand-pull nature of quality information systems brings into the field the ideas of just-in-time (JIT) and kanban. In this approach, it is the customer's need that tells the supplier the time and schedule for an item or service to be delivered. In other words, demand-pull determines the supplier's delivery schedule of information systems input products (data, software, or hardware) or services (reports, access, or communications).

Good-Enough Reliability vs. Zero Error.   The idea of reliability of information systems has received only a cursory treatment, if at all. The prevalent attitude is to develop systems that work reasonably well, and to fix the bugs as they appear after the system has become operational.

The quality information systems framework has zero error as its goal and is based on the idea of "doing it right the first time." All the trial and error processes should take place at the prototyping stage of design, in which all the defects are identified and removed. The goal is to produce zero-error operational systems.

Achieving this goal requires identifying reliability measures, collecting data, and using control charts to discover potential problem areas and take preventive actions.

There are three phases for finding errors:

- Prevention: prevent errors from occurring
- Detection: search for errors while the system is working
- Failure: wait until the system fails

In a traditional information system, the focus of error discovery is more on failure, whereas quality information systems emphasize the prevention and detection phases.

Direct Cost vs. Cost of Ownership.   In a cost analysis of traditional information systems, the direct cost forms the basis of project selection and of resource allocation to various components of a system. Therefore, an increase in the reliability of the system is considered an additional cost, requiring time and money.

According to Taguchi's concept of loss function, one should consider system-wide or even society-wide costs generated by the failure of the product to perform according to its requirements. In quality information systems, the cost of the system is the cost of its ownership, which includes future maintenance and loss due to lack of reliability. The emphasis on quality requires a longer and more careful design phase, leading to a shorter overall development period. Furthermore, the higher reliability of the system reduces the ownership cost of the system by eliminating maintenance costs, crisis management costs due to the failure of the system, loss of customers' goodwill, and all additional human and financial costs generated by defective systems.

1.3.4   Process

One can compare traditional and quality information systems based on the processes involved in their production and use:

- Strategy: Plan vs. Plan for the Vision
- Analysis: User Requirements vs. Voice of Customers and QFD
- Design: Sequential vs. Concurrent
- Manufacturing: Trial and Error vs. Right the First Time
- Service: Use-as-is vs. Planning and Monitoring
- Maintenance: Fire Fighting vs. Recovery Plan

Strategy: Plan vs. Plan for the Vision.   Traditional information systems have recently come to value the role of information strategic planning based on the corporate strategy plan, known as *information engineering* [Finkelstein 1989].

The quality information systems framework expands the idea of information engineering to planning for the working vision of the information systems function, which is formed based on the corporate vision. This gives a more creative and global role to planning for information systems, in that it does not bind the information systems plan to specific and short-term corporate plans. Instead, it provides the IS function with a forum to be innovative and farsighted for planning in order to accomplish the organization's long-term vision.

Analysis: User Requirements vs. Voice of Customers.   The field of information systems has been one of the few that, through a process of trial and error, has come to appreciate the importance of users in ensuring the success of a system. The user requirements analysis plays an important role in traditional information systems.

The quality information systems approach expands on this idea and generalizes users to customers, including internal and external customers. In other words, a programmer or data entry personnel are as much the customer of an information system as are the users of the operational system. Furthermore, the quality dimension adds techniques such as quality function deployment (QFD) and analytic hierarchy process (AHP), which provide a formal structure for requirements analysis in information systems.

Design: Sequential vs. Concurrent.   In traditional information systems, the design phase is just one step in the system life cycle. Thus, the analysis, design, manufacturing, and deployment of a system form a mostly sequential process (with some overlap between two consecutive phases). The cycle has an imbedded iterative trial and error approach to fixing design defects and manufacturing errors.

In quality information systems, the design process is concurrent in that major participants in the subsequent phases take part in the design phase, and plan for their functions as the design progresses. The participants include manufacturers (such as programmers and hardware specialists) and service providers (such as field supervisors and system trainers). Thus, the cross-functional design team includes all those who will, one way or another, be involved with the production, deployment, and use of the system.

The design phase of quality information systems includes two additional aspects that are normally missing in the design of traditional information systems: reliability and robustness. Here, reliability techniques, Taguchi's fractional factorial method, and simulation analysis are among the available techniques for designing reliability and robustness into the system.

Manufacturing: Trial and Error vs. Right the First Time. We can define the development of systems as the manufacturing phase. Manufacturing of traditional information systems takes place in the form of trial and error. If the manufactured system does not have the desired features and lacks adequate reliability, the design and manufacturing cycles are repeated until a good-enough system is produced.

The goal of quality information systems is to manufacture the system right the first time. It means an extensive and careful design phase, and extensive reliability testing at the manufacturing phase.

Furthermore, the manufacturing of systems requires inputs, such as hardware, software (if purchased), data (if acquired externally), and communication capabilities. Suppliers of these inputs have a role similar to that of the suppliers of manufacturing products, with the difference being that the purchase is for the services of these inputs.

For example, the manufacturer of information systems purchases hardware services. Although the payment is for equipment, it is the service input of the hardware that goes into an information system. Therefore, it is the reliability of the hardware and the hardware supplier's insurance for defect-free and continuously improving hardware service that are most important in information systems.

In traditional information systems, we select suppliers based on their reputation, survivability, and price. In quality information systems, we demand a closer relation with the supplier by getting involved, as much as possible, with the internal quality efforts of suppliers.

Service: Use-as-is vs. Planning and Monitoring. Once an information system is put into operation and deployed in the field, it becomes a provider of service—information service. In traditional information systems, we pay little attention to the ongoing operations of information systems. An operational information system is expected to be used *as is*, unless an error or defect is discovered that would require maintenance.

In quality information systems, we plan for measuring and monitoring the service performance of operational systems. Once a system becomes operational, it is monitored by regular collection of data for early detection of service problems. Monitoring data becomes the basis for process improvement before any major problem arises in the system, hence improving the system on a continuous basis.

Maintenance: Fire Fighting vs. Recovery Plan.   One can deal with system errors and defects by:

- Prevention
- Detection
- Failure

In traditional information systems, maintenance is mostly in the form of fire fighting. The discovery of errors is through failure. There is no process in place for discovering defects, shortcomings, or errors. Thus, the system may be working in its defective mode for some time before a disaster, a failure, or a user complaint forces the manager to allocate resources for fixing the system. The system must fail noticeably before a maintenance process is initiated.

In quality information systems, we deal with defects and errors by prevention and detection. We prevent errors by designing reliability into the system, and detect them through constant field data collection and monitoring via control charts and other statistical techniques.

1.3.5   Techniques

Quality techniques add additional technical arsenals to what is already available in the field of information systems. Below is a list of some commonly used techniques in traditional information systems, followed by what quality techniques add to the list. We will not go through the description of either list. A detailed discussion of traditional techniques can be found in texts on systems analysis and design and database management systems. The quality techniques are discussed in this book in chapters that follow.

Traditional Techniques.

- Walkthroughs
- Structured Programming
- Prototyping
- Flow Chart
- Data Flow Diagram
- Entity-Relationship
- Normalization
- Dictionaries
- Data Modeling
- CASE Tools
- Object-oriented analysis (OOA) and object-oriented design (OOD)
- PERT

Quality Add-on Techniques.

- Plan-Do-Check-Act
- Benchmarking
- Brainstorming
- Mental Mapping
- Affinity Diagram
- Pareto Chart
- Interrelationship Digraphs
- Tree Diagram
- Matrix Diagram
- Prioritization
- Quality function deployment (QFD)
- Cause-and-Effect Diagram
- Taguchi methods
- Statistical process control, control charts
- Simulation

1.3.6   Information Systems as Quality Tools

In traditional information systems, little attention has been paid to the type of information systems needed for managing quality. In quality information systems, systems are designed to achieve the corporate vision. Since quality is an integral goal of any organization with a quality commitment, the creation of information systems to serve quality efforts receives high priority. Information systems for managing quality include:

- Database: Internal and External
- Graphics: Quality Graphs
- Intelligent System: Standards and Procedures
- Communications: Removing Barriers
- Systems for Certification and Awards

Database: Internal and External.   Since quality is a fact-driven system, database systems play an important role in managing quality. Database types that aid in managing quality include:

- Internal data for measuring quality processes
- Internal data for employee attitudes
- Internal data regarding training processes
- Internal data regarding information on internal customers
- Internal data for cost of quality

- Internal data for the design of products and systems
- External data for external customers' needs and desires
- External data regarding the performance of products, services, and systems
- Customer complaints and follow-up actions
- External data for benchmarking other organizations
- External data on quality programs of other organizations

Managing quality generates a great deal of data, which at times seems bureaucratic and overwhelming. The role of database systems is to help define what data types are worth keeping and organize them into an easily accessible structure.

Graphics: Quality Graphs.   Many quality techniques are graphical in nature or require graphics, such as control charts, Pareto charts, tree diagrams, cause-and-effect graphs, and quality function deployment (QFD). Graphics services that make these techniques easily accessible for users contribute to quality efforts in an organization.

Intelligent Systems: Standards and Procedures.   In quality management, once a process is established as the best, it must be formalized into a standard procedure to be followed by all. In the complex organizations of today, if the quality efforts succeed, quality standards will mean a mountain of manuals. Managing the wealth of knowledge regarding such standards requires intelligent systems in order to store the knowledge, to function as a reference or guide for employees and to teach the novice. Expert systems for managing quality may be an answer to the mountain of papers that quality standards generate.

Communications: Removing Barriers.   The cross-functional and cross-organizational nature of quality management requires a comprehensive design for communications channels. An information strategy has communications as its fundamental component. It is the basis for what is now called *virtual organizations*, where the units of various companies are interconnected in producing a product or in providing a service to consumers.

The architectural design of telecommunication must include an accelerated integration process prompted by quality management. Peter Keen [1991] defines *reach* and *range* of telecommunication systems. Reach shows the physical possibility of connecting various intra-organizational and inter-organizational units. Range identifies the types of information services that should be shared among the connected units. Quality management has a significant input in both dimensions of the telecommunication architecture.

Systems for Certification and Awards.   Quality certificates and awards, such as the Baldrige and Deming awards, as well as ISO 9000 certificates and Q90 standards, result in extensive data collection and paperwork. We need to develop the conceptual framework of information systems supporting such efforts. These awards and certificates have clear directions in various categories (as demonstrated in the following chapters) and company-dependent implementation that may vary from industry to industry and company to company. Furthermore, one of the areas of emphasis in all awards and certificates is the information system function. Thus, information systems play an important role in supporting quality efforts, as well as in satisfying the requirements of the certificates and standards.

◆ Conclusion

This chapter defined total quality management (TQM) and traced the historical origins of theories that form the foundation of TQM. Quality owes its popularity to a handful of pioneers who have spent their energy in promoting its implementation in the world. This chapter presented a brief introduction to quality gurus, whose works will be referenced throughout this book.

The promotion of quality efforts in production and provision of goods and services has become a global agenda. Quality awards and standards are designed to focus corporate attention on the importance of quality efforts. Among the most prestigious awards are: the Deming prize (Japan), the Malcolm Baldrige award (U.S.), and the European quality award (Europe). The major quality standards are the ISO 9000 series (EC countries), and its equivalent the Q90 series (U.S.). These awards and standards were introduced in this chapter, and will be referred to in the chapters that follow.

We define quality information systems as the framework in which the concepts of total quality management are implemented in the field of information systems. We compared and contrasted traditional information systems and quality information systems in six categories: people, organization, approach, process, technique, and information systems as quality tools. This comparison identifies the areas where TQM adds strength to the field of information systems, and constitutes an introduction to the arguments put forward in this book.

◆ References

1. Boulding, K. "General Systems Theory—The Skeleton of Science," *Management Science*, Vol. 2, 1956, pp. 197–208.

2. Byrne, John. "High Priests and Hucksters," *Business Week*, October 25, 1991, pp. 52–57.

3. Camp, Robert C. *Benchmarking: The Search for Industry Best Practices That Lead to Superior Performance*, Quality Press, Milwaukee, WI, 1989.

4. Crosby, Philip B. *Quality Without Tears: The Art of Hassle-Free Management*, McGraw-Hill, New York, NY, 1984.

5. Feigenbaum, Armand V. *Total Quality Control*, Third Edition, (first edition in 1951), McGraw-Hill, New York, NY, 1991.

6. Feigenbaum, Armand V. "Total Quality Control," *Harvard Business Review*, Vol. 34, No. 6, November-December 1956, pp. 93–101.

7. Finkelstein, Clive. *An Introduction to Information Engineering*, Addison-Wesley Publishing Co., Reading, MA, 1989.

8. Gabor, Andrea. *The Man Who Discovered Quality*, 1990.

9. Ishikawa, Kaoru. *Introduction to Quality Control*, Translated by John Howard Loftus, 3A Corporation, Tokyo, Japan, 1989.

10. Juran, J. M. *Juran On Quality by Design*, The Free Press, New York, NY, 1992.

11. Katz. D. and Kahn, R. *The Social Psychology of Organizations*, Wiley and Sons, New York, NY, 1966.

12. Keen, Peter G. *Every Manager's Guide to Information Technology*, Harvard Business School Press, Cambridge, MA, 1991.

13. Lewin, Kurt. "Frontiers in Group Dynamics: Concepts, Methods, and Reality in Social Science," *Human Relations*, Vol. 1, No. 1, 1947, pp. 5–41.

14. Lewin, Kurt. *Field Theory in Social Science: Selected Theoretical Papers*, Harper and Brothers, New York, NY, 1951.

15. Miller, J. "Living Systems: The Organization," *Behavioral Science*, Vol. 17, 1972, pp. 2–182.

16. Roethlisberger, F. J. and Dickson, W. J. *Management and the Worker*, Harvard University Press, Cambridge, MA, 1939.

17. Roy, Ranjit. *A Primer on the Taguchi Method*, Van Nostrand Reinhold, New York, NY, 1990.

18. Simon, Herbert and Newell, Allen. "Models: Their Uses and Limitations," in L. D. White (ed.), *The State of the Social Sciences*, University of Chicago Press, Chicago, Ill, 1956.

19. Schein, Edgar H. "The Role of the Founder in Creating Organizational Culture," *Organizational Dynamics*, Summer 1983, pp. 13–28.

20. Schein, Edgar H. "Coming to a New Awareness of Organizational Culture," *Sloan Management Review*, Vol. 24, Winter 1984, pp. 3–16.

21. Schein, Edgar H. *Organizational Culture and Leadership*, Jossey-Bass, San Francisco, 1985.

22. Simon, Herbert. *The Science of Artificial*, second edition, (first edition in 1961), the MIS Press, Cambridge, MA, 1981.

23. Taguchi, Genichi. *Taguchi Methods*, American Supplier Institute, Tokyo, Japan, 1989.

24. Taylor, F. W. *Scientific Management*, Harper and Brothers, New York, NY, 1947 (original work was published in 1911).

25. Tichy, Noel M. and Ulrich, David O. "The Leadership Challenge—A Call for the Transformational Leader," *Sloan Management Review*, Vol. 25, Fall 1984, pp. 59–68.

26. Tichy, Noel M. and Devanna, Mary Ann. *Transformational Leader*, Wiley and Sons, New York, NY, 1986.

◆ Questions

1.1. Discuss the ingredients of quality in the context of information systems.

1.2. Review the conceptual developments that form the foundation of total quality management and divide them into technical and behavioral categories.

1.3. Discuss the major contributions of quality gurus.

1.4. What are the differences between quality awards and quality standards?

1.5. What are the major quality awards in the world?

1.6. What are the major quality standards in the world?

1.7. What are the precursors of ISO 9000?

1.8. What are the differences between the ISO 9000 and Q90 series?

1.9. What is the quality information systems approach?

1.10. Identify the areas in which traditional and quality information systems differ.

1.11. Discuss the differences between quality information systems and traditional information systems in dealing with people.

1.12. Discuss the differences between quality information systems and traditional information systems in organizational structure.

1.13. What are the major approaches in which quality information systems and traditional information systems differ?

1.14. What are the major processes that distinctively belong to quality information systems?

1.15. Compare and contrast the techniques in quality information systems with those in traditional information systems.

1.16. Discuss the role of information systems as a tool for managing quality.

1.17. Identify specific areas of information systems that deal with quality-related information and knowledge.

But the harvest are surely those who have the clearest vision of what is before them, glory and danger alike, and yet notwithstanding go out and meet it.

— *Funeral Oration of Pericles*
Thucydidtes, 460–400 B.C.
Translated by Sir Richard Livingstone

The future belongs to those who believe in the beauty of their dreams.

— Eleanor Roosevelt

Self-expression must pass into communication for its fulfillment.

— Pearl S. Buck

If you don't agree with me, it means you haven't been listening.

— Sam Markewich

◆ Chapter Objectives

The objectives of this chapter are:
- To discuss the people aspect of quality management
- To introduce the importance of vision in leadership
- To emphasize the importance of empowerment and the approaches to achieving it
- To demonstrate how the concepts of vision and empowerment are applied to quality information systems

◆ Key Words

Vision, leadership, vision types, questioning, brainstorming, mental mapping, affinity diagram, empowerment, involvement, team development, training, communication, organizational structure, organizational culture

IS Leadership with Vision and Empowerment

2.1 Vision
    2.1.1 Vision as a Guiding Light
    2.1.2 Leadership
    2.1.3 The Nature of Vision
    2.1.4 Private vs. Group Vision

2.2 Creating Vision
    2.2.1 Questioning
    2.2.2 Brainstorming
    2.2.3 Mental Mapping
    2.2.4 Affinity Diagram

2.3 Employee Empowerment and Involvement
    2.3.1 Education and Training
    2.3.2 Team Development
    2.3.3 Communication
    2.3.4 Recognition and Award
    2.3.5 Organizational Structure
    2.3.6 Organizational Culture

◆ Introduction

The behavioral dimension of quality information systems includes people and leadership. This chapter covers the people aspects of quality management. It discusses the difference between leading with a vision and just managing. Here, we cover methods of creating vision with examples related to information systems.

Empowerment and involvement constitute another major people-oriented aspect of quality information systems. This chapter covers the approaches for empowering employees, including training, team development, instituting quality-focused communication, recognition and award, and changing the organizational structure.

This chapter concludes that quality management is about changing the culture of organization. Leadership, with vision and through empowerment, forms just one component of the quality culture. The strategical and technical aspects covered in the upcoming chapters form the remaining parts of the quality puzzle.

2.1   ◆   Vision

Creating a culture of quality and commitment to quality requires more than simply applying techniques, providing massive training, following a set of recommended procedures, or getting certified in quality. It starts with a collective commitment to a vision.

Psychologists have long been aware of the power of personal vision. To accomplish any great feat or create new patterns and habits, the individual should first envision the desirable. To become an accomplished theater actor, the aspiring beginner envisions acting his or her most-cherished part for a big audience, the standing ovation applauding his or her performance, and the rave reviews of critics. A business unit needs a similar vision to channel its collective energy in a common direction.

It is easier to begin defining vision by stating what it is not. Vision is not the prediction of the future based on the present state of affairs, nor is it a pie-in-the-sky notion, or an unfounded dream. The dictionary definitions of vision include "something seen in a dream; the act or power of imagination; unusual discernment or foresight; and the act or power of seeing." Although an operative vision contains elements of these definitions, it goes further in that it embodies the way a unit likes to picture itself in the future.

Vision is the desired or ideal state of the unit. It is a picture of the ideal future. Vision is the answer to the question: Where are we going? What do we look like when we arrive at our desired destination? The "we" in this definition consists of the leaders and members of the unit sharing the vision. The unit could be the entire organization, an IS department, an IS project team, or a software product.

Vision conforms to the dictionary definition of the word in that it contains foresight, is imaginative, and defines the collective dream of the unit. However, the difference between a vision statement and a pipe dream is the collective commitment of the unit members to the vision. It is a dream to which the unit commits to realize, and therefore the vision becomes the guiding light for every action and decision within the unit.

2.1.1   Vision as a Guiding Light

Once defined and committed to, the vision becomes the force behind every undertaking of the unit. In the hierarchy of leadership tools, going from the most macro and aggregate to detailed and micro, vision stands on the uppermost level of the hierarchy, as shown in Figure 2.1. Hence, it is essential to distinguish vision from mission, values, principles, purpose, goals, and plans, all of which are essential in an organization committed to quality.

Mission.   It is easy to confuse vision with mission. While vision identifies *what* the desired state is, *mission* identifies *how* the unit intends to realize the vision. In other words, vision is a state and mission is a set of actions or behaviors. For example, a hypothetical credit information company, called ACCU-INFO, has this vision:

> We provide the most accurate information on credit-worthiness of shoppers within the United States.

The mission of ACCU-INFO is:

> We satisfy our customers by providing an integrated information system that combines reliable data from all possible sources, and by creating an atmosphere of trust and growth for our employees.

Values and Principles.   *Values* are the moral beliefs that the unit collectively holds. Values include integrity, professionalism, honesty, loyalty, respect for people, and fairness.

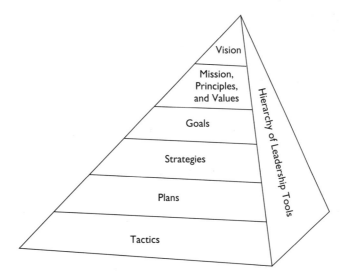

Figure 2.1   Hierarchy of Leadership Tools

Principles consist of a collection of core values upon which the unit operates. Principles guide the behavior of stakeholders.

For example, ACCU-INFO has the following principle:

> We respect the creativity and rights of individuals, and work as teams to improve the quality of our service to internal and external customers.

Purpose.   Peter Senge [1990] differentiates vision and purpose as follows: "Purpose is similar to a direction, a general leading. Vision is a specific destination, a picture of a desired future." Purpose is abstract. Vision is concrete. In the ACCU-INFO example, purpose is advancing customers' capability to explore all possible information. Vision is providing customers with the most accurate credit rating information.

Goals.   *Goals* consist of set values for measures related to the vision. Since vision identifies a state, we should define measures that identify that state. In the ACCU-INFO vision, we have the words the most accurate information. Now, the question is what measures define accuracy. One possible measure is:

> The time lag (in hours or days) between a change in a shopper's credit data and the update of the system to reflect the change.

We call this the *update interval* measure. The smaller this measure, the better the accuracy. Now, a goal could be that this measure should be reduced to 2 within the next two years. Thus, this goal is a value for one measure related to the vision.

A goal is related to a measure and has a time dimension for its achievement. Vision-related goals and measures form a crucial aspect of commitment to realizing the vision. We will come back to the issue of measurement in Chapters 8, 9 and 10.

Plans.   *Plans* determine a set of specific future actions that will move the unit toward its vision. In the ACCU-INFO example, a plan will determine actions necessary for reducing the *update interval* measure. One such plan consists of creating a computer network with access to databases that are the primary repository of shoppers' credit data.

2.1.2   Leadership

The leader's compassionately personal commitment to quality and customer focus is one of the main points in the evaluation process for the Baldrige Award. One of the seven main categories of the Baldrige Award is leadership (that is worth 90 of a total 1,000 points):

> The Leadership category examines senior executives' *personal* leadership and in-volvement in creating and sustaining a customer focus and clear and visible quality values. Also examined is how the quality values are integrated into the company's management system and reflected in the manner in which the company addresses its

public responsibilities and corporate citizenship [Malcolm Baldrige Quality Award 1993].

Deming's first point is the continuity and constancy of purpose. Crosby's first step is the management commitment to quality. The constancy and commitment require vision. Vision sets a leader apart from a regular manager.

History contains accounts of leaders with vision, leaders who were able to communicate and share their vision with their followers and inspire them to realize it. What distinguishes a leader from a manager is that a leader has a vision, which synthesizes the collective energy of the group members toward achieving the vision, while a manager organizes and uses resources efficiently.

A good manager structures work in a logical manner. This logic is normally limited to the micro domain of the manager's sphere of responsibility. A good information systems manager will make sure that the system is designed according to specifications at a reasonable cost. A leader with a vision adds passion and emotion to this logical structure. For the leader, it is not enough to create the system at reasonable cost; he or she strives to create a system that moves the organization toward satisfying and even foreseeing customer needs with zero defect and quality. Vision acts like a compass pushing the organization's activities in a single direction.

A manager puts in place rules, procedures, regulations, and systems to organize employee activities required to produce the intended goods, services, or systems. A leader helps create an inspiring and moving picture of the ideal, and lets the subsequent activities be guided by this compelling picture.

A manager is like a builder who builds foundations, floors, and walls, and does all with the optimum amount of raw materials and manpower, while following the specifications and standards. A leader envisions a house in which people will enjoy living, shares this vision with those involved in the construction, and builds foundations, floors, and walls to create such a house. If you were a construction worker, which of the two would you rather work for? Would you prefer to build a beautiful wall, or a beautiful wall that will be a part of a child's room in which you can almost hear the children's laughter as you put one brick over the next? The actions involved are the same. The difference is that in the first example you are creating just another wall, because you are a good brick layer. In the second case, there is an emotional charge attached to what you are doing, a compelling sense of contributing to the realization of a vision that you share.

Tichy and Devanna [1986] analyzed a dozen transformational leaders of major U.S. corporations, including Burroughs, Burger King, GM, GE, Chase Manhattan Bank, Chrysler, Honeywell, and Imperial Chemical Industries. They found a number of common characteristics among these leaders. They:

- Are visionaries
- Are value-driven
- Identify themselves as change agents
- Believe in people

- Are courageous individuals
- Are life-long learners
- Have the ability to deal with complexity, ambiguity, and uncertainty

John G. Johnson, the recipient of the 1990 QPMA Leadership Award notes that "Leadership is inspiring people to voluntarily pursue a worthy set of mutually held values." He observes that from the moment of announcing the vision and values, all actions of the leader are judged by his/her consistency with the stated values. For the employees to attach any credibility to the vision, the leader must ensure that the vision becomes the focal point for every one of his or her decisions and actions.

John G. Johnson [1991], reporting on the implementation of TQM at the Harris Corporation, states:

> A skills inventory of the current generation of managers may well cause concerns that we aren't equipped to deal with the conflicts noted above. We are very strong on management or control skills (planning, deciding, directing, and so on) but are relatively weak on leadership skills (inspiring, coaching, nurturing and such). In fact, it appears that our processes for developing managers tend to not select those with the kind of leadership skills needed for TQM. Our "left-brained" incumbent managers tend to view those "right-brained" potential leaders with considerable skepticism. In fact, both sets of skills are going to be required to manage in the new culture.

In an interview, Paul Ellison, the Chairman of the American College of Healthcare Executives, was asked: "What skills have helped you to be an effective leader?" He answered: "I'm a perennial optimist and I've tried to instill that in others. In addition, you must have a vision, a sense of fairness, and you must manage with a steady hand." [Wachel 1991].

2.1.3   The Nature of Vision

Vision is a succinct and simple statement. It should be understandable by all employees while inspiring them to realize it. Bennis and Nanus [1976] state that "The genius of the leadership function is articulating a vision of the future that is at once simple, easily understood, clearly desirable, and energizing."

Lynch and Werner [1992] recommend the following features for the vision statement. It should:

- Be brief and memorable
- Inspire and challenge the employees
- Describe an ideal state
- Appeal to and be shared by all stakeholders
- Describe the future business

Examples of Visions:

British Telecom: "Our vision is to become the world's leading telecommunications company." [Odgers, 1990].

Ford Motor Company: "The maker of the highest quality cars and trucks in the world." [Lynch and Werner, 1992].

Johnson & Johnson: "We believe our first responsibility is to doctors, nurses, and patient, to mothers and all others who use our products." [Lynch and Werner, 1992].

Federal Express: "We will produce outstanding financial returns by providing totally reliable, competitively superior global air-ground transportation of high priority goods and documents that require rapid, time-sensitive delivery" [Lynch and Werner, 1992].

Oregon State University: "It is OSU's vision to be recognized as a premier international university." [from the presentation of Edwin Coate on the strategic total quality management at Oregon State University, 1992].

From these examples, one can observe that vision statements vary in clarity and emphasis. One may criticize some as being slogans, a mixture of missions and values, vague, or non-inclusive of all aspects of the organization. But, there is no right or wrong vision statement as long as it articulates a shared vision, determining the common direction.

2.1.4   Private vs. Group Vision

In formulating the vision statement, the question is where to begin. There are three possible approaches:

- Private
- Group
- Mixture of Private and Group

Private Vision.   In many instances, the leader formulates a vision for the unit and then works to convince all stakeholders to accept and share the vision. Don Ciampa [1992] observes:

> *The first step in the creation of the common vision for the organization is a personal vision for the leader; that is, an image in the mind's eye of the leader of a future state that he or she wants most to see created. That future state may not seem practical at the present time or may not closely resemble what currently exists, and the distance between what is and what is desired may well seem daunting.*

This personal vision becomes a passion for the leader. A charismatic leader is able to convey, convince, and transform his or her passion to the employees. This transformation does not take place overnight. It is an ongoing and gradual process, affected by the culture and history of the organization. However, the private vision is of no consequence until it is turned into a shared vision within the organization.

Group Vision.   In many non-profit, academic, or public-sector organizations, the formulation of the leader's private vision may not be the only way to formulate a vision. The unit as a whole can formulate a vision through an interactive process that will be discussed later. The idea of the group vision is that a group of people (all employees or their representatives) attempts to formulate a vision for the unit.

There are instances in which the basic aspects of a unit's vision may have already been predetermined externally. For example, the vision for a hospital is to provide the best quality health care for its patients. The law has determined the vision for the Environmental Protection Agency (EPA).

While the general framework of the vision is already defined, the unit members still can define a more specific vision for the unit. The process of generating group consensus through affinity diagrams and other quality tools is described in a later section.

Mixture of Private and Group Visions.   It is also possible for the leader to start with a private vision, and have the entire unit refine it or make it more specific and relevant to their work.

The *working visions* for departments or products are examples of making the corporate vision more specific. For example, an information systems (IS) department takes the corporate vision and defines its working vision for the IS function. In this case, the involvement of department members in the definition of the IS working vision is quite essential.

In quality information systems and software development, having a mental model of what the end product must be is essential in providing inspiration and direction to the process. Spool [1992] divides software prototypes into *user prototype* and *design prototype*. The user prototype is the user's vision of what the product should be. The vision may be impractical at the present, but it provides guidance for the evolution of the product. Developing a user prototype for information systems serves a similar purpose. Chapter 5 will expand on the use of vision in IS requirement analysis.

2.2   ◆   Creating Vision

Vision is not created quickly. For some companies, it has taken more than a year to arrive at the vision. This is true when the group vision is being defined. Creating a group vision requires extensive interaction and consensus building among the stakeholders.

The process could be helped by:

- Questioning
- Brainstorming

- Mental Mapping
- Affinity Diagram

2.2.1   Questioning

Questioning stimulates the group members to identify the major ingredients of the vision statement. Normally, vision focuses on the performance of the unit, service to the internal and external customers of the unit, and the way the unit is perceived. Hence, the process may be helped by asking questions such as:

- What is the most desirable outcome of our work?
- What is the value of the outcome for us and for others?
- What is the importance of what we do?
- Who are our external customers?
- Who are our internal customers?
- How do we want to be known by our customers?

The purpose of these questions is to identify the nature of what is being produced as well as the internal and external customers of the product.

For example, for an information systems department, in answering the question: "What is the most desirable outcome of our work?" the group may discover that what is important in information systems is whether it improves the quality of the decision or action by every direct or indirect user of the system. In other words, if the information system does not benefit the quality of decisions and products, it adds no value to the organization, even if the system generates the best and most accurate information every time.

Questions such as "What is the value of the outcome for us and for others?" and "What is the importance of what we do?" direct the vision group toward the impact of the system on the overall working of the organization, rather than the technical sophistication of the system per se.

The question: "Who are our external customers?" focuses the vision group on customers. In information systems, external customers are not necessarily external to the organization. For example, external customers of an information systems department could be other departments within the organization, or customers external to the organization.

Internal customers of an information systems department or project are members of that department or project. The question: "Who are our internal customers?" focuses the attention on those who create and maintain the systems. They play a major role in producing and providing information services and should be included in the vision.

The question: "How do we want to be known by our customers?" focuses the group on the way the group would like to be perceived by its customers, internally and externally. The question opens the discussion on the professional pride of the group. Answers such as: "We would like our external customers to see us as the most reliable source of relevant information for their decisions and actions" puts the emphasis on professional pride and quality focus in the vision statement.

2.2.2   Brainstorming

Developed by Osborne in the 1930s [Osborne 1953], brainstorming is often thought of as a meeting in which group members churn out ideas. It is useful only when applied properly.

The philosophy behind brainstorming is (1) to generate a large set of ideas, (2) by a number of individuals, (3) in a short period of time [Jones and McBride 1990].

Brainstorming has four phases:

- Generation
- Categorization
- Discussion
- Selection

Generation Phase.   In the generation phase of brainstorming, ideas are not judged as bad or good. The goal is to produce as many ideas as possible.

Assume that we want to use brainstorming to generate a proposal for the vision statement of an information systems department. The department forms the IS Vision Group and selects 5 to 12 members, some from the department, and some from other units and top management. The time is fixed at an hour for each session.

The department assigns a group leader who is trained in brainstorming techniques. The leader should use the following guidelines for the brainstorming phase:

- No criticism or evaluation of ideas is allowed. Criticism hampers creativity. A humorous or silly idea may end up being the most creative one.
- Free flow of ideas should be encouraged and all ideas must be recorded. Wild and numerous ideas encourage creative suggestions.
- Repeated ideas should also be recorded. Grouping and evaluation will take place later.
- All group members should participate, and the leader must demand that each member contribute as many ideas as possible. The emphasis is on the quantity, not quality, of ideas.
- Record ideas on flipcharts and hang up the filled sheets for members to see.
- To ensure participation, the leader should go around the table again and again and call on every member for an idea. A person who does not have any idea at the moment could say "pass."
- Adopting, stealing, and cross-fertilization of ideas are encouraged. A member may revise, enhance, or reword another person's idea. This process is crucial for generating good ideas.

The idea generation could be facilitated by *priming* or *brainwriting*. In this method, each member is asked to prepare a list of ideas (good or bad). Each list is reviewed by all other members in a short interval. Other members can add new ideas to the list. The list is returned to the original owner. Thus, when members come to the meeting, they already have some ideas on paper.

Categorization Phase. In the categorization phase, the ideas are grouped into categories. The discussion at this phase is to clarify the nature of ideas and group them into a more general category. No criticism or evaluation is allowed during this phase. The owner of the idea may be allowed to elaborate on it. Others can ask clarifying questions.

For example, the brainstorming for the IS Vision Group has led to the following categories of ideas:

1. Produce the best state-of-the-art information systems
2. Provide the most reliable information to other departments
3. Create information systems that enhance the quality of products
4. Be known as a model of information systems departments within the profession
5. Create the best environment for personal and professional growth
6. Make the systems accessible to every internal and external customer

Discussion Phase. In the discussion phase, the categories of ideas are discussed in detail. The discussion phase may be postponed to another session in order to reduce the memory of the ownership of ideas, and collect facts regarding the ideas, if needed.

Evaluation and criticisms are allowed in this phase. The discussions should be based on facts, rather than personal opinions and judgments. The criticism should be directed toward ideas, not the owners of ideas.

In this phase, the group may decide on the criteria for judging the idea categories. For example, the IS Vision Group has decided to judge the idea categories by feasibility, desirability, and profitability criteria.

Selection Phase. In the selection phase, the group members evaluate each category of ideas based on the agreed criteria of the previous phase and then judge every category. That is, each member assigns a number (say between 0 and 1, 1 being the best) to every evaluation criterion for each category. The rating of a category would be the sum of the numbers assigned to its criteria by group members. The group then selects the top-rated categories.

In the example of the IS Vision Group, six categories of ideas were created in the categorization phase and three criteria were chosen in the discussion phase. In the discussion phase, the members have evaluated and criticized every category. Thus, they have a good idea of the nature and implications of every category. In the selection phase, the group members rate each category based on feasibility, desirability, and profitability criteria.

To facilitate the rating process, one can use the evaluation chart as shown in Figure 2.2. This chart shows one member's evaluation chart for the IS Vision Group. The rating of Category 1 is .5, .9, and .2 for feasibility, desirability, and profitability, respectively. The rating of this category by one member is 1.6. The sum of the rating of all members for Category 1 determines the group ratings of this category.

	Criteria			Individual Total Rating
Idea Categories	Feasibility	Desirability	Profitability	
1. Produce the best state-of-the-art information systems	.5	.9	.2	1.6
2. Provide the most reliable information to other departments	.9	.9	.8	2.6
3. Create information systems that enhance the quality of products	1.0	1.0	1.0	3.0
4. Be known as a model IS department within the profession	.6	.7	.5	1.8
5. Create the best environment for personal and professional growth	.9	1.0	.7	2.6
6. Make systems accessible to every internal and external customer	.4	.6	.5	1.5

Figure 2.2   Individual Evaluation Chart for IS Vision Group

A similar process is applied to all six categories, with the results shown in Figure 2.3. According to this evaluation chart, categories 2, 3, 4, and 5 have the highest ratings. They form the basis for this vision statement for our information systems department:

The information systems department creates information systems that enhance the quality of products by providing error-free and up-to-date information services, and is a model of information systems departments with the best environment for personal and professional growth.

The IS Vision Group will propose this vision statement to the department members and the organization for discussion and final approval.

Note that in this evaluation process, the three criteria—feasibility, desirability, and profitability—are given equal weight. In a more sophisticated evaluation process, the

	Criteria			Group Total Rating
Idea Categories	Feasibility	Desirability	Profitability	
1. Produce the best state-of-the-art information systems	5.0	9.0	2.2	16.2
2. Provide the most reliable information to other departments	9.5	9.6	7.0	26.1
3. Create information systems that enhance the quality of products	9.8	9.7	9.0	28.5
4. Be known as a model IS department within the profession	7.0	6.1	4.5	17.6
5. Create the best environment for personal and professional growth	8.5	9.2	8.1	25.8
6. Make systems accessible to every internal and external customer	5.1	5.5	3.9	14.5

Figure 2.3   Group Evaluation Chart for IS Vision Group

members assign different weights to each criterion. This approach will be discussed in Chapter 5.

2.2.3   Mental Mapping

Metal mapping is a method for aiding the creative process and unblocking mental barriers. The purpose of mental mapping is to use unorganized and sometimes seemingly illogical associations in order to tap mental creativity. The associations are intended to mimic the way information is stored in our brain.

This is the least structured method of creating ideas and can be used as part of the brainwriting process for idea generation in brainstorming. Moreover, one can apply this technique at the team meeting during the generating phase of brainstorming.

In mental mapping, we start with the core problem. Applied to vision creation, the core problem is "what is our vision?" Then, one member starts drawing branches out of the box to identify issues to the core problem. The member continues to draw branches from the core or from other branches. Then, other group members join in by suggesting more branches related to the box or to already created branches. The purpose of this method is to generate a mental picture of all issues related to the core problem.

Let us apply this method to the IS Vision Group's efforts to create a vision for the information systems department.

The group starts with the core question "What is the IS department's working vision?" as shown in Figure 2.4. One member starts a branch that indicates users are important for any information system, and then adds branches related to the type of users. This mapping is done on a large board or flipchart so that all members can see it. Another member adds the branch on corporate vision, and says that the IS vision should be within the corporate vision. The first member adds profitability, corporate goals, and strategies as sub-branches to this branch. As the meeting progresses, group members add branches and sub-branches to the mapping. The outcome is a mapping that can be used as a basis for brainstorming or affinity diagram.

2.2.4   Affinity Diagram

Among the major quality tools, affinity diagram is the most helpful in the process of vision creation. It lends structure to the process and encompasses the main aspects of previously discussed techniques.

Affinity diagram is defined as a tool that "gathers a large amount of language data (ideas, opinions, issues, etc.), organizes it into groupings based on the natural relationship between each item, and defines groups of items. It is largely a creative rather than a logical process" [Michael Brassard, 1989]. Michael Brassard provides a concise and useful discussion of this method.

Affinity diagram has its basis in the KJ Method© developed in the 1960s by Jiro Kawakita, a Japanese anthropologist. He needed the method to efficiently organize a large amount of information and to bring out new patterns that might exist in the information.

Affinity diagram is useful when:

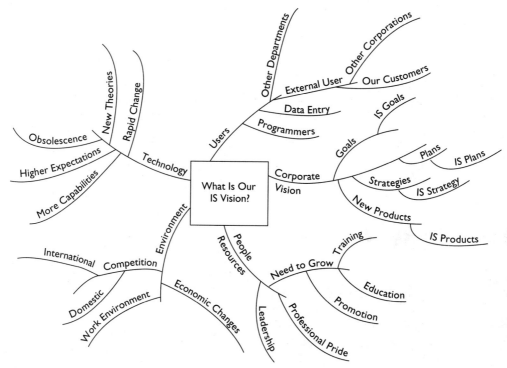

Figure 2.4   Mental Mapping for IS Vision Group

- A team has to deal with the problem
- The issue is complex and chaotic
- Traditional methods of problem solving are of no help
- No easy or quick solution exists

Affinity diagram has phases similar to the brainstorming method. It involves the following steps:

- Assembling the team
- Posing the central question
- Generating ideas
- Grouping ideas
- Assigning headers

Assembling the Team.   The team members should represent diverse views on the central issues and at the same time be able to communicate together smoothly, and know each other's language and concerns.

For example, in the IS Vision Group, the group members should reflect the diverse IS department groups and user groups. At the same time, the members should have worked together previously so that they can communicate well. The team should have about 4 to 12 members. It should have a facilitator, who does not engage in the discussion, but follows the affinity diagram procedure and helps members in the process.

Posing the Central Question.   The central issue or concern should be stated vaguely. Too many details and guidelines could prejudice the discussion. As in brainstorming, the team needs a free flow of ideas and an atmosphere of "anything goes."

In the example of the IS Vision Group, the central issue is "What is the IS vision?" The central issue is placed on the top of a flipchart or a blackboard for all team members to see. When discussions become tangential, this reminds team members what the main issue is.

Generating Ideas.   Small cards or 3M Post-it ^{TM} pads are distributed among the members and they are asked to write their ideas, one on each card or Post-it, in silence. After members are finished, the facilitator goes round the table, asks each member for one idea, and records it on the flipchart. The process continues until all ideas are recorded. Writing ideas on a flipchart or blackboard helps stimulate new ideas in other members.

At this phase, as in brainstorming, no criticism or discussion of ideas is allowed. All ideas are recorded, no matter how silly, humorous, outrageous, or repetitious. Each idea should be on one card or Post-it, and should be as concise as possible. Brassard [1990] recommends that each idea should have a noun and a verb in order to be both concise and clear.

For example, in the IS Vision Group, one member has the following ideas in his or her cards:

- Must serve our users
- Need to keep up-to-date with technology
- Should be the best in the market
- Should minimize errors in the system
- Should have reliable information
- Should define reliability for information systems
- Need guidelines from the top
- Must know information needs early
- Need training on the job
- Need professional training
- Should define what quality is
- Should learn what customers want

Grouping Ideas.   In this phase, ideas are grouped together, as in the brainstorming method. The process involves the following:

- The cards (or Post-its) are posted onto a spacious surface on which they could be reshuffled
- The members are asked to group the cards based on the similarity of ideas
- The member who does not agree with a grouping simply changes the cards
- The process should take place in silence
- No discussions or arguments are allowed
- No force-fitting of cards is allowed. Loner cards with no group are acceptable
- The process should move forward quickly; it is a reflexive rather than contemplative process
- Members should move around and allow others to regroup the cards
- Repeated reshuffling of cards is allowed and encouraged
- In the case of disagreement, cards are moved around until nobody wants to move around anymore cards

Assigning a Header.   In this phase, one of the cards that best represents the group is chosen to serve as the group header. It is possible and common that no such card exists. In this case, the team should come up with an appropriate header card that generalizes the group of cards under that header.

The following points should be followed for header assignment:

- Be innovative in devising the group headers
- Do not use familiar cliches and categories—they have the ring of business as usual
- In devising the header, be sensitive to tones and emphasis of statements on cards; they reflect the direction of change
- The header card should be concise and meaningful by itself
- Discussions and arguments over the headers are allowed

Once the group headers are determined, groups of headers themselves are generalized into a more aggregate header, thus forming a hierarchy of headers and ideas. The idea groups and their headers form a diagram of interrelated components that is called affinity diagram.

For example, the ideas listed in the previous section can be grouped into the following headers:

Header card: Must focus on customers
    Must serve our users
    Should learn what customers want
    Must know information needs early

Header card: Technology changes rapidly
    Need to keep up-to-date with technology

Header card: Quality is essential
    Should be the best in the market
    Should define what quality is

Header card: Should have reliable systems
    Should minimize errors in the system
    Should have reliable information
    Should define reliability for information systems

Header card: Corporate vision is needed
    Need guidelines from the top

Header card: Education and training are essential
    Need training on the job
    Need professional training

The headers Quality is essential and Should have reliable systems may be aggregated into a more general header card: Need a quality philosophy. The final aggregate header for this example is: Components of the vision statement. Figure 2.5 shows the affinity diagram for this portion of the IS Vision Group example.

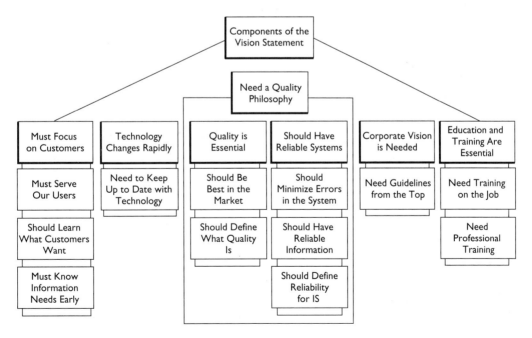

Figure 2.5   Affinity Diagram for a Portion of IS Vision Group

2.3 ◆ Employee Empowerment and Involvement

All quality standards and gurus cite employee empowerment and involvement as one of the major prerequisites of any quality undertaking.

One of the seven categories of the Baldrige Award is human resource development (worth 150 points of the total of 1000 points). It is defined as:

> The Human Resource Development and Management category examines key elements of how the work force is enabled to develop its full potential to pursue the company's quality and operational objectives. Also examined are the company's efforts to build and maintain an environment for quality excellence conducive to full participation and personal and organizational growth. [Malcolm Baldrige Quality Award 1993].

Two of Deming's 14 points are: "drive out fear," and "remove barriers to pride of workmanship" in order to empower employees to perform at their best.

John G. Johnson [1991], who reports on the implementation of TQM at the Harris Corporation states:

> *Each worker must feel accountable for the quality of his or her work, and must have the necessary control over the processes which determine that quality. This level of ownership requires managers to be prepared to give up some control and entrust it to their employees. This is real empowerment, giving over control to the doer for the success of the task and not just asking for suggestions or greater efforts. It's not easy for any manager, and seems to be virtually impossible for some. Nevertheless, employee and team empowerment is an essential element of all values described above. Leaders will be able to do it effectively—managers lacking leadership skills won't.*

An empowered employee gets involved in what he or she does, and will act as an owner of the work, rather than just an indifferent follower of procedures.

Few would disagree about the importance of employee involvement. However, it is easier said than achieved. A Gallup survey of top corporations that had undertaken major quality initiatives, commissioned by the American Society for Quality Control (ASQC), found that "over two-thirds of employees responding indicated that they felt that they were now expected to participate in making work decisions, but less than 15 percent agreed that they had any authority or power to make such decisions" [Hyde 1991].

◆ CASE: Employee Involvement

Total quality management sounds like something managers do *to* employees. Total quality involvement tells it like it is: quality can only be gained through participation and the involvement of everybody.

Over the past two years or so, region nine of the Employment Standards Admin-istration (ESA), U.S. Department of Labor, under the committed leadership of William Buhl, has been implementing total quality involvement in three agencies: Wage and Hour Division, Office of Workers Compensation Programs, and the Office of Federal Contract Compliance Programs (OFCCP). These three agencies are composed of numerous field offices spread throughout the states of California, Arizona, Nevada, and Hawaii.

If we have learned one thing, it is that total involvement is like fusion. It releases energy and vitality. Little or no involvement fizzles the reaction, saps energy, and thickens inertia.

When we use the term involvement, we speak of more than just token involvement, such as roundtable discussions and suggestion boxes. Government has tried the suggestion box for years and ended up with too few good ideas and an abundance of used candy wrappers. For us, involvement means more than just training managers or constructing a parallel organization to drive the total quality process.

Involvement = training. Involvement means training virtually everyone in group pro-cess, meeting management, and quality enhancement skills and then including them on teams, be they task forces, quality circle, cross-functional link, or focused workgroup teams. This way, everyone is more fully empowered, integrated into the organization and has a stake in maintaining momentum.

Yes, like TQM, we are finding redundancies, needless complexities, unmet require-ments, potential bottlenecks, and too much re-work. But, the TQI attention on involvement breeds the energy, flexibility, and willingness to put in the extra effort that is essential to continuously improve our processes and embrace the changes.

Involvement = energy. The more involvement, the more motivated, enthusiastic, confident, creative, expressive, and productive managers and staff became. Let's face it: the single biggest resource we have is human energy. And the only way to harness its full capabilities and power is through involvement and teamwork at all levels of the organization.

Management involvement. Some managers have experienced real involvement as a godsend, relieving them of many tasks and allowing them to focus on long-range concerns. Others have yet to understand clearly their new role as communicator, coach, counselor, and facilitator and understandably are skeptical and hesitant to engage in what they may perceive as a "passing fad." A few just don't think it will work. Yet others are struggling with learning how to "keep their hands in their pockets" and let the teams work a problem.

One manager describes TQI as the most exciting thing that's happened for him in 20 years of service. Another manager has seen communication and trust improve so much in her office that she now takes vacations where she cannot be reached without fearing an office melt-down.

Real breakthroughs have occurred in perception. Some managers have frankly ac-knowledged that, before TQI, they saw staff as 'extensions of themselves' and as units of production, but that has changed. Now many see their team as a brain trust to be nurtured and tapped. One manager puts it this way: "I began to realize that everyone had something valuable to contribute, even if it meant doing things differently from the way I liked to operate. As I started listening more to people, I began to trust what I was hearing."

These managers are discovering that everyone has a wide range of untapped and therefore unsuspected potential—potential that when given half a chance is easily accessed and put to good use by involvement and appropriate leadership.

Staff involvement. Trust, teamwork, enthusiasm, discretionary effort, creativity, confidence, self-expression, empowerment, selflessness, and communication head the list of budding involvement-induced qualities and behaviors. Barely a week goes by without hearing quotes like, "It's almost too good to be true. I'm not sure I quite trust it yet." TQI is like an unproven tonic that has opened a window of hope and begun to rejuvenate the spirit of organization.

Selflessness. Examples of emerging selflessness are the professional staff from two field offices who have moved outside their job descriptions and given creative extra efforts to improve existing computer software in a way that allows their peers in all offices to share the benefits.

Work organized by team. One field office has totally organized itself to handle all incoming work as teams. In an informal survey, the team members rated communication among themselves as excellent. In addition, they reported lower stress levels.

In some of the offices, the way casework is assigned has changed from the best assignment always going to the *stars* of the office to a much more democratic method. The result is that the quality of everyone's work has improved.

The manager of one area office reported: "I've noticed a big change in the confidence level of the staff. I've gone from being the *answer man*, with a solution to every problem, to the role of resource or coach for people to bounce off their ideas." Isn't that what real leadership is about... helping people think for themselves?

In virtually every office where the training has been implemented, most of the staff feels more empowered and willing to break out of the old ways and challenge existing methods, including those required by current procedure manuals.

Involvement at the ESA, Its Mission and Its Work

We have so far maintained and observed that energizing the total quality enhancement process with real involvement builds employee confidence, motivation, flexibility, and creativity. But those aren't the only reasons for emphasizing involvement at the Employment Standards Administration. Two other reasons are: (1) anything less than real involvement is incongruent with the mission and purpose of ESA; and (2) the highly interactive and interpersonal nature of the field investigators' work with corporations is enhanced by learning and utilizing involvement processes.

Congruence with the mission. The mission of ESA is to safeguard the legislated rights of the workers *and* to advocate practices that will maintain or improve the integration and productivity of America's workforce in the face of the extraordinary demographic changes predicted in *Workforce 2000* and *Opportunity 2000* (studies commissioned by the US Department of Labor). One of the core recommendations of the studies is to "invest in people."

Involvement *is* an investment in people, an investment that allows them to participate fully in their organization in a way that fosters harmony, quality, productivity, and continuous improvement of self as well as work processes.

As the standard bearer of fairness and justice in the workplace, the Department of Labor, through ESA, should operate on the cutting edge of labor/management practices. There isn't any doubt that an involved work force is more satisfied and productive. Accordingly, it behooves the Federal agency most concerned with America's work force to set the involvement standard.

The Work Process. The majority of professional staff at the ESA are frontline investigators and fact finders who are charged with enforcing a myriad of regulations designed to protect workers' rights. Their daily activities involve frequent meetings with contractors, complainants, and potential witnesses. Often they interface with CEOs, human resource professionals, and attorneys.

Perceived conflict orientation. These investigators are too frequently perceived as unwelcome intruders upon management prerogatives, especially in the area of employee selection, training, promotion, and compensation. Accordingly, the investigator/employer relationship tends to be adversarial and often results in time consuming and unnecessary conflict, extra work, and drawn out, cumbersome and expensive litigation.

Through training and ongoing membership in TQI teams, the frontline staff will have an ongoing context within which they can learn and/or enhance skills for managing interpersonal relationships, problem solving, meeting management, conflict resolution, and negotiating. These are the very skills that can maximize their effectiveness as change agents, and gain quicker resolutions.

To quote the experience of one OFCCP investigator: "The training has enhanced my presentation and negotiation skills and made me a better listener. I spend less time making assumptions and more time gathering data. By taking a facilitative stance, I can convince a contractor to help me collect data, thereby resulting in a more collaborative approach. This saves time, since the contractor is more familiar with its own data. I try to present such a request as a win-win situation..."

The Next Step

Our spirits have been rekindled by TQI. The challenge now is to sustain that and channel the energy toward delivering the highest quality service at the least possible cost to the U.S. taxpayer. We are currently developing and refining measurements that realistically assess ESA's service to its many customers. The long-term vision for ESA is captured in the following quote from William Buhl, "The strength of our organization lies in our people. Empowerment is the key to unleashing this enormous potential. Our commitment in region nine is to totally empower our staff."

Source: Excerpt from "Is TQM Enough?" Robert Brownstone and Peter Stonefield, *Journal of Quality and Participation*, July/August 1990, pp. 34–36. Copyright (c) by Association for Quality and Participation, Cincinnati, Ohio. Reprint with permission from AQP.

One of the sub-categories of the Human Development and Management category for the Baldrige Award (worth 40 points) requires the applicant to:

Describe the means available for all employees to contribute effectively to meeting the company's quality and operational performance goals and plans; summarize trends in effectiveness and extent of involvement [Malcolm Baldrige Quality Award 1993].

Empowerment requires information, skills, and resources. It is the leader's task to empower the employees by adopting strategies appropriate for the given type of work and environment, and its success depends on, among other things, the personality and leadership style of the CEOs and their managers. However, successful employee empowerment processes have some common ingredients:

- Education and Training
- Team Development
- Communication
- Recognition and Award
- Organizational Structure
- Organizational Culture

2.3.1   Education and Training

Training is a familiar phrase in information systems analysis and design. User training is a critical phase of deploying information systems. In deploying quality in information systems, training has the same prominent place. In quality training, however, *everyone* is educated and trained.

Two of Deming's 14 points are "institute on-the-job training" and "institute a vigorous program of education and training." Part of Crosby's 14-step program is "supervisory training." Juran's breakthrough sequence includes "determine how to overcome resistance to change" with training as its integral part.

One of the sub-categories of the Human Development and Management category of the Baldrige Award (worth 40 points) requires the applicant to:

Describe how the company determines quality and related education and training needs for all employees. Show how this determination addresses company plans and needs as well as supports employee growth. Outline how such education and training are evaluated, and summarize key trends demonstrating improvement in both the effectiveness and extent of education and training.

◆ CASE: Training at Hewlett-Packard

Hewlett-Packard Co. has always had a reputation for selling high-quality computers, test-and-measurement instruments and other equipments. For the most part, customers were willing to pay a premium for those products.

But in 1980, the company found itself facing Japanese competitors selling comparably high-quality products at lower prices. HP had to change, says Rudell O'Neal, manager of corporate quality training and development. "We couldn't expect our customers to pay more than the competitor's price for the products."

To become more competitive, HP in 1983 adopted total quality control, which O'Neal describes as "a management philosophy and operating methodology." The major tenants of Hewlett-Packard's TQC program are process improvement, customer satisfaction, and the use of quantitative tools.

Having settled on a methodology, HP was then faced with the question of how to train its employees to "think quality." But the company did not seek out high-priced consultants to solve its dilemma. Instead, HP looked within.

In 1983 and 1984, HP combed its worldwide operations to learn what individual departments, divisions, and subsidiaries were doing in quality improvement training. The company selected the programs that appeared to work well and adopted them for a corporate quality training curriculum launched in 1985. Many of the courses came directly from HP's operations in Japan, Singapore, and Malaysia.

Quality has become a buzzword at many companies, notes Barry F. Willman, a computer analyst at Stanford C. Bernstein & Co. "What differentiates Hewlett-Packard from the rest is that they have institutionalized quality throughout the corporation."

Worldwide, HP spends between $150 million and $200 million a year to educate its 92,000 employees, according to Neil M. Johnson, director of corporate education. When other costs are included, such as the time workers spend in classrooms and travel expenses, the total cost of education reaches $400 million to $500 million annually.

O'Neal says some 140 HP trainers spend more than 50% of their time running quality education programs. Most, however, are assigned to specific business areas or departments and are experts in certain quality functions—one trainer teaches the employees software inspection, for example. O'Neal's five-member department oversees the decentralized quality education operations.

Quality training must follow up two basic principles to succeed, say HP executives: The training must be closely linked to other corporate education programs, and top management must be involved.

When HP began quality training in earnest in 1985, for example, TQC was taught to the company's work force in separate classes. Later, TQC education was integrated into orientation classes for new employees and training for new managers.

O'Neal believes that the visible involvement of management is the most critical element of implementing quality-improvement training and that any such effort delegated to a company's lower ranks is doomed. HP president and CEO John Young often kicks off employee orientations and other training sessions, describing the company's quality improvement goals and how employees can help meet them.

HP now offers quality-improvement training for employees on three levels: general TQC education, followed by more job-specific quality training, and augmented by continuing education.

HP emphasizes continuing education and keeping employees current in their fields of expertise. Johnston estimates that in the fast moving high-technology arena, almost half of the knowledge possessed by an HP employee today will become obsolete within four years.

While some training is conducted in classroom settings, a great deal is done through consultation between employees and HP trainers, either in groups or one-on-one. O'Neal estimates quality training per employee can total 50 hours.

"People at HP are very eager to learn," says O'Neal. "Just as we respect our processes to continually improve, we expect our people to continuously improve in how to perform their jobs."

Source: Excerpt from "Hewlett-Packard Educates From Within," Rick Whiting, *Electronic Business,* October 15, 1990, pp. 113–114, reprint with permission from *Electronic Business Buyer,* copyright (c) 1990, Reed Elsevier Inc.

There are a number of issues to be considered in planning training:

- Participation at all levels
- Continuous commitment
- Quality vs. functional training
- Professional vs. on-the-job training
- Tailor-made vs. general training
- Training evaluation

Participation at All Levels. All quality gurus—Deming, Crosby, Juran and others—agree that everyone should be trained. The most critical aspect of training is that the CEOs and managers acknowledge its importance by personally taking part in the training process.

Traditional management methods include a great deal of control and enforcement in day-to-day activities. Management in the quality environment involves far less control and enforcement, and much more modeling, facilitating, and coaching. Taking part in training is one way for the managers to model for their employees, as well as acquire the necessary knowledge to become a coach and facilitator in their managerial tasks.

Management by modeling, coaching, and facilitating is even more relevant in managing information systems. Most employees involved in development, maintenance, and delivery of information services have a high degree of technical knowledge, and each system has unique features. These two factors make it very difficult to have common standard procedures and control structures for all systems. Thus, the IS function hardly lends itself to the traditional managerial style of enforcement and control. The same features make the IS function an ideal environment for quality management—managing by modeling, facilitating, and coaching.

Managing quality puts responsibility on managers for removing barriers to employee involvement, facilitating the production of best outputs, and acting as coach in problem solving. Rather than acting as an omnipotent personage who commands what employees should execute, a quality manager stimulates employees ideas, coaches the selection of best ideas, and facilitates the implementation of these ideas. Thus, a quality manager of the IS function is less like an almighty commander-in-chief and more like a mentor. To become one, IS managers require extensive training in quality.

Continuous Commitment.   In the new production age, a company's most valuable asset is its human resources. Companies invest in their machineries to counter obsolescence. Investing in employee development and training is even more paramount in information systems, where human assets have proven to be the most scarce resource in systems development.

Like any investment, training and education of employees should be an ongoing activity, and have a committed budget. It forms the backbone of the organizational commitment to quality. International comparisons of training and education budgets indicate that U.S. corporations spend less on training than do their Japanese and European counterparts.

This is changing however, and top U.S. companies that have made a commitment to quality have recognized training as an essential component of quality.

The director of customer satisfaction at Ford Motor Company of Canada reports that to ensure continuous improvement among the workforce, "Ford increased its training budget, which is now virtually unlimited in Canada. In 1989, the company invested more money in training than in the seven previous years—unprecedented spending levels that expected to grow in the 1990s" [White 1990]. Motorola has allocated 2.5 percent of its payroll costs (about $120 million annually) to training [Ross 1993]. Xerox initiated its Leadership Through Quality strategy in 1983. To support a massive quality effort, all Xerox employees receive at least 28 hours of basic quality training, and many more hours in advanced quality methods. The fact that one of two Xerox businesses alone, Business Products and Systems, employs more than 50,000 employees indicates the magnitude of the company's commitment to training. In four years of its quality implementation, Xerox has spent four million man-hours and $125 million in Leadership Through Quality training [Hunt 1992].

Quality vs. Functional Training.   As the technology progresses, the degree of specialization and technical skills of employees increases. Nowhere is this more true than computer- and information-related jobs. Those who are involved in information systems development and information technology find themselves in need of continuous updates and education. Many companies have recognized this need, and provide technical training for their employees.

Quality education and training cuts across all functional areas, and is as important as technical know-how in information systems. In high-tech companies with a commitment to quality, the training budget is allocated about 50-50 between functional and quality education. Motorola spends about 40 percent of its training budget on quality education [Ross 1993].

The allocation of the training budget between quality and IS functional training depends on the nature of the function and how advanced the unit is in its quality efforts. At the start of quality implementation, there may be a larger portion allocated to quality training. As the quality deployment becomes established, the time and money spent on the two types of training may become more balanced.

One future trend is the combination of advanced quality training with functional and technical training. This, however, is not true for training top managers; training managers in quality leadership and strategies will remain a crucial aspect of quality initiatives.

Professional vs. On-the-Job Training.   A major part of quality training is carried out through formal professional education. However, the relevance of formal training could be driven home by early involvement of employees in prototype quality projects as well as membership in quality teams. In planning the training process, there should be a careful distribution of training hours between various modes of training and development. In some companies, a new employee spends as much as one year working in various teams and departments in order to learn the company's functional as well as quality processes.

In a technical function such as information systems, on-the-job training is an essential and inevitable part of any new employee's job, novice or experienced. The challenge is to integrate on-the-job training of IS-related subjects with quality training.

Custom-made vs. General Training.   Many aspects of quality are universal in all types of functions and companies. However, an organization's vision as well as the technical and functional climate may require tailor-made training, including custom-made qual-ity training. Furthermore, training could be done in-house or may be contracted to universities, professional institutions, or consulting services.

At the start of quality implementation, quality training is mostly general, because the trainees are educated on the principles and philosophy of quality. Depending on the size, timing, and cost of the training process, this phase may be accomplished either in-house or through outside contracts.

This early quality education includes training in-house trainers and facilitators, called *training the trainers*. (The function of facilitators is discussed in the next section.) As the quality implementation advances and the number of quality-educated and in-house trainers increases, the organization can develop custom-made quality courses specifically appropriate for the organization and the unit.

Like every facet of quality deployment, training requires a well-designed plan with specific objectives, budget, and evaluation measures and process. One of the ways to devise a training plan is to benchmark companies that have succeeded in their quality efforts. (Benchmarking is discussed in Chapter 4.)

Training Evaluation.   Quality training is a process, not a project. A program or project has an end, whereas a process is ongoing. Thus, in order to ensure the intended outcome, the focus of attention should be the process—the way the function is carried out. As we will see in Chapter 3, every process can be continuously improved by the Shewhart-Deming's cycle of plan, do, check, and act. We can apply this cycle to the training process.

The previous sections discussed the planning and execution of the training process. In order to continuously improve the process, one should evaluate the training. This requires establishing evaluation measures. The measures should be developed in accordance with the goals of training. Zagarow [1990] states, "the barometer of success for training efforts is whether the employees are using TQM tools and techniques in their process improvement teams and as they execute their job responsibilities."

The training plan establishes the evaluation measures. The execution of the plan includes the regular data collection after each training episode.

For example, at the start of quality training for an IS department, the training plan contains the following measures:

- Number of hours spent by the top managers in quality training per month (week, quarter, or year)
- Hours of training per employee per month
- Dollars spent on training per employee per month
- Employees' ratings of the quality of training per month
- Employees' perception ratings of training's relevance to his or her IS function per course
- Number of hours spent by employees in applying training materials to his or her IS task per month
- Number of hours spent by an employee in on-the-job quality training per month
- Number of in-house trained employees
- Number of hours spent by in-house trainers educating employees per month
- Satisfaction ratings of internal customers of the employees who have participated in quality training, such as internal users of information systems and data entry personnel
- Satisfaction ratings of external customers of the employees who have participated in quality training, such as external users of information systems

Regular collection of data on the quality of the training process identifies areas of possible improvement. For example, if the satisfaction ratings of IS external customers do not increase as IS employees are trained in quality, then the whole training approach must be reviewed for its effectiveness. Or, a low number of in-house trainers spending time to educate other employees indicates the waste of a valuable resource in training.

Every training process should establish its measures and use them to continuously evaluate the training process and to take actions for improving the process. A training process that is not regularly evaluated is bound to fail eventually.

2.3.2   Team Development

Teamwork is a familiar concept in information systems. Almost all systems development activities are performed through teamwork, in order to draw on the various technical and people skills needed for the project. In quality information systems, the idea of teamwork is not limited to systems development; it encompasses all aspects, including development of vision, strategic planning, project selection, system maintenance, service delivery, day-to-day operations, and any process involving interaction with internal and external IS customers.

One of Deming's 14 points is the breakdown of barriers between departments and staff areas. A vehicle for this is the establishment of departmental as well as cross-functional teams. Crosby recommends the formation of quality teams consisting of department chairs, who oversee the quality improvement process. Juran's breakthrough sequence recommends diagnostic and steering groups. Diagnostic teams identify problems and analyze them. Steering teams, which are cross-functional, identify problem causes, find solutions, and implement them [Hunt, 1992]. Yet, another model is to form a quality council consisting of the organization's top decision makers to oversee quality deployment and improvement through teamwork. Teamwork is recognized as a major ingredient of employee involvement.

Lynch and Werner [1992] suggest the following stages for team development:

- Formation
- Familiarity
- Power
- Performance and synergy

Another way of categorizing team development stages is: forming, storming, performing, and norming. It corresponds to the above stages, where storming is a combination of familiarity and power, and norming is equivalent to synergy.

Formation.   The formation stage involves selecting team members and appointing (or electing) a team leader. The team must have a stated mission or charge. In some cases, especially in quality teams, the team has a *facilitator*. The facilitator has expertise in team management and team problem solving tools relevant to the team's mission. The facilitator does not participate in the substance of discussions. He or she provides expertise for guiding team discussions and problem solving efforts. A facilitator plays the role of objective outsider and consultant to the team.

In team formation, one has to balance practicality against necessity. The two listings that follow contain issues to be balanced in team formation. Examples in the parentheses assume that a team is to be formed with the mission of analyzing users' requirements for an IS project.

Practical considerations include issues such as whether team members:

- Are geographically close (e.g., members are located in one building or city)
- Have adequate time and matching schedules for meetings (e.g., the main CEO user may not have enough time to attend the team meetings)

- Share common technical vocabularies (e.g., a programmer and an external customer may have difficulty communicating)
- Have an understanding of the mission (e.g., a manager may require too much explanation for comprehending why the team is charged with analyzing the users' requirements when he or she has already told the designer what the system is supposed to do)
- Have the technical know-how related to the mission (e.g., few users may be familiar with the technical methods for user requirement analysis)
- Have personal conflicts or animosity (e.g., two managers of the user departments have been engaged in a power struggle over the years)
- Lack team spirit (e.g., a programmer who works the night shift alone is not a team player and abhors meetings)
- Should be optimal in number (e.g., a large team is not effective in its work)

The necessity considerations include issues such as:

- Representation of groups who are affected by the team's actions (e.g., all user groups including secretaries, CEOs, and external customers should be represented)
- Representation of groups who have the technical know-how related to the mission (e.g., individuals who have expertise in different user requirement methods should be part of the team)
- Participation by individuals who have factual and procedural information (e.g. a member who is knowledgeable about customer complaints regarding a similar information system is helpful to the team)
- Representation of all points of view related to the team's mission (e.g., a manager who has plausible reasons why the system may not deliver what is promised provides a policing function for the team's analysis process)
- Building a culture of teamwork and involvement within the organization (e.g., membership of the programmer who abhors meetings, in the team that produces valuable and tangible results, can be educational and alter his or her perception of teamwork, thus fostering an environment of involvement and participation)

Familiarity. At the familiarity stage of team development, the members get to know one another, discover each others' talents, points of view, biases, and concerns. The challenge for the leader at this stage is to make sure that:

- There is a complete openness in expression of opinions (Deming's point: drive out fear)
- The leader should establish the criteria of fairness, objectivity, and team norms and values [Parker 1990]
- If there is a team facilitator, his or her role is clearly understood and coordinated with the leader's function
- He or she gets to know the members [Parker 1990]
- The game plan is created for the team [Parker 1990]

Power. At the power stage, team members have already started discussion of the substantive issues and have passed the familiarity threshold, becoming more comfortable in expressing their views and opposing one another. At this stage, conflicts emerge among the members and between members and the leader. The leader's leadership skills are put to the test at this stage. In the role of mediator, teacher, objective observant, and enforcer of the group's values and mission, the leader and facilitator can help the team pass through this phase successfully.

At this stage, the team and its leader must ensure that:

- Meetings are not used to settle scores or personal grievances (e.g., the two managers snicker at each other's comments)
- There is no fear of reprisal against those who oppose a superior's view (e.g., in disagreeing with the CEO, members may feel that they will be penalized)
- No member dominates the discussion and intimidates opposition (e.g., the CEO member tries to force his or her view and dominates the discussion)
- No one enforces hidden agendas (e.g., a member who feels threatened by the new system attempts to derail the discussion)
- Memories of failed attempts do not hamper the team's efforts (e.g., one manager constantly expresses doubt about the usefulness of the team's efforts because he or she had participated in a team with a similar mission, and the designed system was so defective that the project was canceled)
- Criticisms are constructive and impersonal, rather than blaming and personal (e.g., a user blames the inadequacy of the existing system on the IS manager's incompetence)
- There is an atmosphere of sharing and educating, rather than showing off and belittling (e.g., a system designer belittles the users for their lack of technical understanding)
- No unfair or gang tactics are used to shut up the opposition (e.g., the technically-inclined members gang up against other members to demand a feature in the system that is technically sophisticated but is not of importance to the system's users)
- Questions and participation are encouraged (e.g., the leader should recognize the shyness of the lone programmer and encourage his or her participation)

Performance and Synergy. At this stage, the team has overcome the major conflicts and disagreements and started to produce useful results. Parker [1990] suggests that the leader should share the limelight with other members, acknowledge productive contributions, and celebrate accomplishments.

Lynch and Werner [1992] suggest using a team-building feedback sheet that has a detailed list of the behavior types that are helpful to teamwork as well as those that should be changed. Team members are asked to evaluate one another by suggesting whether a member should exhibit more or less of a particular attribute, such as speaking up, being concise, trying to outdo others, and so forth. Alternatively, each member is asked to list the positive attitudes that should be reinforced and negative behavior types that should be changed. The feedback sheets are distributed, discussed, and negotiated in order to increase the cohesiveness of the team.

As the performance level of the team increases, the team commitment, energy, and enthusiasm grow, and synergy emerges. At this stage, the team functions as a unit and its reliance on the leader diminishes. The leader must ensure that team cohesiveness does not hamper creativity, innovation, independence, and critical thinking within the team. At this stage, the leader will have a more active role as the interface between the team and the outside.

Using the IS example for this stage, the team members have become familiar with the process and methods of requirements analysis and have already identified some of the major components of the users' requirements for the information system. They are now ready to work hard to refine the requirements and make them more accurate and representative. The leader must make sure that the members will continue to critique the outcome and not accept each others' views without adequate discussion. The leader of the group reports the team progress and arranges for presentation of the results to the top management.

◆ CASE: Starting Out Right at Memorial Medical Center

Memorial Medical Center in Savannah, Georgia assembled a cross-functional team to expedite the delivery of patients' laboratory tests to emergency department physicians. This is a prime example of how a healthcare organization used team work to address a work process quality issue.

Memorial Medical Center, a 2,000-employee, non-profit hospital, has established an executive *Council of Excellence* to assist in implementing its quality improvement process. The committee considers cross-functional teams to be an integral part of this effort, and searches out opportunities for appropriate projects. The adjoining example demonstrates how Memorial Medical has put this team process to work for the organization and its customers.

Shortening lab turnaround time. One such endeavor has involved a year-long effort to study the turnaround time the laboratory requires to process patients' tests and to devise ways to reduce this. According to Betty Lewis, the center's administrative laboratory director, the cross-functional team included: herself, a pathologist, two general-staff physicians, the director of ambulatory care, the medical director of the emergency department, a medical technologist, a phlebotomist, a nurse, and a unit secretary.

The problem and the target. The group defined the problem as being the turnaround between the time physicians write orders for a lab test and the time results are received by physicians. A target of within 15 minutes was designated for collection of specimens.

Finding the 'what' of the processes. In analyzing the work processes involved, the team discovered that the laboratory was actually being notified three or more times that a test has been ordered; first, a secretary or nurse would input the order into a new computer system that interacted with the lab.

In addition, he or she telephoned the laboratory, and also dialed the beeper of the phlebotomist assigned to the emergency department to notify the phlebotomist that a test needed to be performed.

Solutions and what was learned. The medical center has trimmed duplication by stationing a phlebotomist directly in the emergency department during the busiest part of the day. As a result, employees now have more confidence in test orders that have been entered into the computer. Although wasteful and expensive steps have been eliminated, this hasn't significantly affected turnaround time, according to Lewis.

Nonetheless, after conducting telephone surveys of other nearby hospitals of comparable size, MMC has learned that its laboratory turnaround time is as good or better than its competitors concerning the time interval from when an order is received in the laboratory until results are reported via the computer.

In working together to analyze this work process, the medical center's employees have gained a broader understanding of all the steps required to fulfill physicians' laboratory orders. And they have also acquired a greater appreciation of each other's roles and responsibilities.

Source: Excerpt from "New Quality Challenges for Healthcare," Ron Sepielli and Amy Klausner, *Journal of Quality and Participation*, January/ February 1991, pp. 54–58. Copyright (c) by Association for Quality and Participation, Cincinnati, Ohio. Reprint with permission from AQP.

2.3.3   Communication

Feigenbaum [1951, 1991] defines a quality organization as (1) a channel of communication and (2) a means of participation. In order to internalize quality, extensive and continuous efforts must be made in:

- Communicating quality focus to employees
- Communicating quality demand to vendors and suppliers
- Communicating commitment to quality to external customers
- Communicating dedication to quality to internal customers
- Clarifying the quality control terminology
- Two-way communication up and down the organizational structure, called "catch ball" in the Japanese system
- Communicating standards and expectations
- Communicating recognition for reinforcement of behavior
- Increasing interdepartmental communication

In communicating quality focus to employees, the leader must communicate the vision and the strategies to achieve the vision to employees. This communication involves all regular channels of communication as well as new approaches. One of the most effective ways of communicating vision is the day-to-day actions and decisions of CEOs demonstrating the quality focus.

Quality implementation includes a plan for communicating the focus to suppliers, and internal and external customers, and a clear explanation of terminology and procedures to be used. For example, in an information system, quality terminologies such as nonconformity of a system with its requirements, errors, up-to-date data, or reliable system should be defined and clarified.

A quality organization has two-way communication up and down the organizational structure, called "catch ball" in the Japanese system. This way the top management proposes a policy and asks the lower level of the hierarchy to come up with suggestions and more detailed plans of action, thus involving all organizational levels in the policy-making process.

Denton [1992] reports: "Pepsi's interdepartmental communication and understanding comes from promoting up through the ranks, rotating jobs within disciplines and their management-by-wandering-around (Hewlett-Packard became famous for this MBWA)."

In a quality organization, the extent of communication increases regarding standards, expectations, and recognition among the departments and other functional units.

With the increase in substantive communication, conflicts and disagreements surface and become explicit. An open communication process:

- Recognizes differences and disagreements
- Defines, clarifies, and checks differences
- Initiates a process for resolving differences

Recognizing Differences and Disagreements.   Effective communication requires listening skills. Two-way communication between management and employees requires that managers listen carefully, rather than issuing orders to be followed by employees. Listening skills are even more essential in recognizing differences and disagreements.

Gibb [1961] contrasts *defensive* and *supportive* communication approaches. In a defensive mode, a great deal of energy is given to defending a real or perceived attack, leading to little real listening. Since little attention is spent on preparing and shielding attacks in a supportive mode, it promotes more careful listening.

McLaurin and Bell [1991] contrast the defensive and supportive behaviors as:

- *Judgmental vs. descriptive* (e.g., stating that a given IS design is lousy vs. analyzing the design's capability in meeting the customers requirements)
- *Controlling vs. problem-solving* (e.g., the IS manager directs how the system flaws must be corrected vs. the IS manager creates a consensus on the flaws, solicits solution, and discusses the pros and cons of each solution before selecting the best approach)
- *Scheming vs. spontaneous* (e.g., a programmer is against using a computer language because he or she is not skillful in the language and comes to the meeting with the hidden agenda of arguing that the language is not appropriate for the system vs. the programmer reacts spontaneously and states that although the language is great, he or she will not be able to contribute to the project because of his or her lack of skill, and will need training in the language)
- *Uninvolved vs. having empathy* (e.g., the project manager does not get involved in or care to understand why a user is vehemently against a given design vs. the manager tries to listen and understand why the user is against the design)

- *Acting superior vs. appreciating others* (e.g., the project manager puts on an air of superiority because he or she has more power, intelligence, or experience vs. the project manager acts as a team member and acknowledges others' abilities and expertise)
- *Rigid vs. flexible* (e.g., an experienced designer demands that his or her proposal is the only way: "my way or no way" vs. the designer attempts to see others' points of view and is willing to be convinced and change views)

Defining, Clarifying, and Checking Differences.   The next step in effective communication and conflict resolution is to clarify differences, once their existence is recognized. McLaurin and Bell [1991], in applying TQM at Weyerhaeuser Mortgage Company, recommend the following guidelines for clarifying differences:

- Clarify values (e.g., in this IS design, my value is to best address the user's immediate needs; your value is to have the latest technology)
- Clarify goals (e.g., what I want to do in this IS design is to have a menu-driven system; you want a voice-activated system)
- Clarify methods (e.g., the way I want to implement the menu-driven system is to buy a software product that has the capability; you want to program the system from scratch)
- Clarify beliefs (e.g., I believe that buying software is more cost-effective, you believe that doing the programming ourselves gives us more control and flexibility)
- Clarify experiences (e.g., my experience shows that buying software involves less headaches and errors, your experience shows that buying software makes us dependent on the vendor forever)
- Clarify actions (e.g., my proposed action is to buy the software now, your proposed action is to postpone buying until we have more information from those who have used the product)
- Clarify words (e.g., what I mean by an error is that the software fails to produce the expected answer or menu, what you mean by an error is that the software crashes)
- Disagree with the idea not the person (e.g., I disagree with this design vs. I disagree with Pat)
- Analyze conflicts by being inquisitive (e.g., please explain the reasons why your design will work better)
- Be clear in explaining your own position (e.g., I disagree with this design because it does not allow for the future expansion of the system into networking with other systems)

Initiating a Resolution Process.   The best method for resolving differences is to focus on the target or the purpose, and evaluate every idea, proposal, or belief against the target. Quality provides a clear target, hence making conflict resolution a matter of how to best achieve the quality vision.

2.3.4   Recognition and Award

Crosby recommends that employees and teams with outstanding performance and quality achievement should be recognized publicly and nonfinancially. Deming's point on the employees' pride of workmanship has the same element of award through public recognition and acknowledgement of achievements.

In a technical function such as information systems, technical and professional recognition is of much greater significance to employees. Recognizing the team members for their achievement in improving the design of a system goes a long way in motivating and involving others to do the same. As we will see in Chapter 3, celebrating the successes of quality teams is an essential motivational tool.

The top management should have a clear policy for recognizing excellent performance and reinforce it in all their decisions. For example, the policy that promotions in the IS department are open only to the employees that have been team leaders in a quality improvement team would go a long way in motivating active involvement in teamwork and quality improvement. The job performance review system can be rewritten to encourage teamwork.

2.3.5   Organizational Structure

Cross-functional teams, quality communications, and employee empowerment and involvement have led to a change in organizational structure, making it more flexible, more decentralized, and flatter, with fewer middle managers.

Although the jury is still out on the form of the quality organization, four patterns have already emerged in such organizations:

- Upside-down hierarchy
- Flatter hierarchy
- Cross-functional teams
- Pushed-down decision making

Upside-Down Hierarchy.   In a quality organization, the hierarchy is up-side down, as shown in Figure 2.6. In the traditional hierarchy, the flow is from top to bottom in the form of orders and control. The top management has the most important position in the hierarchy (Figure 2.6-a).

In the quality organization, the hierarchy is upside down (Figure 2.6-b). The customer is the focus and workers serving them have the highest position in the hierarchy. Management's role is coaching, mentoring, and supporting the workers in their quest for quality.

This is a revolutionary approach in management. However, the IS function, with an end-user focus and workers with technical expertise, is one of the first areas where this approach could be successfully implemented. When the vision and goals of a system have been made clear for the IS technical workers, the manager's function becomes providing the tools, supporting materials, and services to the workers and coaching them in their problem-solving efforts.

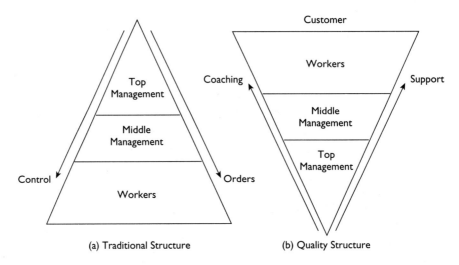

Figure 2.6   Organizational Hierarchy

Flatter Hierarchy.   As Figure 2.6 shows, a quality organization has a flatter hierarchy. The reasons are (1) the emphasis on teamwork, and (2) handing control to those who produce the output to be controlled. These factors reduce the number and layers of middle managers whose main function is to control those below them in the hierarchy.

The information systems function fits naturally with a flat organizational structure because IS design, deployment, maintenance, and service delivery require involvement of various functions and expertise. Teamwork comes naturally to the IS function. Moreover, because of the specialized nature of IS, the IS workers are the most qualified to control the system they create. (The issues related to quality control in the IS function will be discussed in Chapters 8, 9 and 10.) Thus, IS has a natural organizational structure appropriate for quality management.

Cross-functional Teams.   The team emphasis of quality organization is discussed at length in a previous section. Cross-functional teamwork in quality improvement is a hallmark of quality organizations (the role of quality improvement teams will be discussed in detail in Chapter 3). In such organizations, the team spirit goes beyond quality teams, and extends to the day-to-day tasks. Again, IS function is oriented to cross-functional teamwork, and is one of the areas most appropriate for quality deployment.

Pushed-down Decision Making.   The upside-down and flatter hierarchy, as well as cross-functional teamwork, move the decision making closer to the level where the decision is to be implemented, thus making employee involvement a real phenomenon, rather than just a slogan. This process has to be strongly coupled with a clear vision statement, well-defined strategic plan, and well-established communication channels. Otherwise, it will lead to chaos and contradictory actions by employees.

In the IS function, pushed-down decision making means that the person who, for example, provides IS service must be able to make decisions about which customer should be served first. This decision, however, requires guidance from a plan in which the priorities of customer types are clearly spelled out. This way, IS workers will be in control of what they do, but they have enough guidance to make a collective effort in promoting the organization goals and plans.

◆ CASE: Keystone Steel & Wire Company

When Keystone Steel & Wire started its Keystone 2000 program, designed to take the company, profitably, into the next century, there were a lot of things they could anticipate: a certain degree of apathy, a fair amount of resistance to change, but one thing they didn't count on was redefining management's role in the business.

With the establishment of action committees throughout the company, charged with identifying challenges and problems in their departments and both recommending and implementing solutions, it became apparent that the traditional "chain of command" didn't mean much in the new order of things.

"And what that means," explains Rick Cloyd, Keystone's marketing and communications manager, "is that the fellow running the grinding machine may be the guy that writes the appropriation request to the board of directors. If he's the most capable person to do that and knows the situation, he's welcome to it."

"It's a very far reaching change in the culture of the company. It's a major change because we have a readjustment of perspective as to what management's role is. Management has become a coach and a facilitator ... someone to provide the resources. Not to be a cop or somebody that administers a strict rule book. Management just sees to it that people get what they need to get the job done."

"That is the type of management we think is going to be necessary 'cause that's the type of environment people are going to respond."

The Keystone 2000 project was based on the idea of clearing away attitudes that may have existed and starting over because the company simply could not be successful in an adversarial environment.

"It's all about empowerment. If we're going to have a company that's going to be around in the year 2000, *and* be profitable and successful, *and* people are going to see their families grow, they've got to feel secure that their jobs aren't threatened by things that are done internally. We can control the way we relate to each other."

Source: "Keystone Steel & Wire Company: Redefining traditional roles," Victor Bonini, *Wire Journal International*, December 1991, pp. 36-38, reprinted with permission from *Wire Journal International.*

2.3.6 Organizational Culture

Hunt [1992] defines organizational culture as "a prevailing pattern of activities, interactions, norms, sentiments, beliefs, attitudes, values, and products in an organization." The

Department of Defense's TQM Master Plan contains a three-page strategy for changing the organizational culture [Hunt 1992].

The entire total quality management effort strives to bring a cultural change to an organization. Leading with a vision and empowering employees are just two of many facets of quality management that aim to create a new culture in the organization—a culture of striving for excellence with the focus on customers. The upcoming chapters cover other approaches that aid such a cultural change.

◆ Conclusion

This chapter discussed the people aspects of quality management, which consist of leadership with vision and through empowerment. Vision is the guiding light of any quality organization. A vision is a concise and inspiring statement of what the organization wants to be in the future. A leader may start with a private vision, but eventually the employees must buy into the vision. This chapter discussed the nature of group vision as it applies to information systems.

There are a number of methods helpful in the process of creating vision. They include posing questions, brainstorming, mental mapping, and affinity diagram. The chapter discussed these techniques and gave examples of their application in creating a vision for an IS department.

All quality gurus, as well as the Baldrige Award criteria, emphasize that employee empowerment is one of the foundations on which any quality effort rests.

The prerequisites for achieving employee empowerment are training, team development, communication, and recognition, discussed in some detail in this chapter. Employee empowerment leads to an alteration in the organizational structure that is flatter and has fewer middle managers. The chapter ended with a brief discussion of the organizational culture. Changing the organizational culture into one that strives for excellence with the focus on customers is the end result of TQM. This focus is in complete harmony with the reasons why the field of information systems has come to exist.

◆ References

1. Bennis, W. G., Benne, K. D., and Corey, K. E. *The Planning of Change*, Holt, Rinehart, and Winston, New York, NY, 1976.
2. Brassard, Michael. *The Memory Jogger Plus*, Goal/QPC, Methuen, MA, 1989.
3. Denton, D. Keith. *The Service Trainer Handbook: Managing Service Businesses in the 1990s*, McGraw Hill, New York, NY, 1992.
4. Feigenbaum, Armand V. *Total Quality Control*, Third Edition, Revised, McGraw Hill, New York, NY, 1991 (First Edition in 1951).
5. Gibb, Jack R. "Defensive Communication," *The Journal of Communication*, September 1961, pp. 141–148.
6. Hunt, V. Daniel. *Quality in America: How to Implement a Competitive Quality Program*, Business One Irwin, Homewood, Ill. 1992.

7. Hyde, Albert C. "Rescuing Quality Measurement from TQM," *The Bureaucrat*, Winter 1990-91, pp. 16–20.

8. Johnson, John G. "Successful TQM is a Question of Leadership," *The Journal of Quality and Participation*, June 1990, pp. 16–20.

9. Johnson. John G. "Why Aren't Our Managers Better Leaders?" *Tapping the Network Journal*, Spring/Summer 1991, pp. 2–4.

10. Jones, Louis and McBride, Ronald. *An Introduction to Team-Approach Problem Solving*, ASQC Quality Press, Milwaukee, WI, 1990.

11. Lynch, Robert F. and Werner, Thomas J. *Continuous Improvement: Teams & Tools*, QualTeam Inc., Atlanta, GA, 1992.

12. McLaurin, Donald L. and Bell, Shareen. "Open Communication Lines Before Attempting Quality," *Quality Progress*, June 1991, pp. 25-28.

13. Odgers, G. D. W. "Total Quality and 'High Wire' Performance," *Proceedings of the Institution of Mechanical Engineers*, 1990, pp. 17–21.

14. Osborne, A. F. *Applied Imagination—The Principles and Problems of Creative Problem Solving*, Charles Scribners's Sons, New York, 1953.

15. Parker, Glenn M. *Team Players and Teamwork*, Jossey-Bass, 1990.

16. Ross, Joel E. *Total Quality Management: Text, Cases, and Readings*, St. Lucie Press, Delray Beach, FL, 1993.

17. Senge, Peter. *The Fifth Discipline*, Doubleday, Garden City, NY, 1990.

18. Spool, Jared. "Product Usability: Survival Techniques," Professional Seminar of the Greater Boston Chapter of the ACM, Boston, MA, 1992.

19. Tichy, Noel M. and Devanna, Mary Anne. *The Transformational Leader*, Wiley and Sons, New York, NY, 1986.

20. United States Department of Commerce. *The Malcolm Baldrige National Quality Award: 1993 Award Criteria*, Gaithersburg, MD, 1993.

21. Wachel, Walter. "An Interview with College's Chairman, Paul Ellison" *Healthcare Executive*, September/October 1991, pp. 19-22.

22. White, Bruce. "How Quality Became Job #1 at Ford," *Canadian Business Review*, Vol. 17, No. 1, Spring 1990, pp. 24–27.

23. Wollner, George E. "The Law of Producing Quality," *Quality Progress*, January 1992, pp. 35–40.

24. Zagarow, Herbert W. "The Training Challenge," *Quality*, August 1990, pp. 22–26.

◆ Questions

2.1. Why is vision important in quality management?

2.2. What is the difference between private and group vision?

2.3. What is a working vision?

2.4. What is the significance of vision for an IS department?

2.5. Describe the techniques helpful in creating the vision statement.

2.6. Compare and contrast brainstorming and mental mapping.

2.7. Compare and contrast brainstorming and affinity diagram.

2.8. Discuss brainstorming phases.

2.9. Discuss the ways to empower employees.

2.10. What is the significance of employee empowerment in quality information systems?

2.11. What are the characteristics of a successful training process for an information systems function?

2.12. What is the significance of evaluating training?

2.13. What is the role of communication in employee empowerment?

2.14. Discuss various aspects of communicating quality in an organization.

2.15. Discuss the relevance of communication to quality information systems.

2.16. What are the issues and methods in team development?

2.17. What are the differences (if any) between teams in quality information systems as opposed to any other team?

2.18. Describe the organizational culture of a quality information system department.

2.19. Describe an organizational structure in a quality information system department.

◆ Problems

2.1. Assume you are the project leader for an information system project. State your private vision for the project.

2.2. Form into a group, and use brainstorming to develop a vision for a software product to be used by shoppers in identifying the products they need, locating the best place to shop, and making the purchase.

2.3. List possible questions to be asked in questioning technique for Problem 2.2.

2.4. Use mental mapping and affinity diagram for Problem 2.2, and report on your experience in using these techniques.

2.5. Devise a training process for an information systems department.

2.6. How would you evaluate a training process for an information systems department?

Revolution is the Pod
Systems rattle from
When the Winds of Will are stirred
Excellent is Bloom

— Emily Dickinson, 1866

How doth the little busy bee
Improve each shining hour
And gather honey all the day
From every opening flower

— Isaac Watts, *Against Illness and Mischief*

◆ Chapter Objectives

The objectives of this chapter are:
- To introduce the paradigms for information-systems improvement
- To compare the modes of systems improvement
- To present policy deployment and information-systems strategic planning
- To discuss the theory of constraints
- To discuss the ingredients of the continuous improvement process in information systems
- To discuss the linkage between information-systems strategic planning and information-systems continuous improvement process
- To present the quality tools—cause-and-effect diagram, Pareto chart, tree and hierarchy diagrams—that are helpful to the information systems continuous improvement process

◆ Key Words

Systems-improvement paradigm, maintenance, systems life cycle, continuous improvement process, kaizen, information systems policy deployment, information systems strategic planning, hoshin planning, theory of constraints, quality teams, Shewhart-Deming cycle, plan-do-check-act cycle, suggestion handling, cause-and-effect diagram, Pareto chart, tree diagram, hierarchy diagram

Continuously Improving Information Systems

3.1 Paradigms for Improvement in Information Systems
    3.1.1 Maintenance
    3.1.2 Systems Life Cycle
    3.1.3 Continuous Improvement, Kaizen, Innovation, and Reengineering
    3.1.4 Comparing the Modes of System Improvement

3.2 Policy Deployment in Information Systems
    3.2.1 Strategic Planning for Information Systems
    3.2.2 Hoshin Planning
    3.2.3 Theory of Constraints

3.3 Continuous Improvement in Information Systems
    3.3.1 Quality Teams
    3.3.2 Shewhart-Deming Cycle
    3.3.3 Seeking, Handling, and Implementing Suggestions

3.4 Tools for Problem Identification
    3.4.1 Pareto Chart
    3.4.2 Cause-and-Effect Diagram
    3.4.3 Tree and Hierarchy Diagrams

◆ Introduction

Many organizations have made substantial investments in their information systems. Like any other asset type, information systems must be maintained and improved through time in order to retain their value. Otherwise, the systems become obsolete and new systems must be created. Therefore, improving information systems plays an important role in preserving the investment as well in providing quality service to the internal and external customers of the systems.

In this chapter, we discuss the paradigms for changing and improving information systems. We compare three paradigms for change: maintenance, systems life cycle, and continuous improvement process. We argue that continuous improvement starts when maintenance ends and prolongs the life of the system until new innovations make the existing system obsolete.

It is within this context that we focus on the information-systems continuous improvement process. One of the major prerequisites for the success of systems improvement is the existence of an information-systems strategic plan. Therefore, we discuss strategic planning, hoshin planning, and constraint identification through the theory of constraints as the foundations upon which the continuous improvement process should rest.

Quality teams, the Shewhart-Deming cycle, and suggestion handling are the ingredients of the information-systems continuous improvement process that are discussed in this chapter. Finally, we discuss the quality tools helpful to the improvement process. They include the cause-and-effect diagram, Pareto chart, and tree and hierarchy diagrams.

3.1 ◆ Paradigms for Improvement in Information Systems

Faults in information systems may be the result of errors in software codes, errors in system implementation, inadequacy of the system's design, technical obsolescence, organizational growth, and market changes.

Finkelstein [1989] reports that errors in information systems have the following distribution:

- Incomplete requirements: 56%
- Design: 27%
- Coding: 7%
- Other: 10%

Correcting the errors from various sources does not take proportionally the same amount of effort. Errors due to incomplete requirements analysis take a disproportionally larger share:

- Incomplete requirements: 82%
- Design: 13%

- Coding: 1%
- Other: 4%

In other words, a great deal of investment is made in improving information systems to meet customers' needs (82%). This is the non-technical specification of the system, in which the system developer must identify what customers really expect from the system. The technical corrections take only 18% improvement efforts.

Information-systems improvement could take place in one of the following modes:

- Maintenance
- Systems Life Cycle
- Continuous Improvement

3.1.1 Maintenance

One of the most common changes in information systems takes place in the form of maintenance. Maintenance is an on-going process and costs many times more than the cost of system development.

Code Maintenance. Most of the error correction for codes takes place at the maintenance stage. Sometimes, correcting codes may introduce additional errors, which, in turn require further error-correction maintenance.

Many code errors may be caused by:

- Non-modular coding
- Inadequate reliability tests

Non-modular coding causes errors that propagate in an unexpected manner to various parts of the software. Normally, error correction in such systems causes the introduction of new errors. The reason is that when an error is corrected in one part of the software, the changes are not localized to that part and may have unexpected side effects in other parts of the software.

In fact, the non-modular coding is originated in the poor design. It is possible for a system to have general modular structure, but non-modular coding. This happens when the system developer does not spend adequate time at the design stage and leaves the details of programming design to programmers or chooses a language or software that does not lend itself to modular coding.

Inadequate reliability testing of information systems is a common occurrence. There are few formal methods for testing the reliability of information systems. They are rarely fully tested before going on-line. The extent and scope of checking the system before its deployment are at the discretion of the system developer and at the mercy of scheduling and budget constraints. Therefore, it is easy for the system developer, in the rush to put the system into use, to test the reliability of the system in operation. However, when the system is in operation, fixing any error or making any change in the system's structure would be considered an emergency measure, which is much more costly and causes customer dissatisfaction.

Software testing, on the other hand, has numerous models for reliability [Zahedi and Ashrafi 1991, 1993]. These models are mostly mathematical formulation for the computation of a measure that shows the reliability of the software (we will discuss software reliability in Chapter 9). Although software reliability models are used in large software projects, the applications of these models are not common when developing information systems.

Therefore, maintaining programming codes in information systems partly takes the place of software reliability tests. This is analogous to delivering a defective item to a customer and hoping to fix the defects through repair. Such a product can hardly be called a quality product.

Design Maintenance. Many code changes made as maintenance are caused by faulty design. An insufficiently detailed design may lead to using non-modularized codes. A design that does not allow for natural growth of an organization will end up with patchwork expansion of the system. A design that does not anticipate future technological changes and does not incorporate portability to upcoming technologies will require expensive conversions.

A common example of inadequate design is when the customer requires a data item that was not needed before, and the existing system cannot incorporate the new data item without requiring a major overhaul. Another example is when a new site is added to a distributive information system, and the system is so narrowly designed that one cannot easily add the new site to the system.

Customer Requirement Maintenance. Many inadequacies of design are caused by allowing inadequate time for deciding customer requirements. Many enhancement projects for maintaining an existing information system results from a lack of adequate communication with the true customers of the system about their unexpressed needs and future requirements. It is precisely this inadequacy that makes piece-meal maintenance inefficient, eventually leading to another iteration of systems life cycle.

3.1.2   Systems Life Cycle

Once an information system has proven so problematic and inadequate that no maintenance operation could save it, a study is initiated to review the problems and propose a plan to overhaul the system. The decision to study the system is normally made after numerous maintenance operations to fix the system's problems.

The system life cycle has the following phases [Whitten et al. 1989]:

- Feasibility study
- Analysis of current system
- Analysis of customer requirements
- Selection of feasible approach

- Design of the new system
- Acquisition of hardware, software, and manpower
- Construction of the new system
- Deployment of the new system
- Maintenance of the new system

Feasibility Study.   At the feasibility phase, a general analysis of the condition of the system and cost-benefit analysis is carried out. At this stage, the top management must decide whether or not to commit resources to a systems life cycle process. This phase is initiated either by customers who feel the information system performs poorly and inadequately, or by information-systems personnel who may feel that an advanced technology can better serve the customers.

Analysis of Current System.   Once the existing problems prove to be significant, the existing system is analyzed. The systems analyst who carries out this phase documents how the current system works and identifies its flaws and shortcomings. The result of the systems-analysis phase is a recommendation on whether or not a new system is needed.

Analysis of Customer Requirements.   Once it is established that indeed a new system is needed, it is necessary to decide the features of the new system. To make this decision, the systems customers must be consulted to identify their present requirements and future needs.

Selection of Feasible Approach.   With the data on the shortcomings of the current system and the customers' needs, one must come up with alternative definitions and attributes of the new system. This can range from add-on components to the current system to building a new system from scratch, or some alternative between the two extremes. Based on the existing needs and available resources, the feasible approach is selected at this phase.

Design of the New System.   Once the boundary of the new system is determined, the new system must be designed. This phase involves logical design and physical design. At the logical design phase, the details of the new system are worked out without hardware and software considerations. Physical design takes into account the particulars of the hardware and software that will be used in the system.

Acquisition of Hardware, Software, and Manpower.   At this stage, the hardware and software specified by the physical design are acquired and those who will have the task of constructing the system are recruited internally or externally.

Construction of the New System.   At this phase, the new system is created according to the design specifications. Hardware is installed and software is either created or purchased. If purchased, the software may be modified and coded for the implementation of the physical design.

Deployment of the New System.   The completed system goes on line at this phase. The process of deployment may be conversion from the old system in a gradual fashion, all at once, or in parallel. In the gradual mode, the new system goes on line one piece at a time, while the old system is in operation. In the sudden conversion, the old system is stopped and the new system takes over. In the parallel mode, the new and old system work in parallel, until the new system proves to be stable and in good working condition.

Maintenance of the New System.   This phase completes the cycle in that as defects in the new system are discovered, they are then fixed. Although systems maintenance is part of the systems life cycle process, we have discussed it separately because the nature and length of this phase is different from the other stages of the systems life cycle.

Note that in the systems life cycle, there is no formal stage for testing the information systems. The common mode is the iterative approach, where the next phase starts before the previous phase is completely over. The outcome of one phase is the input into the next phase. As defects and shortcomings are discovered in the input of a phase, the work iterates back to the previous step for correction and modification.

3.1.3   Continuous Improvement, Kaizen, Innovation, and Reengineering

The new concern in systems analysis is *systems integration*. Gantz [1987] states, "The challenge: to be able to incorporate the new without losing investment in the old." In other words, waiting for the current system to become useless before undertaking a new systems life cycle leads to the loss of all investments made in the existing system.

The continuous improvement concept is an answer to the challenge of systems integration. It goes beyond just fixing errors and faults. The objective of continuous system improvement is to keep the system current with the needs and wishes of customers.

Kaizen.   Continuous improvement has its origin in the Japanese concept of Kaizen. *Kaizen* means "*ongoing* improvement involving *everyone*—top management, managers, and workers," [Imai 1986]. It works within an organizational culture dedicated to quality, teamwork, and quest for improvement.

Continuous Improvement and Innovation.   Imai compares the modes of change in Japan and western countries. In Japan, Kaizen is equal parts between maintenance and innovation (Figure 3.1), with the involvement of supervisors and middle management. In western countries, changes take place mainly through maintenance by workers and supervisors, and innovation only has the involvement of middle and top management (Figure 3.2).

One can imagine the process of innovation as a step function (Figure 3.3). In this case, the maintenance function keeps the system at the same performance level until a new system is created. Then a major change and innovation brings the system performance up to a new level.

With continuous improvement, the system is first maintained for removing errors. Then the continuous improvement of the system gradually increases the system

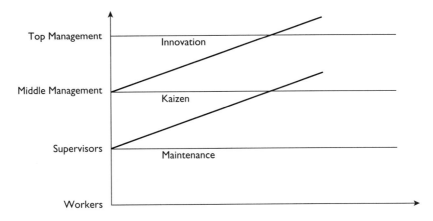

Figure 3.1   The Modes of Change in Japan. Adopted from *Kaizen* by Massaki Imai.

performance, thus prolonging its life and reducing the necessity for major innovations (Figure 3.4).

Continuous Improvement and Quality Circles.   Continuous improvement and quality circles both involve cross-functional teams that identify problems and provide changes to address them. Their main difference is that continuous improvement takes place within the directions provided by the organization's stated strategies and goals.

Continuous Improvement and Reengineering.   Reengineering is a recent concept that runs opposite continuous improvement. Rather than gradually changing the existing processes to improve the system, reengineering recommends tearing down the existing processes within the organization and starting from scratch. It recommends redesign

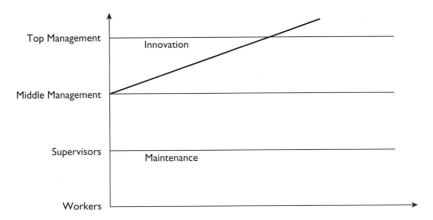

Figure 3.2   The Modes of Change in Western Countries. Adopted from *Kaizen* by Massaki Imai.

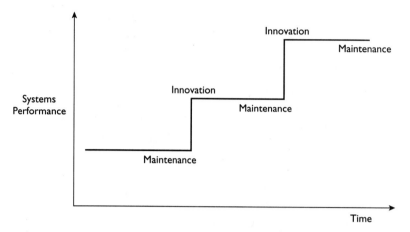

Figure 3.3 Systems Performance with Maintenance and Innovation

of the organization's infrastructure, processes, and modes of interaction. The concept has its roots in American management consulting and was coined jointly by Michael Hammer (president of Hammer & Co.) and CSC Index (another consulting firm).

3.1.4 Comparing the Modes of Systems Improvement

We can compare various modes of systems improvement from various perspectives:

- Ad hoc or planned
- With or without priority

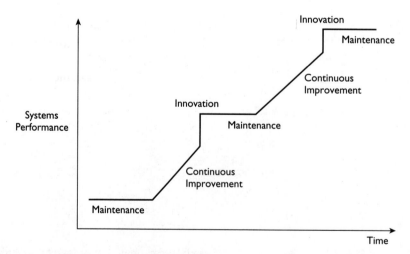

Figure 3.4 Systems Performance with Maintenance, Continuous Improvement, and Innovation

- With or without design
- Static or dynamic
- Passive or active
- Corrective or preventive
- Complaint-driven, champion-driven, or data-driven
- Functional-based or quality-based
- Low or high cost
- Management involvement

The comparative analysis of the three methods of systems improvement—maintenance, systems life cycle, and continuous improvement—reveals the basic differences in these approaches.

Ad Hoc or Planned.   The actions taken at the maintenance phase are mostly a function of random discovery of errors, which are corrected as they appear. Thus, the maintenance process is mainly ad hoc and is driven by how errors are discovered and by customer complaints.

The systems life cycle mode is a planned improvement, once the necessity of another round is established. Since there is no prediction about when an information system requires another cycle, there is no way to plan for the process. Therefore, the systems life cycle mode is a randomly planned process.

In the continuous mode of systems improvement, the reliability of the information system is regularly monitored. The collected data give an early warning signal about the possible problems. This signal provides a chance for planning the improvement process of the system. Therefore, the continuous improvement method is a planned improvement of the system.

With or Without Priority.   Lack of planning leaves little room for selection and choice. Since the maintenance mode is mostly ad hoc and does not work within a framework of a plan with goals and priorities, it would be difficult for the managers in charge of maintenance to assign priority to what errors should be corrected first.

The systems life cycle mode, once started, provides the opportunity to assign priority at the selection of a feasible approach phase. At this stage, the requirements of customers are analyzed against organizational resources and technical capabilities. If the systems life cycle is not initiated within an information strategy, choices made at the selection phase will have little connection to the overall organizational vision, mission, strategies, and objectives.

In the continuous improvement mode, the priorities are determined based on the information systems vision and mission, which, in turn, are based on the overall vision and mission of the organization.

With or Without Design.   As discussed before, many errors in information systems stem from errors in design. However, the maintenance mode of systems improvement does not inherently allow for changing the design of the system. Hence, it is difficult to make effective corrections when the underlying design is faulty.

The systems life cycle mode allows for complete redesign of the information system. The continuous improvement mode makes it possible to keep the old system while making design corrections in the system.

Static or Dynamic.   The nature of changes in the maintenance mode is static, in that the objective of maintenance is to keep the system as is and make it work reliably. Changes occurring in a system in its life cycle are *comparative static* in that changes are made after a relatively long period in a static state. In the continuous improvement mode, changes are dynamic in that the system is being improved upon on a regular basis.

Passive or Active.   The maintenance mode is *passive* in discovering errors. Since the reliability and performance of the system are not regularly monitored, no one is actively looking for possible errors or faults. The corrective actions are taken only when the system fails, a customer complains, or an error occurs.

The systems life cycle mode is passive before the start of a new cycle, and becomes active once the decision is made to start a new cycle. Therefore, we can call it *passive-active*.

The continuous improvement mode is *active* in discovering errors because it regularly monitors the performance of the system, collects reliability data, and provides early warning signals for possible problems. It actively seeks to improve the system. This mode of improvement is *proactive*.

Corrective or Preventive.   The maintenance mode is *corrective*; it responds to errors and failures. The systems life cycle is partly corrective and partly preventive. It is corrective because it initiates a new cycle in response to failures and inefficiencies. Its preventive nature comes into play when it completely redesigns the system to prevent similar problems from recurring again. The continuous improvement mode is capable of introducing changes that can prevent the recurrence of failures or shortcomings.

Complaint-driven, Champion-driven, or Data-driven.   The maintenance mode is mainly driven by customers' complaints. These customers may be internal or external to the information system as well as to the organization (as discussed in Chapter 2). This mode is *complaint-driven* and *subjective*. The louder the complaint is, the faster will be the corrective response.

A new cycle of the systems life cycle normally starts when there is an organizational champion who brings the problems to the attention of the CEO and strongly advocates the investment of resources in starting a new cycle—it is *champion-driven* and *subjective*. The personal opinion of the champion is the force behind the start of a new cycle.

The continuous improvement mode tracks the system performance on a regular basis. Changes and improvements take place based on the information provided by the field data—the mode is *data-driven* and *objective*.

Functional-based or Quality-based.   The maintenance and systems life cycle have a functional-based nature—as long as the system is functional, there is no need to fix it. In the continuous improvement mode, a functional system may be improved to deliver still a better service. The continuous improvement mode focuses on the quality of information systems and the ways to improve the system.

Low or High Cost.   In the short term, maintenance costs are small, but it has been shown that maintenance cost in the life of an information system is many times higher than its original cost. The short-term cost of the systems life cycle is high, but it eradicates the direct and indirect cost of maintaining and using an information system that has become ineffective.

The problem with creating a new system from scratch is that it then becomes necessary to discard the current system, hence losing the investment made in its creation and maintenance. Furthermore, the new system will have bugs that will have to be removed. In short, the maintenance cycle continues.

The continuous improvement mode improves the current system, thus preserving what is already fixed and working in the system. Since its focus is quality and preservation of the current system, its relative cost, compared to replacing the system with a completely new one, is also small.

Management involvement.   Maintenance is a function that requires little involvement by middle and top management. Continuous improvement requires top management involvement for strategy formulation and middle management involvement for the participation in the process and the implementation of improvements. The development of a new system requires extensive involvement of top and middle management.

3.2   ◆   Policy Deployment in Information Systems

The information-systems continuous improvement process is guided by the organization vision, information-systems vision, and information-systems strategic plan for realizing the visions. In Chapter 2, we discussed the process of defining the vision and mission for information systems. Here, we discuss the strategic planning process for information systems. This plan provides direction and sets priorities for all continuous improvement activities.

3.2.1   Strategic Planning for Information Systems

Strategic planning for information systems has the following components (Figure 3.5):

- Vision
- Mission
- Policies
- Goals and objectives
- Strategies and tactics

Information-systems strategic planning starts with the vision and mission statements. In the ACCU-INFO example, we have the vision statement:

We provide the most accurate information on credit-worthiness of shoppers within the United States.

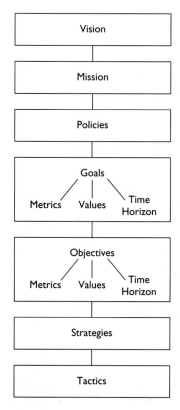

Figure 3.5   Stages of Information-Systems Strategic Planning

ACCU-INFO's mission statement is:

We satisfy our customers by providing an integrated information system that combines reliable data from all possible sources, and by creating an atmosphere of trust and growth for our employees.

Goals and Objectives.   The next step is to identify the needed policies, goals, and objectives for realizing the vision. Policy statements are qualitative guidelines, whereas goals and objectives have a more quantitative nature. For example, some of the policy statements of ACCU-INFO are:

- Our main customers are the commercial banks and credit companies. We develop our information systems with the main focus on the needs of our main customers.
- We seek to expand our market to have customers who themselves are major sources of credit data.
- We aggressively go after new sources of data by developing innovative ideas of joint partnership with those companies that have access to credit data.

- We are committed to be the first in deploying new technology in serving our customers. We seek to become known for our state-of-the-art technology in serving our customers.
- We are committed to integrating our computer networks with our customers' network system. We will provide technical assistance to our customers to achieve this integration.
- We seek to reduce our update time and access time on a continuous basis.
- We seek to be known for the reliability of our systems. To this end, we monitor and continuously improve the reliability of our information systems.
- We encourage innovation and research for measuring and interpreting systems reliability.
- We are committed to providing state-of-the-art technical and quality management training for our employees.

Goals and objectives quantify the policy statements. Objectives have a more immediate and short-term nature, whereas goals are more long-term quantities. To define goals and objectives, we need have [Finkelstein 1989]:

- Metrics
- Metric values
- Time horizon

Metrics are combined measures and variables that quantify a goal. *Metric values* are the numerical values for metrics, and *time horizon* is the period allowed for achieving the goal or objective.

For example, in ACCU-INFO's policy statement we seek to be known for the reliability of our systems, we need to have reliability metric(s) for information systems. We will discuss reliability metrics in another chapter. For the purpose of this example, assume that one metric of systems reliability is the percentage of faults generated by the system (including input errors, software faults, or network faults). We call this metric the systems fault ratio. We compute this metric by counting input errors, software failures, and network failures and dividing them by the number of times the system has been accessed.

Once we define the reliability metric, we can set a goal for this metric by defining a value for it, such as .0001, and deciding that we will go below this threshold within the next five years. Thus, one of the goals for the policy statement we seek to be known for the reliability of our systems is:

We will reduce our systems fault ratio to .0001 within the next five years.

From this goal, ACCU-INFO identifies the annual objectives for systems reliability for the next five years. Assume that the systems fault ratio at present is .01. In other words, every 100 times that ACCU-INFO customers access the system, they encounter one input error, software fault, or network failure. The goal is to reduce this ratio by a factor of 100 in the next five years. The annual objectives for this goal are set as:

- First year: .01, the same as now
- Second year: .005
- Third year: .001
- Fourth year: .0005
- Fifth year: .0001

The first year's objective is set at the present level to allow the company to put processes in place and come up with strategies and tactics for achieving the annual objectives for the subsequent years.

Strategies and Tactics.   After the objectives are identified, the next step is to define strategies and tactics for achieving them. *Strategies* determine *how* to accomplish an objective, and *tactics* are the steps, actions, and tasks for implementing a strategy.

In the ACCU-INFO example, we identified the objective of reducing the system fault ratio from .01 to .005 in two years. Among the possible strategies is to set up a continuous-improvement team to:

- Collect detailed data on the input errors, software faults, and network failure on a regular basis
- Analyze data to identify the area with the highest number of faults and perform a thorough analysis of the problem area
- Consult the customers who are most impacted by the problem area
- Make recommendations for actions to be taken in order to reduce the occurrence of faults

Another strategy is to perform benchmarking of other companies who have a very low fault rate in their system. Benchmarking is the investigation of a company that has a superior performance in an area of our interest. (Benchmarking is discussed in Chapter 4.)

For this strategy, ACCU-INFO may decide to benchmark the information systems for the Tokyo subway system to see how to reduce the system fault ratio and increase the systems reliability.

One of the tactics for the strategy collect detailed data on the input errors, software faults, and network failure on a regular basis is to design an automatic fault-data collection module. This module keeps a log of customer attempts to access the system, asks the customer whether he or she sees any problem with the information or the software, keeps a record of software failures, and keeps a count of unsuccessful network access.

Another possible tactic for ACCU-INFO in accomplishing the above strategy is the design of a subsystem for the quality control of input data. In this tactic, a module collects a random sample of input data on a regular basis. An operator checks the sample against the source of data, and reports discrepancies to the module. The module performs an analysis of input errors, identifies the major sources of problems (such as the data-entry person, the type of data, the time of data entry, so forth), and recommends possible courses of action.

In identifying strategies and tactics, we need processes by which we can continuously monitor the system performance and define strategies, tactics, processes, and actions that move the system toward accomplishing the set objectives. The continuous improvement process serves this purpose.

The precursors of the continuous improvement process are hoshin planning and the theory of constraints. These two concepts help the improvement process by identifying the areas on which the improvement process must focus.

3.2.2 Hoshin Planning

The organization-wide policies, goals, objectives, strategies and tactics, collectively, form a master plan for the organization. Within this master plan, we must identify the policies, goals, objectives, strategies, and tactics that are related to information systems.

Another piece of the planning process is the determination of hoshins. Hoshin karni, translated as hoshin planning or policy deployment, has its origin in Japanese companies [King 1989]. The idea is to choose a number of focus areas for implementation. Each unit determines the hoshins for the unit within the context of the master plan. Hoshins are the most important activities which tie into the top priority components of the organization's plan [King 1989]. The hoshins guide the choices in the continuous-improvement process and focus on the root causes of problems.

The identification and selection of hoshins is a team process and is an integral part of the planning process. Once the plan identifies priorities, the managers determine critical activities that are related to the top priorities.

In the ACCU-INFO example, it is determined that information-systems reliability is a top priority item in the plan. The goals and objectives provide quantitative targets for this item. Now, the managers within the information-systems function should determine their units' hoshins for the year. For example, the database systems group chooses as one of the unit's hoshins the reduction of data-entry errors by 50 percent every month. Another hoshin of this group is to create a system for automatic data collection on input errors. The network group selects the identification of major causes for network fault as one of its main hoshins.

This hoshin is selected by a process in which all managers participate in determining hoshins that will lead to the realizations of objectives and goals. Hoshins guide the continuous improvement activities and require the regular diagnostics and checking that are involved in these activities. There is a process of regular feedback on the implementation of hoshins. This topic will be discussed in more detail in the discussion of the continuous improvement process.

3.2.3 Theory of Constraints

Another concept that aids the continuous-improvement process is the theory of constraints [Goldratt 1990]. To identify where the major focus of improvement should be, the theory of constraints advocates the inspection of the entire system and the identification of constraints that obstruct the systems flow.

Goldratt, in his *theory of constraints*, defines five steps for this approach:

- Identify the system's constraints
- Decide how to exploit the system's constraints
- Subordinate everything else to the above decision
- Alleviate the system's constraints
- If in the previous steps a constraint has been broken, go back to Step 1

When there is a problem with the system, the most crucial step is to identify constraints. Many constraints could be caused by assumptions that are not valid anymore. Therefore, it is helpful to verbalize the unspoken assumptions and see if they are still valid. This is not an easy task. Goldratt in his book, *The Goal*, tells the story of the discovery process involved in identifying system constraints. It is by common sense, observation, and analysis of the observed processes that one can discover the true nature of the system constraints.

The next step is determining how to alter the system constraints and make them opportunities for improvement. Once this determination is made, other processes are subordinated to the target of constraints removal. Resources are allocated to the alleviation of the constraint until it is shown that the identified constraint has been removed. The removal of one constraint triggers another round of constraint identification and removal.

For example, ACCU-INFO shows a high value for the systems fault ratio metric for its information systems. Once analyzed, we find that the input data has the largest share of the blame. One immediate reaction to this finding is to blame the data-entry clerks and recommend a stringent control and redundancy checks for the data-entry process. It turns out that even with added expenses of checking and redundant data entry, the system still has a large fault ratio for input data.

We have identified the core problem as errors in data entry, but the solution of more control and more redundancy has not worked. It even has worsened the systems fault ratio in other areas because it has delayed the updating process and caused customer dissatisfaction.

Goldratt recommends using the cause-effect-cause method as an aid to identify the core problem. For example, in the case of ACCU-INFO, we start with observing the data-entry process. The company receives various types of reports regarding the credit activities of an individual. A supervisor checks the report for validity and acceptance and passes it to the data-entry clerk for entry into the system.

The database system is set up by name and social security number. If the name and social security number on the report do not match any concatenated name and social security primary keys in the database, the clerk creates a new record. Furthermore, credit reports arrive in various forms and sometimes in the form of a letter. The data-entry clerk must read the letter or the form and pick up the data to be entered into the system. Many forms are standardized, such as a delay in paying the mortgage or credit card bill. However, there are cases such as delay in payment due to a dispute or emergencies that require judgment. In such cases, the data-entry clerk must go to the supervisor for a decision. There is a high attrition level in the clerical staff.

Matching both names and social security numbers as a concatenated key leaves out women who change their names after marriage. Furthermore, leaving the interpretation to clerks with a high turnover could create errors and inconsistencies in entering the credit data. It turns out that to alleviate the problem, the software should be changed to allow for name changes, and the data-entry interface must have some intelligence in helping the data-entry clerks deal with the exceptional cases. Furthermore, the company has decided to provide extensive training for the clerks and adopt hiring practices that give more incentive for staying on the job. Therefore, what was first considered a data-entry problem turns out to be problems caused by software and personnel policies.

Now that the constraints and the method of their removal are decided, we must subject other processes to it. That is, we take the measure to change the data-entry interface. For example, we may have to reallocate programmers' time from other projects to create an intelligent module for data entry. Supervisors would allocate time for training the clerks, and the human resource department might have to devise a new hiring and benefit package for the data-entry jobs. This requires teamwork and focused effort for the alleviation of the constraint.

Goldratt [1990] observes that human factors play a crucial role in identifying constraints, finding solutions, and causing the change. He recommends:

- What to change? Pinpoint the core problems, use the cause-effect-cause method
- What to change to? Construct simple, practical solutions, evaporating clouds solutions
- How to cause the change? Induce the appropriate people to invent such solutions, use the Socratic method

Cause-Effect-Cause Approach.   This approach recommends testing the hypothesis that an identified cause is indeed the root cause of a constraint. It has three steps:

- Identity a possible cause
- Observe the effect of the cause
- Look to see if it causes a similar effect in another situation

In the ACCU-INFO example, one of the data-entry errors was hypothesized to be caused by the concatenated key of names and social security numbers in the recent set of errors.

To verify this cause, one can search the database for identical social security numbers to see if there were undiscovered errors caused by the name changes of married women. For the case of the impact of training, we can train a couple of clerks and observe their performance to see how much their errors are reduced. In other words, the constraint identification should be fact-based and tested before making the decision that indeed the core problem has been discovered.

Evaporating Clouds Solutions.   In evaporating clouds solutions, Goldratt advocates simple and intuitive solutions that work like evaporating clouds. To identify such solutions, one has to go to the core of the problem and focus on removing causes, rather than addressing symptoms. In a later section, we see that the cause-and-effect chart can aid this process.

Socratic Method.   Any solution requires changes in attitudes and processes. Goldratt observes that even when we identify the right solution, people would resist the change that the solution brings about. People need to take ownership of the solution. Goldratt proposes using the Socratic method. He suggests that you should pose the question and lead the person to find the solution you have identified. This way, the person will have the ownership of the solution and will not be resistant to the changes it causes.

Sources of Organizational Improvement.   In his book, *Goal*, Goldratt identifies three sources for guiding the improvement activities within a manufacturing setting:

- Increasing throughput
- Reducing operating costs
- Reducing inventory

Applied to information systems, increasing throughput means an increase in the access to and use of the system. Reducing operating cost means delivering the same quality services at a lower cost. An interesting concept is the application of the inventory reduction concept to information systems. One interpretation is that there must not be data, software, and hardware waiting to be put to use. In other words, a lengthy system design and implementation process is like a high-volume inventory—money is invested in its acquisition, but no results are yet produced. Coming up with processes that reduce the length of systems development and implementation has the same effect of reducing inventory in manufacturing processes. Another interpretation is the reduction of excess capacity in hardware and data that are not used.

3.3   ◆   Continuous Improvement in Information Systems

The mode of continuous improvement in information systems requires a firm and long-term commitment to quality and customer focus. This process does not work in a vacuum. It demands leadership for change because continuous improvement is about changing and improving the present system. The idea of "if it is not broken, don't fix it," is not valid anymore.

Lynch and Werner [1992] identify the keys to a successful continuous improvement process:

- Top management's passionate conviction that change is necessary and valuable
- Readiness to seek and accept honest self-assessment
- Spend time communicating with customers and workers and learning skills and tools for continuous improvement
- Develop and work within the organizational vision, mission, and principles
- Work within the strategic plan, and specify the important results that should be achieved through the process of continuous improvement
- Be prepared to deal with the fears and unreasonable expectations that change causes

- Expect, understand, and use cynicism from employees; reduce it by involving all employees in the process, and acting consistently with the vision, mission, and principles
- Remain focused on external customers
- Continuous improvement is a journey. Enjoy the process, and derive satisfaction from the opportunity it provides to learn from mistakes and experience

To put the process of continuous improvement in place, one needs to put in place cross-functional quality teams and provide the teams with the necessary methods and tools, as discussed in the following sections.

◆ CASE: Lessons Learned From Implementing TQM in a High Tech Facility Start-up

Since arriving a little over a year ago at George Marshall Space Flight Center, an IIT Research Institute (IITRI) team has had the opportunity to begin a journey toward excellence in applied research support service. The IITRI team is fulfilling a contract to maintain and operate an on-site Metallurgy Research Facility (MRF) for NASA. IITRI has corporate headquarters in Chicago, Illinois and 17 off-site locations throughout the country. IITRI is a contract organization providing approximately $120 million worth of research services to industry and government annually.

During the first several months of MRF operations, a group of technologists, scientists, and engineers were assembled. Starting with diverse educational and geographic backgrounds, the group has formed into a working team dedicated to excellence in service provided to our customer. This is due in large part to the TQM efforts of both NASA and MRF. It began with a commitment by local and corporate management at IITRI, and was successfully coupled with an emphasis on TQM by NASA.

The services provided by MRF are varied in nature. There are three significant technical focuses: Applied Metallurgy and Alloy Development, Testing and Maintenance, and Real Time Support. These activities are extremely diverse and require different management approaches. Administrative and quality functions are also locally managed.

In order to assure the quality of data generated for NASA, as well as to provide structure to the research being accomplished, a Quality Plan that incorporates TQM principles was introduced. This plan creates a structured approach to what is normally considered a creative process. The following is its outline:

- Task order initiated and approved
- Program plan, milestones, and completion dates developed and approved
- Task work begins
- Interim reports generated as required
- Final task report generated and approved
- Task closed

The *task order* is a document that recognizes a need. It provides an estimate of the amount of work required, an objective, and an estimate of the materials/services purchases required. It is submitted to the NASA Contracting Officer's Technical Representative (COTR) for approval. Once approved, the task work can begin.

NASA Marshall has committed to the quest for continuous improvement in all its operations; both contractors and civil servants are held to this standard. Positioning MRF for excellence in fulfilling our mission was in line with customer expectations.

The first step toward our goal was to establish a joint NASA-MRF Steering Group. The members of this group include NASA's contracting officer, TQM coordinator, MRF program manager, MRF assistant manager and MRF quality manager. This group acts primarily as a policy-making entity, along with facilitating the implementation of TQM in MRF operations.

Getting all the players to speak the same quality language was the next goal. A one-day introductory seminar was held for both NASA and MRF senior staff. As a result of the initial training seminar, a two-week training session was scheduled. The technicians and administrative staff participated in 4-hour sessions over the two weeks, relating to overall TQM concepts and Statistical Process Control (SPC). The engineering and scientific staff participated in training specific to statistically designed experiments. All of the sessions were videotaped, to be used as refresher training for both NASA and MRF employees.

As a result of these workshops, several application projects were identified. Process action teams (PATs) were formed to address several of the projects. Some of the PATs' projects include:

- Measurement capability study
- Test request elimination
- Hardness testing equipment
- Purchasing lead times
- Furnace temperature profiles
- Microprobe variability

Standard operating procedures were developed to aid the employees in applying the statistical tools to specific projects. Both administrative and technical processes have been established. The process actions teams were suggested by the employees working at MRF. Successes achieved by the teams were due in large part to the team members' commitment to doing things better. In addition, demonstrated commitment by both the local and corporate management teams, along with demonstrated support by NASA, have made the team concept work at MRF. Some of the successes achieved by MRF include:

- Measurement capability team: reduced variability measurements among operators by as much as 85%
- Purchasing lead time team: reduced overall lead time by two days, and variability by 3 days

- Test request elimination team: reduced handling of specimens by 10 minutes per specimen
- Hardness test equipment: assured the repeatability and reproducibility of hardness equipment

In order to keep TQM alive at MRF, a monthly newsletter has been developed. Participation by all of the MRF teams in writing, editing, and publishing the newsletter has been an unexpected, but valuable outcome. The newsletter has not only kept TQM a visible part of our operations, but has also opened communications among the staff.

Other valuable achievements include streamlining of MRF operations though greater local control of administrative processes, like purchasing, reporting, and financial management. Time savings, due to reduced testing paperwork will amount to approximately 500 man-hours per year. Standardization of the measurement techniques and equipment used by MRF employees will decrease the amount of redundant testing, and the training time required for new employees. In addition, a supplier trend-analysis for purchasing lead times is now available to MRF. MRF can begin working with its suppliers to assure on-time service.

A recognition system, to encourage improvement suggestions and participation in PATs has been developed. This system recognizes both individual and team efforts. It is a three level-system, with recognition for any improvement idea submitted. Certain criteria have been developed, that allow for awards of increasing value, based on the impact of the improvement idea to the operation of MRF. A quarterly recognition presentation is held, and an annual banquet is held to recognize superior improvement achievements. The local program manager presents the quarterly awards, and the corporate program director presents awards at the annual dinner.

Lessons Learned

One of the most important lessons to be learned is *never be discouraged*. If it doesn't work, throw it out and move on. Not all ideas will bring the desired results.

An example of this at MRF was an ill-fated attempt at posters. Posters were developed so that employees could identify processes, variables, and expected improvements. No one used them. Rather than dwell on the problem of why not, the team decided to attempt something different. Out of this rather obvious failure came the recognition system mentioned above. Sometimes, synergy will produce another, better idea from the remains of a bad idea.

One reason teams are working at MRF is the structured approach in which we:

- Develop an agenda for every meeting
- Set deadlines, assign responsibilities
- Attempt to achieve a clear consensus of team members
- Encourage participation of all members
- Invite only key personnel
- Discourage hidden agendas

- Maintain open communication among members
- Publish minutes

A demonstrable commitment must be made by the most visible management. In our case, the local management team is totally committed to TQM. Our NASA counterparts have been very visible in their commitment to the concepts as well. This commitment cannot be delegated; management must actively show their support, by being involved in teams, and by allocating time, materials, and dollars to the effort.

Do not let the alphabet soup surrounding TQM become an obstacle and do not let current buzzwords hamper your efforts. Decide on common languages and methods, and stick to them.

Finally, TQM *must* have a champion within your organization (and your supporting organization if appropriate). There must be someone within the organization who is absolutely convinced that the concepts will work. General Loh, of the U.S. Air Force said, "This is not a game of home runs—it is a game of singles." Your champion must be there to advance the philosophy all along the line, when results are not yet evident, as well as when they are.

A Look to the Future

At MRF, our goals include further involvement by our NASA counterparts, joint NASA/MRF teams to address technical issues, and further training. Process action teams have been identified in the heat-treating areas, statistically designed experiments are being developed in applied metallurgy and alloy development, and out PATs are continuing to look for even further results.

Our mission is to use statistical tools, common sense, and TQM principles to provide continuously improving services to NASA.

Conclusions

- TQM can work in a high-tech research start-up
- A structured approach is required
- Management support is crucial
- Structured team efforts are valuable
- A champion of the approach is vital

Source: Excerpt from "Lessons Learned From Implementing TQM in a High Tech Facility Start-up" Stephanie Manneback, and E. J. Vesely, *Tapping the Network Journal*, Spring/Summer, 1991, pp. 24–27, reprinted with permission from Quality and Productivity Management Association, Schaumburg, IL.

3.3.1   Quality Teams

The cross-functional quality team is the organizational structure for putting the improvement process in place. We discussed quality teams in Chapter 2. For the improvement process, the cross-functional nature of the team must be emphasized.

Information-systems quality teams must include representatives of the internal and external customers of the system as well as those of the technical, clerical, and administrative staffs. It is important not to limit the team members to those with technical know-how of the system.

The team must be well-informed about the organization's as well as the information system's vision, mission, principles, hoshins, goals, and objectives. It would be within this context that the quality team can plan and prioritize improvement actions.

Another important behavioral aspect of the quality team is to regard improvements as opportunities for learning from mistakes, rather than as a basis for rating the performance of those who might have caused errors or faults.

For example, in the case of ACCU-INFO, assume that the quality team discovers that faults in the network are caused by the errors in forecasting the network's demand. Blaming the forecaster for the error and using it to punish him or her will sabotage the spirit of commitment to change. The team must investigate what caused the forecaster to err. It could be that the forecaster did not have adequate data—customers were not consulted adequately, the top management did not express its intention of providing connectivity to the network for all employees who have a computer, and the organization's plans for future expansions were not shared with the forecaster. Learning from this experience, the policy is adopted that in developing a computer network, planning must take place within the context of organizational and information-systems plans as well as extensive involvement of the existing and potential network customers.

The lack of blame and punishment in the improvement process and allowance for errors and mistakes creates an atmosphere of openness in which employees are willing to identify faults without endangering their own jobs or those of their co-workers.

3.3.2   Shewhart-Deming Cycle

The idea of the continuous improvement cycle was developed by Shewhart and popularized by Deming. The cycle has four components: plan, do, check, and act, as shown in Figure 3.6.

Plan.   In planning the improvement projects, the focus should be on prevention. In other words, a system that is working is not necessarily the best system. It is obvious that when a fault is detected, the system needs improvement. However, a major aim of improvement efforts should be to foresee and prevent faults.

In discovering areas that may need improvement, we can look for signs of trouble such as:

- High variability in performance metrics
- Areas of bottleneck and constraints

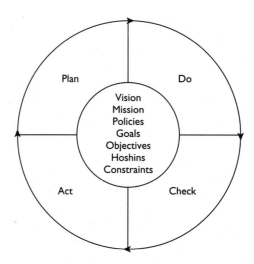

Figure 3.6   Shewhart-Deming Cycle

- High waiting time
- Delays in scheduled services
- Fatigue, frustration, and complaints
- High number of fixing activities
- A culture of fire-fighting and emergency operation

For example, in checking data in the information system, we might discover that data errors have a high variability. To reduce errors, we have to check the data more than once, which leads to delay in updating the databases in the information system.

We can identify improvement opportunities through feedbacks from:

- Employees
- Internal customers
- External customers
- Internal suppliers
- External suppliers

For example, a data-entry clerk at ACCU-INFO complains that the software interface is crowded and ambiguous. This should come as a warning that the interface may cause errors in data entry. The preventive measure is to evaluate the complaint. If it proves valid, the change of data-entry interface becomes one of the potential improvement projects. More importantly, a data-entry clerk may be afraid to complain because of the fear of being branded as a "troublemaker" or "nagger." To alleviate such fears and encourage suggestions and problem identification, such employees should be rewarded and recognized.

Once an improvement item (such as changing the data-entry interface) is identified, its priority in achieving the quality goals and objectives must be determined. The systems analysis and design phases involved in planning for an improvement project ensure that the changes made in the system are congruent with the company's overall information-systems strategy.

In the planning phase, we have to make sure that we have:

- Established the improvement objective (for example, error-free data in the database)
- Have selected the project that is in line with the improvement objective (for example, changing the data-entry interface to reduce errors in data)
- Identified the appropriate team of employees to be involved in the project (for example, systems analyst, system designer, data-entry clerk, programmer, and manager)
- A clear understanding of the existing state of the information system and the desirable state of the information system (for example, we now have a crowded data-entry interface, we want to have a data-entry interface that is clear and easy to understand)
- Identified and involved the customers and suppliers in the improvement project (for example, the software provider, data-entry clerk, external user of the information system on the team)
- Have clearly identified rewards and recognition for the improvement activity (for example, the successful improvement in the user interface will be announced throughout the company and individuals involved will receive a quality plaque)

There are a number of tools for identifying and planning for improvement, such as Pareto, cause-and-effect, and tree and hierarchy diagrams. These tools are discussed in a later section.

Do.   Implementing an improvement plan requires a team, budget, and schedule. There should be a clear and well-established process for implementing the planned change. In the ACCU-INFO example, implementing the change in the data-entry interface requires a software programmer, the data manager, and a data-entry clerk to work on the implementation and testing. Since these employees are pulled out of their regular jobs, their time, as well as any other resources used in the implementation of the change, should be included in the budget. A schedule for the completion of the task is created so that the conversion from the existing system to the system with the new data-entry interface can be planned, and a data-entry clerk can be trained on the new interface.

Check.   One interpretation of the check stage is the inspection of what is created at the "do" stage. Imai [1986] believes that this interpretation "is based on a division of labor among supervisors, inspectors, and workers." He believes that both management and inspectors are responsible for the checking phase of the cycle.

This stage requires establishing the criteria for improvement, such as:

- Functionality
- Usability
- Reliability
- Performance
- Supportability
- Availability
- Prices

In the ACCU-INFO example, the criterion for improvement was to increase the reliability of data in the information system. However, the improvement was expected to increase the functionality and usability of the data-entry interface as well. At this stage, the data manager should collect data for checking whether the improvement has increased data reliability as well the data-entry usability and functionality. The reliability of data can be checked for number of errors in the data before and after the implementation of the new system. Another measure related to reliability is to establish if the variability of errors in the data has decreased after the implementation of the new system. Functionality and usability can be measured in observing data-entry clerks working with the old interface and the new interface.

In all cases, checking must involve factual and objective data. We will see in Chapter 10 that control charts are useful tools in the checking stage.

Act.   The checking stage may show that:

- The implementation has significantly improved the system
- The implementation has not significantly improved the system
- The implementation has improved the system, but more work in the same area is needed.

In the first case, the improvement should be standardized and become an integral part of the system. For example, the new user interface will be used in all input stations, and the old interface is discarded. This constitutes the "act" stage of the Shewhart-Deming cycle.

In the second case, we must go through another round of plan-do-check-act. For example, the change of the data-entry interface did not have any impact on the errors in input data.

In the third case, the improvement is standardized, and the improvement cycle continues. For example, the new interface has eliminated the ambiguity on the screen and is not efficient for experienced data-entry clerks.

3.3.3   Seeking, Handling, and Implementing Suggestions

Employees' and customers' suggestions fuel continuous improvement. Companies in Japan, such as Toyota, have regular employee competition for the highest number of suggestions. The rewards are mostly in the form of recognition; the monetary compensation is small, if any. When the suggestion of an employee is implemented and produces an improvement, the employee receives further recognition.

Encouraging suggestions require putting in place a process to screen the suggestions and to respond to the person who makes the suggestion. This is an excellent method of communication between workers and customers who are directly involved with the system on one end, and managers and decision makers on the other end of the communication line.

For example, a programmer becomes aware of a new, cheap interface module that can increase the clarity of PC screens. It may cross his or her mind that this clarity may help data-entry personnel to see the screen better and improve the quality of data. He (or she) may have different reactions to this thought. 1) Data entry is not my responsibility, so why should I worry about it? 2) If I remember it, I may mention it to the data manager next time I see him (or her). 3) People talk about suggestions, but it is a hassle; I do not know how I should make the suggestion without looking presumptuous. 4) Why bother? Nobody pays any attention to what programmers suggest. 5) My manager was talking about suggestions and their importance; we have gone through a short seminar on how to make suggestions and learned of the recognition and visibility it generates within the company. I will send the suggestion.

The purpose of putting a suggestion process in place is to show employees that their views and recommendations are important and are taken seriously, and to inform them how to make a suggestion.

A permanent unit or team should review suggestions and let the employees know in a short time that their suggestions have been reviewed. Suggestions must be categorized and recorded, and employees rewarded. Moreover, the continuous improvement team should have access to the suggestions pool. This process requires an information system by itself.

3.4 ◆ Tools for Problem Identification

There are a number of tools that can be used in the problem identification stage of the continuous improvement process. They include: the Pareto chart, cause-and-effect diagram, and tree and hierarchy diagrams.

3.4.1 Pareto Chart

A Pareto chart is a simple tool for identifying the value (normally in the form of relative frequency) of the item that has the highest contribution to the problem under study. It is a bar chart of relative frequencies, sorted in descending order of frequency values. The cumulative frequency values are also shown on the chart.

After the main problem area is identified (such as data errors), we choose metrics that can be the indicators of the specific problem areas and their sources. In the ACCU-INFO example, we first identify the source of reported errors, such as redundant records, missing data, discovered errors during quality control, and customer complaints.

We then have to identify the time interval for the data, such as data collected over one week.

The next step is to collect the data. For example, ACCU-INFO has collected the following counts of errors on the input data to its information system.

Error Type	Frequency	Relative Frequency	Cum. Relative Frequency
redundant records	20	.50	.50
missing data	10	.25	.75
discovered errors in testing	8	.20	.95
customer complaints	2	.05	1.00

The Pareto chart is drawn as a bar chart of the data shown in the above table. Figure 3.7 shows the Pareto chart for the ACCU-INFO example. The cumulative relative frequencies are shown on the line connecting the points on each bar.

This chart shows that redundant records are the major source of errors in input data. The process should be repeated for identifying the reasons why redundant records are created. We may discover that using a name as part of the primary key (the field by which we access a record) has caused the creation of redundant data for the same person.

Thus the Pareto chart aids in identifying the main sources of a problem by using objective, factual data. This approach takes personal judgments and political considerations out of the continuous improvement process.

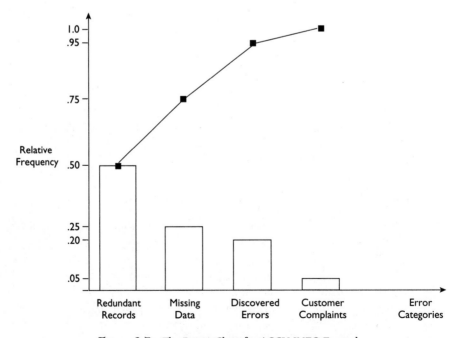

Figure 3.7   The Pareto Chart for ACCU-INFO Example

Figure 3.8   Starting the Cause-and-Effect Diagram

3.4.2   Cause-and-Effect Diagram

The cause-and-effect diagram (also known as the fishbone diagram) was first developed by Ishikawa. It is another tool for identifying the root causes of problems and their constraints. The diagram is used in the brainstorming process.

The diagram starts with a straight line, at the end of which is the problem, such as errors in input data, as shown in Figure 3.8.

The next step of constructing the cause-and-effect diagram is to add major categories in which the sources of the problem may lie. These categories may be people, procedures, hardware, software, network, and data suppliers, as shown in Figure 3.9.

The brainstorming process continues by adding more specific reasons why there are errors in input data. On the people branch of Figure 3.9, one may have the following as the causes of errors:

* Inexperienced data-entry clerks
* Lack of attention by data-entry clerks
* Bad supervision of the data-entry function

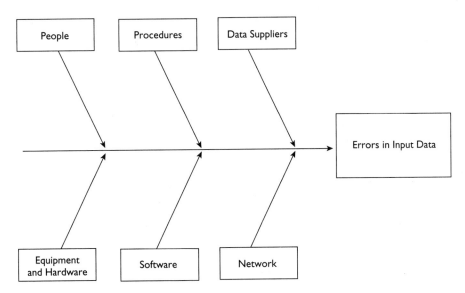

Figure 3.9   Adding Major Categories of Problem Causes to the Cause-and-Effect Diagram

On the procedures branch, we may have:

- Low wages for data-entry clerks
- Lack of training for data-entry clerks
- Lack of adequate data quality control

The possible sources of the problem for other branches are shown in Figure 3.10.

The cause-and-effect diagram is a discussion tool for creating consensus on the possible main causes of a problem. Once the possible root causes are identified, we should collect and analyze data in order to objectively investigate that the hypothesized causes are indeed the source of the problem. The Pareto chart is a simple tool for data analysis.

3.4.3   Tree and Hierarchy Diagrams

The tree and hierarchy diagrams are tools for organizing a sequence of ideas, tasks, or attributes, starting from the most general level, and gradually breaking down into more detail. They are tools for organizing complex structures into manageable and comprehensible forms.

A tree diagram starts with the most abstract and general concept from the left-hand side of the page and moves to the right. A hierarchy has a similar structure with the difference that the most general concept is at the top of the page, and subsequent levels are presented by moving down, as shown in Figure 3.11a.

In some cases, a hierarchy is a more general method of presentation in that it allows a lower-level element (the child) to have more than one parent, as shown in Figure 3.11b, where C has both A and B as its parents.

Tree and hierarchy diagrams can be used in the planning stage of the continuous improvement process. For example, let us consider planning the tasks for change in the data-entry interface in the ACCU-INFO case. The planning tree starts at the top with the plan to change the data-entry interface (Figure 3.12).

The next level of the tree contains decisions regarding the extent of the change and the requirements it should have, the financial resources allocated to the process, and the evaluation of the success of the project.

Once the extent of the change is decided, then the decisions regarding the composition of the teams, schedule, software, and hardware must be made. On the financial branch, the allocation should be divided to the present and future allocation of resources. On the evaluation branch, one has to decide on the criteria, personnel, and schedule for evaluating the success of the project.

We could present the same information in the form of a planning hierarchy by turning it 90 degrees, as shown in Figure 3.13. In the planning hierarchy, however, we can also show interdependency of lower-level elements to more than one element at the top.

For example, the decision on manpower, schedule, hardware, and software depends on the allocated financial resources, as shown in Figure 3.13. This interdependency allows for a more complicated and realistic presentation of the planning process.

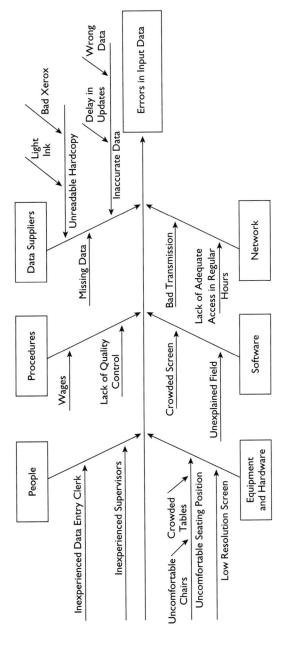

Figure 3.10   Cause-and-Effect Diagram for the Problem of Errors in Input Data

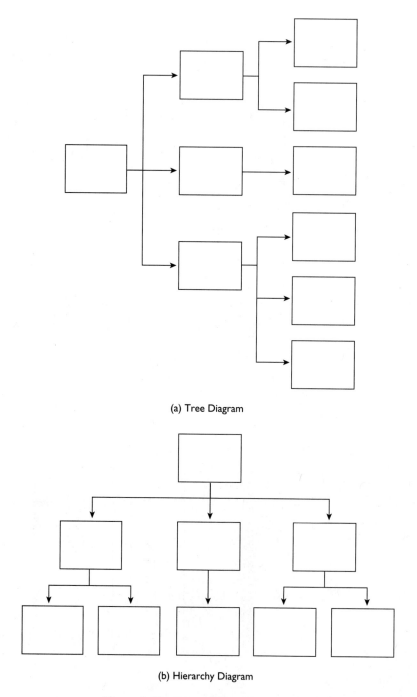

(a) Tree Diagram

(b) Hierarchy Diagram

Figure 3.11   Tree and Hierarchy Diagrams

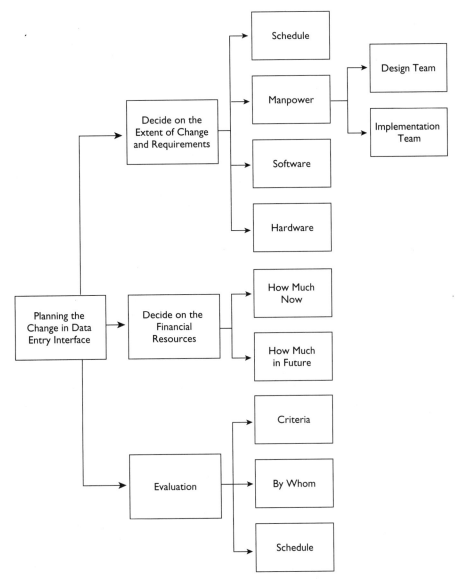

Figure 3.12   Planning Tree for the Data-Entry Interface

◆ Conclusion

In this chapter, we introduced the concept of continuous improvement process applied to information systems. This chapter introduced and compared the major paradigms of information-systems improvement: maintenance, systems life cycle, and continuous improvement process. The chapter focused on the continuous improvement process.

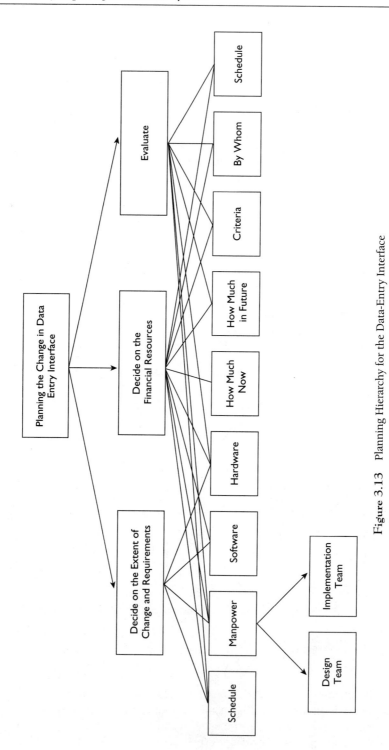

Figure 3.13   Planning Hierarchy for the Data-Entry Interface

The existence of a well-defined information-systems policy within the framework of the overall company policy is a major requirement for the success of the continuous improvement process. The second section of this chapter discussed the concepts of the strategic planning process, hoshin planning, and the theory of constraints. These are planning and diagnostic paradigms that have a major impact on the improvement process.

The third section of this chapter covered the ingredients of the continuous improvement process, which include quality teams, the Shewhart-Deming cycle, and seeking, handling, and implementing suggestions. The Shewhart-Deming cycle of plan-do-check-act forms the underlying foundation of the continuous improvement process, whereas quality teams provide the structure for the process, and suggestions fuel the move toward change and improvement.

The last section of this chapter discussed three quality tools that could be used in the improvement process. These tools are cause-and-effect diagrams, Pareto chart, and tree and hierarchy diagrams. One must note here that the use of these tools in managing quality is not limited to the continuous improvement process, nor does the process rely solely on these tools. The methods discussed in other chapters, including team building and brainstorming, covered in Chapter 2, are quite relevant to the continuous improvement process as well.

◆ References

1. Finkelstein, Clive. 1989. *An Introduction to Information Engineering: From Strategic Planning to Information Systems*, Addison-Wesley, Reading, MA.

2. Gantz, John. 1987. "System Integration: Living in a House of Your Own," *Telecommunication Products + Technology*, Vol. 5, No. 5, May, pp. 32–54.

3. Goldratt, Eliyahu. 1986. *The Goal: The Process of Ongoing Improvement*, Revised Edition, North River Press, Inc., Croton-on-Hudson, NY.

4. Goldratt, Eliyahu. 1990. *Theory of Constraints: And How Should it be Implemented?* North River Press, Inc. Croton-on-Hudson, NY.

5. Imai, Masaaki. 1986. *Kaizen: The Key to Japan's Competitive Success*, McGraw-Hill Co., New York, NY.

6. King, Bob. 1989. *Hoshin Planning: The Developmental Approach*, GOAL/QPC, Methuen, MA.

7. Lynch, Robert F. and Werner, Thomas J. 1992. *Continuous Improvement*, QualTeam, Inc. Atlanta, GA.

8. Sarazen, J. Stephen. 1991. "Continuous Improvement and Innovation," *Journal of Quality and Participation*, September, pp. 34–38.

9. Whitten, Jeffrey L.; Bentley, Lonnie D.; and Barlow, Victor M. 1989. *Systems Analysis & Design Methods*, 2nd Edition, Irwin, Homewood, IL.

10. Zahedi, F. and Ashrafi, N. 1991. "Software Reliability Allocation Based on Structure, Utility, Price, and Cost," *IEEE Transactions on Software Engineering*, Vol. 17, No. 4, April, pp. 345–356.

11. Zahedi, F. and Ashrafi, N. 1993. "A Decision Framework for Selecting Software Reliability Models," unpublished manuscript, University of Wisconsin, Milwaukee, WI.

12. Zahedi, F. 1994. "Reliability Metric for Information Systems Based on Customer Requirements," unpublished manuscript, University of Wisconsin, Milwaukee, WI.

◆ Questions

3.1. What is the strategic importance of change and improvement in information systems?

3.2. Discuss and compare the paradigms of change in information systems.

3.3. What is the significance of information-systems strategic planning?

3.4. What is hoshin planning?

3.5. What is the role of the theory of constraints in systems improvement?

3.6. List the five steps for using the theory of constraints.

3.7. What are the signs of trouble indicating the need for systems improvement?

3.8. What are the ingredients of the continuous improvement process in information systems?

3.9. What is the Shewhart-Deming cycle?

3.10. Why is handling suggestions important in the improvement process?

3.11. What are the sources of improvement?

3.12. List the criteria for measuring the success of systems improvement.

3.13. What is the use of the cause-and-effect diagram?

3.14. How does the Pareto chart help in the information-systems continuous improvement process?

3.15. What is the difference between a tree diagram and a hierarchy diagram?

◆ Problems

3.1. Give three examples of information-systems hoshins.

3.2. Give four examples of possible information-systems constraints.

3.3. Perform a group brainstorming session using the cause-and-effect diagram to identify the possible causes of errors in your university's information systems for reporting student grades.

3.4. Perform a similar session as the above problem for the class schedule system.

3.5. Draw the Pareto chart for the following data:

Error Type	Frequency	Relative Frequency	Cum. Relative Frequency
missing data	10	.25	.25
redundant records	10	.25	.50
discovered errors in testing	18	.45	.95
customer complaints	2	.05	1.00

3.6. Draw a planning-tree diagram for improving the student information system at your university. Assume that the required improvement is the change of manual reporting of grades to computerized reports originated by professors.

3.7. Draw a planning hierarchy diagram for improving the student information system at your university. Assume that the required improvement is the change of manual reporting of grades to computerized reports originated by professors.

Mediocrity knows nothing higher than itself, but talent instantly recognizes genius.

— Sir Arthur Conan Doyle, *The Valley of Fear*

I have found my own definition of criticism: a disinterested endeavor to learn and propagate the best that is known and thought in the world.

— Matthew Arnold, *The Function of Criticism at the Present Time*

Nothing in life is to be feared. It is only to be understood.

— Madame Curie

◆ Chapter Objectives

The objectives of this chapter are:
- ◆ To introduce the benchmarking concept as applied to information systems
- ◆ To discuss planning benchmarking
- ◆ To discuss issues involved in benchmarking data collection
- ◆ To discuss how to use the benchmarking results
- ◆ To relate benchmarking to systems continuous improvement

◆ Key Words

Benchmarking, stages of information-systems benchmarking, information-systems metrics, planning for benchmarking, collecting benchmarking information, analysis of benchmarking results

Benchmarking for Information Systems

4.1 The Importance of Benchmarking
   4.1.1 Benchmarking in Japan and the U.S.
   4.1.2 Relevance to Information Systems

4.2 Benchmark Planning for Information Systems
   4.2.1 Identifying Benchmarking Objectives and Measurements
   4.2.2 Types of Benchmarking
   4.2.3 Selecting the Benchmarking Partner

4.3 Collecting Benchmarking Information
   4.3.1 Types of Benchmark Information
   4.3.2 Methods of Information Collection
   4.3.3 Documentation of Benchmark Information

4.4 Analysis of Benchmarking Information
   4.4.1 Performance Analysis
   4.4.2 Process Analysis
   4.4.3 Policy Analysis
   4.4.4 Structure Analysis
   4.4.5 Iterative Benchmarking

4.5 Using the Benchmarking Results
   4.5.1 Shared Understanding of Benchmarking Results
   4.5.2 Determination of Future Performance and Goals
   4.5.3 Implementation
   4.5.4 Evaluation, Monitoring, and Continuous Improvement

◆ Introduction

Information-systems benchmarking is finding the best industry practices and applying them in continuous systems improvement for achieving excellence and superiority in performance. Xerox CEO David Kearn states, "benchmarking is the continuous process of measuring products, services, and practices against the toughest competitors or those companies recognized as industry leaders" [quoted in Camp 1989].

As discussed in Chapter 3, the process of continuous improvement requires the knowledge of problem areas and weak spots. One of the ways of identifying opportunities for improvement is to look outside the unit and search for the best. This approach provides goals and models that are both realistic, in that they have been achieved by others, and have the highest level of performance.

Benchmarking can be perceived as a step within a series of steps taken for establishing the continuous systems-improvement process. It requires:

- Self-evaluation
- Identification of weak spots
- Definition of metrics
- Identification of processes, policies, and structures of interest

Before commencing benchmarking, we must perform a self-evaluation to identify the weak spots in information systems. In some cases one can identify weak spots qualitatively. In other cases, we need to define performance and evaluation metrics for various aspects of information systems, and identify processes, policies, and structures that have the potential for improvement. This chapter provides a practical guide for performing benchmarking activities.

4.1 ◆ The Importance of Benchmarking

Benchmarking is an effective tool for igniting the process of continuous improvement. Internally motivated improvements are gradual and mostly piecemeal. Internally motivated major changes encounter skepticism and resistance by various factions of the organization, who feel threatened by change. At the same time, a lack of knowledge about whether the improvements are possible, practical, and profitable makes top management reluctant to choose drastic improvements. Benchmarking shows top management, workers, and customers what the best is and how one can achieve it. This is what the drive for continuous improvement is all about.

The reasons for benchmarking include:

- Focus on customer requirements
- Focus on excellence and industry leadership as a goal
- Clear roadmap for continuous improvement process
- Objective and data-driven evaluation

- Competition through a culture of learning
- Developing market-driven metrics of performance and productivity
- External focus for process development

Normally, benchmarking is motivated by almost all of the above reasons because it is another cornerstone in building quality into the fiber of the organization.

4.1.1 Benchmarking in Japan and the U.S.

Benchmarking, as reported by Camp [1989], has a long history in China and Japan. The Japanese word *dantosu* (meaning the best of the best) embodies the idea of benchmarking. The idea is that one should first understand what constitutes a superior performance and then make decisions about improvement changes. Otherwise, change for the sake of change could be destructive and chaotic. Benchmarking allows a company to orient itself to external market innovations and apply them ingenuously for the improvement of its internal processes.

The first known comprehensive benchmarking experience in the U.S. began in 1979, when Xerox's Manufacturing Operations carried out benchmarking by analyzing the xerox copiers manufactured by Fuji-Xerox (Xerox's Japanese affiliate) and other Japanese manufacturers. This study resulted in the identification of significant cost gaps between the U.S. and Japanese manufacturing processes. The company used the benchmarking results for planning and goal setting.

This experience led to the company's formal commitment to quality in the early 1980s. From there, external benchmarking became a common practice at Xerox. Camp [1989] describes the experience of Xerox in benchmarking for L. L. Bean, a catalog mail-order company identified as the best in warehousing and material handling functions. Xerox used the benchmarking of L. L. Bean for improving its warehousing, shipping, and logistics functions. (See the case at the end of this chapter for a more comprehensive presentation of the benchmarking analysis at Xerox.)

Benchmarking is not a theoretical proposition limited to a select number of pioneering companies anymore. In a survey by the American Productivity and Quality Center in Houston, 79 percent of large companies surveyed stated that benchmarking is crucial for their survival, and 76 percent reported an increase in their benchmarking activities [Owen 1992].

4.1.2 Relevance to Information Systems

Benchmarking is crucial to information systems for three major reasons:

- Information systems function has process-based outputs
- Information systems are highly dependent on technology and innovation
- The continuous improvement process plays a crucial role in preserving the value of the existing systems

Process-Based Output.   One can benchmark for products and processes to see how products are made and how the processes function. Benchmarking is highly useful for process-oriented outputs. When the output is a product, one can open it and look into its components to see what it is made of and how it functions. In contrast, there is no way to take apart a process that produces a service output. Close and directed observation is the way to take apart processes in order to learn how they work.

Information systems are a major organizational function that produce critical service outputs from their processes. Benchmarking makes it possible to find the best way to produce quality service by looking into the processes of other units or organizations, within the same industry or outside.

Dependence on Technology and Innovation.   Information systems activities are among the areas that are highly dependent on technological advances and innovations for their continued effectiveness. A system working perfectly well today may quickly become outdated and useless because of market changes that result from the advances in technology.

For example, with the advent of CD ROM and its use for library searches, the market for library information technology has drastically shifted. Prior to the use of CD ROM, libraries subscribed to centralized services carrying publication information. Since a library paid for connection time to the library information service provider, normally a librarian was in charge of the search and was trained in using the system to minimize the search time.

With CD ROM, the publication information is available in the library's own CD ROM and directly accessible to the customer. The library pays for the CD ROM and the customer accesses it with unlimited search time. Thus, the investment in a centralized computer center to hold the information and the remote access to it becomes unnecessary. The service of the library specialist is not needed for searches anymore. The management of information is not the network of terminals connected to a centralized unit. Instead, the production and timely distribution of CD ROM with the latest publication information has become of greatest importance.

To look inside and out for innovative ideas in order to increase customer satisfaction and run a better business is the hallmark of the continuous improvement process. This is even more critical for the information-systems area that has to be on the lookout for unexpected breakthroughs and sudden obsolescence.

Take the example of ACCU-INFO, which allows its customers to access its credit information systems through a remote linkup. The company observes and benchmarks a leading library for its delivery of information. After benchmarking, it decides to deliver credit information to its customers through CD ROM. This decision is the consequence of looking externally to other industries and observing the superior performance of a function that is similar in nature to information systems delivery. Looking outside provides the opportunity to observe a similarity and generate an innovative idea that is not normally apparent when the examination is totally internal.

Benchmarking is a proactive approach to changes that lead to major improvements and increase the competitive edge.

Benchmarking for the Continuous Improvement Process.   In Chapter 3, we discussed the importance of the continuous improvement process in preserving the value of a company's investment in information systems. Benchmarking is one of the best ways to make the continuous improvement process work.

A company may wish to benchmark its information systems because it has discovered a certain ineffectiveness in the system that requires innovative ideas for removing the problem. In the ACCU-INFO example, the customers have complained about the reliability of the system. A performance evaluation of the system has shown a high variability in system reliability, and the quality team has identified the reliability of information systems as a candidate for improvement. The company decides to embark on benchmarking to discover ways to increase the reliability of the system.

Benchmarking Steps.   Benchmarking involves a fact-finding process and has many features of scientific research. It involves the following steps:

- Planning
- Information collection
- Analysis
- Goal setting
- Implementation

These steps are discussed in the sections that follow.

◆ CASE: Eyes on the Prize

Prizewinners are obvious benchmarkers. Though the original guidelines for the National Institute for Standards and Technology's Malcolm Baldridge National Quality Award did not mention benchmarking as a technique for achieving quality, they did insist that winners set the standard for others and share their expertise. In 1992, however, it became an official part of the review process; applicants must work through nine items requiring competitive comparisons and benchmarking.

Companies use the Baldridge guidelines in various ways: to compete internally, as a prototype for functional areas, as a model for a TQM program, or even to prepare for the competition. Take Columbus McKinnon Corp. (Amherst, NY), which makes forging, chains and chain hoists, and tire shredders for farm-equipment builders. Its CEO, H. P. Ladds, Jr., says the company was looking for quality improvement guidelines and a TQM program "long before we ever heard of Baldridge."

Once Ladds studied the guidelines, he decided to play a practice round. An "internal Baldy" [an expert knowledgeable about Baldridge Quality Award] might reduce employee fear of the sheer size of the undertaking. Company divisions generated 83 potential projects, and the race was on. Divisions had always competed with each other to some extent, says Ladds, but now each watches to see how the other attacks a problem and how successful it is. Some plants discovered substandard processes: their managers now know what their TQM priorities must be. These practice runs also produce improvements that cynics could call "soft" or "intangible"—improved morale, capability, and understanding. Soft or not, they got the company's fledgling quality program aloft.

"Once we understood the concept of the internal customer, we took a tremendous step forward," says Ladds. "Learning to think statistically—to see that all work is a series of connected actions—was another big step that let us raise the level of individual output. Now we're developing indexes that pinpoint the improvement in all the processes we studied. Though areas of on-time deliveries have improved, we can't just say we are the best all around." Ladds has learned to keep the heat on: "Because of the enormity of the task, communication must be constant and forceful, so TQM efforts don't get pushed into the background by everyday pressures."

How about the bottom line? Giving each employee eight hours of training annually falls on the expense side of the ledger, but 35 of the 83 pilot projects reduced cycle time, waste, or nonvalue-added activities. "That will soon put some numbers on the profit side," Ladds predicts.

United Electric Controls (Watertown, MA), a 400-employee manufacturer of industrial sensors and temperature-control devices, applied for the North American Shingo Prize for Manufacturing Excellence in 1989, the first year its sponsor, Utah State University, offered it. The reason was practical, says Bonnie Rafuse, manufacturing education manager. "We're a small company and don't spend much on consultants, but we were sure that other companies were using tools we didn't know about. Getting advice from a group of experts for the cost of their meals and airfare seemed like a very good investment."

Though the Shingo examiners didn't visit, Utah State University held a conference the next year that Vice President Bruce Hamilton attended. As he listened, Hamilton identified weaknesses in some areas that he decided should be worked on before the company applied again. Back at the plant, however, he was surprised. The process of applying had stimulated improvements in every problem area. When the Shingo team visited the next year, United won the prize, and Hamilton keeps his own benchmarking skills honed these days as a volunteer Shingo examiner.

The new prize produced a lot of publicity. A member of the US Department of the Navy's Best Manufacturing Practices Program team read an article about the company and asked United to invite BMP in. BMP, a low-profile undertaking, searches the country for defense contractors that are using advanced manufacturing processes and equipment and progressive management techniques successfully or that have overcome manufacturing problems.

Director Ernie Renner runs this very lean government agency with the help of all-volunteer inspection teams: host companies know before a site visit who the inspectors will be, so they can reject someone from a competitor if they wish. The team visiting United, for example, came from Metalworking Technology Inc. (Johnstown, PA), as well as the Navy.

"Many companies struggle with problems other companies have solved," says Renner. For that matter, many divisions within a company struggle with problems other divisions have solved. United stands out, he says, because "they've done a lot of innovative things, made a lot of low-dollar investments, and reaped major benefits."

He cites the company's employee involvement program as a best practice as well because BMP finds that out-of-control processes cause most manufacturing problems. "When people are responsible for tracking their progress, inspecting their product, resolving problems they notice (or the next person who gets their product notices)," Renner says, "when they can shut down equipment if parts are not right, when they can buy something they need, when they get a chance to compete against someone else, you get impressive results."

Source: Excerpt from "Benchmarking World-Class Manufacturing" Jean V. Owen, *Manufacturing Engineering*, March 1992, pp. 29–43. Reprinted with permission from *Manufacturing Engineering*.

4.2 ◆ Benchmark Planning for Information Systems

Embarking on benchmarking without a well-designed plan guarantees its failure. Benchmarking is a search—a search for excellence. Prior to starting it, one should know what the search is about, and what the object of excellence is.

Planning for benchmarking has the following steps:

- The development of the vision and mission statements
- The definition of the objectives and measures involved in benchmarking
- The decision on the benchmarking type
- The selection of the benchmarking partner
- The selection of the benchmarking team and the development of a benchmarking schedule

Benchmarking, like all aspects of managing quality, begins with the definition of the vision and mission statements of the organization as well as the functional area, in this case, information systems. We have discussed the vision and mission statements in Chapter 2. It is worthwhile to repeat again that the vision and mission statements are the driving force for defining the scope and purpose of the continuous improvement process, of which benchmarking is one of the ways to identify areas in need of improvement. We discuss the steps of planning for benchmarking in the following subsections.

4.2.1   Identifying Benchmarking Objectives and Measurements

Benchmarking for the sake of benchmarking is a costly and useless undertaking. Prior to the decision to carry out benchmarking, the benchmarker must decide to have a clear understanding of its own internal processes and should have identified the candidate areas for improvement. The benchmarker must have a clear idea of what its benchmarking objectives are. These objectives determine who to choose for benchmarking and what to benchmark.

For example, Xerox had identified logistics and material handling as the candidate for improvement. It was this objective that led to the selection of L. L. Bean as the best company to benchmark because of its superior warehousing and material processing.

For the example of ACCU-INFO, the objective could be the discovery of ways to increase the reliability of information systems. This objective focuses benchmarking attention on finding a company that has the best reliability for its service delivery that is similar in nature to the service of information systems.

Once the objective of benchmarking is determined, the benchmarker should determine the metrics to use for measuring performance. In the case of ACCU-INFO, the company should decide how to measure the reliability of information systems. Although some of the metrics may be discovered in the benchmarking process, ACCU-INFO should have a clear idea about what it calls reliability, accuracy, or faults.

4.2.2   Types of Benchmarking

One can choose different types of benchmarking partners. We can divide benchmarking into four categories [Camp 1989]:

- Internal
- Competitive
- Functional
- Generic

Internal Benchmarking.   In *internal* benchmarking, the best and most successful unit within the organization is chosen for benchmarking. In large organizations with multiple units, subsidiaries, or multinational divisions, it is possible to identify an internal unit as the best in a functional area and suitable for benchmarking.

For example, the company's European branch has an information system that has proven to be superior in its customer satisfaction and low fault ratios. This information system may be chosen for internal benchmarking.

The advantages of the internal benchmarking are:

- The access to data will be easier than the external benchmarking
- One may receive more extensive cooperation and resource commitment by the internal benchmarking unit
- There will be little problem with confidentiality of the requested data

If the divisions of a company are organized to compete with one another, some of the advantages of internal benchmarking may not be present. Furthermore, using internal benchmarking exclusively may deprive the company of the innovative ideas that exist outside the company. For example, if the world-wide policy of the company is to use one particular hardware or a given set of methods for requirements analysis, exclusive internal benchmarking would deprive the process from investigating the impact of using alternative hardware products, or the innovative ways other companies elicit the true wishes of their customers.

Competitive Benchmarking.   *Competitive* benchmarking involves selecting a direct competitor that produces similar products or services. Normally, in competitive benchmarking, the scope of benchmarking is not limited to one functional area such as information systems. The scope of investigation is much larger, and information systems would be one of many functional areas and processes that are investigated.

The advantage of competitive benchmarking is that it provides a deep understanding of the competitive advantages of the successful competition. The difficulties of competitive benchmarking are that:

- There may not be a comparable direct competitor in the market
- The competitor may not provide the needed data and information
- The confidentiality problem may hamper the benchmarking process
- The competitor may not wish to allocate resources for a true benchmarking partnership

Some of competitive benchmarking's problems could be alleviated by involving an outside consultant who can ensure confidentiality and serve as a liaison for bringing the two companies together in the interest of discovering the best processes and structures.

Functional Benchmarking.   In *functional* benchmarking, the benchmarking partner is selected based on its excellence in a particular function, regardless of its industry, product, or compatibility in other areas. Functional benchmarking may be internal or external. It is the most relevant type for service-oriented areas such as information systems.

The advantages of functional benchmarking are:

- The benchmarking partner is more willing to provide access to data and processes when no direct competition exists between the two companies
- The benchmarking activity is focused and easier to carry out
- The results from dissimilar companies are more acceptable to the benchmarking company [Camp 1989]
- It involves an innovative way of looking at the selection of the benchmarking partner that has the potential for a large payoff in improvement and innovation

Generic Benchmarking.   There are business areas that are the same in most companies, regardless of industry or types of operations. Examples of such generic areas include inventory systems, accounting information systems, and service quality control. Generic benchmarking is the choice of benchmarking partner for functions or processes that are generic.

In many types of information systems, *generic* benchmarking can be used in an innovative fashion. For example, banks, telephone companies, credit companies, and brokerage houses have customer accounts that have numerous activities at any moment and have to be kept up-to-date at all times. Thus, customer account-handling functions in these industries are generically similar. A brokerage house that wants to improve the quality of its customer accounts may look into its own industry or go outside to banking, communication, or credit card industries to find the best way of handling customer accounts.

The difference between functional and generic benchmarking is that the functional benchmarking involves a comparable organizational function in another organization. In generic benchmarking, there is no need for comparability. One may even emphasize looking into dissimilar functions that have basic requirements, such as reliability or timeliness of data.

For example, functional benchmarking of information systems requires both partners to have similar functions in their information systems, such as delivering similar types of information to similar types of customers. The Information system of a bank may be a good candidate for functional benchmarking with the information system of a card company. Or, the customer-service information system of a company may be a good internal, functional benchmarking partner for its marketing information system.

Generic benchmarking of information systems, on the other hand, does not require functional similarities. It requires similarity in certain attributes or needs. The information system of an overnight-mail carrier may be a good generic benchmarking partner for the customer-information system of a bank. The two systems do not have similar functions, but they both need to respond quickly and accurately to their customers' queries.

4.2.3   Selecting the Benchmarking Partner

Selecting the appropriate benchmarking partner requires a careful search. Benchmarking a second- or third-rate company has little benefit and may in fact be harmful because the benchmarker company may find that it is ahead of the benchmarking partner and become lax in its vigilance for improvement.

Although some organizations may have reputations for excellence in information systems, finding the *best* in the industry is not always an easy task. However, there are numerous sources for locating the best:

- Internal experts
- Internal information-systems functional areas
- Professional associations
- Professional journals
- Business and trade journals
- External experts and consultants

One can collect information regarding the choice of the best practice from internal sources, such as internal information-systems experts and those who are working in the information-systems function and keep current with the industry practices. These internal sources can also provide information about the compatibility of the type of information-systems practices to be benchmarked. Involving the information-systems workers in benchmarking helps the implementation of changes that the benchmarking analysis will recommend.

Professional associations relevant to the benchmarking activity are a good source for finding the best in the field. These associations hold conferences, workshops, tutorials, and round-table discussions that are related to the latest developments in the field and to those organizations that have the reputation as being the best.

Professional journals, conference proceedings, trade journals, and business journals occasionally publish articles about practices and companies that have distinguished themselves in the area. Finally, consultants and external experts who are active in the field can be commissioned to identify benchmarking partner(s) for the information-systems function or a particular aspect of information systems.

In reviewing the information and publications for locating a partner, one should look for performance data as well as statements of pride and excellence regarding the information systems of a company. For example, there may be an article in a professional journal that reports close to 100 percent reliability in the data of a company's information system. Or, an information-systems manager of a company may report the innovative ways that his or her company identifies the needs of information-systems users and the level of customer satisfaction attained through this process. Such a company is a potential benchmarking partner.

Once the benchmarking partner is found and approved by the top management, a number of logistical issues must be clarified:

- Could the benchmarking partnership have an adverse public relations consequence?
- Is there a legal problem for benchmarking?
- Is there a confidentiality problem?
- Is there sufficient compatibility between what we want to benchmark and the benchmarking partner's operation?

Answering these questions is essential, because benchmarking is not just a one-time operation. We would like to build on the experience and continue to update the benchmark information. In some cases, the benchmarking partner may want to have a reciprocal relationship. Since the benchmarking relationship may continue for sometime, the choice of the partner must be made with care.

Obtaining the Benchmarking Partner's Consent.   When the benchmarking partner is an external organization, getting the partner to agree can be a delicate task. Camp [1989] recommends establishing contact:

- At the functional level: for example, the manager of the internal information systems contacts the manager of the potential benchmarking partner for the initial introduction. This creates a professional pride in the potential benchmarking partner that will facilitate the agreement

- Through the customer or supplier relationship, if one exists: for example, if the potential benchmarking partner is a bank, it is worthwhile to see if any branch or function of the company is a customer of the bank or provides goods or services to the bank
- Through professional associations: for example, some of the information-systems professionals of the potential benchmarking partner may attend the same professional societies and conferences as those of the internal professionals

Camp [1989] recommends that however the initial contact is made, it is crucial to be clear and honest about the intent of the benchmarking.

4.3 ◆ Collecting Benchmarking Information

Collecting and documenting the benchmarking information should be planned in advance. The planning involves defining and deciding on:

- The types of information to be collected
- The methods of information gathering
- The documentation data and the process of information collection
- Future visits for follow-up

Since benchmarking requires goodwill and close cooperation of the benchmarking partner, careful planning of the information collection process will avoid wasting the partner's time and the benchmarker's resources.

4.3.1   Types of Benchmark Information

Benchmarking information should be clearly defined for the benchmarkers. The types of information to be collected in benchmarking are:

- Performance metrics
- Processes
- Policies
- Structures

Performance Metrics.   Performance metrics are the measures by which the performance of the function or the system are quantified. These metrics are not normally the common measures found in business reports. They are focused on customers, quality, and external environments, and are derived from the vision statement of the organization, as well as that of the functional area, in this case, information systems.

For example, in Chapter 2, the vision statement for ACCU-INFO was:

We provide the most accurate information on credit-worthiness of shoppers within the United States.

ACCU-INFO's mission statement was:

We satisfy our customers by providing an integrated information system that combines reliable data from all possible sources, and by creating an atmosphere of trust and growth for our employees.

As Figure 4.1 shows, we create a hierarchy starting with the corporate vision at the first level, the components of the information-systems vision on the second level, and the components of the information-systems mission on the third level. On the fourth level, we have the physical components that serve the mission and vision components.

For integrated information systems, we have information-system centers, systems, and computer networks. We now can identify the metrics that measure the extent of integration in information systems. As Figure 4.2 shows, we can define the metrics for centers as percentage of centers that are interconnected, average number of messages sent out over the network per center, and average number of messages received per connected center.

Similarly, for the systems we have percentage of systems sharing the same input data and percentage of systems identically available to all information-systems centers. The metrics for networks are: percentage of remotely connected computer nodes and

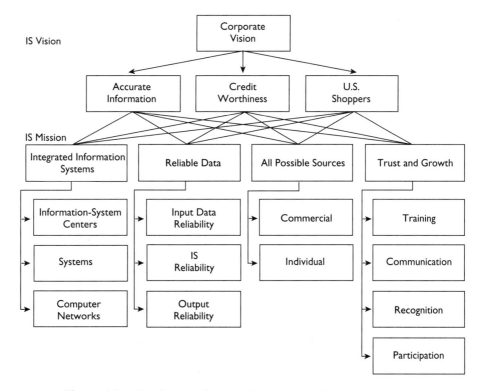

Figure 4.1   Identification of Metrics Categories Based on Vision Statement

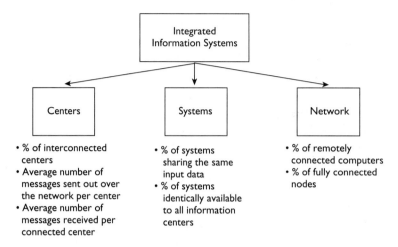

Figure 4.2   Metrics for the Attribute: Integrated Information Systems

percentage of fully connected computer nodes to total nodes. (A computer node in this example is a collection of one or more computers in a site that constitute a node or entry point to a network of computers.) Figure 4.3 shows an example of metrics for the attribute reliable data. Figure 4.3 refers to information-systems reliability metrics covered in Chapter 9.

The definition of metrics is an important step in the benchmarking process. They are arrived at after an extensive consultation with the internal and external sources, such as:

- Internal experts
- Functional managers and CEOs
- Employees of the functional area being benchmarked

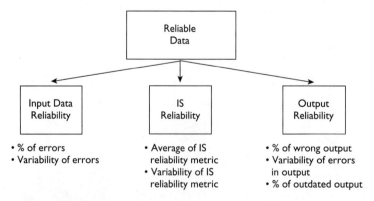

Figure 4.3   Metrics for the Attribute: Reliable Data

- Consultants in the field
- External experts
- Professional publications
- Conference proceedings and professional meetings

Although the metrics should be defined prior to the benchmarking data collection, new metrics may be discovered during the benchmarking data collection. For example, in the benchmarking process, we may discover that the benchmarking partner uses an innovative metric to measure the responsiveness of the system to customer queries.

Quality metrics are not normally the type of routinely collected data. In this respect, both companies benefit from the benchmarking experience. Each has to compute the benchmarking metrics. The benchmarking partner shares its internal performance metrics that later can be used by the benchmarker. This becomes a learning experience for both companies and increases their awareness of their own operations and performance.

Processes.   Another set of benchmarking data includes the processes used by the benchmarking partner that lead to the high performance metrics. In other words, metrics determine what has been accomplished, while processes determine how the superior performance levels are attained.

For example, in the ACCU-INFO case, the processes that the benchmarking partner uses to decide which systems should be integrated and which centers should be interconnected are of interest to the benchmarking team. Another set of processes of interest relate to the maintenance and continuous improvement activities.

We need a hierarchy to identify the processes that go with various aspects of the vision and mission statements. For example, in the ACCU-INFO case, we had integrated information systems as an attribute. We define process types that are put in place for attaining the attribute, such as creation processes, support processes, and systems improvement processes, as shown in Figure 4.4.

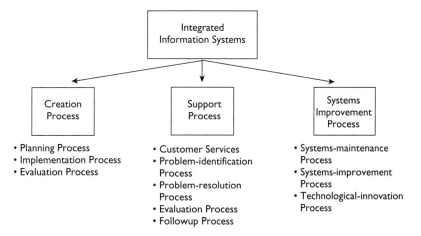

Figure 4.4   Processes for Attaining the "Integrated Information Systems" Attribute in ACCU-INFO Case

As Figure 4.4 shows, underneath each process type, we can identify more specific processes, such as planning process, implementation process, and evaluation process for the creation processes type. Similarly, for support processes, we have the problem identification process, problem resolution process, and customer service process. For the systems improvement processes type, we have systems maintenance process and systems-improvement process.

In the case of process identification, too, various internal and external sources must be consulted before the final list of processes is prepared for benchmarking. It is also possible to discover novel and innovative processes used by the benchmarking partner that will then be added to the list. Since information systems are mostly process-based, benchmarking visits should focus on the discovery of new and innovative processes for quality service production, delivery, and maintenance.

Policies.   While metrics and processes are continuously changed and dynamically improved, policies are the more stable part of business practices. Policies are derived from the vision and mission statements and the underlying culture and value structure of the business.

For example, in the ACCU-INFO case, the benchmarking partner may have the following policies:

- Every customer complaint must be dealt with to the satisfaction of the customer within half an hour
- Customer complaints must be reported and recorded; cases taking more than half an hour must be investigated within one day and reported to the area manager
- The performance of information systems should be regularly monitored, and any abnormality should immediately be investigated
- Integrated systems must be evaluated annually for their usefulness and customer satisfaction

Policies are identified and discussed at the time of benchmarking. However, the categories and types of policies that are candidates for benchmarking can be identified from the vision and mission statements. For example, at the time of benchmarking visit, ACCU-INFO may give a high priority to policies regarding information systems reliability and integration of information systems. Therefore, the questionnaire will focus on questions regarding these types of policies.

Structures.   Organizational and physical structures are another category of benchmarking information. The types of structures that the benchmarker may need to review include:

- Organizational structure within the information-systems function
- The team structures for various processes, such as planning, design, maintenance, and continuous improvement
- The hierarchical level within the company and within the information-systems function

- The location of the information-systems function within the organization
- The extent of participation of the information-systems employees in company-wide projects and functions
- The degree of centralization within the organization and within the information-systems function
- The geographical spread of the information-systems function and services

The documentation of the benchmarked structure is important because many processes can only work within a certain organizational type. For example, the continuous systems improvement process requires cross-functional teams. A highly vertical structure with rigid boundaries among units and functions will have great difficulty accommodating a cross-functional team approach.

◆ CASE: Benchmarking Idea in Banking Information Systems

Quality of information services, as an attribute, is easy to recognize—but awfully hard to benchmark.

However, one of the nation's largest regional banks has taken on the task of benchmarking the quality of the information systems services it provides to its organizations.

The benchmark for First Union National Bank, a Charlotte, N.C.-based regional bank with assets of $49 billion, is being developed by an independent consultant. It is based on customer satisfaction surveys of end-user departments.

"Our uptime is consistently in the 98% range, and we're proud of that. We've even bragged about it," said Judge Fowler, a senior vice president of the bank's Automation Division who oversees all systems development. "But we have to create a culture that says 98% is not good enough. We've estimated that even that 2% of downtime results in 30,000 customers inconvenienced each month."

The quest for quality began last year, when First Union's top management promoted quality as a competitive advantage against other large regional banks, such as NCNB Corp. in Charlotte and First Wachovia Corp. in Winston-Salem, N.C.

In search of role models, Fowler visited IBM's Rochester, Minn., Factory for Application System/400s, Xerox Corp. and textile maker Milliken & Co.—all of which have won the coveted Malcolm Baldrige National Quality Award.

Never-ending Process

"We found a theme of measuring the existing quality, fixing what's broken—and then doing it all over again in a never-ending quality improvement process," Fowler said.

To measure IS quality, First Union commissioned Towers Perrin, a New York-based employee-benefits consulting firm, to develop a survey that would quantify IS services. Now that the survey has been prototyped, First Union has invited other companies to participate in the quality benchmark study. So far, First Union has surveyed more than 100 of its 25,000 employees about IS satisfaction.

If other IS groups jump on First Union's quality bandwagon, the profile and efficiency ratings of their IS operations will be stored in a database at Towers Perrin. Then, those ratings will be compared to those of other IS organizations in various industry segments.

Participants would have to pay $10,000 to $20,000 to Towers Perrin for the survey said Thomas Davenport, a principal consultant based in San Francisco. "First Union has funded the development of the survey," Davenport said. "What other firms will get is a comprehensive analysis of customer satisfaction with their MIS shops."

Source: "Banks Find Ways to Put IS Quality to Test," Jean Bozman, *Computerworld*, November 25, 1991, p. 57. Copyright 1991 by Computerworld, Inc., Framingham, MA 01701. Reprinted with permission from Computerworld.

4.3.2   Methods of Information Collection

One can collect benchmarking data in a number of ways:

- Mail survey
- Telephone survey
- Site visit

Although the site visit is the most representative method of benchmarking, a number of routine or short questions can be asked via mail or telephone survey. In all three cases, a questionnaire should be prepared in advance to assure that the right questions are asked the right way.

Survey design is an important area of applied statistics. Designing surveys and procedures that produce unbiased and accurate answers is critical to the integrity of the benchmarking outcome. The benchmarking process should involve the expertise of a survey designer in developing the telephone and mail-survey questionnaires.

The questionnaire at the site visit is mainly used as a guideline for starting the discussion and making sure that all areas of interest are covered. Of the three methods of data collection, the site visit has the greatest potential for inspiring ideas and creativity.

For example, assume that the ACCU-INFO team is doing a site visit for benchmarking one of the package-delivery services in which the packages are barcoded for keeping track of where the package is. The ACCU-INFO team may come up with the idea that the credit-information document could also be barcoded so that ACCU-INFO can keep track of the supporting documents regarding credit information of individuals and small businesses.

The observation of the system in action, coupled with extensive data collection of the metrics, processes, policies, and structures allow the benchmarking team to gain an insight to the working of the benchmarking partner that would not otherwise be easily possible.

The data and information collection should be focused on performance, process, practice, and structure issues. Discussions regarding price and marketing strategies, as well as customer information, should be avoided. Camp [1989] recommends that all data should be collected on ratios or a per-unit basis in order to avoid asking for sensitive information.

The common sense approach is that if a piece of data is sensitive internally, it would be sensitive for the benchmarking partner as well. For example, in collecting information regarding the data entry practice, if asking for the list of customers is a sensitive issue for ACCU-INFO, then it should be considered sensitive for its benchmarking partner as well and must be avoided.

4.3.3   Documentation of Benchmarking Information

During the benchmarking visit, one of the team members should be in charge of documentation of benchmarking information. This person should take notes on discussions and observations, and make sure that the items of the prepared questionnaire are adequately addressed in meetings and discussion sessions.

Debriefing immediately after benchmarking is essential. The debriefing meeting should be documented on the spot. The documents and notes become the basis of the benchmarking analysis, report, and information summary.

4.4   ◆   Analysis of Benchmarking Information

In the analysis of benchmarking information, the partner's benchmarking data is contrasted with that of the benchmarking company. The purpose of the comparison is to identify:

- The performance gaps between the two companies
- The differences between processes used, and the advantages of implementing different processes
- The difference between the policies applied, and the implications of adopting the partner's policies
- The difference between the underlying structures of the two companies, the relative advantages and disadvantages of each, and the implications of changing the existing structures to the partner's structure

4.4.1   Performance Analysis

In the comparative analysis of benchmarking data, metric values are compared and the difference between the two are computed and analyzed. There are a number of issues that should be taken into account before jumping to a hasty conclusion.

Assume in the ACCU-INFO case that the reliability of input data is .001 (there is one error in every 1000 input data), while the same metric for the benchmarking partner is .000001 (one in every one million items of input data). Should we immediately conclude that the benchmarking partner is one thousand times better than ACCU-INFO in input-data reliability?

One has to perform more analysis before accepting such a conclusion. There are a number of issues to be addressed in the quantitative comparison of benchmarking metrics:

- Randomness of data
- Variability of data
- Comparability of data
- Time interval of data
- The determination of gap

Randomness of Data.   Performance metrics, like almost all business data, are random variables. The reason is that the value of these metrics at any time is affected by uncertain events. For example, one of the reasons for the benchmarking partner to have a high reliability value for input data could be that the data-entry clerks were on strike and all input data has been entered by experienced supervisors. On the other hand, ACCU-INFO had just hired a number of new data-entry clerks, and they were being trained when the reliability metric data were collected.

Because of the random nature of metric values, it is essential to have a number of observations of the same metric and use the average values for comparison in order to average out the random effects.

Variability of Data.   The average values of the benchmarking metrics are not the only basis of comparison. The variability of metrics is another indication of performance problems.

For example, ACCU-INFO and its benchmarking partner may have the same average value for the reliability metric of information systems, say .75. However, ACCU-INFO's metric may vary from .55 to .95 as opposed to its benchmarking partner that has the range of .70 to .80.

At one extreme, ACCU-INFO has the value of .95 for the reliability metric of information systems; one may be tempted to conclude that ACCU-INFO's metric is more preferable. However, the low variability of the metric is the indicator of the stability of the system, and hence it is more preferable.

One can use the lowest and highest observed values of a metric as the measure of variability. However, a better variability measure is the standard deviation of the observed values of the metric, computed as:

$$s = \sum_{i=1}^{n} \frac{x_i - \bar{x}^2}{n - 1}$$

where s is the standard deviation of the metric, n is the number of observed values of the metric, $\bar{x}$ is the mean or average value of the metric, and x_i is the ith observed value. Note that the computation of standard deviation can be easily performed with most calculators or statistical software. We will use standard deviation in the discussion of metrics and control charts in Chapters 8, 9 and 10.

Comparability of Data.   Another issue in the analysis of the benchmarking metric is the comparability of data. In the computation of the metric values, we should use identical definitions of metrics for both companies. Since the processes, definitions, and methods of data collection vary from company to company, collecting comparable data may not always be easy or even possible. In such cases, one has to make every effort to adjust the metrics for such differences.

Almost all benchmarking metrics are in the form of ratios in order to exclude the effect of size. However, in some cases, larger systems have a different set of parameters. For example, ACCU-INFO's information system may have three times as much data and four times as many users and customers as its benchmarking partner. The reliability metric of a large information system may be significantly different from that of a small system because the sheer size and geographical spread of the system make it more difficult to standardize, manage, check, and control.

We can test the validity of the assumption that size and number of computer nodes have impacts on the information-systems reliability metric. This would be possible if we have the metric value for information systems of different sizes and number of computer nodes. When such data are available for the metric r, we can hypothesize that:

$$H_0 : r_1 = r_2$$
$$H_a : r_1 \neq r_2$$

and test this hypothesis statistically.

When there are adequate data and the metric is complex, one can use regression analysis to formally take into account and test the impact of variables that are believed to have a significant impact on the benchmarking metric.

For example, in benchmarking the reliability of information systems, we conclude that size and number of computer nodes on the network have an impact on the reliability metric. In this case, we can hypothesize the model:

$$r = b_0 + b_1 \; size + b_2 \; node$$

where r is the reliability metric, and $size$ and $node$ are the variables for information-systems size and number of computer nodes, respectively. If the estimation of parameters b_1 and b_2 are significantly different from zero, then we can conclude that the data supports the hypothesis that size and number of computer nodes have an impact on the reliability metric.

For example, assume that we have 30 observed values for reliability metric (r) and the corresponding size and number of computer nodes. We run the regression analysis to get:

$$r = .5 + .002 \; size + .001 \; node$$

Assume that the statistical t values for the $size$ and $node$ are 4.6 and 5.3. Since these t statistics are well above the critical value of 2.47, we conclude that the data support our hypothesis of size and node effects. In this case, in comparing ACCU-INFO's metric with that of its benchmarking partner, we should take into account the impact of these two factors.

Such analysis may not be necessary for a small-scale benchmarking project. However, when the benchmarking results have major consequences for an organization, careful comparability analysis is essential for lending weight to the recommendations that result from the benchmarking process.

The number of observations and volume of data should also be comparable in both organizations. For example, having two values for the information-systems reliability of ACCU-INFO as opposed to 30 values for the benchmarking partner makes the comparison inaccurate.

Time Interval of Data. Another aspect of comparability of benchmarking data is that they should be collected during time intervals of similar nature. For example, ACCU-INFO's data may have been collected during the busiest period of its operation, while the data for the benchmarking partner had been collected in a slow season. The data should be adjusted for the seasonality, trend, or any time-related factor.

The Determination of Gap. Once we have computed the average metric value for the benchmarking partner and the benchmarker, the question is how wide a gap is considered significant. In some cases, the distance is so big that the gap is obviously significant and the conclusion that the two companies are far apart in a metric is not disputable. However, there are cases when the significance of a gap is questionable, especially when the metrics have very different variability.

In such cases, we can use statistical hypothesis testing for determining whether the averages of a metric are statistically different for the benchmarker and the benchmarking partner as demonstrated in the following case.

◆ CASE: Testing the Differences

In benchmarking for ACCU-INFO, we have found that the average value of the reliability metric for the benchmarking partner is .80 and standard deviation is .10, whereas those of ACCU-INFO are .70 and .05, respectively. In both cases, the number of observations is 40. Can we conclude that the reliability metric of the benchmarking partner is larger than that of ACCU-INFO?

To answer this question, we can perform hypothesis testing as:

$$H_0 : r_1 = r_2$$
$$H_1 : r_1 > r_2$$

where r_1 is the mean reliability metric for the benchmarking partner and r_2 is that of ACCU-INFO.

We compute the t statistic for this problem as:

$$t = \frac{\hat{r}_1 - \hat{r}_2}{\sqrt{\frac{s_1^2}{n_1} + \frac{s_2^2}{n_2}}}$$

$$= \frac{.80 - .70}{\sqrt{\frac{.10^2}{40} + \frac{.05^2}{40}}}$$

$$= 5.65$$

Since the observed level of significance (or p value) of this t statistic is 0, we can conclude that the data supports the hypothesis that the reliability metric of the benchmarking partner is indeed higher than that of ACCU-INFO, and the null hypothesis is rejected.

4.4.2   Process Analysis

Another type of benchmarking analysis involves comparing and contrasting processes. Process analysis is crucial for those processes in which the benchmarker has performance metrics far inferior to those of its benchmarking partner.

In analyzing processes, it is useful to use the data flow diagram and process diagram tools available in systems analysis and design. In fact, total quality management has borrowed flowcharting and data-flow analysis directly from the field of information systems for documenting, modeling, and analyzing processes.

In process analysis, we use data-flow analysis for showing the flow of data in and out of processes, data storages, and internal and external entities. (Process in the data flow diagram is alternatively called action here to avoid confusion with the business processes that are more general.) The flowcharting tool is used for documenting the details of a particular action or function.

Data Flow Diagram.   The data flow diagram consists of the following components:

- Data flows
- External and internal entities
- Data storages
- Processes or actions

As shown in Figure 4.5, the graphical elements of a data flow diagram include the directed arrow, process, entity, and storage symbols.

The *process* or *action* symbol represents action such as: compute ratings, review report, and enter data. It starts with a verb and identifies the actor and the subject of the action. To make sure that the flow is not mixed up with action, one should use a noun (not a verb) to describe the flow (such as credit report, data request, error message, or customer complaint).

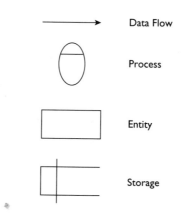

Figure 4.5   Elements of the Data Flow Diagram

The *entity* symbol represents entities that interact with the process and determine its interface with the internal and external environment of the organization. Entities could be *internal* or *external*, such as external customers, internal users, managers, supervisors, regulatory agencies, and suppliers.

The *storage* symbol represents the repository of data and knowledge in the manual and computerized form, which includes file cabinets, computer files, archive systems, and libraries.

We can use these components to document and analyze a process. For example, Figure 4.6 shows the data flow diagram for the data-entry process at ACCU-INFO, and Figure 4.7 documents the same process at its benchmarking partner.

In Figure 4.6, the entities of the process are: credit information suppliers, systems designers, external customers, and internal customers. The benchmarking partner has the same entities, with the exception that system designer is replaced by improvement team.

ACCU-INFO has six processes or actions: checking the information, coding data, entering data, investigating errors, running reports, and update database system. There are five job categories involved: supervisor, coding clerk, data entry clerk, data auditor, and manager.

The benchmarking partner has four processes, of which two are systems—intelligent interface system for data entry and database system—and one process for handling exceptional problems. The two job categories are data specialist and manager.

In comparing the data flow diagram of the data-entry process of ACCU-INFO and its benchmarking partner, we see that the benchmarking partner has fewer actions and job categories, and less hierarchy than ACCU-INFO. The data-entry specialist has the full responsibility of receiving and processing credit information with the help of an intelligent system, and refers to the manager only for exceptional problems. System faults are reported by both the data specialist and the manager to the improvement teams. The data specialist is clearly responsible for the accuracy of data in the system. In ACCU-INFO, more layers of review are involved, and the responsibility of data integrity is shared by four layers: supervisors, data auditors, coding clerks, and data-entry clerks.

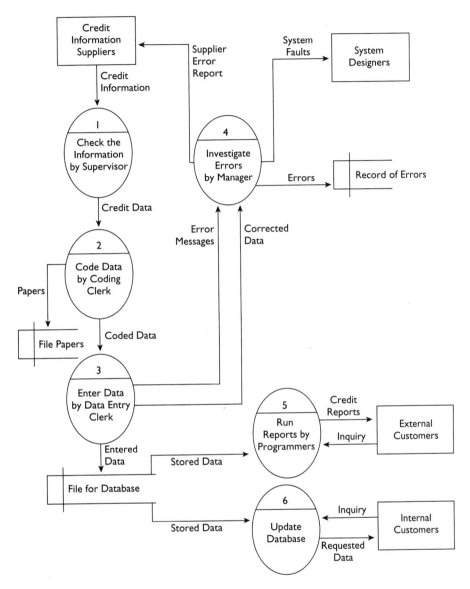

Figure 4.6   Data Flow Diagram for the Data-Entry Process at ACCU-INFO

When the comparison of performance metrics shows that the benchmarking partner is superior, we can investigate how the partner achieves this superiority by using the modeling processes. Using the data flow diagram allows us to analyze and compare processes for the same function, and identify the differences that may be the source of the superior performance.

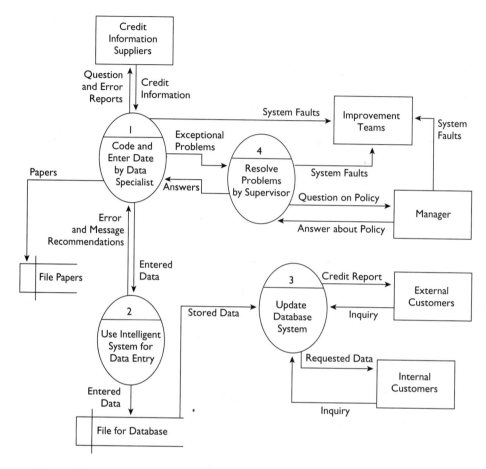

Figure 4.7   Data Flow Diagram for the Data-Entry Process for the Benchmarking Partner

Flowcharting.   Flowcharting is another tool for process analysis. In flowcharting, we use rectangles for actions and diamonds for making decisions. Flowcharts are appropriate for documenting details of an action or computation. Figure 4.8 shows the flowchart for coding and entering data of ACCU-INFO's benchmarking partner.

Differences Between the Data Flow Diagram and Flowcharting.   A data flow diagram and flowchart differ in a number ways:

- A data flow diagram focuses on the flow of data and does not imply sequential time in that many flows may be taking place either simultaneously or at different times. A flowchart documents the sequence of actions and implies a time sequence
- The data flow diagram does not show repetitions, conditions, and choices (such as if, while, for structures), whereas a flowchart shows these decision structures

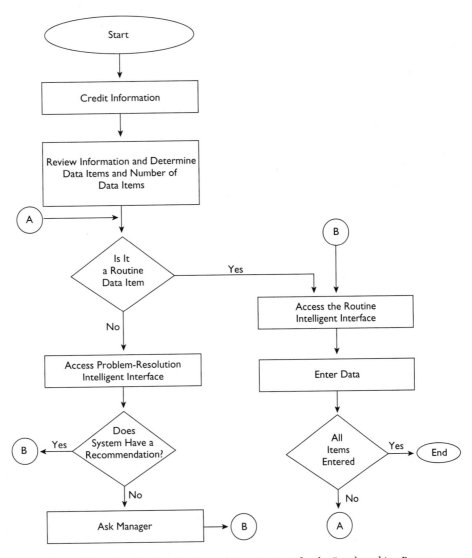

Figure 4.8 Flowchart for Coding and Entering Data for the Benchmarking Partner

- The data flow diagram emphasizes the sources and destination of data—where the data originate and where the data end—whereas the flowchart does not document the external and internal sources of data
- The data flow diagram shows the overall picture of a process with its organizational and environmental links, whereas the flowchart provides a detailed documentation for a given action or computation

Both tools are helpful in documenting and analyzing benchmarking processes.

4.4.3   Policy Analysis

Policy analysis moves the benchmarking analysis from the micro and detail comparison to a more macro level of the overall approach to information systems, because it is the information-systems policies that determine the processes and finally lead to differences in performance.

The benchmarking partner's policies in the following areas would be of interest:

- Customers
- External environment
- Internal communication
- Employee relationships
- Quality
- Innovation
- Maintenance
- Technological changes

These policies are derived from the company's vision and mission statements. The benchmarking team must compare the policies against the benchmarking partner's vision and mission statements, and analyze the process of translating the vision and mission statements into workable policies. Both the process of this translation and the nature of the operational policies are of importance to the benchmarking process. Policies give a great insight to the extent of the top management's fidelity to the company's vision.

For example, both ACCU-INFO and its benchmarking partner have customer satisfaction as a major component of their vision statements. As part of the customer policies, ACCU-INFO has the policy that customers' complaints must be addressed on a first-come first-served basis, within a month. The benchmarking partner, on the other hand, has the policy that customers' complaints must be categorized by their severity and consequences. The severe complaints must be resolved within one day. The partner has an information system for storing and tracking the customer complaints, and the subsequent follow-up for collecting and analyzing customers' reactions to how their complaints are handled. This is a major policy difference between the two companies that may explain the gap in their customer-satisfaction metrics.

On the external environment, ACCU-INFO does not have an established policy regarding how to collect, analyze, and incorporate external concerns into the company's plans and operations. The benchmarking partner, on the other hand, has established a policy of external sensitivity, with regular input from employees across the functional areas to bring up external issues through special info-boxes and monthly forums. A cross-functional team reviews issues raised in info-boxes and forums to decide whether the company must pursue a given issue further.

For example, the company may decide that the publicized concerns over the health hazards of exposure to computer monitors may have relevance to the company. A cross-functional team of programmers, word-processing clerks, health experts, and managers is formed to investigate the concerns and make recommendations to the company's CEOs.

With the policy of actively seeking information regarding any relevant external development and information, the benchmarking partner has become proactive in dealing with new issues well before they become a major problem for the company.

On the quality side, both companies have established quality policies. However, in the benchmarking process, ACCU-INFO discovers that there is a significant gap in the system reliability between the two companies. In investigating the difference between the two companies' quality policies, it becomes clear that the benchmarking partner has an aggressive policy of discovering and establishing new and effective measures of quality and using these measures in planning for major maintenance, technical changes, investment decision, and manpower selection. In other words, the quality metrics are the major decision component in the company's financial commitments, while ACCU-INFO has a passive approach to quality in that it uses quality metrics to inform departments of their performance. For ACCU-INFO, the quality metrics do not normally trigger any major change or decision.

Similarly, a policy comparison regarding the internal communications, employee relations, maintenance, innovations, and technology updates would help the benchmarker to discover the underlying philosophical and fundamental differences between the two organizations.

The major problem in policy analysis is that it is more difficult to collect data regarding the company policies. Among the reasons are:

- Important policies are not always documented, especially if these policies have become so commonplace within the company that the employees implement them automatically
- The benchmarking partner may be reluctant to share some of its important policies because they may be considered the company's major competitive advantage
- Some policies are mixed with the standard operating procedures and strategies. Policy may not be the right vocabulary in a company

To reduce the scope of the problem to a selected number of policies, the benchmarking team may focus only on those areas where large gaps exist between the two companies, such as customer satisfaction, employee performance, or quality metrics. Even this narrow focus may prove a challenge for the team because of the interdependent nature of policies in various areas.

For example, the benchmarking policy regarding external issues may contribute greatly to the employees' pride and satisfaction in belonging to a company that is proactive regarding external issues and regularly seeks their input on much matters. This policy also has influence on the effectiveness of the internal communication. Policy analysis is an area where the benchmarker company needs to use the utmost tact and talent to collect data and perform the subsequent analysis.

4.4.4   Structure Analysis

Another part of benchmarking analysis is the comparison of structures. This analysis is not limited to comparing the organizational charts, but also methods of communication, teamwork, cross-functional cooperation, reward system, and employee training.

For example, in comparing structures, ACCU-INFO discovers that its benchmarking partner has a flat organizational structure (one layer of middle management as opposed to three at ACCU-INFO) and gives considerable independence and responsibility to its operational units. Employees are directly responsible for the quality of their output, and their performance and the reward system is directly tied to the quality of their work.

On the other hand, at ACCU-INFO, the two additional layers of middle management are used to control the quality of the employees' output, while the reward system for employees is not directly related to the quality of their output, but to the quarterly profitability of the unit. In this comparison, the benchmarkers may discover that since the performance measures are based on short-term profitability, major decisions regarding a fundamental change within the unit are almost never initiated by the unit itself. When quality and short-term profitability are in conflict, quality is given up for short-term profitability.

In collecting benchmarking data, the benchmarker has to balance between a comprehensive and costly data collection of structural details and the practical constraints of the time and budget that the benchmarking partner and the benchmarker have allocated to benchmarking. The performance gaps, quality data, and the policy analysis can determine the focus areas of structure that are helpful in determining the reasons for gaps.

4.4.5   Iterative Benchmarking

The discussion of the policy and structural analyses shows that the prior knowledge of performance gaps and differences in processes help the benchmarker team to identify the areas in which the data regarding the policies and structures must be collected. Iterative benchmarking allows the benchmarker to collect data in a sequence of steps.

In iterative benchmarking, the team collects data in the following sequence:

- Collect data on performance
- Analyze performance data and hypothesize the types of processes that may contribute to the difference in performance
- Collect data on processes
- Analyze processes and hypothesize the types of policies that may contribute to differences in processes
- Collect data on policies
- Analyze policies and determine the areas of organizational structure that should be of major focus
- Collect data on organizational structure
- Analyze the organizational structure

The above sequence of iteration is the most ideal list, but it may prove impractical in many benchmarking cases. The benchmarker team and the benchmarking partner may not have the time and financial resources to go through these stages in different visits. In that case, some of these steps could be collapsed into one. However, it is helpful to separate data collection on performance and processes from that of the policy and structure.

4.5 ◆ Using the Benchmarking Results

After the analysis of benchmarking data, the results are used to:

- Create a shared understanding of differences and gaps
- Determine the future performance
- Establish the systems-improvement goals
- Determine the implementation processes, policies, and structural changes

The use of the benchmarking results starts from details and moves upward to change the existing practices and policies.

4.5.1 Shared Understanding of Benchmarking Results

Benchmarking can have a threatening effect on the employees of the benchmarking organization. Resistance to change, doubt in the comparability of benchmarking operations, uncertainty in the thoroughness of the data collection, and doubt in the accuracy of the analysis lead to publicly expressed or privately held skepticism, criticism, and resistance towards benchmarking conclusions. Therefore, it is essential for the benchmarking team to have a comprehensive plan for communicating the benchmarking results to all levels of the company, especially to those whose functions are benchmarked, or will be directly or indirectly affected by changes caused by the benchmarking analysis. Camp [1989] emphasizes the importance of including the customers (internal and external) in the communication loop if they are affected by the benchmarking results.

The benchmarking team should adopt multiple channels of communication including:

- Reports
- Forums
- Functional subgroups
- E-mail and electronic bulletin boards
- Networks of benchmarkers

Written reports are efficient in that they contain details and their distribution is relatively easy. However, written reports are rarely read carefully and offer little opportunity for interaction and feedback.

Company-wide discussion forums allow employees to ask questions and provide immediate feedback about the benchmarking results. Discussion subgroups in functional areas allow the employees of similar functional concerns to exchange ideas regarding the benchmarking results.

E-mail and electronic bulletin boards serve a similar purpose for those who are geographically dispersed and unable to attend forums and face-to-face discussion groups. Camp [1989] recommends the use of the benchmarkers' network, which allows the benchmarker to step outside the company and receive the feedback from other benchmarkers who have gone through similar experiences.

The purpose of communication is to gain acceptance for the benchmarking results, as well as improve the quality of analysis if the feedback indicates the need for more data or better analysis. Since the benchmarking process ideally leads to major changes and improvements, the involvement of employees helps institute changes.

4.5.2   Determination of Future Performance and Goals

The benchmarking gaps between the benchmarker and the benchmarking partner show the possibility of performance improvement in the future. In cases where historical data is available, the analysis of performance gaps in previous years would indicate whether the gaps have been widening or narrowing. A widening gap points to a deterioration of the company's competitive edge and may call for more extensive change.

Once the feasibility of performance improvement has been demonstrated, the company should decide on future performance levels and the time period for achieving them.

The quantitative objectives of the performance improvement would be superficial unless they are accompanied by qualitative and overall goals. For example, ACCU-INFO may set the future performance level for data-entry clerks as one error in $10,000$ data items for the next year. However, this performance-level specification will be superficial if it is not articulated within a long-term goal, such as reducing errors to near zero, and with the reason for establishing such a goal. ACCU-INFO justifies the long-run goal of reducing the errors to near zero as part of its vision of being the most reliable credit-service company in the nation.

Setting such a performance level and goal must be within the context of a comprehensive plan for accomplishing the vision. ACCU-INFO has to attack the issue of reliability from all aspects, not just the input data. It has to make a similar effort to measure and increase the reliability of its software, its applications, its data sources, and its network connection. In other words, the data-entry clerks should not feel that they are singled out as the only source of errors. Instead, it must be communicated to them that their work is a major component of a system whose reliability is of paramount importance to the company, and that every effort is being made to make the entire system work with the highest degree of reliability and stability.

4.5.3   Implementation

Once the performance levels and goals are established based on the benchmarking results, the top management, with the help of the benchmarking and cross-functional teams, has to decide on the processes and policies that would lead to the achievement of the goals. Here, the detailed benchmarking analysis of processes and policies aids the company in making the necessary changes.

Each functional unit should develop an action plan, specifically identifying its share of the implementation. For example, in reducing the data-entry clerk's errors, the human resource department should come up with a plan for recruiting, rewarding, and training. The software-development unit must identify the plan for changes in the data entry software. The data entry unit must come up with the policies, processes, and structural changes for achieving the performance objectives. In other words, each functional area must take ownership of the goals and accept responsibility for their share in achieving the goals and performance objectives.

Making changes without any clue about the outcome can be frightening to decision makers. The benchmarking analysis provides evidence of the effectiveness of the change and gives assurance to the decision makers that another company has excelled by setting the processes and policies prescribed by the benchmarking analysis.

For example, shifting control of the quality of output away from the managers to workers could be unsettling for top management, who are used to hearing reports from middle managers on worker performance. The benchmarking analysis gives assurance to management that if the changes are made properly, there is a good chance of major improvement in performance. Few top managers are willing to be pioneers in a comprehensive change without some knowledge of the possible outcome.

4.5.4   Evaluation, Monitoring, and Continuous Improvement

With benchmarking implementation comes the plan for evaluation and monitoring the results. The performance measures as well as qualitative feedback from day-to-day operations indicate whether the company is on its way to achieving its improvement goals.

It is possible that some of the processes and policies will not work as well as intended. In that case, there would be a need for calibration or even a short benchmarking visit for further observation.

Benchmarking once and implementing the results does not end the process of improvement. It is just the beginning of the continuous quest for improvement. As the cycle of improvement continues, so do benchmarking efforts.

◆ Conclusion

In this chapter, we discussed the importance of benchmarking and its introduction in the U.S. The nature of information systems makes benchmarking an effective tool for continuous improvement.

Benchmarking requires careful planning. The second section of this chapter discussed the need for a benchmarking plan for information systems that includes identifying the objectives and metrics for benchmarking, determining the type of benchmarking, and selecting a benchmarking partner.

In the third section of this chapter, we discussed how to collect benchmarking information, types of benchmarking information, methods of information collection, and documenting the collected information.

The analysis of benchmarking information plays a vital role in the successful use of benchmarking results. The analysis of benchmarking information includes performance analysis, process analysis, policy analysis, and structure analysis. We also presented some techniques that aid these analyses, such as statistical analysis for performance analysis and the data flow diagram and flowchart for process analysis. This section discussed the fact that if benchmarking is done in an iterative fashion, more insight can be gained. However, iterative benchmarking may be costlier and more time consuming.

Using benchmarking results was the topic of the last section. The first imperative of benchmarking implementation is the creation of a shared understanding of benchmarking results among those who are affected by them, including internal users and external customers of the systems. The benchmarking results are used to determine the future performance and goals for information systems. The implementation of these goals requires action plans by all functional areas, which should take ownership of the goals and specify their roles in achieving them.

Evaluating and monitoring bring us back to the concept of continuous improvement. Once the benchmarking results are implemented, the process of evaluation, monitoring, and recalibration should be in place in order to ensure the continuation of the improvement process.

◆ References

1. Camp, Robert C. 1989. *Benchmarking: The Search for Industry Best Practices That Lead to Superior Performance*, Quality Press, Milwaukee, WI.
2. Owen, Jean V. 1992. "Benchmarking World-Class Manufacturing," *Manufacturing Engineering*, March, pp. 29–34.
3. Russell, J. P. 1991. *Quality Management Benchmark Assessment*, ASQC Quality Press, Milwaukee, WI.

◆ Questions

4.1. Discuss the importance of benchmarking.
4.2. Describe the role of benchmarking in information systems.
4.3. What is the origin of benchmarking?
4.4. How did benchmarking start in the United States?
4.5. Discuss the major steps in benchmarking.
4.6. What is the role of vision and mission statements in benchmarking?
4.7. Discuss the types of benchmarking.
4.8. Why is the identification of benchmarking objectives and measurements important?
4.9. Discuss the types of benchmarking information.
4.10. Discuss the methods of information collection in benchmarking.

4.11. Why is the documentation of benchmarking important?

4.12. What are the issues to be considered in selecting a benchmarking partner?

4.13. What are the sources for the definition and determination of benchmarking metrics?

4.14. What are the components of benchmarking analysis?

4.15. What are the important issues in performance analysis in benchmarking?

4.16. Discuss the issues involved in comparing data from the benchmarking partner with that of the benchmarking organization.

4.17. Discuss the techniques used in performance analysis in benchmarking.

4.18. Discuss the techniques used in process analysis.

4.19. What are the differences between the data flow diagram and a flowchart?

4.20. What are the areas of interest in policy analysis in benchmarking?

4.21. What does structure analysis in benchmarking involve?

4.22. Describe iterative benchmarking and the issues involved in this type of benchmarking.

4.23. Describe the steps involved in using benchmarking results.

4.24. What is the importance of creating a shared understanding of benchmarking results?

4.25. What are the channels of communication in communicating benchmarking results?

4.26. How does the benchmarker use benchmarking to determine future performance and goals?

4.27. What are the issues involved in the implementation of the benchmarking results?

4.28. What is the role of benchmarking in the continuous improvement process?

◆ Problems

4.1. Company A benchmarks Company B on the stability of its network systems, and finds that Company B has an average of 3 minutes down time per week over the span of 52 weeks while Company A has had an average of 5 minutes down time per week over 20 weeks. Discuss the issues involved before deciding whether there is a significant performance gap between the two companies.

4.2. In the above problem, test the hypothesis that the two companies have the same value for the stability metric as opposed to the alternative hypothesis that Company B has a significantly better performance metric. Assume both companies have the standard deviation value of 1.

4.3. Discuss the statistical method of regression analysis for taking into account the size difference between two companies.

4.4. Give an example of a metric for the reliability of the information systems.

4.5. Observe the process of maintaining an information system and document it by using a data flow diagram.

4.6. Perform the same task for the maintenance of a building and compare the two maintenance processes.

4.7. Give an example of functional benchmarking for updating the technology of an information system.

4.8. Assume that you are the manager of a large information system, say, an auto manufacturer, and have encountered the problem of customer dissatisfaction. You have decided to perform benchmarking. Identify the types of companies that you may consider as potential benchmarking partners.

4.9. In the above problem, assume that you have the problem of an unreliable system. Discuss the types of companies you will consider as the potential benchmarking partner.

4.10. Write the outline for a benchmarking report in the above problem.

◆ CASE: Benchmarking at Xerox

Xerox created the plain-paper copying industry in 1959 when it introduced the 914 copier. Before that, the most popular office copying techniques were relatively messy and inefficient wet processes, and carbons were big back then. The 914 changed all that and transformed the Haloid Company of Rochester, New York into the Xerox Corporation.

For the next 15 years, Xerox was the victim of its own yearly triumphs. The world's first plain-paper copier was one the most successful new products in corporate history. Xerox had such a stranglehold on the copier market throughout the 1960s and early 1970s that it paid hardly any attention when International Business Machine Corporation and Eastman Kodak Company began marketing high-speed copiers, the most lucrative part of the market. Nor did it when the Japanese began to offer small, inexpensive copiers in the mid-1970s, an area it ignored until recently.

The Xerox of the mid-1970s was a bureaucratic company in which one function battled another, and operating people constantly bickered with corporate staff. Disputes over issues as relatively minor as the color scheme of machines had to be resolved by the CEO. The result was painfully slow product development, high manufacturing costs, copiers which were hard to service, and unhappy customers.

Then, in the mid-1970s, the Japanese camera makers entered the low end of the light-lens copier market. They used aggressive pricing to gain a foothold and proceeded to gain sizable market share. Their strategy—similar to the one they used so successfully in automobiles, cameras, home appliances, calculators, and watches—was to change the rules in the low end of the industry, and gradually move to the profitable mid and high ends.

The Japanese strategy worked well. Throughout the late 1970s, Xerox saw its market share erode at an alarming rate. But the problem was not unmasked for a while because the young industry was still growing. Years of immunity to international competitive vulnerabilities had created a kind of arrogance of entitlement, an abiding belief that whatever was going to be invented or manufactured, America would set the standard, do it first, and do it best.

In fact, when Xerox recognized the influx of Japanese competition into the copier market, it sponsored a conference to determine the magnitude of the Japanese threat. The conference scientists and speakers concluded that the probability of a company manufacturing a copier—in Japan and the U.S.—at a lower cost than Xerox was very low. If any new company entered the market, the conferees concluded, it would lose money because the cost of entry would be prohibitive. Only a few weeks later, however, Canon launched a low-end copier that it sold at a price lower than Xerox's manufacturing cost. The conclusions reached at Xerox's conference proved dangerously incorrect.

By 1980, the problem had become readily apparent. Xerox had to evolve rapidly into a world-wide organization if it were to compete effectively with world-wide competitors in the global market.

Benchmarking: the Genesis of Corporate Renewal

Xerox began to respond by assessing its corporate strengths and weaknesses as well as those of its competitors. An important management step was taken in 1981 when the company instituted a formal benchmarking process to identify the successful practices of top competitors in each of Xerox's operations.

Forms of benchmarking have been used in industry for years. Early in this century, Walter Chrysler would tear apart one of each new Ford model as soon as it came off the assembly line at the beginning of the model year. He sought to determine what components went into the car, how much it cost, and how it was made. Armed with this information, Chrysler had a better understanding of his major competitor's strength and weaknesses.

Competitive benchmarking at Xerox is a tool to identify industry performance standards. It provides insights into how these performance standards can be achieved or exceeded and internal action plans developed. Most importantly, benchmarking is an ongoing learning experience for the firm as a whole. At Xerox, competitive benchmarking looks both inside and outside the reprographics industry.

What did Xerox learn? First, it learned that it took too long to develop new products. Moreover, the products cost too much and did not fully satisfy customers' requirements. This process enabled Xerox to learn how its competitors managed costs and how their cost reduction tactics might be replicated. The firm learned that it needed to overhaul the way the business was managed; to compete successfully, Xerox had to be driven by its customers and its competition.

Internally, Xerox discovered that one of its problems was organization. Xerox had a matrix management structure in the Product Development group. This meant that a product development project must flow through separate function—product planning, design engineering, manufacturing engineering, and service engineering—each operating independently, almost in a vacuum. Significantly, no individual had clear responsibility for the end product.

The matrix structure was installed to prevent errors. Instead, it occasionally had the unintended effect of blocking product delivery. With so many different functions involved, slowdowns were inevitable. Time-consuming committees were needed to address cross-disciplinary issues, and every product was cross-disciplinary. In addition, there was a constant need to review and gain concurrence across the different functions in the matrix.

The product development cycle was so long, in fact, that products sometimes became obsolete in mid-stream because the market needs had changed.

Xerox began the process of renewal by dismantling the matrix organization and its accompanying bureaucracy. The product delivery organization was restructured into Product Delivery teams headed by one manager, called the chief engineer, who is held totally accountable for a product development project, including quality, cost, performance, and schedule. The chief engineer manages all design group, and model shop, and the pilot plan.

Not until 1984, however, did Xerox begin to recover its way back into the market. By then, it had made significant progress in product quality and cost. Before 1980, for instance, Xerox copiers averaged 1.2 defects per unit after installation at the customer's base. Today, on average, only six out of 100 Xerox copiers ever have a defect. In fact, by 1985, Xerox was to reduce its product costs by 50% and increase its product quality by more than 90%. Within five years, it was to regain its market share in the copier market and, just as critically, to be the industry leader in customer satisfaction.

But no sooner had Xerox matched the competition on quality and cost than the rules began to change again. For example, Xerox did reduce manufacturing costs by 50%, but so did Japanese. Xerox improved product quality, but the Japanese had already matched that quality. The new battle was to be on time to market.

Time to Market

Xerox's foremost challenge remains that of improving its product development process and decreasing the time it now takes to bring product releases to market. The prime reason is that technology in the copier industry is changing rapidly. The technology of facsimiles, laser printers, and multi-functional products that will be on the market in a few years indicates that the copier of the future will be more than just a copier. It will be an "intelligent" copier; that is, it will function as a copier, a facsimile machine, and a work station printer. These capabilities will foster other advanced technologies. Xerox had to shrink its product development time to participate in the industry's growth.

For example, consider two products that appear in the market place in 1992, one from a company with a two-year cycle and the other from a company with a three-year cycle. The two-year product incorporates the technology of 1990, the other the older technology of 1989. The result is technological leadership, even though no one has invented anything new. This kind of disparity can dictate success or failure of the new emerging markets.

Magnitude of New Product Problem

Xerox used the traditional productivity tools that increased by five to ten percent annually. But the firm's benchmarking efforts revealed that these may not be sufficient in the 1990s.

In product development, it found that its competitors were using only one-half the development time to launch new products in the market place. Matching this rate was essential to the company's goal of accelerating the rate of new product introductions, and of reducing product development costs. Specifically, Xerox found that, unless it reduced its new product development and introduction cycle from 36–48 months to 12–24 months, the Japanese and other competitors would out-innovate and out-perform the firm. This challenge was based upon the following assumptions:

- The Japanese feel that in a world of high technology, rising yen, and improving Western emphasis on quality, they need to compete not on quality or cost, but on innovation and schedule. Evidence so far indicates that they are being successful.
- On the fundamental need to be efficient, Xerox was at a disadvantage.
- To shorten the product life cycles still further, the Japanese have revised their product delivery processes toward the "Z" curves; i.e., overlapping phases, fewer prototype iterations, design schedules held firm by treating quality and cost as secondary variables to be traded off, etc. Their goal is to reduce design schedules to 12–18 months.

Xerox's response to the Japanese design schedule challenge required nothing less than an internal revolution in all phases of product design, production, and distribution. Some of these are elaborated on below.

The "Kaizen" Approach to Developing New Products

During the mid-1980s, Xerox collaborated with its own Japanese copier venture, Fuji Xerox, to implement actions to close the product delivery gap.

One of the practices adopted was Kaizen, i.e., the incremental and continuous technology transfer process. Short delivery cycles and incremental transfers of technology into new products are strong practices which, if used in tandem, make any company a formidable competitor. In general, Kaizen product planning seems to be the norm for Canon, Hitachi, Mitsubishi, Honda, and others.

Kaizen is a primary strategic element in new product competition in a maturing industry. Within manufacturing, our problems occur not in the early stages of an industry but, once it matures and settles into a cycle of gradual improvements, year after year. In the long run, being successful in this process, known as the manufacturing-development cycle, is as important as a firm's ability to create wholly new products.

It doesn't mean for a moment we should give up our ability to create new products and start new industries. That's our great strength and we want to keep it. American industries have always been good starters. But now, in a much more competitive world, we have to be good finishers as well.

The significance of Kaizen for Japanese advantages in new product development is well-known. In developing automobiles, personal computers, and copiers, Japanese companies begin, not with clean-sheet products, but with variants of existing products or off-the-shelf mature and tested technologies. Variants are members of a family of products to which a company makes incremental changes as it proceeds. New products get launched quickly by this method. The company then makes innovations in technology, features, or cost reduction in the successive generation(s) of those products.

In contrast to the Japanese approach, U.S. industry for the most part uses a "leap-frog" approach. This approach reflects a clean-sheet bias towards new product development. The firm seeks to make large, quantum leaps in product design—that is, home runs instead of singles.

This approach has several shortcomings; notably a lack of conscious, up-front planning for product families whenever a new product is considered, and insufficient use of common architecture, technology, components, and reusable code. Under this system, there is minimum effort to recycle, or borrow, from earlier projects. This method requires a long lead time—as much as five to ten years when the product life cycles are shrinking towards two to three years. After a company completes product development, it often learns that customer requirements may have changed.

The assumption underlying the "Kaizen approach" to new product development is that the more incremental design cycles that can be crammed into a ten-year period, the better the product will be at the end of that cycle. That is, iterative prototype cycles of a single product over a ten-year period will yield a less-advanced product than five full product development cycles. In terms of quality, cost, and development time, the Japanese, with the Kaizen approach, have been trending down a 10–20% learning curve; the leapfrog, clean-sheet approach has historically produced a 5–10% learning curve.

Competitive disadvantages caused Xerox to revamp its product planning process. No longer is each product planned individually. Instead, whole series of products are planned. If a product does not result in variants, it is not a successful product. A product must also have commonality with many other products so that advances in component technology will benefit multiple products. Xerox now redesigns individual sub-systems parts in products instead of blocks of time in redesigning the whole product.

Movement Toward Parallel Design

Most U.S. businesses perform product development steps sequentially. They proceed from product pre-concept to concept planning to concept design. A lot of time is invested in product concept, prototype design, testing, final design, manufacturing, and launch. Authorization to proceed to the next phase can take six months. Another six months pass to secure approval and agreement on manufacturing costs, specifications design, and so on. At Ford, this process takes roughly five years.

In the past, Japanese companies worked sequentially, one step after the other. After the yen shock in 1985, however, the Japanese began performing product development activities in parallel. This practice, called the "Z-curve phenomenon" or concurrent engineering, enabled Japan to reduce the product development cycle substantially. Honda, for example, undergoes fewer phases in contrast to GM and Ford. Before all specifications are determined, the design process begins and changes are made as needed, even in the middle of the process. A prototype is assembled and tested before the design phase is completed. Before design testing is completed, the manufacturing line is set up and tooling begins.

The "Z-curve" process requires discipline; otherwise it can create bureaucratic and organizational turmoil. The Japanese make it work and, as one result, significantly reduce their development time.

The Japanese also reduce development time by decreasing the number of prototype cycles. U.S. businesses use the first design prototype for the engineering feasibility model. Another design is completed for use by other areas that have problems in their designs. Only then are manufacturing blocks, and later the launch blocks, formulated. This process demands up to five years. Currently, Japanese firms are moving increasingly towards one engineering and one manufacturing prototype. Then the product is launched. This requires designing accurately the first time, and use of computer-aided engineering (CAE) to simulate sub-systems and to integrate sub-systems at the computer level.

Xerox is reassessing its design process and reducing its number of design prototypes. Honda succeeded in moving from motorcycles to automobiles partly because of its Z-curve process for new product development.

In its benchmarking, Xerox also discovered, at firms such as Honda, significant differences in the way U.S. and Japanese firms transfer technology within the organization. Honda, for example, moves product designers from the labs into business units as needed. In contrast, many U.S. corporations pass the design concept, not the designers, from the central research unit to intermediary where the design concept is processed and technology further matured. The critical difference is that, in the U.S., the transfer medium is primarily paper, whereas, in Japan, the media are people.

In addition, Xerox, like many other U.S. firms, had an intervening organizational unit to evaluate research and translate the technology into an engineering application. This does not imply that, in Japan, the technology-related activities are not performed. It just means that they are performed in either the central research or engineering groups. In Japan, people are easier to transfer as "technology carriers" because the same grade/job structures exist between research and engineering and the reward mechanisms tend to be identical. Therefore, there are few disincentives to the move from one part of the organization to the other.

When a company moves the paper rather than the people, it can lose one to three years in matching new technology to the product. On the other hand, if a company uses an intermediary unit, it loses another one to three years. As a result, some technologies never come to fruition, while others arrive too late to be useful. A competitive company cannot afford to lose these years in product development. With products such as PCs and copiers that have two-year life cycles, such delays can doom an internally-developed technology.

Need for Quicker Response Time

U.S. businesses typically seek improvements in quality and procedural efficiency but neglect environmental or systemic changes needed to parallel the process changes. Hitachi, a large $20-million company that withstood Japan's yen shock with relative ease, provides one example of such environmental factors. Hitachi's organizational chart lacks the names of some of the company's most influential personnel. The company practices team management, through which these leaders simply stay in their positions while they oversee specific projects or strategic importance.

This organizational concept differs significantly from firms in the West, whose organizational concepts evolved from the Catholic Church and the military, where specific responsibilities are clearly delineated. Job boundaries are also clearly drawn. In contrast, the Japanese delineate work responsibilities in ways that leave boundaries fuzzy. Japanese business define jobs by the personnel performing the work. The result is that employees work on problems rather than just on what a job description dictates. The Japanese also bring in workers to oversee a project. A "hawk organization" is formed specifically to complete the project and, therefore, disbands quickly. Hawk organizations frequently accelerate the speed of response.

Japanese and U.S. businesses differ in other practices as well. Strategic planners in the U.S., for example, typically remain in that function for the duration of their careers. They may move from division to division, receive promotions, and eventually retire. In Japan, however, workers seldom leave their divisions. They move from job to job within the same division—from finance to production to procurement to personnel to sales, and so on. Fifty percent of section managers may be rotated each fiscal year and the next-level managers may be moved every two years. As a result, managers acquire detailed knowledge of every function within their division and solve problems with great speed. A very heavy emphasis on generalist, job rotation, and overlapping responsibilities is one of the reasons Japanese firms adjust so quickly to shocks, such as energy crises, currency fluctuation, advances in production technology, and other major discontinuities. U.S. businesses, by contrast, form quality improvement teams and invest as much as six months analyzing a problem and seeking solutions. Still, the situation may not change because companies often fail to implement proposed solutions, and the response time continues to mount.

Japanese business practices increase the speed of response. When major upheavals occur in the market place—such as the yen shock of 1973 and 1979, or a tariff barrier like that imposed against Canon by the European common market—Japanese businesses respond quickly. Western companies need to improve their response time. For example, several U.S. companies launched project teams in 1985 to overtake the Japanese whose profits had declined because of the yen shock. It took several of these companies a year to launch the project team and another year to develop solutions. By then, it was too late. The Japanese rebounded and are stronger today than they were before the yen shock.

Speed of response is a key factor in market success. Decision making, too, must be quicker in all components of the organization. Although Xerox is a greatly improved company over what it was in 1980, it is not standing still. It continues discussions with other U.S. companies, including Ford and GM, who began a process of change five years earlier than Xerox because they faced Japanese competition that much earlier. Although these companies, like Xerox, now measure up to Japan in quality improvement, they still battle the problem of response time. Xerox is making other fundamental changes as well, changes relating to its environment, the culture of the company itself, the tools of productivity, and the way in which Xerox thinks and plans.

As a result of all this, Xerox can now deliver products in substantially less time. Engineering productivity has more than doubled since 1985. For example, Xerox needed only two and a half years and 300-350 employees to develop its top-of-the-line 9900 copier, a high speed machine. By previous standards, the project would have taken five years and more than 1,500 people.

After a decade of effort to develop the strategies and put in place the systems for Xerox to be a world-class competitor, it has significantly narrowed the advantage held by Canon, Ricoh, Sharp, and Minolta, stemming their advance in Xerox's market. This was recognized by the U.S. Department of Commerce when it awarded Xerox the Malcolm Baldridge National Quality Award in 1989. But for all this effort, there is more to be done, especially since the competition is still a target moving forward. Xerox may no longer be the company it once was, but it is not yet the company it wants to be.

Source: "Back from the Brink," Mohan Kharbanda, *CMA Magazine*, July–August 1991, pp. 9–14. Reprinted with permission from The Society of Management Accountants of Canada.

Case Questions

1. Relate Xerox's benchmarking analysis to managing the information systems function.
2. Identify the major areas that the Xerox benchmarking has covered and discuss their role in the organization functions.
3. Identify the major conclusion in the Xerox benchmarking analysis.
4. Assume you are the manager of the information systems function at Xerox. Develop an action plan for the information systems department in achieving the objectives identified in Xerox's benchmarking results.
5. Assume that Xerox is your competitor. Develop a proposal for how to compete with this company.

For want of a nail the shoe is lost, for want of a shoe the horse is lost, for want of a horse the rider is lost.

— George Herbert, *Jacula Predentum*

Life is a progress from want to want, not from enjoyment to enjoyment.

— Samuel Johnson, *Letter to Lord Chesterfield*

◆ Chapter Objectives

The objectives of this chapter are:
- The review of the concept of requirements analysis for information systems
- The identification of the customers of information systems
- The review of the existing methods of requirements analysis
- The use of quality function deployment (QFD) in requirements analysis
- The use of QFD in systems planning
- The use of analytic hierarchy process for elicitation of customers' preferences
- The discussion of software requirements analysis

◆ Key Words

Requirements analysis in information systems, requirements analysis methods, customer focus in quality information systems, quality function deployment, application of quality function deployment in information-systems requirements analysis, house of quality, analytic hierarchy process, software requirements analysis.

Quality Management in Requirements Analysis

5.1 Requirements Analysis in Information Systems
    5.1.1 The Elicitation of Needs
    5.1.2 The Anticipation of Needs
    5.1.3 The Verification and Validation of Needs
    5.1.4 The Purpose of the Information System
    5.1.5 Making Decisions on Processes and Tools

5.2 Customer Focus in Quality Information Systems
    5.2.1 End-User Involvement in Information Systems
    5.2.2 Customers of Quality Information Systems

5.3 Requirements Analysis Methods
    5.3.1 Concrete Methods for Requirements Analysis
    5.3.2 Abstract Methods for Requirements Analysis

5.4 Requirements and Technical Analysis Using Quality Function Deployment (QFD)
    5.4.1 Customer Requirements
    5.4.2 The General Structure of QFD
    5.4.3 Systems Planning with QFD

5.5 Weight Assignments via Analytic Hierarchy Process (AHP)
    5.5.1 Hierarchy Structure
    5.5.2 Simple Rating of Attributes Within the Hierarchy
    5.5.3 Computing Global Ratings
    5.5.4 Pairwise Comparisons (Optional)
    5.5.5 Group Weight Assignments (Optional)

5.6 Software Requirements Analysis

◆ Introduction

This chapter discusses requirements analysis in information systems. The stages of requirements analysis are divided into the elicitation, anticipation, verification, and validation of needs. We review end-user involvement in information systems, and expand it for quality information systems to include all internal, external, direct, and indirect customers of information systems.

This chapter introduces quality function deployment (QFD) in requirements analysis. QFD allows us to plan the systems requirements directly from what customers express as systems' important attributes. In QFD, we build the house of quality that connects customers' requirements to system requirements. QFD makes it possible to give a clear and formal guideline for the development of the system, identifies the important components of the system, and shows the consequence of subsequent changes in any component of the system.

The house of quality in QFD requires customers' ratings of attributes. The ratings quantify the relative importance of various system components in satisfying the customers' needs and requirements. To facilitate the elicitation of customers' preferences, we can use the analytic hierarchy process (AHP) method. AHP produces the input to the first house of quality for systems planning.

Finally, this chapter discusses the importance of software requirements analysis and the use of similar techniques in planning the software components.

5.1   ◆   Requirements Analysis in Information Systems

As in any technical service industry, the customer plays the most crucial role in defining the information systems service. The process of eliciting customers' needs is called *requirements analysis*, and includes:

- The elicitation of needs
- The anticipation of needs
- The verification of needs
- The validation of needs

5.1.1   The Elicitation of Needs

Knowing what you want or need seems obvious. But in many business—and even personal—decisions, the discovery of exactly what you need requires a careful analysis and formal process. Although people normally live and sometimes adjust to choices that do not reflect their true needs, errors in identifying the true needs of customers could prove to be very costly for business. Since products such as information-systems services are thoroughly defined by whether they address a real need, the elicitation of the needs of information-systems customers determines the success or failure of the system.

5.1.2   The Anticipation of Needs

In a technology-driven area such as information systems, it is not enough to elicit the existing needs or "care-abouts" of customers. Advances in technology often create new markets and customer needs. In some cases, customers' lack awareness of the existence or applicability of a technology could prevent them from expressing a need. Once the customer becomes aware of what the new technology can achieve for him or her, he or she may see a new need that did not exist a short while ago. Therefore, the anticipation of the customer's future desires is as important as the elicitation of his or her present requirements.

5.1.3   The Verification and Validation of Needs

After the preliminary elicitation of customer needs, one has to make sure that what customers have stated as their requirements are indeed what they need, rather than a wish list with little practical use, or miscommunicated statements.

The *verification* of customer needs involves making sure that the customer's statements are correctly communicated and interpreted. The *validation* of customer needs assures systems designers that customers' stated preferences reflect their true needs and wishes, and are not motivated by political, spur-of-the-moment, or other spurious factors.

As an example of the verification problem in the ACCU-INFO case, consider a customer who expresses a strong preference for the fast response attribute of the information system. The analyst may interpret that the customer wishes the system to respond instantly to on-line queries, whereas the customer may mean that the system must respond quickly to requests for new updates. A fast response to on-line queries requires more capacity for hardware, while the fast response to request for new updates requires more frequent and wider access to data-suppliers' databases.

Another example is a customer who states that he or she prefers to interact with the system using a pen rather than the keyboard. At the verification stage, the analyst may discover that the customer meant to convey his or her lack of skill in using the keyboard, rather than the preference for using a pen.

As an example of a validation problem, consider an ACCU-INFO's customer who, in a meeting attended by his supervisors, insists that his most urgent need in using the information system is the system's ability to generate a multi-media output. It may turn out that the motivation for this urgently expressed preference has been to obtain multi-media equipment for his office that otherwise would be unavailable to him.

The challenge is to determine if the customers mean what they say, and to assure that their statements are understood, transmitted, and interpreted correctly.

There are system attributes that the customer may take for granted and therefore fail to mention as important attributes. For example, the availability of the system at all hours may be such an obvious requirement that it could be completely omitted from the list. Now, if the system is to be working over a computer network, this attribute may make a big difference in the cost of the information system. The verification of customer requirements should make the list of information-system attributes complete and comprehensive.

To validate the customer needs, the analyst looks into other companies with similar functional requirements in order to:

- Help anticipate customer needs
- Make sure the list of requirements is complete
- Check whether the stated needs are doable, reasonable, and cost-effective
- Avoid repeating mistakes already committed by other companies

Benchmarking information, discussed in Chapter 4, is helpful for the validation of the customer's information systems requirements.

5.1.4   The Purpose of the Information System

To give direction to requirements analysis, the purpose and objectives of the system should be clearly defined in advance. As the analysis progresses, the scope of the system is defined more concretely. However, it is crucial to have a general framework for the system before commencing the analysis. Otherwise, the requirements analysis becomes an aimless and hence useless exercise. Furthermore, the purpose of the information system determines who would be the system's customers.

For example, in developing the credit information system for ACCU-INFO, the purpose of the system could be to establish credit ratings of individuals. This defines the system customers as the companies who subscribe to the system for checking their applicants' credit status. If we enhance the system's scope by including the justification of credit ratings and the provision of credit information to the individuals whose credit is being rated, we have added a completely different group of customers, whose needs would be quite different from business subscribers.

5.1.5   Making Decisions on Processes and Tools

Simple information systems require simple requirements analysis. Similarly, complex systems demand careful analysis. The challenge is the identification of the complexity parameters in an information system. In most cases, complexity is a relative concept for each company. A company with long experience in developing complex systems has a higher tolerance for complexity than a company that is undertaking its first project in developing an information system.

The elements that play a role in the complexity of an information system include:

- Size of the system
- Diversity of data, information, and functions within the system
- Previous experience of the company in developing such systems
- Experience of the system developers
- Type of system customers

Size and diversity of information as well as the system's functions are system-dependent attributes. The decision makers and developers can control complexity by manipulating these attributes and starting with a smaller or less diverse system.

The impact of the previous experiences of the company and its system developers can be controlled by bringing in outside consultants and hiring experienced individuals for the project.

In the above list, the customer types are the least-controllable factor in the complexity of the system. The customer types and their contributions in the complexity of information systems are discussed in the next section.

5.2 ◆ Customer Focus in Quality Information Systems

After the loss of investment in early data-processing systems that failed to serve the needs of their users in the 1950s and 1960s, the field of information systems has become one of the staunch advocates of involving end-users in developing information systems. Therefore, the customer focus of quality management blends with and enhances the user orientation of information systems.

Traditional information systems view the end-user as the owner of the system. Quality management defines customers of information systems as all those who come in contact with the system and are impacted by it. This expanded definition of information-systems customers makes the requirements analysis more comprehensive in that the system should embody the needs of a larger group of impacted individuals. It makes the system more durable and less susceptible to sudden obsolescence, preserves the integrity of the system, and fulfills the intended purpose of serving all customers' needs.

5.2.1   End-User Involvement in Information Systems

End-user can be a deceiving term in that it covers heterogeneous categories of people or even systems. To offer just a sample of the diversity of this group, consider that users can be:

- Computer-expert or computer-illiterate
- System-expert or system-illiterate
- Permanent or temporary
- Frequent or occasional
- Local or long-distance
- Internal or external
- Friendly or hostile
- Participative or non-participative
- Human or machine

In analyzing users' needs and requirements, the users' knowledge and the degree of their diversity impact the complexity and length of the analysis.

For example, an end-user may be a computer expert, which makes it easier to elicit the technical needs and wishes of the user. On the other hand, unfamiliarity with the information system, even for a computer expert, may make the need elicitation more difficult.

Furthermore, the temporary or occasional end-users may have little incentive to participate actively in requirements analysis. Analyzing the needs of temporary users requires a careful identification and assembly of users. Such users are normally more diversified, and one has to make sure that the analysis is performed over a representative sample of users.

For example, in requirements analysis for a computerized real-estate information system, one has to have a representative cross-section of various types of house-buyers in different regions. The needs of such a diversified group could be quite varied and, at times, contradictory. A similar, though less acute, problem exists when the users only use the system occasionally. An example might be airline travelers or tourists who use the service of an information system for scheduling trips.

When users are internal or local, eliciting their needs is easier than from those who are external to the organization or are geographically dispersed. Both externality and geographical diversity introduce variety to customer needs, which makes requirements analysis more challenging. Geographical diversity combined with cultural heterogeneity could make the job of requirements elicitation a major undertaking.

Sometimes the users may not be friendly. For example, users of an information system may include the company's competitors or legal adversaries. Requirements analysis in such cases is a politically intricate task.

There are also cases where the information system is accessed by another system, or its output is the input of an automated manufacturing process. In this case, the needs analysis requires a careful specification of yet another system that adds more complexity to the process.

Thus, in cases where the users are knowledgeable about the computer, the system is local and internal, and its customers have well-defined needs, requirements analysis can proceed using simple methods. However, there are cases where the system attributes and users' profiles make requirements analysis more complicated. As we will see in a later section, there are formal methods that make requirements analysis more manageable in these cases.

5.2.2   Customers of Quality Information Systems

In quality information systems, the definition of customers encompasses more than just end-users. Customers of quality information systems include those who directly or indirectly come into contact with the information system, and include:

- End-users
- Systems developers
- Programmers
- Developer-users

- Indirect internal users
- Indirect external users

We have discussed end-users as a major category of information customers in the previous section. However, end-users are not the only category of customers. Systems developers and programmers are the customers of the information system in that they develop and maintain the system. Their technical expertise about upcoming technology and market trends are an important input to the requirements analysis. The developers' and programmers' views are always incorporated into the system. By not formalizing their roles in the process, one can only create hidden agendas and biases in the development of the system.

Developer-users are those users who are the main champion of the new system. They play an important part in getting the funding for the project, in developing the system, and in using it after completion. Having developer-users for a system makes the requirements analysis easier in that these types of users know their own "care-abouts" better than others. However, if developer-users are not the only users of the system, their dominance in dictating what the system should do makes the inclusion of other users' needs more difficult, especially when the needs of other users conflict with those of the developer-users.

Indirect internal and external users are often neglected in the requirements analysis, which may become a source of controversy or rapid obsolescence at a later date. An example of the indirect external users can be found in airline reservation systems. In such systems, travel agents are the direct end-users of the system. They are the ones who access the system, search the database, and enter the reservations. However, the indirect users of the system are travelers. If a particular company is shown first on the screen, it does not affect the agent, but it affects the traveler's decision. Therefore, in this case, the indirect user—the traveler—is as important as the direct user—the travel agent. Neglecting travelers' requirements for unbiased access to airline information may prove a costly oversight.

Another example is an expert system for credit authorization of credit-card holders. The direct users of such a system are the credit-card company staff who issue authorization. However, both credit-card holders and store clerks who ask for authorization are the indirect users of the system. Assume that the system finds out the credit card is a stolen card and the customer is a suspect in major credit-card crimes, and recommends the arrest of the customer. Although the authorizer is the direct user of the system, the customer and the store clerk are impacted far more than the direct user.

Requirements analysis for a system with numerous indirect users or extensive public impact requires careful analysis and far more resources than systems with no indirect users.

◆ CASE: The Voice of the Customer

In the last few years, a growing number of companies have recognized that improving quality by meeting or exceeding customer expectations will keep them ahead of the competition and help assure superior profitability. Many of these organizations have turned to technology for help.

Information technology can be a powerful tool for providing better service to customers, but some companies that have invested in new systems are not getting the results they expected. The chief reason, I believe, is that they focus more on the technology itself than the benefits it will bring to the customer. As a result, they end up with state-of-the-art systems that do little to increase customer satisfaction. In some cases, they may actually erode customer relationships.

One very costly mistake in this regard has to do with understanding customer needs. Most companies don't know what their customers want. A major insurance company assumed its customers would appreciate faster processing and payment of claims, so it invested in an expensive computer system to speed claim transactions. Later, the company found out that its customers were less concerned about fast payment than simply being assured of a date when they could expect payment.

Technology can help a company's quality-improvement efforts only if it is solidly grounded on customer needs. Businesses serious about quality listen to the collective voice of their customers and make sure that voice is heard throughout the organization. Only then do they attempt to develop and apply technology to the process of exceeding customer expectations.

But even understanding customer needs doesn't guarantee success. A case in point is the apparel industry, where the average retail store is out of stock on 30% of its items at any one time. This creates disappointment and frustration for customers, headaches for retail buyers, and chaos among suppliers as they scramble to produce and ship more products. Efforts to solve this problem have involved harnessing technology to speed reorders. Requests from sales clerks to retail buyers to distributors and, finally, to manufacturers were processed faster, but the out-of-stock situation continued.

Giving Customers Control

A more customer-focused solution was adopted several years ago by VF Corp., maker of Wrangler, Jantzen and other famous-name apparel. Lawrence R. Pugh, the company's chief executive, said the firm realized the answer wasn't simply to apply technology to an old process. The entire response system had to be fundamentally changed.

VF devised and implemented an innovative system that feeds back customer purchase data simultaneously to VF's sales, marketing, production, and distribution departments. As stock on any item in any store is depleting, everybody in the distribution chain is alerted at the same time and can take the appropriate action to ensure that customers will find the products they want, in the right sizes and colors every day. Pugh says VF ultimately can achieve a 40% reduction in order cycle time, a 30% reduction in total inventory and a 20% reduction in cost.

A third obstacle that stymies many quests for quality, particularly in businesses that have direct contact with customers, is relying too heavily on technology and forgetting that the human touch is still what counts most. In my experience, this imbalance is most often the result of poor training. This was exemplified recently by a registration clerk I encountered while checking in at a prestigious Chicago hotel. I asked the clerk why staff members were setting up microphones and speakers nearby.

"I don't know," he said, as he continued punching keys on his terminal. "Who would know?" I pressed. "I'm not sure," came the reply. "Maybe the assistant manager."

When he was finished on the computer, he handed me the room key and said in a sincere voice, "Thank you very much, Mr. Whiteley. My name is John. If there's anything I can do to help you during your stay, please let me know."

Incredulously, I looked at him and said as politely as I could, "John, I just asked you for help and didn't get it."

John's training had obviously focused on how to process customers and not how to please them. So he processed me much as a machine processes data, sausage, or cheese. He did not make a distinction between following his script and using initiative to create a happy customer. As a result, although the check-in was speedy and technically perfect, the customer was not well-served.

In quality organizations, the customer drives every decision. Information technology can be a valuable ally in creating a customer-focused company, but systems and their applications must be linked directly to customer needs and expectations. Otherwise, the investment is wasted, and rather than creating satisfied customers, it may very well drive them away.

Source: "You Can't Process Customers Like Data," Richard C. Whiteley, *Computerworld,* September 16, 1991, p. 23, reprinted with permission from Richard Whiteley.

5.3 ◆ Requirements Analysis Methods

Simple methods for requirements analysis in information systems include interviews with users. If an information system already exists, the information gathering for requirements analysis would include the review of the existing system's documents and observing the present system in action.

Although simple methods may suffice for straightforward information systems where the needs of customers can be easily identified and elicited, more complex systems require formal methods of needs elicitation, anticipation, verification, and validation.

Numerous methodologies and tools for systems development are reported in the information-systems literature and are used in practice [see, for example, Gutierrez 1989; and Mohda, Gwinnett, and Bruce 1990]. We can categorize the formal methods of requirements analysis into two broad categories: concrete and abstract.

5.3.1 Concrete Methods for Requirements Analysis

In the *concrete* methods, the requirements analysis is carried out based on a concrete and tangible system that could be real or made-up. The analyst and the user work with the concrete model to identify, anticipate, verify, or validate the requirements. The methods that fall in this category include [Gutierrez 1989]:

- Object-oriented
- Games

- Simulation
- Prototypes
- Pilots
- Operational experiments

The *object-oriented* method requires the customers to identify the real objects (physical or conceptual) and the attributes about which they wish to have knowledge, information, or data. This method focuses customers on real-world entities and information services about them and away from technology and gadgets. The object-oriented method can be used in all four levels of needs elicitation, anticipation, verification, and validation.

In the *games* method, the analyst creates a manual prototype of the system so that the customers can play the game of pretending to use the system. For example, in the credit-checking information system, the analyst can create connection gadgets and paper sheets for pretending to access the information system for a customer query. As the customers play with the props that pretend to be various facets of the system, they become aware of whether a feature of the system works for them. The significant contribution of the game method is in verifying the customers needs, although it may be used for needs elicitation and anticipation as well.

In the *simulation* method, the physical props are coded as modules of a system simulation program. The computer simulation of an information system is more realistic and costlier than the game method. This method is useful for the verification of customer needs.

In *prototyping*, a working but much reduced version of the information system is created that allows customers to work directly with a scaled-down, working model of the system. This method helps in the elicitation and verification of customer requirements.

In the *pilot* approach, a completed information system is installed in a few selected areas as a pilot prior to becoming fully operational in all areas. Because a pilot is quite advanced in the system development cycle, its use in requirements analysis is to validate the customers' needs.

In the *operational experiment* method, part of the information system in implemented in a few areas for a short time, and data for the system performance and customer reactions are collected. The final list of customers' needs are based on the analysis of the data generated by these experiments. This method helps in the verification and validation of customers needs.

5.3.2 Abstract Methods for Requirements Analysis

In the abstract methods of requirements analysis, customers focus on the abstract, conceptual attributes of the system, rather than working with real or simulated aspects of the system or its real-world objects. This category includes [Gutierrez 1989]:

- Delphi
- Surveys
- Repertory grids

The *Delphi* method helps in the creation of consensus about requirements among a diverse group of customers. In this method, the analyst sends a questionnaire to a sample of customers who are representative of the system's customer profiles. The answers are collected, tabulated, and distributed among the respondents again, asking for the change in their view with the objective of reaching a consensus. The process continues until there is no change from one set of questionnaires to another.

In the *survey* method, customers are surveyed using the statistical survey approach. The statistical analysis of the responses identifies the features of the system that are most important to the majority of customers. This is a helpful method for eliciting needs from numerous, diverse, and geographically scattered customers of the information system.

In the *repertory grids* method, the analyst develops a matrix of system attributes (on the rows of the matrix) and the system's constructs for supporting those attributes (on the columns of the matrix). The relationships of the rows and columns determine the relationships between the system's attributes and constructs as an individual respondent sees it. We will see later that the idea of repertory grids is utilized in the quality function deployment in a more elaborate fashion. The repertory grids method is helpful in connecting the users' requirements with the system-specific features.

◆ CASE: Using QFD in Requirements Analysis

Palmtop computers are one of those seemingly can't-miss ideas that have done little else but miss. To date, pioneer products from Poqet Computer Corp. and Atari Corp. have generated far more hype than sales.

But analysts are bullish about a new offering from Hewlett-Packard Co. Some say sales for the 11-ounce gizmo aimed at on-the-go users of Lotus Development Corp.'s 1-2-3 spreadsheet could hit 300,000 in its first year.

What's different? Quality function deployment (QFD), for one thing. "We wanted to get the customer's words for what they wanted, rather than our words," says Kent Henscheid, marketing manager at the Corvallis, Ore., division where the computer is made. "And we found out that people considered such a product an extension of their identity—so it has to look good. We didn't realize the needs for personalization."

As a result, the company added engraved nameplates to the back of the unit, a "Lotus 1-2-3" logo on the front, and a screen that flashed the customer's name, company, and title before the actual application comes on. And although some execs wanted the product to sport the gold color scheme of preceding products made at Corvallis, the QFD team ultimately decided to go with a cool black—and even added some unnecessary weight to avoid any "plasticky" feel.

Source: "Case Study: A Customer-Defined Palmtop PC," Peter Burrows, *Electronic Business*, Vol. 17, No. 12, June 17, 1991, p. 74, reprint with permission from *Electronic Business Buyer*, copyright 1991, Reed Elsevier Inc.

5.4 ◆ Requirements and Technical Analysis Using Quality Function Deployment (QFD)

Quality function deployment was developed in Japan at Mitsubishi's Kobe shipyard in 1972. It was later enhanced by Toyota, and has been used extensively in numerous industries in Japan.

QFD was first introduced to U.S. industry by Don Clausing [Clausing 1988] after his visit to Fuji-Xerox Ltd. in Tokyo. Eureka and Ryan [1988] note that the term QFD is a nondescriptive and inexact translation of six Chinese and Japanese characters:

- *hin shitsu* meaning qualities, features, or attributes
- *ki no* meaning function
- *ten kai* meaning deployment or diffusion

Note that the term *hin shitsu* means qualities and attributes, not quality. QFD was developed to:

- Reflect the customer voice
- Formalize integration of the planning, design, and implementation stages of development
- Serve as a knowledge repository of various customers' requirements and technical specifications
- Be a communication medium among customers, technical staff, and cross-departmental units

In developing an information system, QFD can be used to formalize and manage the transition from requirements analysis to technical specification and design of the system. In information systems, it is common to use a new technology just because it is new, others are using it, and vendors are pushing it. This can lead to costly projects with little value added to the company. Using QFD allows the analyst to see whether a new technology is needed and what its priority should be. This approach creates an objective evaluation of the value of any new process, tool, or technology to be used in the development of the information system.

5.4.1   Customer Requirements

The traditional and experimental methods of requirements analysis concentrate on the elicitation and anticipation of customers' needs, and few (with the exception of repertory grids) offer a formal method of matching needs with technical resources. QFD fills this gap.

Requirements Hierarchy.   QFD starts with the most general form of customers' needs. For example, in the ACCU-INFO credit information system, the industry customer group may state that it wants credit information that is quick, accurate, up-to-date, and easily accessible, regarding the credit-worthiness of the applicants. These are the general attributes from the point of view of a group of customers. Figure 5.1 shows the second layer of the customer-requirements hierarchy.

Normally, these terms are general and vague. They may have different meanings for each customer or analyst. However, it is important to start with general attributes that would form a framework for categorizing and summarizing detailed attributes.

The next step is to translate these general terms into tangible and specific attributes. Otherwise, the ambiguity of the general terms makes them useless in QFD.

For example, in the ACCU-INFO case, the question is the meaning of quick in the context of credit checking. There might be many different types of queries from the database, such as first-time query, update query, and queries that are not common and are specific to a particular type or circumstance. Individuals with police records, queries for correction of errors, or applicant complaints could be examples of such queries. Therefore, we should breakdown the query types into more specific categories in order to define what quick means within each category. Figure 5.1 shows this break down as one-day turn-around for a new name, 30 minutes for an update, three days for unusual queries, and two days for error correction and complaint resolution.

Similarly, credit information can have a limited or expanded dimension. Here, we assume that the requirement is a credit rating based on the credit card and mortgage payments history of an individual, while covering as many individuals as possible. The accuracy requirement is defined at the next level as the maximum error of 2 percent across the population, the maximum error of 30 percent for one person, and an error-free entry system. The up-to-date attribute of the information system can be specified as

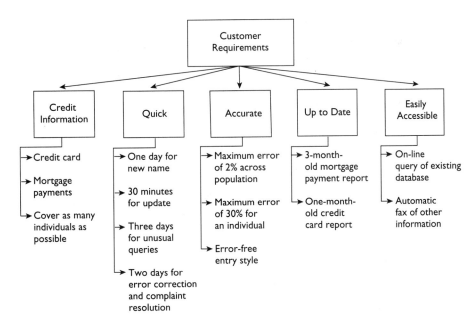

Figure 5.1   The Hierarchy of Customer Requirements for ACCU-INFO's Information System

reflecting a 3-month old mortgage payment and one-month old credit-card payment. The attribute easily accessible is described as on-line query of existing database and automatic faxing for all other communications.

If the extent of detailed attributes at the third level is not adequate, one can extend the hierarchy to four or more levels, as shown in Figure 5.2. The process of adding levels to the hierarchy should continue until both customers and the development team feel comfortable with the degree of details in the requirements.

Relative Importance of Customer Requirements.   QFD requires the rating of the relative importance of the attributes at the lowest level of the hierarchy. The method of eliciting the relative ratings using the analytic hierarchy process (AHP) will be discussed in a later section in this chapter. Here, we assume that customers have assigned relative importance to each one of the attributes at the lowest level of the hierarchy. As shown in Figure 5.3, the assigned relative ratings have a value between zero and one, and add up to one.

Note that the relative importance ratings of the attributes on the second level of the hierarchy in Figure 5.3 are equal to the sum of the importance ratings of the elements at the third level for each second-level attribute. For example, credit information has a relative rating of .60, which is the sum of ratings of credit card information (.20), mortgage payment (.10), and over as many individuals as possible (.30).

5.4.2   The General Structure of QFD

The general structure of QFD consists of a series of tables (or matrices) with borders that make them look like a house. Each house moves the customer requirements towards the more detailed technical design and then implementation of the system, as shown in Figure 5.4.

The sequence of QFD matrices (or quality houses) captures the stages of:

- Systems planning
- Systems design
- Systems implementation

The use of QFD in systems planning is discussed in this chapter. Chapter 6 covers the use of QFD in systems design and implementation.

5.4.3   Systems Planning with QFD

In systems planning with QFD, we connect the customers' requirements with the systems requirements using QFD, as shown in Figure 5.5 and described below.

Voice of Customers.   The house of quality for systems planning starts with the voice of customers on the left border of the house. This border contains the information developed in the customers' requirements hierarchy. The outer border has the most

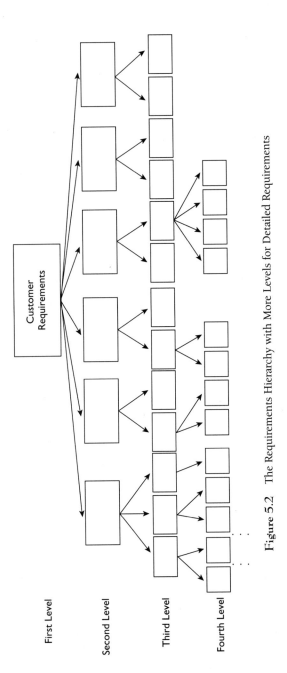

Figure 5.2   The Requirements Hierarchy with More Levels for Detailed Requirements

First Level

Second Level

Third Level

Fourth Level

Customer Requirements

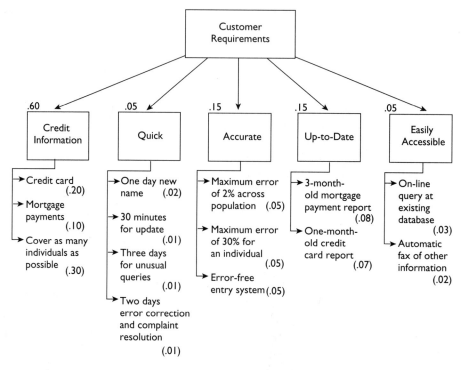

Figure 5.3   Customer Requirements with Priority Ratings

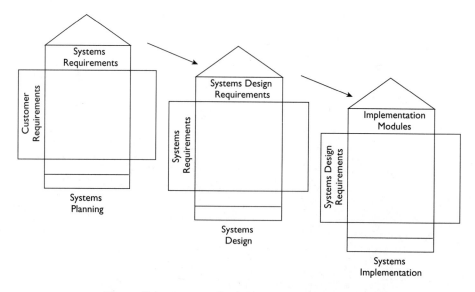

Figure 5.4   QFD in Information Systems Development

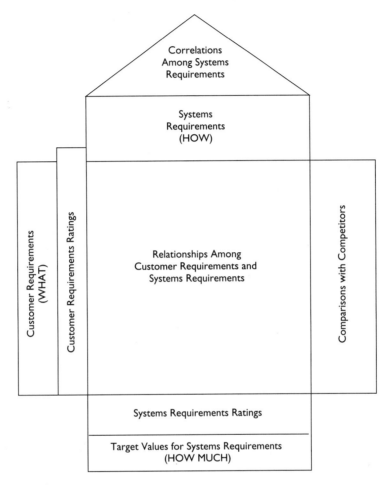

Figure 5.5   The Components of a House of Quality for Systems Planning

general requirements. The next layer of the hierarchy is shown in the next border, and finally customers' requirements ratings are shown in the innermost left border of the house.

For example, Figure 5.6 shows the left border of the house for systems planning for ACCU-INFO. The information in Figure 5.1 is reflected on the two left borders of the house, starting with general requirements and then moving to more detailed attributes. The ratings of customers' requirements are shown on the innermost left border of the house, reflecting the ratings developed in Figure 5.3.

In sum, the left border of the house shows the "care-abouts" and their priorities as expressed by customers.

Systems Requirements.   The upper border of the house consists of the systems re-quirements that show *how* the customers requirements must be fulfilled, as shown in

Figure 5.5. The application of the house of quality shown in Figure 5.6 reflects systems requirements for the ACCU-INFO case:

- Central and local computers
- Central database system and credit ratings
- Local accounting and data-entry systems at local branches

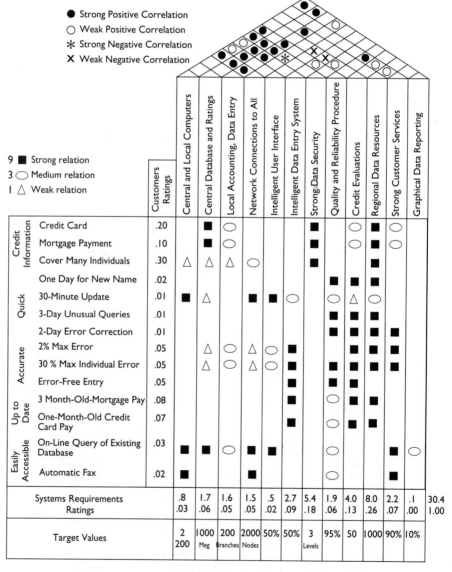

Figure 5.6   Systems Planning for ACCU-INFO's Information System

- Network connections to customers and local branches
- Intelligent user interface
- Intelligent data-entry system
- Strong data security
- Quality and reliability procedures
- Credit evaluators
- Regional data resources
- Strong customer services
- Graphical data reporting

Systems requirements identify the general components of the system. The intention is to show how the system components address customers' needs.

Relationships of Customers and Systems Requirements.   As Figure 5.5 shows, the body of the house (or contents of the matrix) contains the values that reflect relationships of customers and systems requirements. The example of Figure 5.6 makes this more clear.

The three symbols in the matrix indicate the strength of the relationship as strong, medium, and weak. One can use numbers to quantify strength of relationship (9 for strong, 3 for medium, and 1 for weak). The idea is to identify the role of each system component in satisfying the customers' needs. The column with no symbols, or sparse symbols showing a weak relationship, indicates that the component of that column is not really needed by customers.

For example, graphical data reporting has only one medium relation symbol in it. This example shows that this system component is not needed, that the analysis of customers' requirements has not been thorough, or that this feature is an anticipation of a need that has not yet been expressed by customers.

Correlations of Systems Requirements.   Some systems components are correlated positively or negatively. To recognize and formalize such correlations, the roof of the house of quality is used to document them (Figure 5.5).

In the ACCU-INFO case, the intersection of the parallel lines drawn from each system component shows the existence of a correlation. Circles indicate positive, and asterisks indicate negative correlations (Figure 5.6).

For example, network connection to all has strong positive correlations with central and local computers, central database and ratings, and local accounting and data entry. However, it has a strong negative correlation to data security because of the more widespread access to the system.

The correlation roof of the house brings to the attention of systems planners the interdependencies of components. In making the decision to change one component, the roof reminds decision makers to take into account the impact of the change on other components of the system.

For example, in the case of ACCU-INFO, any change in the intelligent user interface requirement impacts on the database software and hardware requirements, as well as the training of personnel as credit evaluators.

Ratings of Systems Requirements.   Requirements of an information system do not have equal importance. Data compression, for example, may not be as important as data security in a database of confidential data. The challenge is the determination of system components with the highest priorities, to which more resources should be allocated.

There is a natural tendency in developing information systems to allocate the most resources to those parts of the system in which the latest technology can be used. While this tendency makes sense for companies whose information-systems vision statement includes technological leadership as a major feature, it could be a costly luxury in others that do not have such a vision. In all cases, system components should be prioritized based on customers' ratings of needs and the strength of the relationships of needs with each component of the system.

We can derive the ratings of system components by multiplying the customers' rating values by the relationship values on each column and summing the result. More formally, the rating of component j—c_j—is:

$$c_j = \frac{\sum_{i=1}^{n} r_i s_{ij}}{\sum_{i=1}^{n} \sum_{j=1}^{m} r_i s_{ij}} \qquad \text{for all } j = 1, 2, \ldots, m$$

where n is the number of attributes stated in the customers' requirements, m is the number of systems requirements, r_i is the customers' ratings of attribute i, and s_{ij} is the strength of relationship between customer-stated attribute i and system component j.

A simpler explanation of the above formula is to multiply the column of ratings by the column of component j, and sum the results. Divide the resulting value by the total of all such values in order to normalize the ratings. These values should be in the zero-one range and sum to one.

For example, in Figure 5.6, the ratings of the first column are computed by multiplying the elements of the customers' ratings by the value of symbols (9 for strong relation, 3 for medium relation, and 1 for weak relation). The sum of this multiplication for the first column is equal to .8 (rounded to the nearest first decimal). Then, .8 is divided by 30.4, the sum of all c_j values, in order to normalize it. Therefore, the rating of central and local computers in the first column is .03. The ratings of the other 11 columns are reported in Figure 5.6. Note that the ratings of the system requirements add up to one. This normalization is needed so that the ratings can be used in the next house of quality for systems design (discussed in Chapter 6).

Target Values.   In the specification of system requirements, one may need to specify the target value for each component. The lowest border of the house contains the target values for system requirements. The target values may have any unit that is appropriate for the component. It may include time spent on designing the component, units needed, the target capacity, or target performance level.

In the ACCU-INFO case in Figure 5.6, the lowest border shows the target values for the twelve system requirements as:

- 2 central computers and 200 local PC's
- 1000 meg worth of data storage
- Accounting and data entry for 200 branches

- Network serving 2000 nodes
- Intelligent users answering 50 percent of users' questions
- Intelligent data-entry systems catching 50 percent of errors and entry questions
- 3 levels of security system—central, network, and local
- Quality and reliability procedures reaching at least a 95 percent level
- 50 trained credit evaluators
- 100 data resources for accessing data
- Customer services capable of addressing 90 percent of customer calls right away
- Graphical data reporting to 10 percent of customers

These target values are not necessarily design parameters and may change in the process of design. They serve to specify the scope of the project and provide a guideline for the next stage of system design. This also helps in budgeting and financing the information-system project.

Comparisons with Competitors.   Another important analysis in system planning is the comparison of the performance of the existing system with that of competitors. The right-hand border of the house (Figure 5.5) contains the competition analysis. This border is completed when there is already an existing system in place.

Customers are asked to compare the existing system's attributes with those of the best or average in the market and rate them accordingly. The attributes used in this analysis are those identified in customers' requirements. For information systems, this task is difficult in that customers may not have been exposed to competitors' information systems. Even if they have used other information systems, it would be hard to compare them attribute by attribute. However, even a crude and anecdotal comparison of the present system with some other systems helps the system planners identify the major shortcomings of the system in the eye of customers.

Figure 5.7 shows the example for ACCU-INFO. Here, we assume that ACCU-INFO has an existing credit information system and has asked its consumers to compare attributes of the existing system with those of its major competitors A and B based on the 14 customer-stated requirements. The rating is between 1 to 5, 5 representing the best.

For example, in its coverage of credit-card information, ACCU-INFO's existing information system is rated as 4, while competitor A is rated 5, and B is rated 3. In credit information, ACCU-INFO is the worst performer in the number of individuals it has in its database. The strength of ACCU-INFO is in responding to unusual queries and keeping the credit-card payment data up-to-date.

Connecting the symbols representing ACCU-INFO creates a curve that shows where ACCU-INFO is the weakest compared to its competitors and by itself. The trough in the accurate shows that ACCU-INFO is performing poorly in general as well as in comparison with its competitors. This analysis reveals that the new system should put a great deal of emphasis on quality and accuracy of the system.

In the case of the attribute easily accessible, ACCU-INFO is performing poorly, but it is ahead of its competitors. This is an indication of a real need for a new technology

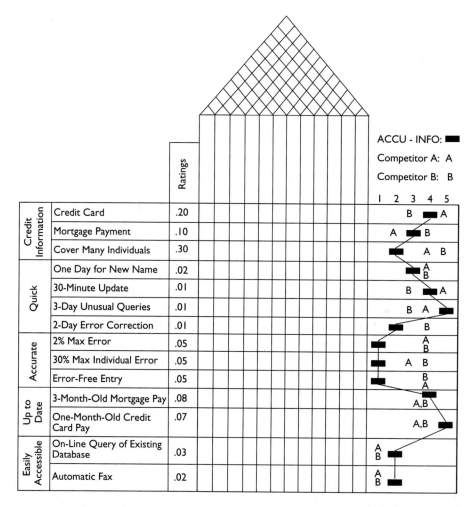

Figure 5.7 The Comparison of ACCU-INFO with its Competitors

or innovative method that would make access easier for customers. This is an indication of a major business opportunity. If ACCU-INFO can find a way to make access to the information system easier, it can create a crucial competitive edge.

However, before making a major commitment to a project for better access, one has to look at the fact that the easily accessible attribute carries only a 5 percent relative weight, while accurate has 15 percent and cover many individuals has a relative weight of 30 percent. While accessibility requires a new technology that may have zealous advocates in the company, the investment in expanding the data resources to have information on more individuals in the database may be far less glamorous and more tedious, but may yield a much higher benefit in customer satisfaction.

The construction of the house of quality takes more than one iteration because there are crucial aspects of the system that customers may take for granted and fail to verbalize. For example, in the case of ACCU-INFO, the data security and confidentiality are of great importance to any credit information system, yet these features are not listed in Figure 5.6. Another round of review and revision or the addition of the deleted features to the system requirements could remedy this defect. Going through another round is a better approach because adding requirements to the system not expressed by customers opens the door for adding features that are not requested by customers. Therefore, any later addition to the list of system requirements should have obvious and undisputable reasons.

In sum, using QFD helps systems planners make choices that will enhance customer satisfaction, and avoid running after glamorous technologies that have little long-term returns. Furthermore, the house of quality documents the major ingredients of systems planning in a formal fashion. This method not only helps the process of planning for the information system starting from the "voice of the customer," but it also provides a knowledge base and documentation for any future review and improvement. We will see in Chapter 6 the continuation of the use of QFD in systems design and implementation.

5.5 ♦ Weight Assignments via Analytic Hierarchy Process (AHP)

In the previous section, we discussed the quality function deployment for requirements analysis. One of the major set of inputs to the house of quality is the ratings of customers' requirements. These ratings are the basis for the computation of all the subsequent ratings of systems, design, and implementation requirements. They dictate the priority rating of improvements of existing systems as well as the amount of attention and resources that should be allocated to different modules of the system. Therefore, it is important to make sure that weight assignments indeed reflect the true preference of customers.

The decision-analysis methods are designed to address the preference elicitation of individuals and groups. One of the important and widely used methods of decision analysis is the analytic hierarchy process (AHP). AHP was first developed by Saaty and has been applied in varied and numerous decision making circumstances [Saaty 1977; Zahedi 1985, 1986a, 1987, 1989, 1990; Zahedi and Ashrafi 1991].

5.5.1 Hierarchy Structure

AHP begins with a hierarchy of decision structure, such as that shown in Figure 5.1. In other words, the hierarchy structure of AHP fits well with customers' requirements for QFD.

The hierarchy starts with the objective of the analysis at the highest level. In this case, customers' requirements analysis is the objective of constructing the hierarchy. The next level contains the general attributes important for customers. The lowest levels break down the attributes into more detail and specific requirements.

In Figure 5.1, the attributes on the third level of the hierarchy are dependent exclusively on one element on the previous level. For example, credit card, mortgage payment, and coverage are dependent only on credit information on the previous level.

There are cases in which the lower level attributes may depend on more than one element on the previous level. AHP is able to address such cases as well.

For example, in the design of the ACCU-INFO information system, one may decide to use AHP in rating various data-resource types in providing data. We take the first branch of Figure 5.1 and expand it to include data resources:

- Banks with national reputation
- Local banks
- Independent mortgage companies
- Mortgage departments of banks
- Card-issuing department stores
- Card-issuing oil companies

It is obvious that all six data resources have something to offer in the three requirements credit card, mortgage payment, and coverage of as many individuals as possible. AHP is capable of dealing with the hierarchy of network structures like that of Figure 5.8. This figure depicts a network connection of the lower elements to the elements on the previous level.

5.5.2   Simple Rating of Attributes Within the Hierarchy

It is difficult to rate the detailed attributes of customers' requirements without a reference to a more general attribute. For example, the customers may have a difficult time determining the rating of error-free entry system in the abstract, with no reference to a more general category of accurate. It would be easier to start with the elements on the highest level of the hierarchy and then move down to the more specific attributes. We demonstrate this in the ACCU-INFO case and Figure 5.1.

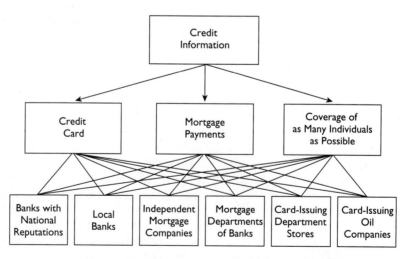

Figure 5.8   An Example of Network Dependency of Elements

Level 1.   To determine the ratings of the 14 attributes on the third level of the hierarchy, we start with the first level, which has only one element: customers' requirements. We are to assign rates at each level such that their sum is 1. For the first level, since there is only one element, its rate will be 1.

Level 2.   Moving to the next level, there are five attributes: credit information, quick, accurate, up-to-date, and easily accessible. There are two ways to assign ratings to these five elements: simple rating and pairwise comparison. We will discuss simple rating here, and the pairwise comparison will be discussed in Subsection 5.5.4.

   With simple rating, we ask the customers to assign a value between zero and one, reflecting the importance of each attribute in satisfying their requirements. The rates assigned should add to 1. For this example, the assigned ratings for the five attributes on the second level of Figure 5.3 are:

$$wq_{1,1} = .60$$
$$wq_{2,1} = .05$$
$$wq_{3,1} = .15$$
$$wq_{4,1} = .15$$
$$wq_{5,1} = .05$$

where wq represents relative weight of the general requirements, indexed by i, 1 identifying the importance of the ith element ($i = 1, 2, \ldots, 5$) in satisfying the parent attribute 1 on the previous level. Since there is only one parent element on the previous level, we have only one set of such ratings for Level 2.

Level 3.   At the third level of the hierarchy, we ask the customers to rate the role of each set of elements in satisfying the requirements at Level 2. For example, we ask the customers to rate the role of credit card, mortgage payment, and coverage in satisfying the credit information requirement. Now customers have a point of reference in rating these three elements. Assume that they give us the following ratings:

$$wd_{1,1} = .33$$
$$wd_{2,1} = .17$$
$$wd_{3,1} = .50$$

where wd is the *local* relative weights of the three detailed requirements for the credit information. The index 1, 1 represents the first attribute credit card and the first attribute on the previous level credit information. In other words, customers believe that covers as many individuals as possible has the relative importance of .50, while the other two take a one-third and two-third share of the remaining points.

   Note that the ratings add to 1 for these three elements. Table 5.1 shows the local relative weights for all elements of Level 3. These relative weights are called local because they are not yet combined with the relative weights of requirements on the previous level. We will show the aggregation process in the next section.

Table 5.1   The Local Relative Weights of Level 3

Weights of Elements Serving				
Credit Info.	Quick	Accurate	Up-to-date	Easy Access
$wd_{1,1} = .33$ $wd_{2,1} = .17$ $wd_{3,1} = .50$	$wd_{4,2} = .40$ $wd_{5,2} = .20$ $wd_{6,2} = .20$ $wd_{7,2} = .20$	$wd_{8,3} = .33$ $wd_{9,3} = .33$ $wd_{10,3} = .34$	$wd_{11,4} = .50$ $wd_{12,4} = .50$	$wd_{13,5} = .50$ $wd_{14,5} = .50$

5.5.3   Computing Global Ratings

The local relative weights of the elements at the third level are easier to attain because they reflect the relative importance of each element at the lower level in satisfying a general requirement at one level higher. However, as shown in Table 5.1, the local relative weights of Level 3 do not add up to 1 and do not contain the relative importance of the elements at Level 2—the general requirements.

We aggregate the relative weights of the two levels by multiplying the local relative weights of elements at Level 3 by the relative weights of their respective parents to get the *global* relative weight of the elements at the lower level.

For example, local relative weights of the three elements credit card (local weight .33), mortgage payment (local weight .17), and cover as many individuals as possible (local weight .50) are multiplied by the relative weight of credit information (relative weight .60) to arrive at the global weights for these three elements as: .20, .10, and .30. Figure 5.3 and Table 5.2 show the global relative weights for the 14 detailed attributes of customer requirements.

The global relative weights of the elements at the third level reflect the relative ratings of detailed customers' requirements and are the input to the first house of quality for system planning, as shown in Figure 5.6.

5.5.4   Pairwise Comparisons (Optional)

In many cases, customers may have difficulty assigning relative weights to elements. The analytical hierarchy method, developed by Saaty [1977], offers the method of pairwise comparison and the *eigenvalue* method for helping customers express their preferences.

In the method of pairwise comparison, the elements of each level are compared pairwise for their role in satisfying one of the elements on one level higher. Take the five

Table 5.2   The Global Relative Weights of Level 3

Weights of Elements Serving				
Credit Info.	Quick	Accurate	Up-to-date	Easy Access
$gw_{1,1} = .20$ $gw_{2,1} = .10$ $gw_{3,1} = .30$	$gw_{4,2} = .02$ $gw_{5,2} = .01$ $gw_{6,2} = .01$ $gw_{7,2} = .01$	$gw_{8,3} = .05$ $gw_{9,3} = .05$ $gw_{10,3} = .05$	$gw_{11,4} = .08$ $gw_{12,4} = .07$	$gw_{13,5} = .03$ $gw_{14,5} = .02$

elements on Level 2 of the hierarchy in Figure 5.3. Customers may have a difficult time assigning relative weights directly to these elements. To help them in their preference elicitation, we can ask them to compare the elements pairwise, asking typical questions such as: "Is credit information equally important as the Quick requirement? If not, is it twice as important? Half as important?" The answers to the pairwise comparisons form a table (or matrix) as shown in (1).

$$
\begin{array}{c}
\begin{array}{ccccc}
\text{credit inf} & \text{quick} & \text{accurate} & \text{up to date} & \text{easy acc}
\end{array}\\
\begin{array}{c}
\text{credit inf}\\ \text{quick}\\ \text{accurate}\\ \text{up to date}\\ \text{easy acc}
\end{array}
\left(
\begin{array}{ccccc}
1 & 9 & 4 & 4 & 9\\
\frac{1}{9} & 1 & \frac{1}{3} & \frac{1}{3} & 1\\
\frac{1}{4} & 3 & 1 & 1 & 1\\
\frac{1}{4} & 3 & 1 & 1 & 3\\
\frac{1}{9} & 1 & \frac{1}{3} & \frac{1}{3} & 1
\end{array}
\right)
\end{array}
\tag{1}
$$

The elements on the lower diagonal are always the inverse of those symmetrically located from the main diagonal. For example, the last element in column 1 is the inverse of the last element in row 1. So we do not need to get the pairwise comparison for the elements of the main diagonal. This is the basis of the eigenvalue method developed by Saaty in 1977.

The eigenvalue method takes the above matrix and computes the local relative weights from the following formula:

$$A = W \cdot \lambda_{max} \tag{2}$$

where A is the matrix of pairwise comparisons, W is the vector (or the list) of estimated local relative weights, and λ_{max} is the greatest eigenvalue of the matrix. There are algorithms which compute W and λ_{max} for any given A.

Note that the user can be inconsistent in expressing pairwise values. For example, in the input matrix (1), credit information is 9 times more important than quick and 4 times more important than accurate. This means that quick should be 4/9 or .44 as important as accurate, but instead we have 1/3 on the second row and third column of the matrix.

When a pairwise matrix is fully consistent, the computation yields λ_{max} equal to the size of the matrix. In the case of matrix (1), the size is 5. The inconsistency of an input matrix could be computed as

$$\text{inconsistency measure} = \frac{\lambda_{max} - n}{n - 1} \tag{3}$$

where n is the size of the matrix (or the number of elements being compared), and λ_{max} is computed from (2).

There is a software product on the market called Expert Choice (Decision Support Software, Pittsburgh, PA) which takes in the pairwise comparisons from the user and produces local and global relative weights for the elements on the hierarchy.

Using Expert Choice for the input matrix (1), we get the relative weights of general requirements (WQ) as:

$$\begin{array}{cccccc} & \text{credit inf} & \text{quick} & \text{accurate} & \text{up to date} & \text{easy acc} \\ WQ = (& .57 & .06 & .16 & .16 & .06 &) \end{array} \qquad (4)$$

and the measure of inconsistency is .003. It is recommended that if this measure goes above .1, the user should try to check the input matrix to reduce the inconsistency. The pairwise comparison helps in identifying the relative weights when the evaluator has difficulty rating the attributes.

We can repeat the same process in the ratings of the elements on the third level. At this level, we will have five input matrices of pairwise comparisons, because the each set of elements at the third level are compared pairwise for their role in satisfying each one of five requirements on the second level.

For example, the first matrix on the third level could be:

$$\begin{array}{c} \\ \text{credit card} \\ \text{mortgage pay} \\ \text{coverage} \end{array} \left(\begin{array}{ccc} \text{credit card} & \text{mortgage pay} & \text{coverage} \\ 1 & 2 & .5 \\ & 1 & 4 \\ & & 1 \end{array} \right) \qquad (5)$$

Using this information in Expert Choice, it will give us the local relative weights (WD) for these three requirements as:

$$\begin{array}{cccc} & \text{credit card} & \text{mortgage pay} & \text{coverage} \\ WD = (& .29 & .14 & .57 &) \end{array} \qquad (6)$$

The local relative weights show the relative importance of the above three attributes in satisfying the credit information requirement.

The global relative weights (WG) of the same requirements are computed by using Expert Choice as:

$$\begin{array}{cccc} & \text{credit card} & \text{mortgage pay} & \text{coverage} \\ WG = (& .16 & .08 & .33 &) \end{array} \qquad (7)$$

We need a matrix of pairwise comparisons for each set of elements below quick, accurate, up-to-date, and easily accessible requirements. A process similar to the above procedure will give us the local and global relative weights of the remaining detailed requirements.

5.5.5   Group Weight Assignments (Optional)

In eliciting customers' requirements, in almost all cases, one is working with a group, rather than an individual. When the group is homogeneous in their "care-abouts," it is relatively easy to arrive at relative weights that reflect all customers' preferences. However, when the customers are heterogeneous in their needs and the relative importance of each need, a formal method of consensus generation would be needed.

There are a number of methods for generating consensus among decision makers [see, for example, Zahedi 1986b]. AHP offers a simple method for group decision [Aczel and Saaty 1983]. In this method, the customer-requirements hierarchy includes all attributes that are deemed important by the group members. Then, we need to have one matrix of pairwise comparison for each individual or homogeneous subgroups who have common interests. To form a group matrix, we compute the geometric mean of the corresponding elements on all matrices generated for the same set of attributes.

For example, assume there are three subgroups of customers with common interests for ACCU-INFO: external users, internal users, and individuals whose credit ratings are determined by the system. To begin with, the customers' requirements hierarchy should include the "care-abouts" of all three subgroups. Let us assume that Figure 5.1 indeed reflects the concern of all customers.

In generating matrices of pairwise comparison, in place of each matrix we will have three matrices—one for each subgroup. For example, instead of matrix (1) in the previous section, we have three such matrices, one for each subgroup. Then the group matrix is formed by multiplying the corresponding elements of the three matrices (say, the three elements on row 2 and column 3) and raising it to the $\frac{1}{3}$ power. This becomes the element on row 2 and column 3 of the group matrix. This process continues until the three subgroup matrices are combined into one group matrix. Once the group pairwise matrix is formed, the rest of the AHP methodology applies to it as before.

5.6 ◆ Software Requirements Analysis

In many instances, the creation of information systems involves either the development of software from scratch or programming using a special-purpose software, such as DBMS, spreadsheets, or expert-systems software products. In all such cases, the software requirements analysis plays a crucial role in the right design of the software in the first try and in avoiding costly and time-consuming revisions at later stages of software production.

Many techniques discussed for the requirements analysis of information systems equally apply to software requirements analysis. Major companies, such as AT&T Bell Laboratories, Digital Equipment Corp. (DEC), Hewlett-Packard, IBM, and Texas Instruments have already undertaken to use QFD in their software development [Zultner 1989, 1990]. The principles of applying QFD in software requirements analysis are the same as those discussed for the information-systems requirements, with the difference that the customers are the software customers and their needs and "care-abouts" are specific to the software project.

Software requirements analysis is an important topic. However, because of the information-system focus of this book, this topic is not discussed here at any depth.

◆ Conclusion

In this chapter, we discussed the stages of requirements analysis for information systems, which include the elicitation, anticipation, verification, and validation of customers' needs. In requirements analysis, it is important to define the purpose of information systems. In quality information systems, the purpose of information systems is directly connected to the vision statement for information systems, which in turn is derived from the company's vision statement.

Quality information systems has customers as its major focus. This focus fits well with the end-user involvement in the development of the traditional information systems, and expands it to include all internal, external, direct, and indirect customers of information systems.

Customer focus requires formal methods. There are a number of methods in requirements analysis that we have divided into concrete and abstract methods and provided a brief review of the major methods in each category.

In quality information systems, we use quality function deployment (QFD) for linking customers' requirements to the components of information systems. The house of quality in QFD enables us to incorporate customers' requirements into systems planning components. In Chapter 6, we see the connection of systems-planning house of quality to those of systems design and implementation.

One of the major quantitative inputs to the house of quality for systems planning is the customers' ratings of the information system's desired attributes. The analytic hierarchy process (AHP) aids the assignment of weights to the desired attributes. AHP involves the development of the attribute hierarchy, ratings process of attributes within the hierarchy, and the computation of the global ratings. AHP involves the pairwise comparisons of elements, facilitates the rating process, and uses the eigenvalue method to compute the final weights. In the case of customer groups with heterogeneous interests, AHP offers a method for group weight assignment that was briefly discussed in this chapter.

Finally, this chapter briefly mentioned the importance of software requirements analysis in developing software or programming the existing software products needed in the development of information systems.

◆ References

1. Aczel, J. and Saaty, T. 1983. "Procedures for Synthesizing Ratio Judgements," *Journal of Mathematical Psychology*, Vol. 27, pp. 93–102.

2. Bossert, James L. 1991. *Quality Function Deployment: A Practitioner's Approach*, ASQC Quality Press, Milwaukee, WI.

3. Brown, Patrick G. 1991. "QFD: Echoing the Voice of the Customer," *AT&T Technical Journal*, Vol. 70, No. 2, March-April, pp. 18–32.

4. Clausing, Don. 1988. "Quality Function Deployment," in *Taguchi Methods and QFD: Hows and Whys for Management*, ASI Press, Dearborn, MI, pp. 63–76.

5. Doll, W. J. and Torkzadeh, G. 1990. "The Measurement of End-User Software Involvement," *Omega: International Journal of Management Science*, Vol. 18, No. 4, pp. 399–406.

6. Eureka, William E. and Ryan, Nancy E. 1988. "QFD and You," *Taguchi Methods and QFD: Hows and Whys for Management*, ASI Press, Dearborn, MI, pp. 67–87.

7. Gutierrez, Oscar. 1989. "Experimental Techniques for Information Requirements Analysis," *Information and Management*, Vol. 16, pp. 31–43.

8. Hauser, John R. and Don Clausing. 1988. "The House of Quality," *Harvard Business Review*, Vol. 66, No. 3, May-June, pp. 63–73.

9. Modha, J., Gwinnett, A., and Bruce, M. 1990. "A Review of Information Systems Development Methodology (ISDM) Selection Techniques," *Omega: International Journal of Management Science*, Vol. 18, No. 5, pp. 473–490.

10. Saaty, Thomas L. 1977. "A Scaling Method for Priorities in Hierarchical Structures," *Journal of Mathematical Psychology*, Vol. 15, No. 2, pp. 234–281.

11. Saaty, Thomas L. 1990. *Decision Making for Leaders*, RWS Publications, Pittsburgh, PA.

12. Zahedi, F. 1985. "Database Management Systems Evaluation and Selection Decisions," *Decision Sciences*, Vol. 16, No. 1, Winter, pp. 91–116.

13. Zahedi, F. 1986a. "The Analytic Hierarchy Process—A Survey of the Method and its Applications," *Interfaces*, Vol. 16, No. 4, pp. 96–108.

14. Zahedi, F. 1986b. "Group Consensus Function Estimation When Preferences are Uncertain." *Operations Research*, Vol. 34, No. 6, November–December, pp. 883–894.

15. Zahedi, F. 1987. "Qualitative Programming for Selection Decisions," *Computers and Operations Research*, Vol. 14, No. 5, pp. 395–407.

16. Zahedi, F. 1989. "Quantitative Evaluation of Micro vs. Larger Database Products," *Computers and Operations Research*, Vol. 16, No. 6, pp. 513–532.

17. Zahedi, F. 1990. "A Method for the Quantitative Evaluation of Expert Systems," *European Journal of Operational Research*, Vol. 48, No. 1, September, pp. 136–147.

18. Zahedi, F. and Ashrafi, N. 1991. "Software Reliability Allocation Based on Structure, Utility, Price, and Cost," *IEEE Transactions on Software Engineering*, Vol. 17, No. 4, April, pp. 345–356.

19. Zultner, Richard E. 1989. "Software Quality Engineering: The Deming Way," *American Programmer*, Vol. 2, June, pp. 13–24.

20. Zultner, Richard E. 1990. "Software Quality Deployment: Applying QFD to Software," *2nd Symposium on QFD Transactions*, ASQC and GOAL/QPC, Novi, MI. pp. 132–149.

◆ Questions

5.1. Discuss stages involved in requirements analysis.

5.2. What is the importance of elicitation, anticipation, verification, and validation of needs in requirements analysis?

5.3. What is the importance of identifying the purpose of information systems?

5.4. What are the major determinants in defining the purpose of an information system?

5.5. What are the factors affecting the complexity of an information system?

5.6. Discuss the differences between the end-user involvement and customer focus in information systems.

5.7. Discuss the types of end-users and their impacts on the creation of the system.

5.8. Discuss the types of information-systems customers and their role the defining the nature of an information system.

5.9. List the major types of requirements analysis methods.

5.10. What are the differences between the concrete and abstract methods in require-ments analysis?

5.11. List and contrast the concrete methods.

5.12. List and contrast the abstract methods.

5.13. What is QFD?

5.14. What is the requirements hierarchy?

5.15. Discuss the general structure of QFD.

5.16. Draw a typical house of quality for systems planning with QFD.

5.17. What are on the borders of the house of quality?

5.18. What is the importance of comparing the customer-stated attributes of the existing information system with those of the competing systems?

5.19. What is the role of AHP in customers' requirements analysis?

5.20. What is the hierarchy of customers' requirements?

5.21. Describe the ratings process in AHP.

5.22. What is a pairwise comparison matrix in AHP?

5.23. What is the difference between the local and global relative weights?

5.24. What is the output of AHP in requirements analysis and what is its use?

5.25. What is the inconsistency measure in AHP?

5.26. Discuss the importance of software requirements analysis.

◆ Problems

5.1. Assume that the five attributes credit information, quick, accurate, up-to-date, and easily accessible in Figure 5.3 have relative ratings of .40, .15, .20, .20, and .05. Recompute the ratings of the 14 elements on the third level of the hierarchy.

5.2. What is the consequence of the changes in the previous question in the house of quality in Figure 5.6?

5.3. Use your own preference to come up with the remaining pairwise comparison matrices in the example of Section 5.5.4.

5.4. Develop the customers' requirements hierarchy for an airline-reservation informa-tion system.

5.5. Develop the customers' requirements hierarchy for the intelligent-user interface component of ACCU-INFO's information systems.

5.6. Develop ratings for the second level of the hierarchy in the above question and discuss the local and global ratings in the context of this problem.

◆ CASE: QFD in Action

Before you can build a product that delights your customers, you have to know what it is they want. "The first step in any quality improvement program is to understand the voice of customer," says Robert L. Klein, president of Applied Marketing Science Inc. in Waltham, Mass. "Building things right is only part of the battle. Building the right things is just as important, and only the customer can tell you that."

Quality function deployment (QFD) can help in the search for the optimum product, but QFD findings are only as good as the market research on which they are based. As a result, QFD is driving a new approach to market research. "Before QFD the object was to reduce customer input into a few key thoughts that could be used for an ad campaign or to position a product," says Klein. "But an engineer needs more guidance than that to really understand the customer."

Just ask Ford Motor Co. During initial research for the Taurus product line in the early 1980s, market research showed that drivers wanted fuel-injected engines, but QFD studies done later revealed that drivers really meant they wanted more powerful engines. Or ask BEN Communications Corp., a communications manufacturer in Cambridge, Mass. When the company sent its engineers out to both existing and potential customers in preparation for QFD on an upcoming product late last year, they found to their surprise that a key component of "ease of use" was having ports on both the front and the back of the unit.

Given the very real chance of misinterpretation, many QFD users try to identify over 100 customers care-abouts, rather than the 20 or 30 concerns typical of traditional research campaigns. "Customers don't always know exactly what they want, so they can't give you a recipe for success themselves," says Gary Podwalny, a Hewlett-Packard Co. Industrial design engineer in Corvallis, Ore., who worked HP's recently unveiled 11-ounce palmtop PC. "They may want a product to have 'enough memory,' but the software engineer still has to figure what that means in terms of RAM."

To get this kind of detailed knowledge, QFD practitioners are increasingly relying on face-to-face contact such as focus groups, informal visits, periodic phone surveys, and one-to-one interviews—especially between engineers and customers. The goal should always be to capture the customer's intent; some consultants suggest that interviews be taped, so that exact customer quotes appear on the QFD matrix rather than engineers' translations. Digital Equipment Corp. goes so far as to invite customers to help fill the QFD chart.

This new wave in market research emphasizes qualitative input over sheer numbers. For example, when Charles Scott, president of Westford, Mass.-based Whistler Corp., wanted to find out what was wrong with a poor-selling remote-controlled dock light, he opted to go straight to the customer: He sent waves of engineers, marketers, and salesmen to marinas up and down the East Coast to isolate the reason for the poor sales. The result was a new view of customer care-abouts. Rather than low price, customers were willing to pay for a product that offered longer battery life and was easy to see from far away.

The key, says MIT professor and QFD expert Don Clausing, is to "find the reasons why customers want what they say they want." QFD makes you ask, like an inquisitive two-year-old, "Why, why, why, why?" And while you run the risk of annoying some customers, many of the most mature electronics companies are finding QFD an effective way to get inside the head of the customer.

Source: "The First Step Toward Total Quality," Peter Burrows, *Electronic Business*, Vol. 17, No. 12, July 17, 1991, p. 73, reprint with permission from *Electronic Business Buyer*, copyright 1991, Reed Elsevier Inc.

Case Questions

1. Discuss the points made in this case regarding the application of QFD in real-world applications.
2. Connect points made in this case to the discussion of the validation and verification of customers' needs.
3. What are the similarities and differences between marketing research and information systems requirements analysis?
4. What is the danger of misinterpreting customers' needs, and what are ways to prevent such misinterpretations?

◆ CASE: Shortcomings of QFD

The U.S. electronics industry has a dubious but time-honored tradition of making technologically excellent products that bomb simply because customers don't need them—Xerox's first-generation, $22,000 PC, for example, or IBM's heavy-handed first attempt at a laptop. The reason: product design has long been dominated by product designers, not by customers. "Our company's biggest problem has been that we spend lots of money on talented engineering to make not-quite-right products," says Robert Anderson, president and CEO of test-equipment maker GenRad Inc. in Concord, Mass.

That's why GenRad and many of the biggest names in electronics are working with a powerful management tool called quality function deployment (QFD) to put the drawing board back into the customer's hands. Digital Equipment Corp., Hewlett-Packard Co., IBM, Intel Corp., and Texas Instrument Inc., have all announced or plan to announce products developed using this technique. QFD makes extensive use of matrices to translate "customer care-abouts," gleaned through rigorous market research, into products that most nearly fulfill customers' wish lists.

Here's how it works. A matrix is drawn on a large piece of paper that is mounted on a wall. A cross-functional team from throughout the product-development organization is assembled, including representatives from R&D, hardware and software engineering, manufacturing, quality assurance, marketing, sales, service, and others as deemed appropriate. The matrix is then labeled: Customer care-abouts (performance, appearance, or reliability, for example) are listed down the left side of the matrix in order of customer priority. Technical requirements (such as amount of memory or number of parts) are listed along the top of the matrix. Competing products are listed along the right side for comparative analysis.

The team begins with structured brainstorming and then fills in the cells of the matrix, applying a weighted value to each cell. The relationship between "reliability" and "self-checking software," for example, might warrant a 9 on a 10-point scale, while the relationship between "ease of use" and "self-checking software" might get only a 1. If market research shows that reliability is the number-one priority, engineers know they have to find a way to include self-checking software in the product. Once all the cells have been completed in this manner, engineers have a road map by which to make the necessary trade-offs related to cost, time to market, and resource allocation.

In essence, QFD can help companies make the key trade-offs between what the customer wants and what the company can afford to build. "QFD does nothing that people didn't do before, but it replaces erratic, intuitive decision-making processes with a structured methodology that puts things down on paper," says Dan Walsh, a marketing manager with GenRad. "It helps you make sense of it all so that everyone is working in the same direction."

Sound easy? It isn't. Many a company (including DEC) have ended up with 100-by-100 matrices—that's 10,000 cells to fill in—wasting months of precious time. Team members get caught up in the details of the exercise while the market window closes on them. As a result, many companies—especially younger ones with roots in the more customer-oriented 1980s—are highly skeptical of the formality and intense attention to detail required by QFD. "It all depends on where you are in terms of corporate culture," says Larry Abernathy, vice president of quality for Convex Computer Corp. in Dallas. "We started out with a focus on the customer, so we don't feel we have to be quite so formalized."

When properly done, QFD can raise a company's product batting average by weeding out misguided concepts before they enter the development pipeline. In other words, it replaces the "voice of engineer" with the "voice of customer," according to consultant Michael T. Anthony with Pittiglio Rabin Todd & McGrath in Weston, Mass. He tells the story of one company who took two years to add eight functions to a statistical multiplexer without going to the customer to find out if the added functionality was wanted. By the time the product was released, another company had introduced a cheaper, more focused product with fewer bells and whistles. The company scrapped its project after spending millions on its development.

"Companies almost always put in too much functionality," says Anthony. "It seems that engineers don't understand that customers don't get as fired up about features as they do, and what QFD is all about—finding out what the customer is willing to pay for."

Despite horror stories of frustrating, time-wasting days in front of wall-size QFD matrices, many lessons have been learned since U.S. companies began experimenting with QFD in the mid-1980s:

- Assume a time limit of about three months for each QFD exercise
- Keep teams ideally between 5 and 8 members, and always less than 10
- Limit the number of elements in each matrix to less than 50-by-50
- Use the customer's exact words. Translations or paraphrases can end up mimicking the engineer more than the customer
- Stick to paper. While QFD software programs exist, many experts say that working with pencil and paper encourages interaction and helps build consensus and team understanding
- Start off slow, on a subsystem or on an upgrade rather than on a brand-new product. Experience is the best teacher here
- Appoint a "facilitator"—normally a nontechnical staffer with strong interpersonal skills and a clear understanding of the process—to shepherd the team
- Don't expect miracles. Research shows that only about 20% of QFD users realize identifiable short-term advantages in the marketplace, but over 80% get strategic benefits such as increased understanding of the customer, increased communication and shared vocabulary among divisions, fewer downstream engineering changes, and faster decision-making

And QFD can also help morale. "Even engineers like to know that they are building products that people want to buy," says Bob Hinden, a core-team leader and engineer at BBN Communications Corp. in Cambridge, Mass. The key thing to remember, experts say, is to have the courage to customize. "QFD is not about completing charts," says K. J. McAllister, a facilitator with HP's division in Corvallis, Ore. "You have to make it fit your needs."

Indeed, QFD consultants are offering a wide range of versions. PRTM hawks what it calls S-QFD (simplified QFD), which focuses more on honing projects already in the pipeline and less on start-from-scratch concept design. The American Supplier Institute in Dearborn, Mich., a Ford spin-off that introduced QFD to Ford and the nation in the early 1980s, offers a four-phase system that helps make trade-offs throughout the development cycle. GOAL/QPC in Methuen, Mass., suggests a system of 32 interwoven matrices to improve decision-making throughout a company. "Capturing the voice of the customer is an important piece of it," according to Bob King, executive director of GOAL/QPC. "But the real value of QFD extends far beyond that." For example, it can be used to determine the optimum benefits package, the best strategy to satisfy government regulators, or even the best food service.

Unfortunately, U.S. practitioners have not closed the gap with their Japanese competitors, many of whom have a twenty-year lead in QFD use. The technique was invented in Japan in the mid-1970s and has become so ingrained in some companies that it is no longer thought of as a separate way of doing things. "Many companies over there would look at you funny if you asked them about QFD because they are no longer aware they use it," says Lawrence Sullivan, chairman of ASI. "At Toyota, for example, they've developed such heightened communications skills that they no longer even have to write all the stuff down on a chart."

But this level of expertise cannot be rushed. Take it slow, do it right, but don't forget that you still have a product to build, say the experts. "It's worse to oversell this than to give people a realistic view of what it can do," according to Doug Daetz, a QFD veteran with HP's corporate quality department in Palo Alto. "If it backfires—as it has—you can end up killing off something that could have been a great product, because a bunch of people got bogged down."

Source: "In Search of the Perfect Product," Peter Burrows, *Electronic Business*, Vol. 17, No. 12, June 17, 1991, pp. 70–74, reprint with permission from *Electronic Business Buyer*, copyright 1991, Reed Elsevier Inc.

Case Questions

1. Discuss the problems that may arise in the improper use of QFD in information-systems requirements analysis.
2. Discuss the validity of the recommendations made in this case for the appropriate use of QFD in information systems.
3. What are the differences between the application of QFD in Japan and in the United States?

The mechanics of running a business are not really very complicated when you get down to essentials. You have to make some stuff and sell it to somebody for more than it cost you. That's about all there is to it, except for a few million details.

—John L. McCaffrey

Don't buy a £10,000 solid gold sledgehammer to drive in a two-cent thumb tack.

—John Bear, *Computer Wimp*, 1983

◆ Chapter Objectives

The objectives of this chapter are:
- To provide a foundation for designing quality information systems
- To introduce the concept of reengineering and the role of information systems in the reengineering process
- To show the importance of concurrent engineering in information systems
- To introduce parallel design in the design of information systems
- To show the application of quality function deployment (QFD) in information systems
- To discuss the important role of engineering usability in information systems
- To apply the Taguchi methods in information systems
- To discuss the loss function and robust design for information systems

◆ Key Words

reengineering, concurrent engineering, parallel design, quality function deployment, usability engineering, usability assessment, the Taguchi methods in information systems, system robustness, loss function.

Quality Management in the Design of IS

6.1 Designing Value into IS Through Reengineering
    6.1.1 Characteristics of Reengineering
    6.1.2 Process Design in Reengineering
    6.1.3 Concurrent Engineering
    6.1.4 Parallel Design

6.2 Designing Utility in IS by Applying QFD
    6.2.1 Technical Requirements
    6.2.2 Subsystems
    6.2.3 Interrelationships
    6.2.4 Components

6.3 Engineering Usability into IS
    6.3.1 Usability Criteria
    6.3.2 The Technology of User Interface
    6.3.3 Methods of Assessing Usability

6.4 Reducing Cost by Applying Taguchi Methods
    6.4.1 The Taguchi Loss Function for Information Systems
    6.4.2 The Taguchi Measure of Quality
    6.4.3 Robust Design in Taguchi Methods

◆ Introduction

This chapter deals with designing quality information systems. The focus in such designs is how to design quality into the system.

The quality of design (and the quality of information systems for that matter) depends on the acceptance of the system by the direct and indirect customers (Figure 6.1). Direct customers are those who are directly affected by the system, including the direct users. Indirect customers are those in the general public who have an interest in the system, are affected by it, and whose views are important to the successful use of the system.

The acceptance of the system by the system's direct customers depends on a number of system characteristics (Figure 6.1):

- Value
- Use
- Cost
- Reliability

The use of the system could be divided into its utility and usability. We define the *utility* of the system as the satisfaction and the perceived benefits derived from using the system. The system *usability*, on the other hand, refers to the extent to which the system interface serves the users' needs and wishes.

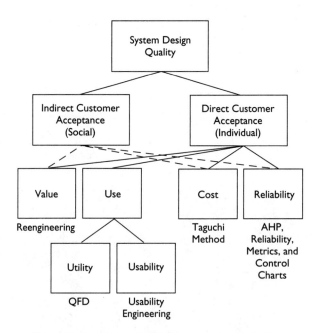

Figure 6.1   Components of Systems Design Quality

The system *integrity* is a component of its usability. A system with integrity performs as designed, within its existing specifications and standards. The system integrity becomes an important characteristic when hiring outside experts as there is often an integrity gap between what they propose to deliver and what is actually delivered. This could be a greater problem when a separate marketing division promotes the information-system services.

This chapter discusses the quality methods that we can apply in designing information systems. These methods help in incorporating quality into the system, hence increasing its acceptability. Here we cover the four areas identified in Figure 6.1, except for reliability, which is discussed in Chapter 7.

The first section of this chapter (Section 6.1) shows how the application of reengineering concepts can improve the value of information systems within an organization. This section discusses the characteristics of reengineering and process design in reengineering and their application in information systems. The concept of concurrent engineering and parallel engineering are of importance to the design process of information systems.

The second section (Section 6.2) discusses the use of quality function deployment (QFD) in designing utility and integrity into the system. This section continues with the requirements analysis discussed in Chapter 5 and connects customers' needs and wants directly to the design of the technical components of the system. This section takes customers' requirements and translates them into technical requirements and technical components of the system. The subsystems and interrelationships of the subsystems are also covered in this section.

The third section (Section 6.3) demonstrates how to enhance system usability via usability engineering. In this section, we discuss the criteria for usability, the evolution of the user-interface technologies, methods for assessing usability and, finally, the usability standards.

The fourth section (Section 6.4) uses the Taguchi methods for dealing with the long-term cost characteristic of information systems. In this section, we discuss the Taguchi loss function in information systems, the Taguchi measure of quality, and the concept of designing robustness into information systems.

6.1 ◆ Designing Value into IS Through Reengineering

In dealing with the changing environment, many large and successful corporations have taken a revolutionary approach to organizational and functional design that Hammer and Champy have called *reengineering* the corporation. In the book with the same title, *Reengineering the Corporation* [1993], they define reengineering as:

> *The fundamental rethinking and radical redesign of business processes to achieve dramatic improvements in critical, contemporary measures of performance, such as cost, quality, service, and speed.*

In such undertakings, information systems play a critical role in implementing the innovative and creative approaches in business processes. Successful reengineering of organizations requires a dynamic and proactive information-systems function that aids the reengineering of the organization in order to keep its services of value to its users. The information system itself should also be reengineered to keep its services of value to customers.

In other words, information systems get involved with reengineering at two levels:

- At the corporate level
- At the functional level

At the corporate level, information systems play the role of broker, in that almost all creative ways of redesigning business processes require an innovative way of using information systems. For example, getting rid of inventory and having a just-in-time system in which the supplier delivers parts as needed is not possible without an information system that links the buyer's production schedule to the supplier's production-information system.

At the functional level, the information-systems function has to look at its own processes and operations to find out the innovative ways of delivering services to its users. For example, while there is no policy of just-in-time at the corporate level, the reengineering of the information system and improved delivery of its services may lead to a substantial reduction in the corporation's inventory investment.

Corporate-level reengineering has a *top-down* policy implication—there is a general design of the business processes at the top, and the information system is designed to fit within that business-process design. On the other hand, function-level reengineering is a *bottom-up* process in that the information-system function comes up with innovative methods of service delivery that would add value to the corporation, and has the potential to become an impetus for reengineering business processes.

In most cases, a successful reengineering process requires both top-down and bottom-up approaches. It could be that what starts as a bottom-up proposal by an information-system group ends up triggering a top-down reengineering process, and vice versa. The most important point is that the IS group should be a proactive participant in the reengineering efforts.

6.1.1   Characteristics of Reengineering

Hammer and Champy have observed some common features among all major corporations that have undertaken reengineering. They have found that reengineering is:

- Focused on process
- Sweeping and extensive
- Rule-breaking
- Reliant on the innovative use of information systems

Process Focus.   Reengineering in these corporations focuses on processes, and questions the underlying assumptions on which the existing processes are built. Compared to continuous improvement, reengineering does not lead to partial or gradual improvement. It creates a radically different and innovative way of looking at a function or process.

In our example of ACCU-INFO, one can look at the design of the information system within the context of a wider design change of providing information services to customers. In this reengineering process, the focus is on taking a hard and searching look at the entire process of selling credit information and the beliefs and assumptions under which the business operates. The following are the operating assumptions:

- There is one information system for each type of information needs: one for credit ratings, one for individual inquiries about credit ratings, one for risk analysis for mortgage insurance, and so forth.
- Each information system has its own customers and accounts.
- Each information system has its own data-entry and systems-maintenance group.
- There is a legal, financial, and operational wall between the corporation and its data suppliers that makes any data communications possible only through written reports or mail-delivered computer tapes.

A continuous-improvement approach keeps the existing norms and attempts to make improvements in each of the systems. In contrast, a reengineering approach would question the validity of these assumptions and ask:

- Why should we have one information system for each type of information?
- Do we gain more customer satisfaction, efficiency, productivity, and savings by combining these systems into one?
- Do we gain by combining the data-entry and system-maintenance groups into one?
- Is there an alternative way of setting up the data-entry and maintenance groups? For example, rather than waiting for the data suppliers to send us their data, can we directly access their records and automatically transfer the data as soon as it gets generated to our files, thus eliminating most of data-entry requirements?

In other words, the redesign of the information is not limited to just the computerized systems, but also the entire function within which the information system operates.

Sweeping Change.   The design of the new process is normally sweeping and revolutionary, and involves an entire function in its general framework, rather than a unit or small department.

In the ACCU-INFO case, the design would involve changing the way information services are being offered to customers, not just the design of the credit-rating information system. It involves a fresh look at the interaction with the suppliers and customers. Do the customers get all they need, when they need it? Is there a dramatically different method of service delivery that would serve their needs better?

Rule-breaking.   Reengineering requires breaking the well-accepted rules and turning the system inside out. For example, one of the assumptions is the concept of inventory and its related inventory information systems. In a continuous improvement approach, we try to develop a better inventory system that reduces waste and cost while satisfying the customers' needs.

In reengineering the process of moving goods from the supplier to the customer, we may question the whole concept of inventory and ask if we can rely on suppliers to make sure that we get goods or services on time to our customers. This turns the concept of inventory information system into supplier-customer link up, and would demand a new way of looking at the design of inventory systems. We will see more on this concept in the discussion of "just-in-time" in Chapter 7.

Reliance on the Innovative Use of Information Systems.   The successful reengineering cases that Hammer and Champy investigated involved innovative use of information systems in their reengineering undertakings. In other words, innovative information-systems design is an integral part of any reengineering project at present. This puts information systems in the forefront of any major changes in the corporation, and demands innovation and creative thinking in the design of the system to accommodate the reengineering requirements.

In the ACCU-INFO example, the reengineering task force has noticed the substantial paperwork generated by the correspondence related to individuals' information requests for their own credit rating and their complaints regarding the inaccuracy of their credit history or rating. A great deal of time is spent tracking down the correspondence and responding to people's telephone messages or subsequent followups.

Part of the new design will require the credit information system to have data about where each piece of paper is. This requires the information-system design team to take a creative look at the way the system should be designed to accommodate this need. Part of this creative thinking could be an innovative imitation of other industries' information systems. For example, one of the industries that traces papers most efficiently is overnight package delivery, which includes companies such as UPS and Federal Express. Benchmarking the leaders of the industry can give ACCU-INFO innovative ideas on how to develop a computerized trace on the paperwork of individuals' inquiries about their credit ratings.

Another innovative approach could be the complete elimination of paperwork by entering queries into the system at the origin, such a receipt of a letter or telephone message. One could then trace the query in the computer, rather than by a paper trail. In this approach, ACCU-INFO may investigate how other industries handle customer requests, such as mail-order queries. In yet another approach, the individual may be given access to a portion of a credit-information system that contains input data for rating the customers' credit. Such an approach would eliminate the paperwork completely, but would require safety features to protect the system from abuse.

6.1.2   Process Design in Reengineering

Hammer and Champy, in their analysis of corporations that undertake reengineering, have observed that there are common features in reengineering processes. They include:

- Combining jobs
- Empowering employees as decision makers
- Multitrack process
- Natural and common sense development and placement of the work
- Reducing costly controls and checks
- Reducing the number of external-contact points
- One point of contact through case manager
- Using a combination of centralized and decentralized structure

Combining Jobs.   In the reengineered processes, many jobs are combined into one. Combining jobs allows one employee to do more than one job, increases the responsibility of the employee, and reduces the tedium of doing a small task repeatedly.

Empowering Employees as Decision Makers.   Employees have more responsibility for making decisions and less supervision, and are responsible for their actions. The concept of empowerment discussed in Chapter 2 should be practiced in the reengineered process.

Multitrack Process.   One of the most interesting aspects of a reengineered process is its multitrack feature. Hammer and Champy observe that many complexities of the existing processes exist because they are designed to accommodate all contingencies in one track. While in 80 percent of cases, the process is simple and straightforward, the inclusion of the other 20 percent makes the process complex and cumbersome for everybody.

In a multitrack process, there is a simple track for the simple cases and other tracks for more complicated cases, hence simplifying the job for 80 percent of the customers. Those customers who have complex problems are cognizant of the complexity of their cases and are willing to wait longer. Multitrack processes make it possible to have a more accurate and less variable estimate of the time it takes to respond to a customer request. Customers would like to have this knowledge in almost all cases.

For example, in the ACCU-INFO case, the design should involve multiple tracks, depending on the type of credit information the customer requests. If it is a straightforward credit rating of an individual in the database, the system should be able to respond automatically and quickly. If the credit request is for an individual for whom little data is available or has an interrupted credit history, then there is a need for additional analysis before an answer can be provided. The design must have a separate track for taking care of such requests. This approach makes the design for the simple cases easy and fast, while a separate track is designed for complicated cases.

Natural and Common Sense Development and Placement of the Work.   Hammer and Champy report that in reengineered processes, the development of the process follows a common sense approach and the work is placed where it is most natural. For example, in the ACCU-INFO case, one may place the data entry as close to the data suppliers as possible, so that resolution of data can take place quickly. This method of thinking may lead to innovative ideas such as sending the data-entry persons to the source of data, having the data suppliers enter the data directly into the system, or asking the data suppliers to redesign their system such that as soon as credit-related data is updated, the system sends it to the ACCU-INFO system.

Reducing Costly Controls and Checks.   There is a sacred axiom in business stating that we should eliminate abuse by establishing strict control. The strict enforcement of controls is a costly operation. Upon investigation and data collection, corporations have discovered that they spend many orders of magnitude to control small amounts of abuse. In other words, the cost of enforcing this axiom far surpasses its possible benefit.

In establishing checks and controls, one must analyze the direct and indirect cost of operationalizing a belief. For example, the strict enforcement of abuse minimization involves direct costs such as wages for supervisors and controllers, and indirect costs due to delays and dissatisfaction. If the cost of control is well above the value of the asset being protected, then this axiom does not add value to the system and must be modified to fit the circumstances. The reduction of control in reengineered processes involves shifting responsibility to employees, and making aggregate and minimum checks. This change means that a small degree of abuse may occur, but its costs would be much lower than the absolute control. Therefore, the rule of *minimization of abuse* is replaced by *optimum control*, with the objective of minimizing the total system life cost.

Reducing the Number of External-Contact Points.   Another feature of reengineered processes is the reduction of external-contact points and thus the reduction of the need for reconciliation. For example, ACCU-INFO sends out requests for data about an individual. Once it receives the data, it has to check against the request to make sure that the data is for the same person as requested, enter the data, and then pay the supplier for the information. Here there are three points of contact with the supplier of data: request for information, checking against what was requested, and payment. Each external-contact point, according to Hammer and Champy, adds overhead to the system because of the need to check and reconcile discrepancies.

The goal of reducing the contact points may lead to the proposition that the data supplier should have direct access to ACCU-INFO's database. Once the name and other identifying data are entered into ACCU-INFO's database, the system automatically generates a message asking for information from the data suppliers. The supplier who has the data enters it into the system, while an intelligent component of the system makes sure that the I.D. of the supplier and individual match those in the system in order to ensure that the right person is entering the right information about the right individual. The system automatically credits the supplier for the data entered into the system.

If a second supplier attempts to enter redundant data, the system accepts it as a confirmation and credits the second supplier. If the second supplier enters conflicting data, then the system issues a warning to both suppliers about the discrepancy and asks them to resolve the conflict and re-enter the data, while keeping a log of all the transactions.

This way, there is little need for reconciliation by ACCU-INFO, except in cases where the suppliers are unable to resolve their differences. In this case, an expert investigator at ACCU-INFO gets involved to resolve the problem and come up with a decision. This approach reduces the number of external-contact points to a minimum, hence reducing the need for checks and reconciliations.

One Point of Contact Through Case Manager.   Another method of reducing the number of contact points is to assign case managers to handle a problem from beginning to end. For example, in the ACCU-INFO case, the individual who has complaints about his or her credit rating may contact the customer service department. Based on the nature of the complaint, he or she may be directed to the data-entry supervisor, a credit investigator, or the suppliers who have provided data on the individual. Upon the subsequent followup by the complainant, a paper chase ensues to determine the status of the investigation. The complainant may be bounced from one department to another in the pursuit of his or her complaint.

Assigning a case manager to a complaint reduces the contact point to one person, and that one person is responsible for providing a satisfactory answer to the complainant.

Using a Combination of Centralized and Decentralized Structure.   Hammer and Champy also found that the corporations with reengineered processes use a combination of centralized and decentralized structure to handle the need for local autonomy and the enforcement of central standards and controls. Again, this has been possible with the innovative use of technology, such as a network of local or portable computers connected to a centralized system. The local or portable computer gives autonomy and mobility to satisfy the need for decentralization, while the central system enforces uniform standards and control over a wide range of decentralized units.

Hammer and Champy describe the case of a major company that wanted to decentralize its purchasing process, in order to give its regional offices the authority to make their own purchase decisions, but still keep the substantial discounts that the company would receive from bulk purchase. To address this dilemma, the company created a central database for various parts and negotiated contracts with approved suppliers based on forecasts from various regions. The regional units could place their orders by using the information from the central database, and receive the parts directly from the supplier.

In the ACCU-INFO case, giving the data suppliers the power to enter the data directly into the system is a form of decentralization, while the central system enforces uniform standards and policies.

6.1.3   Concurrent Engineering

Concurrent engineering is one of the approaches for changing the way a system is designed. The idea of concurrent engineering was used in the early developments of car design [Jo, Parsaei, and Sullivan 1993, p. 5]. The modern specialization in design of various components of products and systems has led to the increase in the probability of poor overall designs.

Concurrent engineering in its recent revival has its origin in the Advanced Project Group at Lockheed, known as the "Skunkworks," in early 1960s. This idea was implemented in the development of the SR-71 Blackbird project [Wong et al., 1991].

In 1988, the Defense Advance Research Projects Agency (DARPA) launched a program called DARPA Initiative in Concurrent Engineering (DICE) in cooperation with a consortium of a dozen manufacturers, software companies, and universities. By 1991, about $60 million was spent on developing enabling technologies for concurrent engineering. The overall goal of the project is to develop an architecture for concurrent engineering in which various team members can communicate, share, and access information. This technology is developed in conjunction with a number of pilot concurrent engineering projects. West Virginia University has established the Concurrent Engineering Research Center in conjunction with DICE. General Electric Aircraft Engines and Westinghouse Electronic Systems Groups have been among those who implemented concurrent engineering in their pilot product development projects [Ashley 1992; Reddy et.al. 1991]. The Skunkworks' approach was to rely on teamwork and concurrent design in manufacturing.

◆ CASE: Benefits of Concurrent Engineering

The Institute for Defense Analysis conducted an investigation to assess the claims of improved competitiveness in the commercial industrial base resulting from the use of concurrent engineering. The results indicated that increased functionality, better quality, lower costs, and decreased deployment time were obtained for both high- and low-production runs, for example components as well as complex systems, and for military as well as commercial products. Some of the more notable reported benefits were:

- Manufacturing cost reductions by as much as 30 to 42 percent
- Improved design quality that resulted in engineering change-order reductions of greater than 50 percent
- Scrap and rework reduced by 75 percent
- Product development time reduced by 35 to 60 percent
- Defects reduced by 30 to 87 percent
- Savings of 30 to 60 percent below bid

Some of the specific benefits certain companies attribute to concurrent engineering are as follows: Boeing reduced the number of engineering changes per drawing from 15–20 changes to one change and reduced the floor inspection ratio from one hour per 15 hours of direct labor to one hour per 50 hours of direct labor. Design analysis changes that took 2 weeks to evaluate can now be done in less than an hour. Mcdonnell Douglas reduced its life-cycle cost by 60 percent and had a 40 percent product cost savings on a short-range missile program. Deere and Company reduced its development time for new products by 60 percent and had a 30 percent reduction in development cost. At Hewlett-Packard, the field failure rate decreased 83 percent; productivity improvements of 300 percent have been reported; manufacturing cycle times have been cut up to 95 percent; and product development times have been reduced by up to 35 percent. Other companies, such as Ford, IBM, AT&T, ITT, Northrop, and Aerojet Ordinance have made claims about improvements by concurrent engineering.

Source: Excerpt from "Cost Modeling for Concurrent Engineering," Robert C. Creese and L. Ted Moore, *Cost Engineering*, Vol. 32, No. 6 June, 1990, pp. 23–27, reprinted with permission from *Cost Engineering*.

Design has been an important step in the development of information systems. Concurrent engineering emphasizes an active role for programmers and system users in the design of information systems. In other words, the design team includes system developers, as well as representatives from those who are to manage and maintain the system.

Furthermore, concurrent engineering brings into focus a number of important design issues. Although most of these issues are not novel to information-systems design, they receive a more critical place in the design phase. There are a number of design objectives that should be addressed in the design [Jo, Parsaei, and Sullivan 1993]:

- Simultaneous process planning
- Design for manufacturability
- Design for assembly
- Design for maintainability
- Design for reliability
- Design for engineering analysis
- Cost estimation

Simultaneous Process Planning.   Simultaneous process planning requires that the design include processes involved in the operational information system. In other words, when the information system becomes operational, its day-to-day operation requires a number of processes. These operational processes should be developed during the design phase.

For example, in the ACCU-INFO system, the system design should contain processes for:

- When the system goes down
- When the network fails
- When a segment of the system should be changed
- How the system should be maintained
- How to respond to customer complaints
- How to update, check, and protect the system

The active involvement of those involved in running and maintaining the implemented system and their participation in the process planning facilitates the simultaneous process planning.

Design for Manufacturability.   There are two types of manufacturing involved in the development of an information system:

- Creating the system and making it operational
- Producing and delivering information service to its customers

The design should incorporate both types. The participation of those who will implement the system at the design stage ensures the manufacturability of the system in the first category. However, it is equally important to ensure the manufacturability of the service (the second category). The design of the service-delivery process must make sure that the system's customers receive the intended service.

The second manufacturability design is mostly ignored by system designers who design a system assuming flawless performance of all components and individuals involved in producing the information service for customers. The lack of design for delivery of the information system leads to a brittle system that malfunctions frequently.

Design for Assembly.   Design for assembly applied to information systems deals with creating independent components that can be changed without the need to overhaul the entire system. At the programming level, modularized design has been a popular concept for many years. However, the principle of modularity could be applied to the design of the entire system by attempting to reduce the dependencies of various system components.

Design for assembly should be one of the principles in guiding the design. For example, this principle emphasizes the choice of hardware-independent software, a machine-independent operating system, an open network structure, open architecture, or a software-independent data-entry system. This principle makes improving the system much easier and gives the system a longer life.

Design for Maintainability.   In designing an information system, one must design maintainability into the system. Design for assembly partly takes into account the issue of maintainability in that it makes various components of the system as independent as possible. However, the design for maintainability should go even further and include additional gateways for enhancing the system at different levels of sophistication.

Maintainability should be among the design objectives, and should be considered explicitly in the design decisions. For example, in choosing between an object-oriented (OO) method of modeling and implementation versus a functional-based approach, the OO method should receive a higher selection rating for the system, if it provides more maintainability. If a particular software provides more flexibility for upgrading or switching to another product, it should be given more preference on the basis of maintainability.

Design for Reliability.   In a quality system, reliability should be designed into the system, instead of being inspected after the system implementation. The principle of design for reliability dictates the specific design rules. The system should:

- Be robust
- Have a database component for its own performance data
- Be self-monitoring
- Be fault-tolerant

A *robust* information system is not sensitive to external interferences outside the control of the system. For example, when the design of a system allows for the possibility of data entry and user error and incorporates adequate functionalities to catch, signal, or correct such errors, then the system is made robust towards data-entry error problems that are outside the system. Similarly, if the system network is designed such that if a server fails, there is another server to take over, or when a line fails, there is an alternative line, then the system is made robust to such failures. The more a system is made robust, the higher its reliability.

The automatic collection of *performance data* for the information system keeps a record of the system's quality. It involves the collection of data on various components of the system as well as customers' opinions on the quality of the system's service. The performance data could be used for constant monitoring of the system quality. Chapter 7 discusses how one can develop reliability metrics for the system based on such performance data.

A *self-monitoring* system goes beyond the collection of data on its own performance; it takes action to deal with problems. For example, a system could have an intelligent component that checks the performance data. When the index of its performance falls below a certain critical level, it notifies the system manager, alerts the maintenance team, or even shuts down the system.

A *fault-tolerant* system is designed to continue operation even if some of its components fail. In such systems, there are alternative versions of critical system components such that if one fails, the system reverts to the back-up component. A fault-tolerant system also has the capability to check for errors and to provide correction opportunities for the system customers.

Obviously, it is not possible to have back-ups for all modules of the system and to check for errors in every action the system customer takes. It is the function of the system designer to maximize the system's tolerance for fault with the minimum number of error-checking and redundant modules.

Design for Engineering Analysis.   The principle idea behind design for engineering analysis is that one should be able to analyze the design easily. In other words, the design should be simple and clear. Complicated designs are breeding grounds for errors, omissions, and faulty implementations. Examples of such designs include those that assume less dependency among their components, have fewer modules, and have modules that are designed for only one independent task.

Suh [1990] states that there are two design axioms that are essential for a good design: (1) the system's functional-requirement modules should be independent, and (2) the information content of the each module should be at minimum. The latter is a formal specification of what we intuitively identify as a "simple" design.

Cost Estimation.   System design based on concurrent engineering should contain a relatively accurate estimate of the system's life-cycle cost. Since the design team would include system managers and maintenance groups, it would contain all those who contribute to the total cost of the system. Section 6.7 in this chapter, as well as Chapter 7, revisits the issue of system cost.

6.1.4   Parallel Design

Design is an art and requires a great deal of creativity. This statement is particularly true at the earlier stages of design, when the basic approach is not yet formed. Therefore, the design team goes through a number of iterations for checking the validity of the basic design idea before finalizing the basic approach.

For example, in designing the system for ACCU-INFO, it may take a number of design iterations to determine whether connecting to the information systems of the data suppliers is a good idea, and if so, what the best method would be. The iterative nature of the design is embedded in the design process and adds to the design time.

Businesses are finding that the time it takes to get a product on the market is an essential parameter for competition. Therefore, the approaches that reduce time to market or time to operation would be of value. Parallel design is one of the methods used to reduce the design time. The initial design team is divided into two to five teams. Each team attempts to come up with the design ideas independently. At a later stage, the design concepts are compared and the best design is selected. In many cases, the best design combines a number of proposals.

The parallel approach has a number of advantages:

- Brainstorming in a large group for creativity in design is not effective. The small team environment is more conducive to brainstorming about design.
- In many creative designs, one has to break out of the existing paradigms and underlying assumptions in order to come up with a novel and revolutionary approach. This is more likely to occur in smaller teams in which team members have a better chance to put forward outlandish and rule-breaking ideas that may lead to a new design approach.
- Friendly competition among groups may generate more novel ideas.
- If the same idea is generated by a number of teams, the design carries more validity.

The problem with the parallel design method is that it may seem more costly to have more than one team doing the same job. The purpose of parallel design is to reduce the time and number of iterations. Therefore, the management of the multi-team approach and the decision on when to stop the parallel process and bring the teams together is critical to the success of the approach.

Furthermore, combining the designs may become costly and difficult. Again, it is important to make sure that the teams understand that the final design may be a combination of different design ideas, and remain open to alternative approaches.

6.2 ◆ Designing Utility in IS by Applying QFD

After the completion of the house of quality for systems planning, one can use its output in the system-design stage. The columns and their related ratings become the left border of the house of quality for systems design. The columns of the house consist of the requirements of the design. The output of this house of quality becomes the input to the house of quality for the design of technical details.

6.2.1 Technical Requirements

Once the customer requirements are specified (as discussed in Chapter 5), the system-design team develops a general design approach via involvement in reengineering and early parallel design. An example of such a general design strategy is when a company decides that the system is going to be distributed over a wide-area network, and geographically dispersed divisions will have control over their own data, but within a centralized design.

The general design now has to become specific, and the technical components of the system should be identified and put together. When the details of the technical design are identified, it is crucial to relate and rate them with respect to their role in satisfying customers' requirements. This rating process allows the design team to concentrate effort and allocate resources to those technical components that play a crucial role in satisfying customers' requirements.

The quality function deployment (QFD) allows us to identify critical technical components. In this section, we continue with the discussion of QFD from Chapter 5 and use the approach to translate customers requirements into the design of technical components.

House of Quality for Systems-Design Requirements.   As we move from more general specifications of systems planning to more technical details of systems design, the house of quality expands in size. It may be helpful to break down the design components into recognizable categories, such as hardware, software, procedures, and so forth. Although the process becomes more lengthy and consequently tedious, it is important to have the development team working on the house of quality for design, so that everybody can see the role of each module in satisfying the systems requirements and their relative importance in the information system as a whole.

Figure 6.2 shows a part of the house of quality for the system-design stage of ACCU-INFO. The left border of the house has the system requirements imported from the columns of Figure 5.6 in Chapter 5, and their relative ratings from the lower border of the same figure. Here, system requirements become the input demands for the systems-design stage. This follows closely the principle of quality management that group

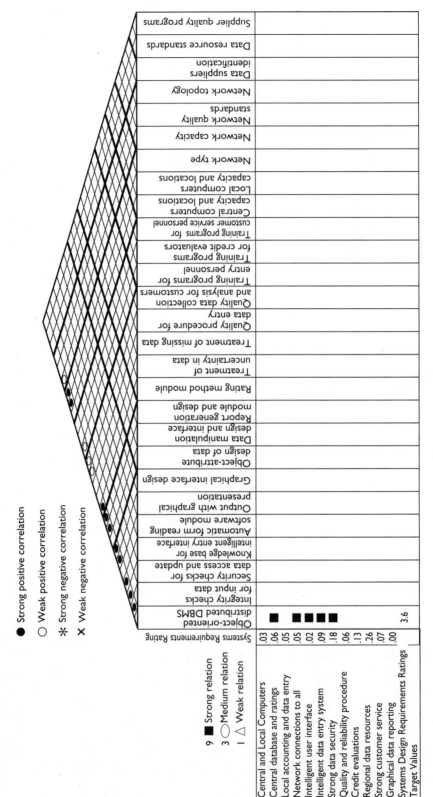

Figure 6.2 Systems Design using QFD for ACCU-INFO's Information Systems

members in stage A of the development process form the customers of stage B; the output requirements of stage A become the customer requirements of stage B.

The design requirements for ACCU-INFO include (Figure 6.2):

- Object-oriented distributed database management system
- Integrity checks for input data
- Security checks for data access and update
- Knowledge base for intelligent data-entry interface
- Automatic form-reading software module
- Outputs with graphical presentation
- Graphical interface design
- Object-attribute design of data
- Data manipulation module and interface
- Report-generation module and design
- Rating method module
- Treatment of uncertainty in data
- Treatment of missing data
- Quality procedures for data entry
- Quality data collection and analysis for customer access
- Training programs for entry personnel
- Training programs for credit evaluators
- Training programs for customer-service personnel
- Central computer capacity and location
- Local computer capacity and locations
- Network type
- Network capacity
- Network quality standards
- Network topography
- Data supplier identifications
- Data resource standards
- Supplier quality program

Attached to the house of quality for systems design is a detailed documentation of design for each column. For example, in Figure 6.2, there are 27 components; hence there should be 27 design documents detailing the design requirements.

Borders of the House of Quality.   Pairwise relations among systems requirements and design requirements provide the basis for rating the design requirements. Applying the same method as that in systems planning, one can combine the systems-requirements ratings (carried forward from the systems planning phase) with the pairwise relations to get the design requirements. These ratings show the importance of each design component in the entire information system.

For example, in Figure 6.2, the relations of the first column to the system requirements lead to the pre-normalized rating of 3.6. In order to get the normalized rating, this value should be divided by the sum of such values computed across all 27 columns.

The significance of the relative ratings of technical modules is that it provides the system developers a guide to the significance of a module in satisfying customer information needs, and keeps the customer focus throughout the process of technical design. This focus is important because in technical design one can easily change the focus from what customers want to what designers may think of as technical necessity or elegance.

The target values on the lower border of the house document the design parameters. For example, the target value of the object-oriented distributed DBMS software in Figure 6.2 could be the number of objects, attributes, and local connections that it can support.

The roof of the house shows the interrelations among the technical modules, discussed in a later section.

6.2.2   Subsystems

Another way to specify the technical components is to break them up into general categories prior to listing all components. In the ACCU-INFO example of Figure 6.2, an easier design approach is to break down the technical requirements into the subsystems:

- Database
- Data model
- Quality
- Training
- Hardware
- Network
- Data suppliers

A tree diagram can be used to identify the relationship of subsystems and the technical requirements of the system, as shown in Figure 6.3. The advantage of breaking down the technical requirements into subsystems is that one can better discover the omissions. For example, in Figure 6.2, the cluttered nature of the technical requirement list does not easily allow us to see that the hardware subsystem is lacking requirements for peripheral units, whereas one can easily see the under-representation of the hardware subsystem in Figure 6.3.

Note that the subsystem breakdown may consist of more than two layers. For example, the database subsystem itself could be broken down into subsystems: user interface, security, and integrity prior to listing the modules. Obviously, the number of subsystem layers depends on the complexity of the system to be designed.

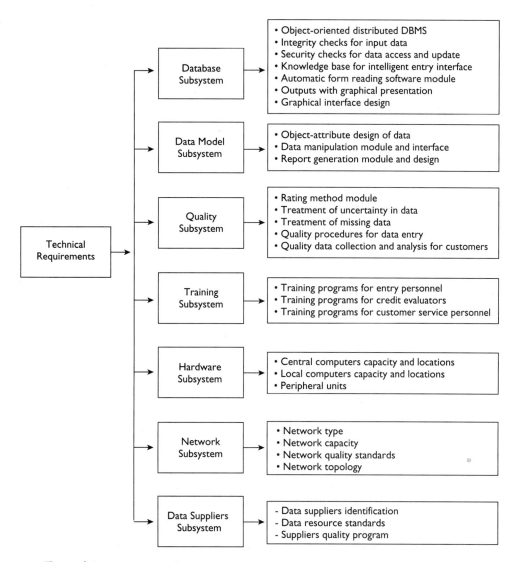

Figure 6.3 Tree Diagram for Technical Requirements Subsystems in ACCU-INFO Example

6.2.3 Interrelationships

As in the systems-planning phase, the borders of the house contain additional information regarding the design. The roof of the house shows the correlations among the design components. The specification of these correlations is important in deciding whether a design component should be changed. A design change of a component that has numerous and strong correlations with other components may be too costly. Therefore, the roof brings out the hidden cost of design alteration. Furthermore, when the design of one component is altered, the roof can be used as a checklist to make sure that the designs of all affected components are also adjusted accordingly.

For example, in Figure 6.4, we see that the object-oriented distributed DBMS (the first column) has a strong correlation with ten components and a weak correlation with four others. This correlation implies that the choice of DBMS software should be made carefully because any change could be costly. Furthermore, a design change regarding this component requires a careful analysis of 14 other design components.

Since a presentation such as that in Figure 6.2 could be quite cluttered for large projects, the interrelationship analysis could be documented separately. Figure 6.4 expands the roof of the house of quality in Figure 6.2, and includes the subsystems of Figure 6.3.

6.2.4   Components

The breakdown of the technical specification continues with a series of QFDs. In the subsequent house of quality, the columns of the previous house become the rows of the new house, and the columns are the detailed technical specifications. This process should continue until the columns of the house consist of specific tasks, programs, or actions such as design of a procedure for a given software product, installation of a specific type of hardware, or specific training courses for employees.

Each house of quality carries its importance ratings from one house to another. In other words, the row next to the last in Figure 6.2 (ratings of the column elements) becomes the second column (ratings of the row elements) in the next house of quality. This way, the role of each specific action, task, or program in satisfying customers' needs is quantified. This method keeps the customer focus in place even for the most specific components of the information system.

The extent of design specificity using QFD depends on the design team. More detailed houses of quality with appropriate ratings and interrelation roofs make the design more clear and keep the customers' needs in focus. However, detailed specifications require time, money, and dedication. The more time is spent at the front end to make the details of the design more clear, the less time will be spent in correcting errors and patching up the system later. However, the minutia of the QFD might deter its use in design. The design team decides how much detailed specification by QFD is productive for a given project.

6.3   ◆   Engineering Usability into IS

The usefulness of information systems has two components: utility and usability [Grudin 1992], Figure 6.1. In this section, we address the usability feature of the system.

Nielsen [1993] distinguishes utility and usability in the following way: "Utility is the question of whether the functionality of the system in principle can do what is needed, and usability is the question of how well users can use that functionality." In Nielsen's definition, users are not limited to the end users, they include those who have to install or maintain the system.

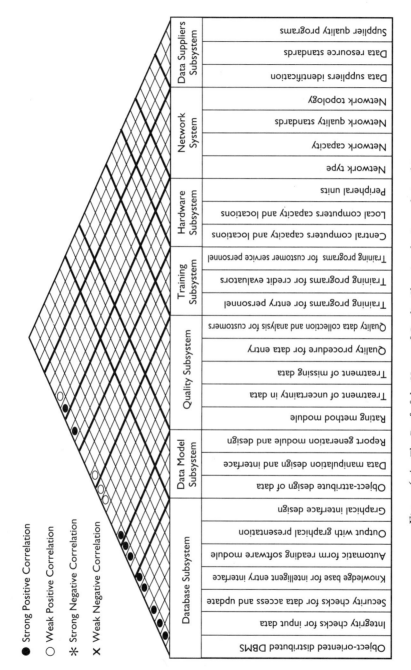

Figure 6.4   The Roof of the House of Quality Showing the Interrelationships

6.3.1   Usability Criteria

Usability is not limited to the design of the user interface [Nielsen 1993]. It includes:

- Ease of use
- Ease of reuse
- Efficiency
- Few user errors
- Self-learning
- Satisfying and pleasing
- Favorable customer perceptions

The interface must be easy to use and the user should be able to easily reuse the system with little effort. The access to the needed information should be efficient and require the least amount of time and effort on the customer's part. The design should be such that it would minimize the number of customer errors to near zero. Using the system should require little or no training, so that the user-interface should have self-learning capability for the customer.

The subjective aspects of the interface are equally important in determining the usability of the system. The interface should be satisfying to the customer as a communication medium, and the experience should be pleasant to the customer. The customer should have a favorable perception of the system. The latter category embodies all other subjective views of system customers with respect to the use of the system, such as the *perception* or expectation that the system will operate efficiently, whether or not the system is indeed efficient.

6.3.2   The Technology of User Interface

Nielsen [1993] traces the technology available for developing user interface as:

- Batch
- Line-based
- Full screen
- Graphical
- New technologies

The batch systems provided little interface for users in that the user had only one chance in each submission to request changes or information. The recent use of files in e-mail and faxes are modern examples of batch-like user interfaces.

Line-based interfaces allowed the users to interact with the system by line commands. This was later changed to include the full screen with hierarchies of menus. Graphical user interfaces increased the visual representations and opened multiple windows to the system.

New technologies move user interfaces towards multimedia and multisensor interactions, such as animation, video, and audio, as well as spatial dimensions such as virtual reality.

In 1971, Shackel reported that about 3 percent of a system-development budget is allocated to usability, while Nielsen [1993] reports this figure to be 6 percent to 10 percent in 1993, and increasing. At present, according to Nielsen, users typically weight usability at 30 percent. This rate will increase as new technologies open new opportunities for making information systems more accessible to non-technical and computer-illiterate customers. In such systems, the quality of the user-interface is an increasingly important component of the general level of system quality.

6.3.3   Methods of Assessing Usability

Nielsen [1993] provides an extensive discussion of the methods for assessing usability design. It is essential to assess the quality of the user-interface design prior to its implementation. The mode of testing could range from cheap and simple modes, such as paper mock-ups of the interface, to elaborate computerized prototypes of the interface tested in usability laboratories. The complexity of the system, the degree and extent of its use, and the allocated financial resources determine the level of testing.

The methods of assessment are:

- Usability heuristics
- Usability testing
- Other methods

Usability Heuristics.   Nielsen [1993] developed usability heuristics. Through statistical analysis, he identified ten rules out of numerous rules for checking the quality of interface design. The test customers are asked to review the interface design and identify interface problems using these ten rules as the guideline.

The ten heuristics state that the interface should: [Nielsen 1993]:

- Be simple and contain natural dialogue; should not contain irrelevant and rarely needed information
- Speak customer's language; the concepts should be familiar to the customer
- Minimize the customer's memory load; instruction should be easy to follow
- Be consistent; the customer should not wonder if a word has different meanings in different contexts
- Provide feedback and keep the customer informed of what is going on
- Provide a clearly marked exit
- Accommodate both novice and expert customers by providing shortcuts and accelerators, unseen by novice customers, to speed up the interaction for expert customers
- Have good error messages, which tell the customer what the error is and how to resolve it

- Prevent errors by not allowing the customer to make mistakes
- Offer help and documentation, which the customer can search based on the task at hand; be clear about steps to be taken; should not be too large and complicated

Usability Testing.   Usability testing involves developing the user interface and formally testing it with real customers, without providing them with the heuristics mentioned above. In usability testing one provides statistical data on various aspects of the user interface. There are reliability and validity issues related to these tests, as discussed by Landauer [1988], Holleran [1991], and Nielsen [1993].

Other Usability-Assessment Methods.   There are a number of other methods to evaluate the quality of the user interface design. They include:

- Protocol analysis
- Observation
- Interviews
- Group analysis
- Logging the actual use

In *protocol analysis*, the customer is asked to verbalize what he or she is doing and what problems he or she is encountering. In the *observation* method, an evaluator observes the actions of the customer and notes the problems that he or she is encountering. In the *interview* method, the customer is debriefed after the experience with the interface in order to identify the problem areas. In *group analysis*, a group of customers who have used the interface discuss their experience and share the problems they have encountered. In *logging actual use*, the use pattern of the interface is logged (by computer or manually) in order to identify the problem areas.

6.4 ◆ Reducing Cost by Applying Taguchi Methods

The poor communication system of Japan after the Second World War caused the Allied Forces to recommend the establishment of a research facility similar to Bell Laboratories in the U.S. for the improvement of the system. This led to the creation of Electrical Communication Laboratories, where Dr. Genichi Taguchi carried out his research for systems improvement. A follower of Deming, Taguchi developed methods that are now widely used in Japan with impressive results. While there are some who believe that Taguchi's methods in experimental design are not novel, there is no question that his methods, combined with his philosophy of design, have made a significant impact on design activities in Japan.

Taguchi's methods were originally developed for product design. In this section, we explore the avenues by which the gains in product design through the use of Taguchi methods can be replicated in the design of information systems. Like any advanced method, the Taguchi methods may not be appropriate for every system, especially if the system is small in size and simple in type. However, they provide us with additional tools for designing quality information systems.

Applied to information systems, Taguchi's philosophy in design consists of the following:

- We should minimize the loss function that is the total cost of the system in its life and all its direct and indirect impacts
- Quality measure is defined as the minimum variation from the design targets
- Quality should be incorporated into the design of the system, not inspected afterwards
- The design should be robust to the adverse, uncontrollable elements that impact the performance of the system

In the following section, we explore these principles in the context of information systems.

6.4.1   The Taguchi Loss Function for Information Systems

One of the major contributions of the Taguchi methods is the concept of *loss function*. The underlying idea is that the system should have the minimum loss to society over its entire life cycle. The cost analysis and comparisons of products and services should take into account all of the following costs:

- Planning
- Design
- Implementation
- Warranties
- Maintenance and support
- Disposal, upgrade, replacement
- Harm to the public and environment

Planning, Design, and Implementation Costs.   In information systems, the concept of the system's life cost is not new. The costs of planning, design, and implementation are the development costs, which are normally used in determining the development budget.

In analysis of development costs, there are hidden quality costs that should be taken into account. These are:

- The cost of non-conformance
- The cost of lost opportunities

The cost of non-conformance is when the system is under-designed or over-designed. An under-designed system lacks some of the features that are of value to the system customers. An over-designed system has features that system customers do not need or use. A bad design could be both under-designed and over-designed at the same time, in that it lacks what customers value, and offers what customers do not need or use.

The cost of lost opportunities are the lost profits or benefits due to the failure of the information system to provide its customers with the needed information. Although this cost is not an easy cost to estimate before the system becomes operational (or even after it has become operational), its existence should be a significant incentive for the development team to invest adequate time in requirements analysis and careful incorporation of the requirements into the system design.

Warranty Cost.   Information systems normally do not provide warranties because damage due to wrong information could be hard to assess and is potentially limitless. However, when the information system provides sensitive information to customers or contains information of high value to the corporation, it may take measures to protect against risks, such as buying insurance or extra security measures that would add to the life-cycle cost of systems.

In many systems with external customers, the service provider offers customers the option of canceling their service or getting a full refund. A poorly designed system could generate a substantial cost in this respect.

Maintenance and Support Cost.   Since maintenance and support represent a large share of information-systems projects expenditure, it is natural to include the maintenance and support cost in the analysis. The projects in which development time is severely limited may require a significant amount of maintenance and support, because systems that lack adequate investment in analysis and design will require a much greater degree of correction and customer support than those with more careful design. Therefore, it is essential to include the maintenance and support cost for various scenarios of systems development in order to give the project decision makers a more realistic sense of trade-offs involved in scheduling and resource allocations in various stages of systems development.

Disposal, Upgrade, and Replacement Cost.   Disposal of products such as autos and house appliances is a major environmental concern for those manufacturing companies that have a quality-based culture and a proactive approach to social issues. Is there a disposal cost for information systems?

It is interesting to observe that information systems have disposal, upgrade, and replacement costs of a different sort. An information system has three major physical components: hardware, software, and people. Once an information system is obsolete, one may ask: What are the costs of disposing of these components?

Hardware: The cost of disposing hardware is similar to the cost of disposing any obsolete machinery. Selling, scrapping, reusing, or storing the machinery would involve a cost to the company as well as to the society and environment. This cost is more critical for large projects involving many small computers, specially designed network connections, special input and output devices, or related office equipments. When a company goes into the buying mode for the hardware of a project, it should have a plan that includes the disposal cost and disposal strategies once the equipment becomes outdated.

For example, in the ACCU-INFO case, the company plans to create a network of three main central and 200 local personal computers for its branches, as well as a computer hook-up to about 100 data resources across the country. The project cost analysis must include this equipment in the system's life cost.

The design of the system must answer questions, such as:

- What is probability of obsolescence?
- What is the strategy to postpone the obsolescence?
- What is the cost of disposing the hardware once the equipment is obsolete?

This long-term view of the information-systems project gives a better perspective for making choices. For example, although a computer model may be more powerful or less expensive at present, the lack of possibility of a seamless migration to another platform or to higher models may be a major shortcoming.

Software: Similar consideration should be given to the obsolescence and disposal of software. The cost of disposing software once it has become obsolete is an even thornier issue. Aside from the investment in preparing the software for the system that now has no value, the obsolete system includes data and knowledge that should be transferred to the new system.

Again, considering the issue of obsolescence may have an important impact on the design decisions of the software. For example, the system that allows for a seamless data migration or knowledge transformation could prove to be a cheaper option, although its initial cost is higher than competing products.

People: Disposing an information system is also costly for the people who interact with the system:

- End-users will lose all their invested time in learning how to work with the system
- Programmers' and technical people's skills in working with the software will be lost
- All customers will have to incur the cost of dealing with a completely different environment
- The internal and external customers need to be retrained for the new system

The cost of disposing an information system is so high that the company may end up working with an obsolete system for a long time. This is a hidden cost in that it is rarely taken into account in the optimistic cost estimation of developing a new system. Furthermore, the formal treatment of disposal costs provides incentive to introduce obsolescence-prevention factors in design decisions, hence postponing obsolescence and making disposal less costly.

For example, in designing ACCU-INFO's hardware, the consideration of obsolescence leads system developers to decide that the system will be open and modularized in the critical components, such as input, storage, and network modules. If the future voice- and character- recognition technologies make it economical to have direct voice and handwriting data entry, the existing input modules may become obsolete. In this case, ACCU-INFO can replace the existing input modules with modules that have the new technology with little interruption to the system. That is, the concept of continuous improvement (as discussed in Chapter 3) should be implemented in the design of the new system.

Harm to the Public and Environment.   The experience in manufacturing has proven that companies with public and community consciousness have a better chance of survival in the long run. There are a number of factors that make this even more crucial in today's market environment:

- Consumers have an increasing awareness of public and environmental rights and safety
- Consumers demand companies to exhibit social responsiveness
- Global competitiveness and technical convergence among companies have led products and services to have the same basic attributes, making other concerns, such as social issues, one of the "care-abouts" of customers and the differentiating factor in products and services
- Adverse publicity due to products and services that harm customers physically or infringe upon their rights has major financial consequences for the company as a whole

With the increasing importance of information systems in various facets of consumers' lives, the social impact of an information system and its social costs are important factors that should be taken into account in the system life-cycle cost.

For example, in the ACCU-INFO case, social costs are incurred to those individuals whose credit is incorrectly rated by the system, or in cases where the data supplier has infringed upon the right of an individual by accessing his or her confidential files. In other words, in the zeal for getting the best and most up-to-date data and producing an output in the shortest time, the company has to make sure that the system does not incur a high social cost. Well-publicized lawsuits have proven that social costs have the potential of turning into major financial losses and publicity nightmares when social consciousness is ignored.

In sum, the idea of the loss function is that the cost of a system should not be narrowly defined as the developmental cost. Only by considering the life-time cost of the system as well as all its impacts can one make project selection and design decisions that minimize cost and loss in the long run.

◆ CASE: Taguchi in Action

When the soldiers of Desert Storm crouched in the sand to scout Iraqi troops, they took their night-vision goggles for granted. But their advantage hadn't come easily. In 1989, the manufacturer, ITT's Electro-Optical Products Div., had struggled with leaky seals on the goggles' phosphor screens. ITT fixed the problem—which was due to variations in a ceramic sealing compound—with the help of a design technique pioneered by Genichi Taguchi, one of Japan's quality masters.

Taguchi's credo is to create products so "robust" that they can withstand random fluctuations during manufacturing that might lead to defects. Say a kiln produces warped tiles because of humidity or erratic temperatures. Instead of sinking more cash into the factory, Taguchi, 67, a consultant with the Ohken Associates in Tokyo, would tinker with ingredients of the clay. "To improve quality, you need to look upstream in the design stage," he says. "At the customer level, it's too late."

Sounds simple, but it isn't. Taguchi identifies the controllable and uncontrollable variables most likely to affect quality. Instead of relying on trial and error, Taguchi uses some statistical magic to design an experiment to find the most resilient combination of those variables—say, the best processing temperature and key ingredients that are likely to work almost no matter what else goes wrong. Auto parts maker Nippondenso, for example, tests variables for making electronic parts. The extra trouble pays off later in lower repair costs and loyal customers.

The biggest value is in the design stage. Fuji Xerox applied Taguchi's methods to its best-selling 3500 copier in the late 1970s, cutting development time from an anticipated five years to two. Later, engineers took on the paper-feeding system of the company's high-speed copier, the FX-7700. The design is so robust that it easily handles thicker recycled paper, while some competitors have had to redesign their machines.

Such concepts began taking shape in 1950, when Taguchi was recruited by a research lab set up by General Douglas MacArthur in the postwar occupation to help fix Japan's chaotic phone system. He quickly zeroed in on the time and money wasted on hit-or-miss experiments. His statistical tools for designing experiments won the Deming award for individuals in 1960, and he has won three more Demings for research papers. His lessons have helped such blue-chip manufacturers as Hitachi, NEC, and Toshiba elbow aside U.S. competitors.

The quality whiz keeps a hectic pace, consulting in Japan, The U.S., and elsewhere. Clients say he has mellowed from the days when a misstep invited a stinging rebuke. Yet even at home, he's Mr. Quality, taste-testing recipes for his wife, Kiyo, and daughter, Kumiko—both cooking instructors.

Taguchi was little known in the U.S. until 1984, when Ford Motor Co. spun off a unit it had formed to train its engineers in his methods. The American Supplier Institute in Dearborn, Mich., teaches hundreds of engineers and advises the likes of Uniroyal, Polaroid, and AT&T Bell Laboratories.

Now, Taguchi wants to turn his methods to basic research. Since the U.S. invests so heavily in the lab, Taguchi says the U.S. could benefit most from robust research. But he's not optimistic that Americans are ready for the challenge. "They want something easy," he says. "But this is not easy."

Source: "A Design Master's End Run Around Trial and Error," Karen Lowry Miller and David Woodruff, *Business Week*, October 25, 1991, p. 24, reprinted from October 25, 1991 issue of *Business Week* by special permission, copyright (c) 1991 by McGraw-Hill, Inc.

6.4.2   The Taguchi Measure of Quality

Taguchi defines quality as the minimum deviation from target value. For example, assume that one of the quality measures of an information system is its response time, with the target value of four seconds. Obviously the response time is not always at four; many factors impact the response time at any one try. It is a random variable with the possible distributions shown in Figure 6.5. Since there are many factors impacting the response time, one may safely assume that the variable has a normal (bell shape) distribution.

In looking at the distribution of the response time, the average of the distribution may fall well above the target value (Figure 6.5-a). This difference means a significant

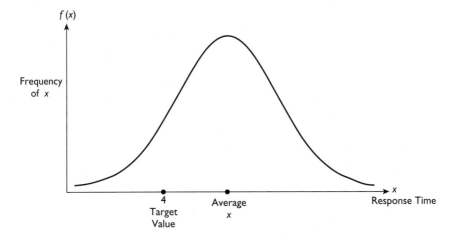

(a) Target value is below the distribution average

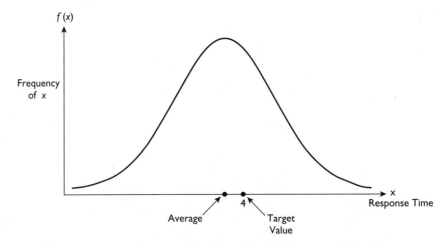

(b) Target value is around the average

Figure 6.5   Target Value and The Distribution of the Information System's Response Time

quality cost. In Figure 6.5-b, the target value is close to the average of the distribution that reflects lower quality cost. But closeness of the target and average values is not a sufficient measure. There may exist substantial costs because of a large variability in the response time.

In determining the target value for the response time, it is a given fact that the system will not constantly be on the target value. Therefore, we establish the acceptable upper and lower limits for the response time—as shown in Figure 6.6.

The traditional way of interpreting values of the system's performance measure is that if the distribution of the measure falls outside the upper and lower limits (as in Figure 6.6-a), then the system is out of its allowable range. If a system is within its determined range (as in Figure 6.6-b), then the system's performance is satisfactory. Taguchi disputes this conclusion. He argues that any deviation from the target value is a loss. Therefore, the loss associated with the distribution in Figure 6.6-c is far less than that in Figure 6.6-b.

Based on the desirability of reducing the variability, Taguchi draws the loss function as the loss due to deviation from target value, shown in Figure 6.7.

For cases where both positive and negative deviations from the target are considered undesirable, the loss function has a quadratic form, as shown in Figure 6.7-a. If only positive (or negative) deviation is unwanted, then the loss function consists of half of the quadratic function, as shown in Figure 6.7-b for the case when the negative deviation from the target is undesirable and 6.7-c when the positive deviation from the target is undesirable.

Taguchi argues that the major focus of the design should be in reduction of the variability of performance. For example, if the reduction in the response time translates into more variability in response time, then the system's performance goes down. This is especially crucial for information systems, where large fluctuations in a system with a good performance record could be considered worse than a fair but consistent and predictable performance. Compare accessing a system that gives a response in one second or in ten minutes as opposed to another system that the responds in five seconds 99 percent of the time. Most people would prefer the system with five-second response because of its predictability.

Thus, in designing a system, it is not enough to consider the average performance parameters of the system; the important factor in the design is the variability of the system performance.

According to Taguchi methods, the loss function of deviating from the target can be measured by:

$$L = C \cdot D^2$$

where C is the cost of unit deviation and D is the amount of deviation from the target.

Furthermore, quality is not what we measure and control after the system is implemented. Instead, quality should be designed into the system. This is a concept that is not commonly addressed in the design of information systems, partly due to the lack of a formal method. The next section discusses using the Taguchi methods in designing systems that have low variability and are robust with respect to uncontrollable environmental factors.

(a) Outside the limits

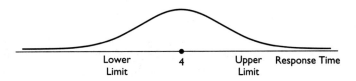

Lower Limit   4   Upper Limit   Response Time

(b) Within the limits

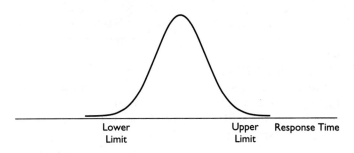

Lower Limit   Upper Limit   Response Time

(c) Inside the limits

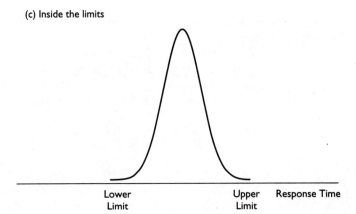

Lower Limit   Upper Limit   Response Time

Figure 6.6   The Variability of the Information System's Response Time

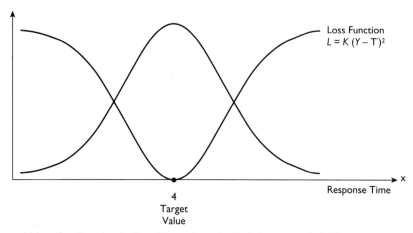

(a) Loss function when both positive and negative deviations are undesirable

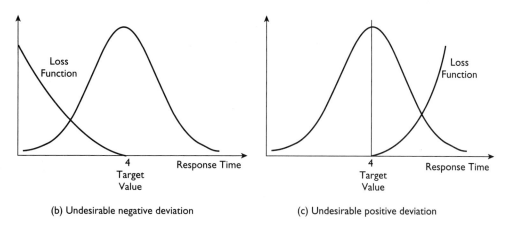

(b) Undesirable negative deviation   (c) Undesirable positive deviation

Figure 6.7   The Quality Loss Function

6.4.3   Robust Design in Taguchi Methods

The main focus of Taguchi methods is in design that is robust with respect to internal and external disturbances. The disturbances to an information system include:

- Error by customers who do not follow the instructions for using the system
- Data errors entering the system
- Error by employees who do not follow the required procedures
- Failure of the network on which the information system operates
- The decision to alter one component of the system, such as the manager of a node in a distributed database deciding to change its database software or add a data item to its database

- The data not being updated on time
- Hardware failure

According to the Taguchi methods, the design of the system should minimize or preferably eliminate the possibility of such disturbances. Taguchi suggests the measure of *signal-to-noise ratio* as a measure for guiding the design [Taguchi and Clausing 1990]. Signal is what the system is expected to produce, and noise is an undesirable output. A robust design attempts to maximize signal-to-noise ratio.

For example, the user interface could be designed such that it would not allow the customer to make a mistake—or, if he or she does make a mistake, corrective actions are immediately provided to the customer. Similarly, the intelligent data-entry interface stops the data-entry clerk from entering the wrong data. If the data is not updated on time, the system could send a warning signal to the system manager and in sensitive cases, could even shut down the system. In the case of network problems, such as a failure in a link, one can design alternative routes in case one link in the network shuts down. In the case of a hardware failure, such as a node or a server becoming unoperational, a back-up node or server may take over the function without interrupting the system's operation.

Information systems are among the best candidates for implementing Taguchi's robustness idea. A robust information-system design has an intelligent component for self-control and self-management. Although various fragments of self-management, such as intelligent user interface and intelligent database-entry systems are recognized as necessary modules of a system, there are no common and well-accepted design principles for a self-management unit as a major and necessary component of information systems.

In designing a self-management unit, the following principles are essential. The unit must:

- Prevent entry errors in data and information
- Provide warning signals for unusual entries
- Offer system customers a chance to reverse a mistake
- Help system customers correct their mistakes
- Minimize errors by customers
- Give customers warnings about unusual actions
- Warn the system manager of unusual circumstances (such as all customers taking a long time to perform a given function)
- Contain alternatives in case of a system malfunction
- Collect data on various system performance and reliability metrics
- Perform data analysis on system performance metrics and give warnings about persistent low performance and reliability of system modules

The purpose of the self-management unit is to increase the system robustness with respect to environmental and external factors, and to self-evaluate the system performance and reliability well before the customers become dissatisfied with the system.

Measuring Signal-to-Noise Ratio of Design Factors.   The signal-to-noise ratio is a powerful metric for designing various components of the system. If we could identify the value of this metric for each system module, the design decisions would become straightforward and simple. The field of information systems has not begun to address the measurement issues related to quality metrics. Therefore, for the time being we need to use the signal-to-noise ratio as a metaphor to compare various design options. Although we cannot measure the signal-to-noise ratio, we can identify design components that increase its value.

The following design principles could contribute to the enhancement of the signal-to-noise ratio:

- Reduce the interaction of components
- Encapsulate each component
- Create interface standards
- Include safeguards against faulty components
- Do not implement a system that barely meets the set standards or goals
- Use lowered performance variability as a metric for robustness
- Incorporate a self-manager module into the design of information systems

Encapsulating each component of the information systems and reducing the interactions among them helps reduce the chance of a faulty component contaminating the performance of others. Therefore, the signal-to-noise ratio of each component will be determined by the design of that component, rather than the value of the signal-to-noise ratios of others.

The standard interaction makes it possible to change a component without affecting the design of others. Therefore, if the signal-to-noise ratio of a component is low, one can redesign that component without affecting the signal-to-noise ratio of other components.

Including safeguards for a faulty component allows the system to switch to a backup component if the signal-to-noise ratio of a component falls below a predetermined level, hence maintaining the overall performance of the system.

The design should not barely meet a minimum acceptable level of signal-to-noise ratio because a small variation in the performance of one component pushes the system performance below the acceptable level. Among the major goals of the system should be the reduction of variability in the signal-to-noise ratio and staying on the target level all the time. Similarly, designing a self-manager module into the system increases the signal-to-noise ratio of the system.

Orthogonal Arrays.   Selecting the best and most expensive alternative for each component of the system may not guarantee the highest and least variable signal-to-noise ratio for the system. For example, a system with almost unlimited capacity for data may make the retrieval and access to data least efficient and highly variable. An elaborate self-manager unit that sends warnings and signals for the slightest deviation may make the task of data entry very cumbersome to the point that the data-entry personnel and system manager may ignore all warnings of the system and find a way to bypass the system checks. This defeats the purpose for which the self-manager unit is designed. Furthermore, since the system is designed to rely on the self-manager for error checks, there may not be any manual checks. Therefore, bypassing the self-manager unit may lead to a drastic reduction in the signal-to-noise ratio of the system. Thus, it is essential to measure the impact of various design options on the overall signal-to-noise ratio of the system.

One way to measure the impact of various design options is to create prototypes of the system in which various combinations of design elements are tested. Alternatively, one can simulate the system and test the combination of various design options. In order to reduce the number of required prototypes at the same time, to test all major design options in prototypes or the simulation of the system, one can use Taguchi's orthogonal arrays.

The power of orthogonal arrays could be best demonstrated with an example. Assume that the design of an information system has 10 main components, each with 3 design options. To test all possible combinations of these design options, one has to test 3^{10} or $59,049$ combinations. Taguchi's orthogonal arrays recommends 27 combinations. Taguchi's orthogonal array does not find the exact optimum combination of design elements, but will reveal enough about the design components to lead to a very good design. (For a discussion of orthogonal arrays, refer to Roy 1990.)

The use of orthogonal arrays in the design of information systems would be for the design of complex systems in which either simulation or prototyping of the system is in order. In such cases, one can use orthogonal arrays to find the optimal design that maximizes the signal-to-noise ratio of the system.

◆ CASE: Quality and Engineering

To many engineers, quality improvement means standards and controls. And that means loss of creative freedom.

But that view among engineers is rooted more in perception than in reality, say managers who oversee engineering and product-development operations within electronics companies. "The notions of quality and creativity are not in conflict at all," says Bob O'Donoghue, VP of development at Epoch Systems Inc. in Westborough, Mass.

Which leaves managers with a problem. How to instill a quality culture among engineers, a class of employees with very different training, needs, and viewpoints from other employees. Quality-management programs that may work in the executive suite or on the shop floor will likely fall flat within a company's engineering or product-development operation.

"Sometimes getting engineers to understand this stuff is difficult," acknowledges Berkeley Merchant, chief quality officer and continuous-improvement division vice president at Mentor Graphics Corp. "Engineers are a special breed."

Curt Wozniak admits that he was "rather surprised at the [low] level of quality awareness in engineering" when he moved from Sun Microsystems Inc.'s manufacturing operations to become vice president of engineering in 1987. He observed that there was a greater awareness of quality concepts in manufacturing than in engineering—and he says the problem is not unique to Sun.

Managers, nevertheless, are finding ways to make their engineers think quality and continuous improvement: Introduce total quality management (TQM) in a language engineers can understand; show engineers how they can analyze and improve their job performance; make engineers aware of who their customers are; and offer incentives to encourage change.

Terry Rock, senior vice president of operations at Convex Computer Corp., suggests skipping what he calls "the rah-rah" often associated with TQM programs. "Engineers are very practical people," he says, and they are more perceptive to the nuts and bolts of quality improvement. Cheerleading will only make them disdainful of TQM efforts.

"We've sold it simply as a way to get their jobs done more effectively," says Bill Daughton, until recently the engineering director at NCR Corp.'s Microelectronics Division in Colorado Springs, and now an assistant vice president of the company's Semicustom Products Business Unit.

Sometimes the problem is one of language, creating a gulf as wide as any parent-teenager rift. "There is a nomenclature problem when dealing with engineers," says Jim Weaver, assistant to the director of research at Eastman Kodak Co. At Mentor Graphics Corp., managers even avoid the word "quality" when discussing engineering operations, opting instead for "continuous improvement."

"When engineers talk about quality, they tend to talk about product quality rather than process quality," says Peter Hoogerhuis, director of consulting services at Mentor. "When we talk about TQM, [engineers] see it as statistical process control, which they associate with manufacturing. It just doesn't sit well with them."

A critical step is reassuring engineers that TQM and continuous improvement apply to the engineering process, not the creative aspects of their jobs. "The innovation is still there because standards generally refer to the implementation of ideas, not the ideas themselves," says Kevin McDonough, engineering vice president at semiconductor designer Cyrix Corp., Richardson, Tex.

"You must focus on what's in it for them, how quality management makes their job easier, and how it improves their more mundane tasks," says Mentor's Hoogerhuis. "It frees them up for more creative tasks, and *that* they get excited about."

One way companies are doing that is to break quality improvement down into more nuts-and-bolts, cause-and-effect issues that engineers can understand. At NCR Microelectronics, engineers study the individual steps of lengthy semiconductor design processes, allowing them to better see how quality improvement applies to their own particular job. "That's how we install quality within development," Daughton says. "It takes advantage of the natural inclination of engineers toward order and discipline."

National Semiconductor Corp. calls the technique "process mapping." Earlier this year the company's embedded control group, looking to improve-to-market and product-design quality, assigned a team of engineers from different functions to examine the entire product-development process and create a schematic detailing each step, from product definition and design to evaluation, qualification, and testing.

Team members also developed a map outlining how the design process *should* work, says Mike Berezuik, vice president of the embedded control group. They discovered that many steps were carried out serially rather than concurrently, which stretched out the development cycle. From this work, quality improvement blueprints were developed for each step and for the entire process, blueprints that Berezuik's division is now implementing.

National Semiconductor generally realizes cycle time reductions of 30% to 40% within the first year by using process mapping and other techniques, according to Tim

Thorsteinson, director of quality performance. He believes that the time needed for some design and development projects could be cut by two-thirds within two years.

Process mapping has the added benefit of allowing engineers, who otherwise are occupied with narrowly focused tasks, to understand how they fit into the overall process and how the quality of their work has an impact on others. "Personally it's given me exposure to areas that I had not looked at before," says Nick Stanco, an analog reliability engineer at national Semiconductor who served on the cross-functional team. "I hadn't seen the overall picture. By doing this, you get to know the kind of problems other people have, in addition to the problems you experience in your own little world."

Hewlett-Packard Co. has taken this idea a step further in its Manufacturing Test Division in Loveland, Colo., where manufacturing engineers occasionally swap places with R&D engineers to give both a better understanding of the complete engineering process. That improves R&D–manufacturing cooperation and the quality of product designs, says Tom Christen, manager of manufacturing engineering.

Another facet of instilling quality in engineers is to make them more aware of their customers. "We're trying to teach our engineers who their customers are," says NCR's Daughton, "both internally and outside the company."

Intel is making extensive use of quality function deployment (QFD), a means of determining what features and functionality customers want in new products. In the past, engineers have relied heavily on their own knowledge and intuition when deciding which products to develop and which features to include, says Pam Olivier, strategic planning process manager in Intel's Microcomputer Product Group.

Using the QFD technique, Intel engineers began meeting with customers in 1989. "Originally the design engineers were a little shy about it and were worried that we were taking away their domain of creating products," Olivier says. "But they eventually came around." Intel, for example, developed the 80386SL microprocessor for notebook computers using QFD.

"This [QFD] methodology has really helped us document input from customers and explain to upper management just what customers wanted," says Dave Vannier, a 14-year engineer at Intel and manager of strategic development at the company's Entry-level Products Group in Santa Clara, Calif.

When a customer has a problem with a Sun Microsystems workstation, the company tries to have the customer work directly with the designing engineer. "Engineers take it personally when something doesn't work out the way they had expected," says Sun's Wozniak. "So it may cause some pain, but it's worth it."

Sun takes the same approach when it comes to engineers' internal customers, particularly manufacturing. Wozniak says Sun is putting more emphasis on design-for-manufacturability to avoid design-related problems during production.

Sun is not alone in driving home the customer idea. "Engineers have to understand that they are a support group for production, just like other segments of the company. They're not some elitist group," says George Dalich, process-engineering manager with Praegitzer Industries Inc., a Dallas, Ore., manufacturer of printed circuit boards.

At Varian Associates Inc.'s ion implant systems operation in Gloucester, Mass., production is halted once a month while engineers report to assembly line workers—their customers—progress in resolving product design problems. Materials/operations manager

Steve Armstrong, who oversees manufacturing engineering and subassembly at the plant, considers himself to be an engineering customer, "and there are times when I'm not a satisfied customer," he says of his high standards.

Varian engineers are further reminded of quality goals by the abundance of graphs and charts lining the walls of the plant's engineering and assembly areas, detailing improvements—or setbacks—in cycle time, scrap and rework, problem resolution, and the status of individual projects. Vice president and general manager Chuck McKenna admits that the latter introduces a measure of peer pressure and competition into the process.

To bring quality to software design and development shores, Mentor is relying heavily on concurrent engineering and standards developed by the Institute of Electrical and Electronics Engineers for improving software functionality, usability, reliability, performance, and supportability. Using these and other techniques has reduced development-cycle time and improved product quality, says Merchant.

For its Idea Station design software, for example, Mentor reduced the "build cycle," the stage where software components are assembled into a complete program, from 20 people working five days to two people working for one day.

Giving engineers the right tools and training are critical aspects of quality improvement. Sun began training its engineers in design-for-reliability and design-for-manufacturability as early as 1987, with emphasis on getting engineers to think of their job as a process.

"Engineers want the opportunity to develop quality products," Wozniak says. "They just need the right training." Sun also operates a "Sun University" for its employees with about 40 of the 200 courses targeted toward engineers, some of those covering aspects of quality improvement.

Praegitzer puts its engineers through 36 hours of training in statistical process control and runs four-day seminars on design-of-experiments, the latter a tool for pinpointing and identifying the causes of problems. Other companies are training engineers in statistical process engineering, another technique for dissecting problems to discover their root cause.

Giving engineers the right incentives to think quality is equally crucial. More and more, electronics companies are making quality improvement part of their employee-evaluation process. At NCR Microelectronics, for example, such metrics as first-pass success—the rate at which an engineer's design works on the first try—is part of the evaluation criteria. Daughton says first-pass success helps strengthen engineers' understanding of the link between quality and personal performance.

At Sun, engineering teams beginning a project set goals for cost, time-to-market, and quality, and bonuses are awarded for meeting those goals, Wozniak says. As an incentive to improve the quality of their work, Texas Instruments Inc.'s Defense Systems and Electronics Group offers engineers and other technical professionals their own career ladder, separate from the corporate management ladder where engineers are rarely found.

Many electronics companies are using engineering teams to oversee development projects from start to finish. Epoch Systems' O'Donoghue says that instills a feeling of "ownership" of the product among engineers. Many companies keep the same team together for years to manage a product line throughout its entire life cycle.

"Engineers are starting to think that there is something to all this," Convex's Rock says of total quality management. But he believes that recognition is dawning very slowly.

Dennis Schnabel, corporate software quality, assurance, and test director at Mentor and a Malcolm Baldridge National Quality Award examiner, agrees. "Ultimately, what this is all about is changing behavior, and, boy, is that tough."

Source: "Engineers Say 'Prove It!' " Rick Whiting, *Electronic Business*, Vol. 7, No. 20, October 7, 1991, pp. 89–92, reprinted with permission from *Electronic Business Buyer*, copyright 1991, Reed Elsevier Inc.

◆ Conclusion

This chapter discussed designing quality into information systems. It covered the quality methods that could be applied in designing stage of information systems. Section 6.1 discussed how the application of reengineering concepts can improve the value of information systems. In this section, the topics of concurrent engineering and parallel design were covered and applied to the design of information systems.

Section 6.2 showed how quality function deployment (QFD) could be applied in designing utility into information systems. This section continued with the requirements analysis discussed in Chapter 5. It showed how customers' requirements could be designed into the system by using QFD. The application of QFD in design was expanded to include the design of subsystems and components, as well as the interrelationships among various subsystems or components.

Section 6.3 discussed the design of usability into information systems. The usability topic included the usability criteria, the technology of user interface, and the methods for assessing the usability of information systems.

Section 6.4 introduced Taguchi's methods and the ways one can use them to reduce the life-cycle cost of information systems. This section showed that the Taguchi loss function is applicable to information systems. The Taguchi measure of quality and robust design were also covered in this section.

This chapter presented design approaches that are helpful in increasing the value and use of information systems, while reducing the life-cycle cost of the systems at the same time.

◆ References

1. Ashley, Steven. 1992. "DARPA Initiative in Concurrent Engineering," *Mechanical Engineering*, Vol. 114, No. 4, April, pp. 54–57.

2. Card, David and Glass, Robert L. 1990. *Measuring Software Design Quality*, Prentice Hall, Englewood Cliffs, NJ.

3. Grudin, J. 1992. "Utility and Usability: Research Issues in Development Contexts," *Interacting with Computers*, Vol. 4, No. 2, August, pp. 209–217.

4. Hammer, Michael and Champy, James. 1993. *Reengineering the Corporation*, Harper Business, New York, NY.

5. Holleran, P. A. 1991. "A Methodological Note on the Pitfalls in Usability Testing," *Behavior & Information Technology*, Vol. 10, No. 5, September–October, pp. 345–357.

6. Jo, Heyon H. and Parsaei, Hamid. 1993. "A Design Trade-Off Methodology for Concurrent Engineering Practices," in *Concurrent engineering*, Peihua Gu and Andrew Kusiak (Eds.), Elsevier, Amsterdam, Netherlands.

7. Landauer, T. K. 1988. "Research Methods in Human–Computer Interaction," in *Handbook of Human–Computer Interaction*, North–Holland, Amsterdam, The Netherlands, pp. 543–568.

8. Nielsen, Jacob. 1993. *Usability Engineering*, Academic Press, New York, NY.

9. Noori, Hamid. 1989. "The Taguchi Methods: Achieving Design and Output Quality," *The Academy of Management EXECUTIVE*, Vol. III, No. 4, pp. 322–326.

10. Parsaei, Hamid R. and Sullivan, William G. 1993. *Concurrent Engineering: Contemporary Issues and Modern Design Tools*, Chapman & Hall, New York, NY.

11. Reddy, Ramana; Wood, Ralph T.; Cleetus, K. Joseph. 1991. "The DARPA Initiative: Encouraging New Industrial Practices," *IEEE Spectrum*, Vol. 28, No. 7, July, pp. 26–30.

12. Roy, Ranjit. 1990. *A Primer on the Taguchi Methods*, Van Nostrand Reinhold, New York, NY.

13. Ryan, Nancy. 1988. *Taguchi Methods and QFD: Hows and Whys for Management*, ASI Press, Dearborn, MI.

14. Shackel, B. 1971. "Human Factors in the P.L.A. Meat Handling Automation Scheme: A Case Study and Some Conclusions," *International Journal of Production Research*, Vol. 9, No. 1, pp. 95–121.

15. Suh, Nam P. 1990. *The Principles of Design*, Oxford University Press, New York, NY.

16. Taguchi, Genichi and Clausing, DOn. 1990. "Robust Quality," *Harvard Business Review*, January–February, Vol. 68, No. 1, pp. 65–75.

17. Wong, Julius P.; Parsaei, Hamid R.; Imam, Ibrahim N.; and Kamrani, Ali K. 1991. "An Integrated Cost Estimating System for Concurrent Engineering Environment," *Computers and Industrial Engineering*, Vol. 21, Nos. 1–4, pp. 589–594.

◆ Questions

6.1. What are the major system characteristics contributing to system acceptance?

6.2. Discuss the levels at which information systems become involved in reengineering.

6.3. List and discuss the characteristics of reengineering.

6.4. What are the common features in reengineering processes identified by Hammer and Champy?

6.5. Why is the reduction of the number of external contact points an important feature in reengineering processes?

6.6. Discuss concurrent engineering and its relevance to information systems.

6.7. What are the design objectives that should be considered in concurrent engineering?

6.8. Discuss the concept of design for reliability.

6.9. What is a parallel design?

6.10. What is the difference between parallel design and concurrent engineering?

6.11. What is the significance of QFD in the design of information systems?

6.12. What are on the borders of the house of quality?

6.13. When should we use subsystems in setting up the columns of the house of quality?

6.14. How are interrelationships formalized in QFD?

6.15. What is the use of knowing the interrelationships among the technical components of a system?

6.16. What is usability in information systems?

6.17. What are the usability criteria?

6.18. List and discuss the methods for assessing usability.

6.19. What is loss function?

6.20. What are the cost components in a loss function?

6.21. Does an information system have a disposal cost?

6.22. Can an information system be harmful to the public or environment?

6.23. What is Taguchi's measure of quality in design and how does it apply to information systems?

6.24. What is a robust information system?

6.25. How can we design a robust information system?

6.26. What is Taguchi's formula for loss function?

6.27. What is the method of orthogonal arrays?

6.28. What is the use of the orthogonal-arrays method in information systems?

◆ Problems

6.1. Complete the house of quality in Figure 6.2 and compute the design requirements rating for this figure.

6.2. Identify target values in the last row of Figure 6.2

6.3. Complete the roof of the house of quality in Figure 6.4.

6.4. Identify the subsystem of the technical requirements for a bank-loan application system.

6.5. Identify the technical requirements of a bank-loan application system.

6.6. Draw the loss function when the cost of deviation is 1, 4, 8, and 20. Discuss the effect of the increase in the cost of deviation.

His Head,
Not yet by time completely silvered o'er,
Bespoke him past the bounds of freakish youth,
But strong for service still, and unimpaired.

— William Cowper, *The Timepiece*

◆ Chapter Objectives

The objectives of this chapter are:
- To discuss the factors distinguishing the delivery of information services as service breakthroughs
- To offer methods of evaluating information-system workers' performance that reinforce quality in delivering information-systems services
- To introduce the structural changes in developing and delivering information-systems services that are in line with changes in the economy and the market
- To apply the just-in-time concept to information systems
- To introduce the concept of meta-information systems and their role in providing just-in-time information-systems development and delivery
- To discuss the idea of meta-database systems and their role in quality information systems
- To discuss the nature of information systems in learning organizations and approaches for creating a culture of learning in information systems
- To emphasize the importance of supplier relationships in information systems, especially that of data, information, and knowledge suppliers.
- To present the concept of recovery plans for information systems and their role in customer satisfaction and continuous improvement of the system

◆ Key Words

Breakthrough services, IS workers' performance evaluation, flexible information systems, meta-information systems, meta-database systems, just-in-time information systems, unstructured information systems, meta-knowledge base systems, learning organizations, information-systems supplier relationships, information-systems recovery plans

Quality in Manufacturing and Delivery of IS Services

7.1 Breakthrough Service in Information Systems
    7.1.1 Change Factors
    7.1.2 Added Value of Information Systems
    7.1.3 Customers as Performance Evaluators

7.2 Structural Changes in Information Systems
    7.2.1 Flexible Information Systems
    7.2.2 Meta-Information Systems
    7.2.3 Meta-Database Systems

7.3 Just-in-Time Information Systems
    7.3.1 Background on Just-in-Time Systems
    7.3.2 Creating Just-in-Time Information Systems
    7.3.3 Unstructured Information Systems
    7.3.4 Meta-Knowledge Base Systems

7.4 Information Systems in Learning Organizations
    7.4.1 Using Errors as Learning Experiences
    7.4.2 Learning Customer Needs and Creating Enlightened Customers
    7.4.3 Training as a Part of the Employment Pact
    7.4.4 Information System Infrastructure for Learning

7.5 Supplier Relationship
    7.5.1 Data, Information, and Knowledge Suppliers
    7.5.2 Hardware and Software Suppliers
    7.5.3 Network and Communication Suppliers
    7.5.4 Consulting Services
    7.5.5 Dependence vs. Independence in Supplier Relationships

7.6 Information-Systems Recovery
    7.6.1 Recovery as a Source of Customer Satisfaction
    7.6.2 Information-Systems Recovery Plan
    7.6.3 Implementation of the Information-Systems Recovery Plan

◆ Introduction

In the past four decades, public and private organizations alike have learned the painful lesson that, regardless of technical content sophistication, an information system does not add value if its services are not used by its customers. In this section, we discuss the issues that directly impact the quality of manufacturing and delivering information-systems services. The use of the word "manufacturing" is intended to emphasize the fact that information services, like any other product and service, are created or manufactured, and their services are delivered to the customers. Therefore, information systems can benefit from the quality concepts that have been developed for manufacturing and delivering product services in the market.

This chapter begins with a discussion of the nature of breakthrough services in information systems. Section 7.1 identifies the change factors in the market, identifies the sources of added value in information systems, and offers a novel method of performance evaluation for information-systems workers that is directed toward customer satisfaction.

Section 7.2 discusses the structural changes that are needed in information systems in order to deal with the new realities in the global market. In this section, the new concepts of flexible information systems, meta-information systems, and meta-database systems are discussed as approaches to dealing with the changing nature of business in the 1990s and beyond.

Section 7.3 continues the focus on structural changes in information systems with a discussion of just-in-time information systems, applying the idea of just-in-time to information systems. It provides a brief background on the just-in-time concept and discusses its relevance to information systems. Unstructured information systems as well as meta-knowledge base systems are among two additional approaches for dealing with the demands of just-in-time information systems.

Section 7.4 covers the role of information systems in learning organizations. It covers approaches to creating a culture of learning in an organization, including using errors as a learning experience, learning customers' needs and creating enlightened customers, training as a part of the employment pact, and information-systems infrastructure for learning.

Section 7.5 emphasizes the supplier relationship as an important factor in quality information systems. The suppliers of information systems include data, information and knowledge suppliers, hardware and software suppliers, network and communication suppliers, and consulting-services suppliers. The section ends with a discussion of the dilemma of preserving independence versus closer cooperation with information-systems suppliers.

Section 7.6 discusses the importance of information-systems recovery plans. It shows why recovery plans are a source of customer satisfaction, how to create information-systems recovery plans, and how to implement them.

7.1 ◆ Breakthrough Service in Information Systems

With the increasing strategic importance of information systems, offering breakthrough service quality makes a significant difference in the competitive position of any organization. The question is how we can create breakthrough service and service delivery for information systems.

Heskett, Sasser, and Hart [1990] in their book entitled *Service Breakthroughs* observe that:

> *Outstanding service organizations are managed differently from their merely good competitors. Missions are stated differently. Managers act differently. Actions are based totally on different assumptions about the way success is achieved. And the results show it, both in terms of conventional measures of performance and the impact these services have on their competitors.*

A service encounter occurs when the customer comes into contact with the service provider, encompassing the people, machinery, system, and service. In information systems, a service encounter takes place when the customer comes in contact with the system. In this encounter, from the machine's point of view, the user interface plays a crucial role. However, the attitude of humans in this service encounter is just as crucial. In the earlier days of data processing, the war stories were abundant about the information-systems customers being turned off by the arrogance of data-processing personnel who thought their technical know-how had given them the sole proprietorship of data, programs, and systems and a license to look down at customers who were solely interested in getting information and did not wish to be bothered by the technical wizardry involved. There is no convincing evidence that all residues of this attitude have been chased from the office corners of information-systems providers.

An information system is as good as its customers think it is. In providing the information, having a cutting-edge system with the latest bells and whistles can have no value if it does not satisfy the needs of customers. In other words, the quality of information-system service delivery can solely be measured by how its customers view its added value. Thus, we start with the premise that an information system provides high-quality service to its customers *only* when customers judge the service to be of high quality. The delivery of a quality information system must be focused solely on its customers.

In this section, we explore the ramifications of this premise and discuss the processes that support the implementation of customer-focused quality information systems.

7.1.1 Change Factors

The concept of user-friendly information systems is not new and predates the existing quest for quality. However, a customer-focused quality information system puts the power entirely in the hands of system customers.

There are a number of changes that make this focus more imperative:

- Globalization of the market economy
- Short product and service life cycle
- The pace and direction of technical changes
- The role of information systems

Globalization of the Market Economy.   The market economy has been persistently moving towards open market since the Second World War. This trend has impacted and in turn been accelerated by:

- The phenomenal success of Japan and Germany in successfully competing in the international market
- The failure of communism as a viable economic option to the market economy
- Increasing numbers of nations moving toward democracy and capitalism
- The increasing popularity of regional free trade zones, such as the common market and North American (U.S., Canada, and Mexico) Free Trade Agreement (NAFTA)
- Successful completion of GATT (General Agreement on Tariff and Trade)
- The phenomenal free movement of capital around the world, and the equally impressive subsequent increase in the movement of labor within regions and to a lesser degree at the international level
- The technological advances that have made geographical distances irrelevant in many instances
- Dependency of industrial nations' profitability on mass markets

A global economy is highly dependent on the immediate capture and flow of information at all levels. As the scope of markets expands, with it increases the volume, complexity, diversity, and type of information that serves the decision-making processes in these markets.

This trend not only directly affects large companies with international markets, but even companies with local markets as well. With the open-door policies of the global market economy, profit-margin-hungry international companies are constantly looking to take advantage of opportunities missed by local companies. Therefore, global competition affects everyone in the market.

In this market, information systems are not a luxury—they constitute the backbone of the business. There is no question that a business needs to have an information system to serve a global market that demands, on an unprecedented level, speed, accuracy, breadth, and ease of use for various types of customers.

The question is: what is the value added of an information system? Does the quality of an information system promote or hamper the competitive position of the business?

The Pace and Direction of Technical Changes.   Interacting with, responding to, and sometimes leading the market demand are the pace and direction of changes in technology. Personal computers and workstations have moved computers out of centralized basements into every office, and with them came the capability of connecting individual workstations through local and wide-area networks, and more recently, through the client-server technology.

The pace of technological changes has quickened because the technology market is now approaching a mass market, and those who do not keep up with the pace are quickly pushed out. The profit to be gained for each technical advance is short term—it must be improved or a competitor will improve upon it in price or quality.

The direction of technical changes is toward increasing connectivity at the micro level—putting to use the ability to connect individuals through computers and networks. To accomplish this demands more simplification of technology and increases in speed, and, in turn, generates sophisticated and demanding customers.

In other words, the customers of information systems will not be satisfied with minimum access to what they need. They demand instant and easy access to a wide range and variety of information. Information systems that satisfy the needs of such customers must be fully focused on customers, and nothing else.

Short Product and Service Life Cycle.   The life span of products and services in the markets are now considerably shorter than before. This means that we cannot afford to wait for a new system to be developed in one or two years; by then the nature of the product, service, and sometimes, the business itself, may have changed drastically. We need information systems that have the capability to provide relevant information on new opportunities, and can be rapidly deployed as new ideas, products, and services are formulated.

The Role of Information Systems.   Steve Pruitt (from Texas Instruments) and Tom Barrett (from EDS) write [1991]:

The traditional equation of 'labor + raw materials = economic success' is rapidly changing as American business approaches the global, highly competitive markets of the twenty-first century. Strategic advantage now lies in the acquisition and control of information.

They continue to explore their vision of the future structure of organizations as:

We believe that cyberspace technology will be a primary drive toward new corporate architectures. The technology will enable multidimensional, professional interaction and natural, intuitive work group formation. The technology will evolve to provide enterprise with what we call Corporate Virtual Workspace (CVWs) as a highly productive replacement for the current work environment. . . Having no need for physical facilities other than the system hosting the CVW, the cyberspace corporation will exist entirely in cyberspace.

With little need for startup capital, cyberspace corporations will form quickly around an individual or group of individuals who have identified an opportunity and formulated a market plan. Additional cyberspace workers will quickly be gathered from previous endeavors or new talent will be recruited. Profit shares will be apportioned across participating members.

The cyberspace corporation may provide a single product or service and then disband, or it may be formed with a longer-term vision and remain to serve the product's market. Other cyberspace firms may specialize in assuming ongoing maintenance of products if the developer decides to pursue other market opportunities.

As organizational structures change toward inter-functional groups formed around processes, products, and services operating at the global level, decentralization is almost an inevitable structure. The increasingly crucial question in such organizations is how to preserve the culture, standards, and, more important, the organizational knowledge and expertise across the decentralized units. A significant solution to this dilemma is the network of information systems that captures and disseminates information, standards, and knowledge across the independent units.

In an operational sense, the units of operations do not differ much in the large and small businesses. What gives large organizations' units an edge over their small-business counterparts is their access to the organizational resources in the form of knowledge and expertise. As such, economies of scale in large organizations can be realized through information systems. This puts a heavy responsibility on information-systems specialists as innovators, creators, and generators of added value to the organization.

In his vision of the knowledge-management structures in the new organization, Tom Peters [1992] reasons that:

- The marketplace requires decoupling and agility as never before
- To achieve decoupling and agility, we must eliminate headquarters functional staffs
- The marketplace requires expertise as never before
- To develop the needed expertise, we need functional staffs without headquarters bureaucracy and with global reach
- To create functional staffs without bureaucracy, we must develop spartan, global knowledge-management structures
- The essence of an effective knowledge-management structure is advertising, marketing, incentives, big travel budgets, and psychodynamics of knowledge management

Through his case analysis, Peters shows that the knowledge-management structure must have the right design, and must be marketed in the same spirit as other services that are sold to customers.

7.1.2 Added Value of Information Systems

Heskett, Sasser, and Hart in *Service Breakthroughs* [1990] note that:

> *If there is a moment at which service managers most often are moved to act in seriously seeking service breakthroughs, it's the moment at which they first realize the true cost of poor service.*

One of the oft-cited disadvantages of information systems is the lack of metrics for the value and quality of service delivered. Products and services are sold competitively in the market. Therefore, customers' responses in buying a product or service determine its ultimate value and quality. Hence, markets are the ultimate judge and the disposer of products and services that do not pass the test of value and quality. In the case of information systems, there is no active market, direct price structure, and comparable alternative services for the internal customers and, in many instances, for the external customers. Therefore, there are not many metrics for gauging the value and quality of information systems, or are there?

Let us once again consider the sale of products in the market. When we buy a car, do we buy it because it is a car? Or do we buy its capability to transport us from one place to another with a specified degree of comfort, dependability, and status? As Heskett, Sasser, and Hart put it, when we pay for a screwdriver, we are buying holes in the wall, not the hardware per se.

Thus, we pay for the value and quality of the product's service throughout its useful life. Selling a product is identical to offering the service of an information system. The difference is that in the case of selling the product in the market, customers determine its value by their willingness to pay the price, whereas in information systems, normally customers are given little chance to have input in evaluating the system's service.

To create incentive for customers' evaluation input, a number of schemes have been proposed:

- Have the customers pay for the development of information systems out of their operational budget
- Have the customers pay for information-systems services

Customers' Investments in Information Systems.   Having customers of an information system invest in its development puts the control of the system directly into the hands of its customers. It creates a customer focus from the start. The information system has to incorporate customers' needs and have a close and continuous communication with its customers from the start.

This scheme, however, is possible only when the system has only internal customers, and the organizational structure and culture would allow it to succeed. When the system is used by external customers, normally there is little chance that one can get an investment commitment from customers.

Furthermore, in hierarchical organizations where the customers of information systems are functional areas separated by invisible walls from the information-systems function, the control wars over resources could damage the underlying objective of getting customers to invest in the information system.

In a hierarchical organization where control over budget translates into control over one's destiny, the functional area that uses part of the system may wish to develop its own little system internally to avoid paying for the information-system function that has proven to be costly, and whose productivity is doubtful. The information-systems function will also fight the scheme because it finds its customers incapable of realizing the benefit of the new system until they see it work. Moreover, having your budget approved by numerous customer areas could be an impossible undertaking. Hence, the organizational politics may corrupt the reason behind the customer investment in information-systems projects.

Customers' Payment for Information-Systems Services.   Another scheme to gauge the value of quality of information-systems services for its customers is to have them pay for the service as they would pay for any other products or services.

This scheme is most appropriate when the customers are external to the company. In some cases, companies use information-systems services as additional competitive features for their products and services. For example, banks offer ATM and automatic information access to accounts as part of their banking services.

Although it is possible to have internal customers pay for the information services they receive, the pricing mechanism could be a hindrance to the scheme. Breaking down the cost of an information system among its customers does not accomplish much because, in most cases, there is no market and thus no competition to set the right price for the service. Some companies have given their decentralized units the option to pay for internal information services or outsource it. This scheme does not address the case when the information could be obtained only from an internal system. Furthermore, diverse and incompatible information systems across decentralized units could constrain any integrated and seamless approach in providing data, information, and knowledge across decentralized units.

None of the above schemes will incorporate the views of customers who are not end-users of the system. For example, we have discussed programmers, systems analysts, and data-entry clerks as customers of the information system. Since they are not the direct end-users of the system, they cannot reflect their views through their decision to invest in the project or pay for the service.

7.1.3   Customers as Performance Evaluators

The problem with the customers paying for either the investment in or the service of information systems is that it focuses purely on the direct and final users of the service, who have separate budgetary sources of their own. It does not include the intermediary and indirect users discussed in Chapter 6. The market pricing mechanism has this shortcoming to some degree, although the product liability lawsuits and increasing public sensitivity to the environmental and public impacts of products and services are changing the nature of market prices to some extent.

One scheme to counter the dilemma is to have customers evaluate the performance of the information-system workers as well as the information system itself.

◆ CASE: IBM Plan

The $382 million in net earnings that IBM reported for the fourth quarter of 1993 has given the computer giant its first taste of black ink in more than a year. And Chief Executive Louis V. Gerstner Jr. wants more in 1994. Having slashed overhead, hired new top managers, and rejiggered the organization, he's now turning to the 30,000 men and women around the world who sell IBM products and services. This year, they'll be asked to bring home the bacon—not just sales but profits. In an unprecedented move, IBM is tying 60% of sales-force commissions to the profits they bring in.

That's a sharp departure. Last year, only 20% of compensation above the base salary—the bulk of a salesperson's pay—was tied to profits The year before, it was 6%. "We have gone from different sales objectives to financial objectives," says Robert J. LaBant, the senior vice-president in charge of sales and marketing in the U.S. and Canada. In the past, IBM has adjusted the compensation plan every January—usually to boost sales of specific products or raise market share in targeted areas. Mainly, Armonk wanted to hit revenue targets—however it could. "In the old days, we'd give a branch manager a revenue quota, and that would be it. We'd see him at the year-end, and he'd tell us how he did," Says Duke N. Mitchell, general manager for IBM's New Jersey trading area.

Smiling Customers? The switch to pay-for-profit is intended to stop the sales force from cutting deals without understanding what they—and IBM—stand to make on the order. And to make sure that sales reps don't simply push fast-turnover, high-margin products. LaBant is linking the remaining 40% of their commission to customer satisfaction. By doing that, LaBant & Co. are sending the right message to IBM's salespeople, says Marc Butlein, chairman of market-watcher Meta Group. "It makes them more like business managers," he says.

Part and parcel of the compensation program is a new information system to let the salesperson know what the margins are on various products—until now, closely guarded secrets. Since 1991, headquarters has given IBM reps some latitude on pricing so that they could close deals. But they had no way of knowing how much profit they were giving up—and had little reason to care.

Another benefit of the new compensation scheme is that it begins to simplify how the company evaluates its salespeople, says LaBant. Until recently, it wasn't unusual to find 240 separate measurements for a branch manager because different product groups would set quotas to spur sales of their gear. "We used to have a lot of real goof-ball measurements," LaBant concedes. Now, he says, the sales representative only needs to worry about two things: satisfying customers and profits.

Pay-for-profit isn't unique. It's a growing trend. But few companies have tied so much pay to profits. Computer services giant Electronic Data Systems Corp. has based a portion of its sales commission on the profits in a deal, but it's only one of several gauges. And rival Digital Equipment Corp. is moving managers that oversee large territories in that direction. But DEC will not extend that plan to individual salespeople. Most computer companies are closer to the model used at Hewlett-Packard Co. HP pays salespeople a variable commission of up to 40% based on the overall revenue from a deal. "It's pretty aggressive," says Alan D. Bickell, an HP senior vice-president, of IBM's plan. "My worry about something as high as 60% focused on profitability is that I have a feeling the customer could be the loser."

High Marks. IBM's insurance against overzealous salespeople is that big chunk of pay linked to customer satisfaction. At 40% of compensation, Big Blue's payback for customer satisfaction is about the highest around. "I give them high marks for that—most organizations only have that up to 20%," says Craig Ulrich, a compensation specialist with consultants William M. Mercer Inc. Moreover, Ulrich says, it makes good sense to give the sales force the same accountability as top executives have. Already, Gerstner has tied 75% of the compensation—above base pay—for members of his executive committee to corporate profits. And the general managers underneath those executives have 35% of their pay tied to profitability.

So far, customers like the idea. "The notion of driving profitability measurement as far down in the organization as you can is superb," says John D. Leowenberg, CEO of Aetna Information Technology, the computer arm of Aetna Life & Casualty Co. And with so much money tied to customer satisfaction, he expects to be satisfied indeed.

Source: Ira Sager, Gary McWilliams, and Robert D. Hof. "IBM Leans on its Sales Force," *Business Week*, February 7, 1994, p. 110, reprinted from February 7, 1994 issue of *Business Week*, by special permission, copyright (c) 1994 by McGraw-Hill, Inc.

Customers as Performance Evaluators of Information-Systems Workers.   In the traditional hierarchy of organizations, it is common that the managers evaluate the performance of information-systems workers, including systems analysts, systems designers and developers, programmers, systems maintainers, database administrators, network managers, and so forth. Although part of the basis for performance evaluation is the performance of the system and customer satisfaction, as long as the information-systems workers keep their respective managers happy and convinced that they work hard and are conscientious and knowledgeable, they keep their jobs and receive high performance marks. When the organization has a flat and cross-functional teamwork structure, one cannot easily rely on managers to be the sole evaluators.

In delivering value and quality to information-systems customers, there is no reason why one should not use the customers as the performance evaluators. Here we focus entirely on customers—direct, indirect, internal, external, and intermediate. This approach raises a number of questions, such as:

- Who is the customer for each type of information-system worker?
- How do we identify our customers?
- What is the relative importance of the performance rating expressed by various customer types?
- Are customers knowledgeable enough to make a fair evaluation?
- What is the transition process from management evaluation to customer evaluation?

Although answers to these questions are not easy, they are the questions that should be raised anyway. The performance-evaluation process gives these questions the deserved high priority and makes them real for each and every information system worker.

Who Is Thy Customer?   The most important individuals involved in the identification of information-systems customers are the information-systems workers themselves. They are knowledgeable about who their immediate and ultimate customers are. For example, for system designers, the immediate customers of their design are those involved in the implementation of their design—including language programmers, database administrators, network managers, software programmers, hardware specialists, and data managers. The ultimate customers of the system designer are the end-users and those who are affected by the use of the system.

The immediate customer of a language programmer may be the person in charge of the maintenance of the system. The immediate customer of a system maintainer could be the end-user and network manager.

To make the matter more complicated, the customer of an information-system worker may change from one period to another. For example, at the start of a project, the customers of the system designer could be the representatives of system customers who participate in the determination of the customer-requirements analysis (discussed in Chapter 6), the system analyst, and the decision makers who are involved in the determination of the system's scope. As the information system's scope becomes more concrete and the design parameters are determined, language and software programmers, as well as hardware specialists and data managers, become the system designer's immediate customers.

In other words, the performance evaluation for each information-system worker is done by the group of people who is the recipient of the worker's output. If the flow of output changes from one period to another, so does the evaluator group.

Who Is the Final Judge in the Selection of Customers?   The process of identifying the customers of each type of information-systems worker is a cross-functional teamwork activity that requires an extensive degree of consensus building and ownership by those who are affected by it. Its success is in the leadership of the company, which should make sure that organizational politics and maneuvering do not destroy the objectives of the process. Discussions of Chapters 1 and 2 have an immediate application in this case.

What Is the Relative Importance of Customers?   One must expect each type of information-system worker to have more than one type of customer. Are customers equally important? For example, if an information-system worker has a CEO, a programmer, and an end-user as his or her customers, should we give equal weight to the performance evaluation of these three types of customers?

The relative weight of the evaluation rating of an internal customer (internal to the function and organization) is his or her relative closeness to the external customer of the company, who pays for the products or services that the company generates.

Let us consider the three types of customers in the above example for the case of ACCU-INFO, which sells credit information. The end-user of the information system could be the person who sends the update to the customer. The programmer writes the program that generates the updates, and the CEO negotiates the contract with the external customer. In this case, since the CEO and end-user are in direct contact with the external customer who pays for the company's product, they get equal relative importance; the programmer who is one stage removed from the paying customer gets a lower relative weight in his or her evaluation of the information-system worker's performance. If the CEO does not have any contact with the paying, external customer, his or her relative weight would be lower than the end-user's and the programmer's.

In other words, the power of each person in evaluating information-system workers' performance is in direct proportion to their direct exposure to the external, paying customer of the company. This approach is the direct consequence of what Deming referred to as turning the organizational hierarchy upside down, removing the power from the bureaucrats and putting it in the hands of customers, and those who serve them directly.

Are Customers Knowledgeable Enough to be Fair Evaluators?   One of the criticisms of the customer evaluators is that the customers may not have the right perspective, knowledge, and understanding of the information-system worker's tasks and capabilities. This is the shortcoming of the company, not the customers. For example, how could programmers accomplish what they are supposed to if they do not have a clear perspective, knowledge, and understanding of what systems designers do? It is the job of the system designer to educate his or her customers. The company's plans and projects should incorporate the time and process of educating customers of each group. The cross-functional teams should make sure customer education is incorporated into their action plan.

This does not mean that every worker should have all types of expertise—nor do managers in the hierarchical structures. However, customers of each information-system worker should be knowledgeable about what to expect from the worker and judge the value and quality of his or her deliverables. In other words, an educated customer is the best ally for information-system workers. This idea is in line with that of the "learning organization," which will be discussed in a later section.

The Transition Process From Managerial to Customer Performance Evaluation.   The transition process from managerial to customer performance evaluation for information-system workers can be accomplished either at once or in a gradual manner. If the structure and culture of the organization has been altered to reflect that managers are not controllers and bosses, but rather facilitators and guides, then the customer performance evaluation process can easily be implemented into the system. However, if the company has not achieved a complete cultural change, a percentage of performance ratings could be allocated to the information-systems workers' customers, with a plan for increasing the share of customers and reducing that of managers as the cultural change takes hold.

In this process, an interesting practice is to identify how the performance of managers and team leaders is evaluated. Here too, the same concept of evaluation by customers applies. It would be the workers or the team leader who should evaluate the manager's performance. This is indeed the organizational hierarchy turned upside down and inside out.

7.2   ◆   Structural Changes in Information Systems

Tom Peters, in his view on "beyond hierarchy" in his book *Liberation Management* [1992], deduces twenty seven "organizing propositions," many of which have direct and indirect impacts on information systems. Two of his propositions speak directly to the nature of information systems for the 1990s and beyond:

> *Information technology is everything, and nothing. Utilizing the new technologies is essential to success. Applying the new technologies to outmoded organizations is a design for disaster.*
> *Real-time access to all information, including information from 'outsiders,' is a must for everyone in the organization. Phenomenal amounts of time and money must be spent*

on communication required to hold slippery, temporary networks together. That includes information technology—and face-to-face meetings and a big travel budget.

Hannan and Freeman [1989] in their book *Organizational Ecology*, and Tom Peters in his *Liberation Management* [1992] distinguish between two modes of organizational strategies: r-strategy and K-strategy. The firm with r-strategy is small and nimble and grows rapidly in an open environment and the condition of rapid change (like flies and mosquitoes). Its flexible structure allows it to respond quickly to a market opportunity and change; or it is destroyed as conditions change.

The firms with K-strategy are larger and more energy goes into creating each one of them (like whales and humans). They have the capability of capturing large markets and withstanding fierce competition. K-strategy is appropriate when change in the environment is slow. The present conditions in the market environment favor firms with r-strategy.

The market is changing, fluid, and open. In an open market, the opportunities should be exploited rapidly and with utmost flexibility. Therefore, organizational structures that are flexible, fluid, and smart can exploit such opportunities. The challenge for information systems is to operate successfully under such conditions. Every time the information needs of the firm change, can IS afford a lengthy system analysis, design, and implementation process? Can it even wait for prototyping? If the organization needs to respond fast, the information systems should already be in place in advance to provide and feed the information about an opportunity that has just been discovered. In other words, the information system should have an almost instantaneous response to requests of an unforeseen nature.

7.2.1   Flexible Information Systems

The dilemma is the design of an information system that is as flexible and responsive to market opportunities as it is to organization units, otherwise it has no value to r-strategy firms. The major characteristics of such information systems include:

- Should be able to respond quickly to the new needs of the organizational units as they move into new markets, new processes, and new products and services
- Should be able to assist the organizational units in identifying new opportunities and new strategies
- Should be the repository of the internal knowledge and expertise as the organizational units try new strategies and gain new experience in various markets, products, and services
- Should act as an early detector of unexpected problems
- Should be the communication broker among various disparate and diverse organizational units, each operating under its unique market circumstances
- Should create trust in and educate its customers about the system's capabilities and stimulate their interest in taking ownership of the system, having input to the system, and helping improve the system

In sum, the information system in a flexible organization reflects the mode of the organization and becomes a close partner of the organization units. IS is the bond that brings the decentralized organizational units together and creates the economy of scale for the large organization with decentralized units. It is the oil that facilitates the operation of various components of an engine.

In this light, let us look into the type of information systems that could facilitate this process. Here we consider a number of avenues that can be followed for creating flexibility in information systems. The emphasis is the movement toward the ideal, not its immediate attainment, because the field is just beginning to address this issue. The approaches for flexible information systems include:

- Meta-Information Systems
- Meta-Database Systems
- Just-in-Time Information Systems
- Unstructured-Information Systems
- Knowledge-Repository Systems

7.2.2   Meta-Information Systems

The advent of workstations and networked personal computers goes hand in hand with the increasing decentralization and independence of organizational units. Even organizations with a large and centralized information system find out that their independent units have set up small systems of their own to address their unique, local information needs. This trend is accelerating to the point where there are few organizations that can claim to have a completely centralized information system.

A *meta-information system* is an information system about information systems. In other words, as new local information systems are developed, they become entries to the meta-information system, Figure 7.1. Let us investigate the nature of such systems. The meta-information system:

- Keeps track of the performance of all information systems across units of the organizations
- Contains the information on the hardware, software, databases, network types, data suppliers of the system, customers of the system, and the reasons for creating the system
- Keeps a record of problems encountered in the system, the way they were resolved, and the individuals who are knowledgeable about the problem and its solution
- Contains the information and expertise gained in developing the system, pitfalls for avoiding them, and the best practices
- Provides information to enter and use an information system, individuals to contact, procedures to follow, authorizations to obtain
- Provides standards for developing a new system in the form of guidelines, and should contain information about the reasons for cases in which the guidelines and standards were not followed

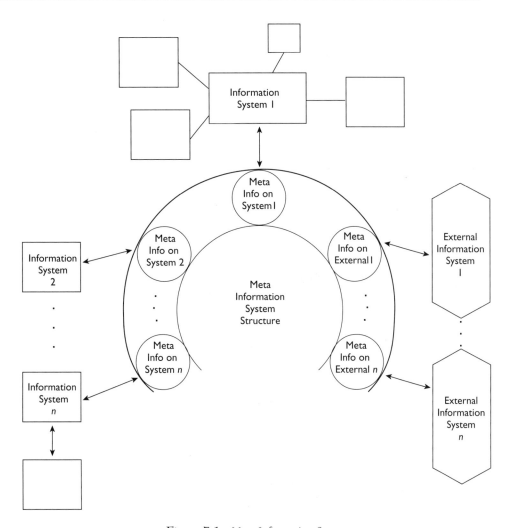

Figure 7.1   Meta-Information System

The role of a meta-information system is not to police information systems across the organization. Instead, it should act as a facilitator for spreading information regarding the availability of information in various systems across the organizational units. When a new unit starts its operation, needs to enter a new market, or initiates a new process, it can use the organizational expertise captured in information systems across the units. Furthermore, it can rely on the internal information regarding the standards for developing a new system, the pitfalls to avoid, and the experts to use.

Mixed-Meta Information Systems.   The basic structure of meta-information systems is focused on the collection, organization, and connection of the internal information systems. However, there is no reason why external information systems should not be included. In this sense, one can divide meta-information systems into three categories:

- Internal-Meta Systems
- External-Meta Systems
- Mixed-Meta Systems

In the *internal-meta systems*, all information systems belong to the corporation that own the system. In the *external-meta systems*, information systems are all external to the corporation.

In today's complex organizational world, it has become increasingly difficult to define the boundaries of organizations. For example, when the supplier has access to its customers' information systems, are these systems internal to the supplier's meta system? The answer will not be easy and it is not of major significance. We should expect that most of meta systems will be *mixed*, in which the internal and external information systems are connected.

Mixed- and external-meta systems have the flexibility of offering their customers the access to a wide variety of resources in a disciplined fashion. If the internal resources lack the information the user is looking for, an external resource may compensate for it.

The problem of external-meta-information systems is that there are so many information resources that including access to all of them and defining the appropriate interfaces to them become a prohibitive and impossible task. In meta-information systems, the choice of inclusion of external systems should be guided by the vision and long-term plan of the organization and that of the information-system function. The choice of external sources reflects the corporate's planned future ventures. Furthermore, the structural design of the meta-system should be flexible enough for quick addition or deletion of new external or internal information systems.

For example, in the case of ACCU-INFO, if the corporation has the vision for entering international credit checking, the meta-information system designers should begin to identify and incorporate the information systems that are useful in an international credit-checking venture.

Furthermore, as ACCU-INFO enters the international credit-checking market, there should be a model for creating information systems appropriate for each country. Furthermore, country-specific information systems should become a part of the corporate meta-information system that, in turn, will make each country-specific information system available to all organizational units across the globe.

Thus, as business moves into new markets, new products, and new processes, so does the meta-information system and its local components. In some cases, the meta-information system may precede the business operation in order to provide the background information needed for effective decision making and operation. In the case of ACCU-INFO, if the company decides to create a credit-checking business in, say, Japan, the meta-information system should provide the background information for the feasibility of such a venture, should offer a model for creating a Japan-specific business, and a design for making the Japan-specific information system a component of the corporate's meta-information system.

Adding systems to the meta-information system without deleting outdated and irrelevant systems could make the meta system inefficient and eventually useless. Therefore, it is important that as information on new information systems is added to the system, the old information should be deleted from the system, and the performance of the existing systems should be monitored to make sure they provide the needed information to the meta system's customers.

7.2.3   Meta-Database Systems

Meta-database systems form a major component of meta-information systems. A meta-database system contains information regarding the data in various databases in the organization. Meta-database systems can be:

- Internal
- External
- Mixed

An *internal-meta-database system* contains information on databases internal to the organization. An *external-meta-database system* has the data on databases external to the organization. A *mixed-meta-database system* contains data on a combination of internal and external databases.

The internal-meta-database system catalogues the data in various database systems across the organization. The difference between a meta-database system and the distributed database systems is that a meta-database system provides a system for binding together database systems that are already independently designed and may already be operational. It does not force a uniform or even compatible design for various databases. Instead, it takes the designs that exist and creates an overall structure through which the access to individual database systems could take place. In a distributed database system, on the other hand, there is an overall design for the entire database, and it is the location of data that is distributed across various nodes.

In other words, the meta-database system provides a transparent access to independent database systems. This requires more than just the information on the available data. It requires knowledge of the type of software, design of the system, and access to the system.

The external- and mixed-meta-database systems contain information on a variety of external databases. As in the case of internal-meta-databases, meta-database systems do not contain any actual data themselves. Instead, they contain information and data descriptions of databases to which the meta-database is connected, or can provide connection on demand (more on this point in the next section's discussion on the just-in-time information systems).

In addition to the reasons common to creating meta-information systems, the development of meta-database systems is necessitated further by:

- Accommodating the needs of diverse customers
- The increase in the volume of data
- The diversity of data types
- The need for the most accurate and up-to-date data
- The increase in the number of available databases containing data of various types

- The spread of data over a large geographical area, decentralization of data
- The impossibility of foreseeing data needs of an organization in a rapidly changing environment
- The need for increased flexibility and response to data needs
- The increase in the requirement to stock data, hence tying up money in computer storage and updating data
- Diversity of platforms and software products
- Continuous changes of technology
- Inertia and investment in legacy systems

Accommodating the Needs of Diverse Customers.   For a long time, information systems were expected to be uniformly designed to meet the information needs of all customers. Once the system is implemented, it becomes the task of customers to learn and adapt to it, and to live with its design shortcomings until its next round of life-cycle improvement.

This view of information systems is being drastically altered with changes in technology, the nature of business, market opportunities, and approaches to management that treat employees as the most crucial organizational resource. Now more than ever, it is important to customize information systems for each customer type in order to empower customers to achieve their highest potential. Information systems have to move out of their uniform, monolithic shell into the workplace of their users, adapting quickly to their needs and wishes, and responding on time to changes in the market and technology. To accomplish this requires customer-specific databases that are linked to a meta-database system accessible to all.

Volume of Data.   With the increase in the complexity of corporate structures and diversity of markets, the volume of generated data has been steadily increasing. As the markets become more global, the volume of data will increase at an even higher rate. While no one database would be capable of containing all data, the users need to access data in diverse databases via one system. Otherwise, identifying, locating, and accessing data from various sources would be an impossible task for a typical user of data.

The Diversity of Data Types.   As the volume of data grows, so does its diversity. Data is not limited to numerical values anymore. Most of the existing knowledge is in non-numerical form. Therefore, we increasingly have information in the form of texts, rules, patterns, graphics, pictures, and sound.

Obviously, we cannot expect all data types to be accommodated by one database system. It is quite natural to have newer database systems that contain later forms of input data, while the existing legacy systems house mostly the numerical data types. The question is whether we can have one system that allows us to access all types of data. The meta-database system is an answer to this question.

Accurate and Up-to-Date Data.   The speed of interactions and decisions has reduced the window for updating data close to zero. If the data is generated by an outside source, to utilize it effectively, one cannot wait until the data is imported into the internal system. The most up-to-date and accurate data is that which is closest to its source. This means that once the data is entered into a database, there is no reason to transfer it to other databases for access. Access should go directly to the source. This means that a meta-database should know where the origin of data is and make it available to the customers of the system.

Similarly, most of the internal data is captured and stored in local information systems before being sent to a centralized database. Instead of moving data across the system, thus losing time and accuracy in the process, a meta-database can reach the local database and make it available to the customer.

It should be emphasized that meta-database systems do not replace distributed systems. In the distributed systems, one may need to collect and aggregate data from various nodes, while the meta-database does not contain data of its own. Distributed database systems are part of a meta-database system (Figure 7.2).

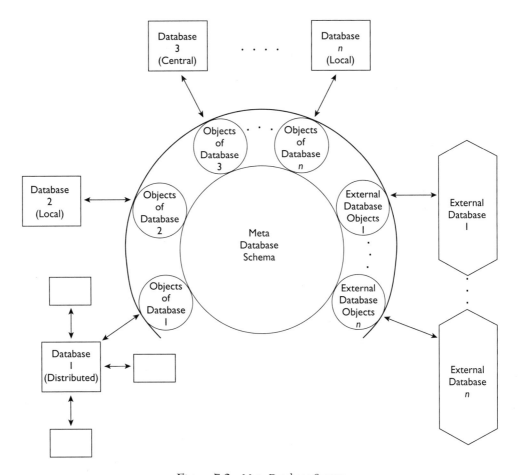

Figure 7.2   Meta-Database System

Available Databases.   Meta-database systems would not be necessary if we did not have not so many internal and external databases. There are numerous companies whose main functions entail the collection and organization of data. Similarly, as organizations have decentralized, independent database systems have mushroomed within them, each using the software, hardware, and design that are the favorites of the local unit.

These systems are organizational assets. Meta-database systems make the resources such systems provide accessible to all units. This way, large organizations are able to share their collective information and knowledge across units, while avoiding the straitjacket of a uniformly designed system.

The Spread of Data.   Another factor that makes meta-databases inevitable requirements is the fact that with the increasing global scope of business operations, databases are spread across national boundaries and continents. Although distributed database systems are designed to connect geographically distributed databases, their requirements for a uniform or coherent design creates constraints and limits the flexibility and freedom of the diverse local databases. Meta-database systems allow full flexibility for local databases, and at the same time create a highway across the diverse and independent database systems.

Thus, meta-database systems respect the complete independence and the diversity of local units, while providing a channel for the access to all such databases inside and outside the organization.

For example, in the ACCU-INFO case, assume that the company has expanded to Mexico, which has its own unique laws and regulations for checking credit. Therefore, the Mexico branch has to develop its own unique database system for credit checking in Mexico. The U.S. operation needs to have access to the Mexico database system because the company needs to check the credit of Mexicans who work or do business in the U.S. Creating a meta-database system that allows for smooth access of all units (U.S., Mexico, and Europe) to all credit-checking systems makes the independent, uniquely created, and local database systems into an integrated system that is accessible to all units.

Quick Access.   Global competition requires an increase in corporations' adaptability to change in market conditions. As the business response to market changes and opportunities quickens, so does the speed by which a successful unit obtains information regarding such changes and opportunities. The information may be internally generated or externally acquired. In many cases, the unit does not have time to wait until its needs are assessed, the right database designed and populated with data. In many cases, what the unit needs may be available somewhere inside or outside the company. Even if the needed data is related directly to the specific operation of the unit yet to become operational, it can obtain an approximate match by benchmarking with other units inside or outside the company. A meta-database system provides the access to the existing databases that provide adequate, if not the best, data for decision making.

Rapid Response to Changes.   When the data needs of the company change, one can undertake the life-cycle analysis of information needs of the company to revise and upgrade the system. This undertaking will take quite some time. On the other hand, one can add or delete database systems from the meta-database system. Meta-database systems do not require the abandonment of the existing systems. That is the decision of the independent units using them. When the use of the database system by the entire organization proves to be of no value, that database system is dropped from the meta-database system. On the other hand, when a new need arises, the company does not need to revamp its entire system to accommodate the new need. Instead, a new database system is created locally and then is added to the meta-database system.

This way, the information system of the company is able to respond quickly to market changes of the company without requiring extensive changes in its overall information-system structure. This does not mean that new developments do not take place, but it reduces the need to redesign the entire system and throw away the legacy systems once the technology, needs, or type of business change.

Investment Requirements.   The need to add to the diversity and volume of data for decision making has created an extensive investment in hardware, software, and storage. It is very difficult to change over from one system to another without extensive reinvestment. A meta-information system allows the legacy systems to stay in operation while new systems are added. This way, customers access new systems without losing the service of the old system. The changeover is gradual and natural. As the new system takes hold, is debugged, and altered to address the needs of its customers, the old system gradually dies down, or may remain part of the meta system until the lack of use makes it a candidate for elimination from the meta system. Thus, changeovers from one system to another would involve minimum discontinuity, and the resistance to the new system because of possible risks and disruptions disappears.

Diversity of Platforms and Software Products.   Customers invest in learning operating systems, software, or interface, for which they develop an ease and attachment. With the existing diversity of products and platforms, it is impossible for any organization, large or small, to enforce a uniform product line. This difficulty leads to uncontrollable variety in the platforms and products within an organization. On the other hand, there is an ever-increasing need to access information across various systems within an organization. Thus, there is a conflict between keeping the diversity of products and services and satisfying the need to have an inter-system connectivity.

The client-server model of information systems addresses this dilemma at the access level, in that one can access various systems and products over the network. Meta-information systems go beyond pure access; they provide a unifying, overall design for integrating heterogeneous systems and making the access transparent for meta-system customers.

Continuous Changes of Technology.   Another factor that constantly defeats any attempt to create uniformity of structure, design, access, and interface is constant changes in technology. No matter how well-designed an information system is, changes in technology and methodology reduce its comparative advantage. Any structure that inherently is based on just one technology is bound for rapid obsolescence. In the present approaches to information systems, even in the client-server model of cooperative processing, the underlying technology binds the flexibility of the system to the introduction of new technology in a seamless manner.

The structure of a meta-information system is inherently open to the addition of any new technology to the system without structural changes.

Inertia and Investment in the Legacy Systems.   Closely related to the issue of technological change is the inertia of the existing systems. Changing an existing system is a costly and disruptive proposition at best. Even when there is no doubt that a system is inadequate and obsolete, and all of its customers are asking for changes in the system, there are elements that create resistance and inertia in changing a system. These elements include:

- Inertia from the type of use
- Inertia from the volume of investment
- Inertia from partial obsolescence

In the *inertia from the type of use*, the obsolete system has evolved beyond its originally intended use. Every system creates its own environment of dedicated secondary users and customers who use the system in creative ways that were not intended or even known by the original designers. This is especially true for large systems with multiple user types, accessible from a central computer system or over a large network.

Incorporating the needs of these second-tier customers into the new system may not be easily possible or even desirable in the immediate future. Some companies have gone as far as creating the system and keeping the legacy system available to the second-tier users, allowing them to gradually migrate to the new system. The problem is that there is no structure to provide a framework of managing the two systems and deciding when the legacy system has practically died or should be phased out from general access.

The meta-information system structure incorporates the new system and manages the old system in the same environment. Since the meta-system keeps track of use and quality of each of its component systems, phasing out the old system will be more manageable.

In *the inertia from the volume of investment*, there is a reluctance in the organization to get rid of obsolete systems because of the extent of investment channeled into the maintenance of the system. The idea of completely getting rid of a system that has worked over the years for a normally unproven system could be troublesome for conservative CEOs. On the other hand, this reluctance creates a barrier to the introduction of new systems that could boost the corporation's competitive advantage. This is the dilemma of the old and tried vs. the new and uncertain system. It leads to the creation of small new information systems accessible only to a relatively small percentage of potential users and customers. Alternatively, the CEO is forced to abandon his or her conservative position after the ineffectiveness of the old system has become painfully obvious in the performance of the business and the extent of the lost opportunities.

The possibility of keeping the legacy systems in a meta-information system allows the introduction of new systems and technology without going to one of the two extremes in dealing with the investment concerns of CEOs.

The *inertia from partial obsolescence* is the case, in which a system is kept for longer than necessary because it is partially obsolete. A great deal of investment may go into dealing with the partial obsolescence because abandoning it completely is not justifiable. In a meta-system, each addition is considered a component of a system. In the case of partial obsolescence, the decision alternatives are to either not improve or create a new system. The comparison is between the cost of improvement and the cost of building a small, new system that can make up for the partial obsolescence of the old system. If the latter case proves to be more attractive, the new, small system is added to the meta-system. The new system may grow in time as the old system gradually becomes obsolete.

For example, in the case of ACCU-INFO, it may be that the present information system is partially obsolete because it cannot accommodate direct access to data suppliers' databases. Ordinarily, the decision involves the comparison between building a new system that has this feature, or leaving the system as is without any direct connection to the suppliers' database. If ACCU-INFO had a meta-database system, it could create a small system that has the capability of interacting with the suppliers' databases and connecting to the meta-system. Since the existing system is also part of the meta-database system, the present system could access data from the new system and continue its operation as before.

In sum, the creation of a meta-information system accommodates the inertia of the existing systems while allowing for the incorporation of new technology and new systems. Thus, meta-database systems can be used as a structure for the continuous improvement of information systems.

7.3 ◆ Just-in-Time Information Systems

There are two forces behind the creation of an information system and the supply of its service: supply push and demand pull. In the *supply push*, it is mostly the technology suppliers and systems developers who champion the acquisition of new hardware and software technology and the creation of a new system. Historically, this has been the major underlying force in the creation of new systems. In many cases, there is a champion of change in the organization who takes it upon himself or herself to convince the decision makers and users that a new technology and system is good for the organization and system users.

In the *demand pull* case, the major force is the demand of customers and users in creating a new system, and offering new information services. With the increasing literacy of systems customers and users regarding the need for and the role of information systems, demand pull is a more attractive force in creating a new system.

A demand-pull information system means that both the *creation* as well as the *delivery* of information services are based on demand pull. The delivery of information on demand has been the hallmark of computerized information systems. The on-line and real-time systems have long been created for the delivery of the information on demand. However, this delivery is based on an existing structure and one or, at most, two methods of delivery.

For example, a credit-checking query to ACCU-INFO is answered through the existing structure of the credit database, an existing set of data in the database, and a couple of pre-set interfaces, such as menu and command interfaces, as well as report generations. ACCU-INFO's information system does not have any capability to respond to queries for which it lacks data, such as the query of a customer for a person's combined individual and business credit rating.

Normally, if such questions are isolated and infrequent, we need to set up a manual process to deal with them. When such questions are frequent and there is a large enough market in volume and price that makes it profitable to have an information system to answer them, we need an approach that can rapidly respond to information demand. In this case, we need to look into information systems that are "just-in-time."

7.3.1   Background on Just-in-Time Systems

The idea of just-in-time has its origin in Japan in the 1960s as a method to handle inventory problems—to eliminate the need to store parts and materials for use in the future. However, this is not the only interpretation of just-in-time. It is also interpreted as an approach to quality control as well as production scheduling, including the *kanban* card system. In the kanban system, a visual signal such as cards, colored lights, or colored balls signal the need for additional production or parts. Such signals are triggered by customer demand.

Just-in-time is also a strategy or philosophy for producing high quality products and services. As a philosophy, just-in-time espouses many of the quality concepts, including close relationships with customers and suppliers and continuous improvement in the flow of product and services. The most important contribution of just-in-time to information systems is its focus on creating a system for response to customers' needs and demands.

7.3.2   Creating Just-in-Time Information Systems

If we consider the implementation of information systems as *manufacturing* information systems, we see that some just-in-time concepts in manufacturing have direct relevance to the manufacturing of information systems.

Manufacturing information systems in the traditional form is mostly triggered by new technology and is mostly supply-pull in the sense that the system developers initiate it. While this may be inevitable in information systems that are created for the first time, there are many instances where a corporate unit needs to enter a market quickly and requires a rapid deployment of a relatively well-understood and previously designed information system.

In such a case, we need a standard procedure, as well as an underlying structure, to have a rapid deployment capability in manufacturing an information system based on the choice of a predetermined design and an infrastructure to connect the deployed information system to the entire system. This creates a *just-in-time* capability for manufacturing information systems.

Manufacturing just-in-time information systems stretches the systems analysis beyond a specific project or an immediate need. Instead, systems analysis and the subsequent designs are carried out for the implementation of corporate vision and its corresponding information-systems vision. In this approach, there is a grand system architecture that embodies the present needs and requirements, as well as the future requirements dictated by the corporate vision. It has an open architecture to include and connect all future information systems—the meta-information system discussed earlier in this chapter.

Coupled with the meta-information system infrastructure is the set of standard procedures and systems for the rapid deployment of new information systems and plugging them into the corporate meta-information system. These information systems are created for the rapid response to customer demand, and their creation should be based on the same principles as the just-in-time manufacturing of products. These principles include:

- Fast response to customer needs
- Flexible structure to purge old and add new
- Open system and connectivity
- Accommodating diversity

Fast Response to Customer Needs.   The globalization of markets requires corporations to have a rapid deployment capability to enter a market and take advantage of the window of opportunity before the competition drives the profit margin to zero. This requirement puts an unprecedented demand on the information-systems function to rapidly respond to its customers' needs. The information-systems function can no longer take a relatively long time to perform systems analysis for every new information system. On the other hand, organizations cannot afford to allow new information systems to mushroom uncontrollably across the geographical spread of the corporation without any standard and capability of interconnection.

Therefore, corporations encounter the dilemma of the need for fast response and the need to have a well-organized and inter-connected information-system structure. The meta-information-system concept provides the underlying structure for a just-in-time information system.

Even without a meta-information system, the company should create standard designs for rapid deployment of information systems. Such standards could evolve from the design of existing and successful systems. Standard designs should be updated as design-related new knowledge is gained in the workings of present systems. The standard design could also be for cases where the real operation has not yet started, but the corporate vision shows a commitment to such projects. Benchmarking similar operations could also be helpful in creating design standards for rapid deployment.

Flexible Structure to Purge Old and Add New.   Another focus of just-in-time manufacturing is the emphasis on cost reduction. In other words, it is not enough to create new systems rapidly. The new systems should be deployed in the most cost-effective manner. This includes purging what is not needed to free resources for new systems.

Every computer network and structure has limited resources of hardware, software, manpower, and physical space, as well as network capacity. Managing just-in-time information-system manufacturing requires a careful analysis and plan for purging the information systems, databases, and data that are not needed anymore. This itself requires careful planning, standard setting, and a design for retiring old systems. Again, the idea of meta-information systems could be very helpful in this respect.

Connectivity to Customer Organizations.   The geographical spread of markets requires internal connectivity of information systems within the boundaries of a corporation. However, the expansion of organizations beyond their legal boundaries has put another layer of demand on the infrastructure of information systems—that is, the demand for connectivity with external suppliers' and external customers' systems. This requirement makes it very costly and technically undesirable to design inter- and intra-organization connectivity for every one of the information systems within the organization. There has to be a meta-information system infrastructure to which each information system is connected.

The standards for the manufacturing of just-in-time information systems need to address the connectivity requirement of various designs of information systems.

Accommodate Diversity.   As corporations decentralize and make their way into various types of markets, they recognize that each market has its own unique needs and requirements. The information systems that are created based on the just-in-time concept have to accommodate these diversities. The diversity may have a number of sources:

- Diversity in size
- Diversity in complexity
- Diversity in the extent of structure

The size of operation dictates the size of the needed information system in many cases. Just-in-time manufacturing of information systems should standardize the design for various size operations, such that small-size operations could get into the meta-information system as fast and easily as the large information systems.

The diversity in complexity is another form of variability in information-systems needs. Modularized design based on an object-oriented approach could deal with the complexity issues. Again, it is important to identify the main objects and components that should be put together in order to deal with the rapid deployment of complex information systems.

The diversity in the structure is yet another source of variability in information-systems needs. In some cases, complete flexibility and lack of structure are needed in dealing with some customers' information needs. This requires creating a design for unstructured information systems, as discussed in the next section.

7.3.3   Unstructured Information Systems

Traditionally, information systems have been created to provide a formal structure for storage and use of data and processing of information within an organization. Therefore, the idea of an unstructured information system sounds like a contradiction in terms.

The need for unstructured information systems is due to the expansion of the role of information systems to the medium of group interaction and group work. It is not enough to use information systems to access and process data and knowledge that are logically organized in the system. Today's information systems are expected to provide a communication link for people across geographical and organizational boundaries.

At the start, the role of information systems in communication was limited to providing a passive channel of communication similar to that of telephones. The success of information systems as instruments of communication has led to the expansion of this role into providing software and bulletin boards and capturing the information created through the communication process. In other words, information systems are increasingly turning into active participants in communication. In this sense, information systems are now a major component in addressing the communication needs of any organization with a commitment to quality programs.

Areas in which information systems have assumed an active role in communication include:

- Unstructured databases
- Groupware
- Internet
- Knowledge collection and dissemination
- Agents: Robo Software

Unstructured Databases.   Unstructured databases contain the captured information of dialogue among communicators over the system, disseminate of the information to everyone who wish to access it. A good example of such a database system is Lotus's Notes, in which the communicators may write notes on various subjects. The software captures the notes, organizes them, and makes them accessible to participants who have an interest in the subject within a network. The software shares the notes with other networks.

The amount and complexity of the information that is created through the unstructured databases is tremendous, and the field of information systems has not yet begun to address the design issues of such systems. However, a meta-information system has to be able to deal with unstructured databases in an efficient manner. Otherwise, the mushrooming of unstructured information may exhaust the resources, or the premature purging of information could lead to the loss of valuable information.

Groupware.   As the geographical dimension of the workplace expands, the idea of the office as a fixed location becomes less commonplace. Employees work in various locations, such as at home, on the road, at the customer's office, in hotels, and in geographically dispersed offices. To have any type of group meeting or group discussion requires additional software and structure to capture and disseminate group members' exchange of ideas. *Groupware* products are designed to facilitate group communications. Increasingly, information systems are required to have the groupware facility such that the discussion of the group can be captured and structured as a source of information.

Internet.   Another source of unstructured information is bulletin boards, many accessible via Internet. Gibbs and Smith [1993] state that "The simplest way to describe the Internet is with one word—communication. To some people, it's just a way to send electronic mail to other people—a pipeline from here to there. To others, the Internet is where they meet their friends, play games, argue, do work, and travel the world." With the expansion of the Internet into what is called the "information superhighway," it seems that the latter description of Internet will be the operating mode of communication in the future.

Meta-information systems not only have to be connected to the Internet or any expanded version of it, but they also have to provide meta systems for guiding customers through the relevant types of information available to them. There is a need for a user interface to guide customers through the maze of ever-expanding information on the Internet and its related bulletin boards. There are now companies in the market that offer intelligent access to Internet.

Knowledge Collection and Dissemination.   We are living in an age of knowledge workers. Any job that can be performed routinely without the need to use judgment and knowledge will eventually be automated, if it hasn't been by now. The success of any organization lies in its ability to increase the job-related knowledge of its workers.

Therefore, another important component of unstructured information systems is the need to capture and disseminate learned experiences and know-how that are created continuously within the organization. Sharing valuable lessons learned through experience, mistakes, and innovations creates a culture of learning and sharing among employees, increases the employees' knowledge of the organizational know-how, and reduces the chance of costly mistakes. We will discuss this subject further in a later section on the learning organization.

Depending on the nature of its business, the organization's knowledge base takes different shapes and forms. In the case of ACCU-INFO, for example, the organization knowledge base could contain the following modules:

- The knowledge on how to report the rating for an individual who has gaps in his or her purchases and payments
- The issues that are sensitive for customers who request a credit rating
- Legal ramifications of errors and the best ways to deal with them
- Best practices in dealing with data suppliers
- Best practices in dealing with customers' complaints and error
- Best practices in dealing with individuals' rating complaints

- New issues and hot topics in credit ratings
- The list of in-house experts, their expertise, and the best time and way to approach them
- The list of external experts, their expertise, and the best time and way to approach them

Notice that a great deal of the organizational knowledge base contains information that is time-sensitive, and requires regular updating and purging. Furthermore, the knowledge base belongs to all who work in the organization. All experts and workers need to take ownership of the knowledge base, have input to it, and use it as a resource in their decision process. In a later section, we will discuss the idea of meta-knowledge base as an approach to disseminating organizational knowledge.

Agents: Robo Software.   This type of software has intelligence beyond the ordinary software products and is able to carry out complex tasks, such as the personnel systems developed by Hewlett-Packard, discussed in the following case. Robo software products capture organizational knowledge by using artificial intelligence, expert systems, and neural networks, which are the methods for creating intelligence in computerized systems.

◆ CASE: Agent Systems and Software

Robots have long captured man's imagination as tireless, eternally loyal servants. But even today, with many factories having gone robotic, few people have ever seen a true robot, much less owned one that they could boss around.

All that may change now, as a new kind of robot starts prowling the digital highways and byways of cyberspace. It's what computer scientists call an "agent"—a kind of software program that's powerful and autonomous enough to do what all good robots should: help the harried humans by carrying out tedious, time-consuming, and complex tasks. Software agents just now emerging from the research labs can scan data banks by the dozen, schedule meetings, tidy up electronic in-boxes, and handle a growing list of clerical jobs. In the next couple of years, experts predict, agents will be available from all major software companies and quite a few startups as well.

Superhighway Surfeit. At Hewlett-Packard Co., an agent supplied by Edify Corp. is already helping automate a quarterly wage-review process that covers approximately 13,000 salespeople. Edify's software, running on a PC, performs essentially the same tasks that a team of 20 administrators has been doing by hand. First, the agent program dials into the HP personnel system and gets a list of who works for each of 1,200 sales managers nationwide. The agent then electronically mails each manager a list for his verification. It collects any changes by e-mail and enters them back into the personnel system—exactly as if a human were working at a terminal.

Now, the agent repeats the entire process, but this time it includes proposed salary changes supplied by management for each employee. Managers can approve the changes or alter them simply by phoning the PC and keying in new data in response to the Edify agent's synthesized voice prompts.

An entire menagerie of software agents is starting to debut—some sophisticated, some simple, some quite visible, others programmed to work strictly behind the scenes. Ideally, they will mimic just what an intelligent human would do, except with greater stamina and accuracy. This might be the only way that mere mortals will be able to cope with the widely hailed Information Superhighway and its cornucopia of services and machine-generated messages demanding immediate attention.

The windows-icon-mouse interface that Alan Kay and other computer scientists developed at Xerox Corp. in the 1970s isn't keeping up with the complexity of networks. Unassisted, people can keep track of only so many graphical icons, for instance. "You'll be connected to millions or billions of different resources," predicts Kay, now a research fellow at Apple Computer Inc. "One of the biggest problems is to find information. We don't believe you can browse for it." To find what you need, he says, the computer "has to be flexible enough to take on many of your goals. You either tell it or teach it what you are interested in, and dispatch agents. The agents will find things and screen them."

Plausible Lies. To make that happen, agent developers are building on the past decade's research in artificial intelligence (AI). Agents are incorporating techniques for understanding human language and learning their masters' wishes by observing how they search for information. Says Ted Selker, a researcher at IBM and professor at Stanford University: "We want to create a tight feedback loop between the user and his computer assistant." That way, an agent might scour a large network of data banks to answer a difficult question, such as "How's the Asian retail market doing compared with Europe's?"

Until recently, even simple agents weren't practical, although AI researchers had sketched out the concept in the late 1950s. "The way you do research is to make up lies that are plausible—then invent the technology to make them true," Kay quips. Now the technology is in place: sprawling networks of powerful computers that are capable of running complex software. In the next few years, everything from personal digital assistants (PDAs) to desktop PCs and supercomputers will likely run some form of agent software. Just how big a market it will be is hard to estimate: The term "agent," like AI 10 years ago, is being applied to new products quite sloppily—in this case, to just about any program that works on your behalf.

In the tradition of those wise-cracking robots in sci-fi movies, software agents are also subject to much anthropomorphizing—and in some cases for good reason. At Carnegie Mellon University, Stanford University, and software think-tank International Research Corp., researchers are trying for "believable agents"—programs that embody human character and present themselves as animated cartoon faces that react to stimuli with convincing human expressions. At Carnegie Mellon, a family of such agents called Woggles—Shrimp, Bear, and Wolf—populates a whimsical virtual world. For entertainment, people can interact with them via another, mouse-controlled Woggle. One day, similar agents may make computers more human by giving their operating systems believable screen personas–frowning if you do something foolish, say. "We want to create agents that gain our confidence," says Joseph Bates, senior research computer scientist at Carnegie Mellon.

Not all agents strive for humanity, though. The Internet, connecting thousands of research computers around the world, relies on agents called gophers, which automatically retrieve information from all over the network. And Rupert Murdoch's News Electronic Data Inc. is getting ready to unleash Oliver, which will fetch personalized news and travel information. It's to appear on screens later this year as a Labrador retriever: "Oliver is loyal," says John Evans, president and CEO. "He retrieves personalized information for me. He is tireless, and he doesn't make a mess. But he's a stupid dog: If you throw two sticks, he'll get confused as hell. We're just trying to lower people's expectations" about agents.

American Telephone & Telegraph Co., meanwhile is heavily promoting the intelligent software assistants scheduled to be available on its forthcoming PersonalLink Computer network. They'll be programmed with software from General Magic, a Silicon Valley startup that's funded by AT&T, Sony, Motorola, and several other large electronics companies. The agents will help consumers communicate and purchase information, goods, and services from companies such as Mead Data Central Inc. A mail agent might have you paged when important e-mail arrives. A personal shopping agent could browse electronic malls for you and even make purchases using your credit-card number. Who knows? Perhaps in the future people doing business in cyberspace will just say: "Have your agent talk to my agent."

Source: John Verity and Richard Brandt "Robo-Software Reports for Duty," *Business Week*, February 14, 1994, pp. 110–113, reprinted from February 14, 1994 issue of *Business Week* by special permission, copyright © 1994 by McGraw-Hill, Inc.

7.3.4   Meta-Knowledge Base Systems

Tom Peters [1992] refers to employees as "knowledge workers," whose knowledge is the productive force in any manufacturing and service industry. A knowledge worker, by his or her nature, needs quick access to ever-expanding repositories of information and knowledge. Identifying the source of information by itself has become an important factor.

The function of identifying information sources used to be in the realm of librarians. Although library science has been increasingly revolutionized by computer systems, the specific needs of an organization and the mass sources of knowledge require that a part of the corporate information system be dedicated to the identification of knowledge sources that are of interest to the knowledge workers in the organization. That is, the meta-knowledge base should be a component of the corporate meta-information system.

We can define a *meta-knowledge base* as a knowledge base about knowledge. It contains information on the *sources* and *methods of access* for the knowledge on various domains that are in the organization's sphere of interest.

For example, in the ACCU-INFO case, the meta-knowledge base could contain the *sources* related to:

- Credit evaluation methods
- Legal issues in credit rating

- Ethical and social issues related to credit rating
- Technology of credit rating
- The use of business credit rating
- Differences in individual and business credit rating
- Industry differences in credit rating
- National and regional differences in credit rating
- Experts in credit rating

Various knowledge bases created in the organizations that deal with any one of the above topics would be included as a source in the meta-knowledge base. However, internal and formal sources will be only a part of the meta-knowledge base. It also includes outside sources related to the same topics, methods of access, and persons who should be contacted.

Again, it is the knowledge workers' involvement in the identification and use of the meta-knowledge base that makes it a useful source of knowledge for the entire organization.

7.4 ◆ Information Systems in Learning Organizations

Tom Peters [1992] quotes from David Maister, a Harvard Business School professor turned consultant, on Maister's evaluation of his personal stock that "Left untended, knowledge and skills, like all assets, depreciate in value—surprisingly quickly... " This is true for consultants as well as corporate professional and knowledge workers—an increasing proportion of the corporate workforce.

Peter Senge, in his book *The Fifth Discipline: The Art and Practice of the Learning Organization*, has brought into focus the idea that only organizations that learn will be able to survive in the long run. Although the concept of the learning organization makes a great deal of sense in the abstract, creating a culture of learning in an organization is not an easy process.

Training in information systems includes user training, occasional retooling of information-systems workers, and on-the-job training of new hires, which have been in practice in most information systems shops. The question is whether organizational "learning" is the same as worker and user "training" in information systems.

Training is certainly an important part of organizational learning, but learning goes far beyond the formal technical training of new users and workers. It involves:

- A culture of learning within the information-systems function and the organization—using errors as learning experiences
- The internal and external customers of information systems—learning customer needs and creating enlightened customers
- Ongoing and regular training of knowledge workers—training as a part of the employment pact
- Capturing and disseminating what is learned—information systems infrastructure for learning

7.4.1   Using Errors as Learning Experiences

When an error or fault is discovered in the information-system design or implementation, the common practice is to:

- Find the problem
- Identify and blame the guilty parties
- Remove the fault or error
- Consider the problem as an abnormal incidence and forget about it

In a learning organization, the discovery of errors and faults is a good opportunity to identify the faults in the *process* that have caused the problem. Therefore, in a learning organization, the preferred practice is:

- Find the problem
- Identify the involved workers
- Identify the process in which the error has taken place
- Get the involved workers participate in removing the fault or problem
- Use the involved workers as an educational source in finding the cause of the problem in the process
- Take corrective action in removing the cause of the problem and improving the process
- Enter the incident as a learning experience in the organizational knowledge base and inform others about the problem—how it was discovered, how it was fixed, what the cause was, and how the cause was removed

Once faults, errors, and problems are considered as opportunities for improvement and learning experiences, then individuals will not be hesitant to identify and report problems before they turn into crises. With a learning and non-blaming approach to problem identification, real causes of problems could be identified more quickly and be resolved more effectively.

For example, in the ACCU-INFO case, it is discovered that 20 percent of all social security numbers entered by a new data-entry clerk have errors. The common practice is to correct the entry errors and fire the clerk.

Considering ACCU-INFO as a learning organization, the data-entry clerk is used as a resource to study what led to the entry error and identify the processes involved. For example, the entry person is a novice; maybe the training process should be improved. The data-entry person has been tired and stressed; maybe the scheduling and work process should be investigated. The data-entry person has never worked with a keyboard; maybe the hiring and human-resource process should be examined. The data-entry screen does not give enough information regarding the format of the social security data item; maybe the data-entry interface should be improved.

Thus, the discovery of a mistake leads to an opportunity to improve the system far beyond fixing the error. Furthermore, the experience and the approach to resolving it should be disseminated so that the discovery experience and the approach to dealing with it become part of the organization's human, as well as computerized, knowledge base.

7.4.2   Learning Customer Needs and Creating Enlightened Customers

Another aspect of a learning organization is getting to know the customers' needs, as well as educating and enlightening the customers about what services are available to them. This is true not only about the external and direct customers of the organization's products and services, but also (and maybe more importantly) the customers within the organization.

Previously in this chapter, we talked about a reward system in which the performance of workers is evaluated by their customers. Another piece of the customer-focus strategy is that workers are partners of their customers in learning their needs and in educating them.

The field of information systems has always emphasized user-training. But such training is normally for the end-user and comes after the system is developed and implemented. In a learning organization with a customer focus, customers are not limited to end-users of the system; they include a host of internal and external customers discussed in Chapter 6. Furthermore, learning customers' needs and educating customers is an on-going process and does not end with the completion of systems design.

For example, an information system has internal customers such as programmers, data-entry personnel, system-maintenance personnel, and network-maintenance personnel. Learning about the needs of these workers is important to the successful implementation of the system.

Take the case where the data-entry clerks are the customers of a systems designer. The designer needs to learn about the needs of data-entry clerks. At the same time, if there is technology that would make the life of the data-entry clerk easier, then the designer should take time to educate and enlighten the data-entry clerks about the possible services that may be available and how they could simplify their work.

7.4.3   Training as a Part of the Employment Pact

Investing in the workers' knowledge is one of the hallmarks of business in the 1990s and beyond. Knowledge depreciates, and the business needs to reinvest in it in order to keep their knowledge workers current. This point is particularly true for technology-oriented areas such as information systems. The information technology changes so fast that a five-year gap in training could make a worker obsolete. Therefore, if a worker is laid off or leaves the job, he or she must invest time and money for retooling.

In a learning organization, the employment pact between the employee and employer contains the understanding that the employer provides learning opportunities (both formal and on-the-job) for the worker in exchange for the worker's dedication, loyalty, and creativity for the tenure of his or her employment in the organization.

Formal training for information-systems workers involves both technical and organizational training, and the training is not just limited to the skills immediately needed for a project, but also a continuous improvement and update of general and specific skills, as well as the latest organizational and managerial issues and approaches.

7.4.4   Information System Infrastructure for Learning

Peters [1992] divides learning into four areas:

- Learning with clients
- Learning with outsiders
- Learning within the organizations
- Capturing and disseminating knowledge

Information systems can play a crucial role in capturing and disseminating knowledge systematically. This requires an information system infrastructure that facilitates the learning process within large and geographically scattered organizations. This infrastructure may have different components:

- Computer networks to facilitate communication
- Formal processes for collection and dissemination of learned information
- Knowledge bases that are the repository of knowledge
- Meta-knowledge bases that identify the sources of knowledge relevant to the working of an organization
- Access to computerized training and courses

The components of the above list are already discussed in the previous sections.

The information-systems infrastructure can be gradually put in place as the learning awareness increases within the organization. Tom Peters [1992] reports a number of ways that a learning infrastructure could be created:

- "Systematic capture of knowledge," as Peters has observed at McKinsey, where a small group of knowledge managers collect and disseminate knowledge within the organization as it is created through experience
- "Joint Learning," as Peters has observed at CRSS (an architectural firm with more than $400 million revenue) that has made *listening* one of its most serious job descriptions
- "Schoolhouse," as Peters has observed at Quad/Graphics and Johnsonville Foods, where the learning has the same structure as in universities
- "Total integration/and symbiosis," as Peters has observed at the Buick Reatta Craft Centre and its paint supplier PPG, where PPG employees worked closely with their GM counterparts to improve the painting process
- "Learning network," as Peters has observed at MCI and Apple, where these corporations keep networking and partnering with outsiders in order to learn and expand their know-how and find new ways of adding value by creating new bundles of products and services

The information-systems infrastructure for capturing and disseminating knowledge in the above modes of learning may vary in formality and extent of detail. It is important that information-systems managers recognize the mode of organizational learning, and provide facilities, including the appropriate information-systems structure, to support and enhance the learning process.

7.5 ◆ Supplier Relationship

While customer focus is of great importance in quality information systems, relationships with suppliers are equally important for such systems. In product manufacturing, raw materials and parts play an important role in the production. Therefore, the quality of input materials, as well as the relationship with the suppliers of the input materials, are of great importance in manufacturing. Information systems do not have the same type of raw materials, while the role of suppliers in manufacturing information services has been underrated and has gone mostly unnoticed.

The supplier relationship becomes even more crucial for the creation of meta-information systems and the rapid deployment of new systems that are part of the meta-information system. As in the case of manufacturing, just-in-time information-systems creation and implementation requires a strong tie with the suppliers who provide parts, methods, input, and solutions for producing information-systems services.

Manufacturing information-systems services requires input from a variety of suppliers:

- Data, information and knowledge suppliers
- Network and communication suppliers
- Consulting services
- Hardware and software suppliers

7.5.1 Data, Information, and Knowledge Suppliers

In an era that is labeled alternatively as the "information age" and "knowledge age," it is obvious that the suppliers of data, information, and knowledge play an important role in the quality and usefulness of an information system. Yet these suppliers normally are taken for granted. In traditional systems analysis and design, little attention is paid to how one should identify sources of data, information and knowledge, methods and techniques for collecting the relevant information and knowledge, and relationships with such suppliers.

Perhaps knowledge engineering in expert systems brought forth the importance of identifying and eliciting knowledge from experts. However, the importance of knowledge suppliers is not limited to expert systems. Once we go beyond the traditional data-processing systems, such as payroll systems or accounting systems, any new system requires information that may not be readily and freely available. Therefore, a close relationship with suppliers of data, information, and knowledge to the system is of great importance.

The suppliers of data, information, and knowledge include:

- Internal generators
- Internal experts
- Internal customers of information systems
- External suppliers
- External generators
- External experts
- External customers of information systems

For example, in an information system that has a customer-service component, the internal and external customers of the information system provide information regarding what they need and the extent of their satisfaction with what the system provides.

For example, in ACCU-INFO, the caseworker who investigates the credit worthiness of an individual with little credit history is the internal generator of information. The external generator could be investigative agencies. The external suppliers could be the banks and credit-card companies who send their credit data to ACCU-INFO. Internal and external experts are those whose expertise is used in the system for checking the quality of the credit rating.

The identification of such suppliers, and the creation of close cooperation with them to ensure the quality of what they deliver to the system, are important factors in the quality of information systems.

7.5.2   Hardware and Software Suppliers

Creating a working supplier-customer relationship with producers of language compilers, software, and hardware products is also crucial in the smooth working of an information system. With the rapidly changing market and regular upgrades of all products, the relationship with these suppliers may keep the system from quick obsolescence.

7.5.3   Network and Communication Suppliers

Network and communication suppliers play an important role in the globally and nationally networked computers. With the existing variety of choices in selecting network and communication carriers, the information-systems function can create a close partnership with the supplier and receive help from the network supplier in determining the best communication topology and improved services as the technology changes.

7.5.4   Consulting Services

Outsourcing various aspects of information systems to outside consultants is common in the creation, and even the delivery, of information-systems services. One of the important functions of consulting services is the learning experience that could be shared between the corporate and consulting organizations. Such close cooperation will allow the internal workers to gain knowledge and experience from the process. Furthermore, the consulting organization will integrate its work more closely with the needs and requirements of the information system and its customers.

7.5.5   Dependence vs. Independence in Supplier Relationships

In creating a close relationship with various suppliers of information systems, there is always the danger of becoming dependent on the supplier to the point that the system becomes locked into the supplier's technology, procedures, and prices. In other words, close relations may breed inflexibility that could be costly and debilitating in the long run. Therefore, there are those who advocate keeping distance from the suppliers in order to preserve the corporation's independence and flexibility.

To address this dilemma, one should notice that a close relationship with a supplier does not necessarily mean the purchase of non-standard and custom-made products and service. The dependence is created when the supplier alters its products and services to suit the buyer's needs. Since this type of tailor-made services is costly, the supplier expects payoffs in the form of a long-term contract, higher prices, or both. To avoid such dependencies, the buyer can always insist on purchasing the supplier's standard product and services. The close relationship comes into play when the supplier gets involved in the design and implementation of the buyer's information system, becomes educated in the true needs of the system, and can offer the standard products and services that best suit the needs of the buyer's system. This partnership also becomes part of the buyer's and seller's learning network, discussed previously.

7.6   ◆   Information-Systems Recovery

In traditional information systems, fire-fighting is the order of the day. That is, those in charge of maintaining the system get complaints regarding the system's fault and try to fix the problems, assigning priority to the customers who complain the loudest.

The creation of a recovery plan allows for a more systematic method of delivering quality information-systems services.

7.6.1   Recovery as a Source of Customer Satisfaction

Heskett, Sasser, and Hart [1990] in their book *Service Breakthroughs: Changing the Rules of the Game* identify three critical points:

- Whether or not the service is delivered poorly
- If service is poor, whether or not a complaint is elicited from the customer
- If there is a complaint, whether or not there is a recovery plan in place to deal with the complaint.

To create quality information-system service delivery, it is crucial to collect data on customer satisfaction. Information-systems customers, as in other service delivery, do not normally complain directly to the service provider, unless there is a system crash. Instead, they may try to avoid using it, create their own little systems that make them independent from the corporate-created information system, suffer and complain about the system to others, or all of the above. The negative impact of poor information-system service delivery goes beyond disgruntled customers. The lack of use may reduce the quality of the customers' decisions, impact the quality of their work and hence the corporation, or create ill will that would hamper their cooperation in any new systems developments. In the case of external customers, the negative impact on customer satisfaction and consequent loss of business is already documented extensively.

7.6.2   Information-Systems Recovery Plan

Creating an information-system recovery plan requires a mechanism to elicit customer complaints at the time of system delivery. This mechanism could be an automatic collection of customer responses to a few simple questions regarding their possible dissatisfaction and reasons for it before completing the service. Alternatively, customers could be polled on a regular basis (such as an agent system, discussed previously, sending and collecting e-mail messages to the customers). The most important factor is to elicit the complaint before it becomes a crisis.

Heskett, Sasser, and Hart [1990] observe that "return on investment for complaint handling units can be substantial." Repeated complaints about one feature of the system could point to a major fault in the system that should be looked into carefully.

The recovery plan for the information system should contain appropriate responses to various types of complaints, and the types of actions that should be taken once a repeated complaint points to a major fault in the system. In other words, the recovery plan is a part of the system's maintenance and continuous improvement process.

The components of the information-systems recovery plan include:

- The categories of possible system faults and customer complaints
- The appropriate actions in responding to customer complaints
- Priorities of customer categories for recovery action
- The time window for each type of response
- The composition of teams and individuals who should be involved in each type of complaint or fault
- A log of recovery actions
- Periodic review of recovery actions for continuous improvement planning and implementation, as well as for the evaluation of the recovery plan itself
- Followup of the recovery action to make sure that the cause of the complaint has been removed

7.6.3   Implementation of the Information-Systems Recovery Plan

Implementation of the information-systems recovery plan relies on a culture of blameless discovery of errors, learning from errors, and opportunities to improve. It requires dedicated frontline workers who welcome the opportunity to help customers and improve the system. The frontline workers should be educated in various methods of dealing with complaints, performing drills and dry runs, and sharing experiences with one another.

More importantly, the successful implementation of the recovery plan depends on top executives' belief in the critical role of quality information systems, and on their dedication to ensure quality service to internal and external customers of information systems. If continuous improvement should become a habitual aspect of the information system, the impetus should be from the implementation of the recovery plans, not the loudness or the status of the customer who has decided to make his or her dissatisfaction known.

◆ Conclusion

This chapter discussed the issues and methods important to the manufacturing and delivery of information-systems services. The changes in the global market economy has necessitated a new way of doing business and, consequently, a new way of dealing with information-systems customers. The customer focus was the underlying theme in developing approaches to creating and providing information-systems services.

The structural changes in the market economy necessitate structural flexibility in information systems. An approach to creating structural flexibility in information systems is the creation of meta-information systems and meta-database systems. These approaches become even more useful when we apply the concept of just-in-time to information systems. Furthermore, just-in-time information systems lead to enhancing the role of information systems beyond their traditional territories to include unstructured information systems, as well as meta-knowledge-base systems.

Another aspect of quality is creating and institutionalizing a culture of learning in the organization and its information systems. We discussed approaches that aid this process, including using errors as learning experiences, learning customers' needs and creating enlightened customers, training as a part of the employment pact, and the information-systems infrastructure for learning.

Another component of creating quality information systems is the relationships with the suppliers of the system, including data, information, and knowledge suppliers, hardware and software suppliers, network and communication suppliers, and consulting-services suppliers. We also discussed the issue that close cooperation with information-systems suppliers may lead to dependency and loss of financial and technical flexibility, and offered a solution to this dilemma.

Finally, in delivering the service of information systems, errors and faults may occur. Having recovery plans for dealing with faulty services is one of the hallmarks of breakthrough services. We discussed the nature of a recovery plan for information systems and issues related to its implementation.

◆ References

1. Benedikt, Michael. 1991. *Cyberspace: the First Steps*, the MIT Press, Cambridge, MA.
2. Gibbs, Mark and Smith, Richard J. 1993. *Navigating the Internet*, Sams Publishing, Carmel, IN.

3. Hannan, Michael T. and Freeman, John. 1989. *Organizational Ecology*, Harvard University Press, Cambridge, MA.

4. Heskett, James L.; Sasser W. Earl Jr.; and Hart, Christopher W. L. 1990. *Service Breakthroughs: Changing the Rules of the Game*, the Free Press, New York, NY.

5. Lubben, Richard T. 1988. *Just-in-Time Manufacturing: An Aggressive Manufacturing Strategy*, McGraw-Hill Book Company, New York, NY.

6. Peters, Tom. 1992. *Liberating Management: Necessary Disorganization for the Nanosecond Nineties*, Alfred A. Knopf, New York, NY.

7. Pruitt, Steve and Barrett, Tom. 1991. "Corporate Virtual Work Space," in *Cyberspace: the First Steps*, Michael Benedikt, the MIT Press, Cambridge, MA.

8. Scheniederjans, Mark J. 1993. *Topics in Just-in-Time Management*, Allyn and Bacon, Boston, MA.

9. Senge, Peter M. 1990. *The Fifth Discipline: The Art and Practice of the Learning Organization*, Bantam Doubleday Dell Publishing Group, New York, NY.

10. Zahedi, Fatemeh. 1993. *Intelligent Systems for Business: Expert Systems with Neural Networks*, Wadsworth Publishing Co., CA.

11. Zahedi, Fatemeh. 1994. "Meta-Information Systems: A Structure for Heterogeneous Distributed Information Systems" Working Paper, University of Wisconsin, WI.

◆ Questions

7.1. What are the new market factors that necessitate a new approach to the creation and delivery of information systems?

7.2. How does the globalization of the market economy affect information systems?

7.3. What are the sources of added value in information systems?

7.4. What are the methods of incorporating the voice of the customer in the performance of information-systems workers?

7.5. What are the reasons for structural changes in information systems?

7.6. What is a flexible system?

7.7. What is a meta-information system?

7.8. What are the types of meta-information systems?

7.9. What is a meta-database system?

7.10. What are the factors that necessitate the development of a meta-database system?

7.11. How do meta-database systems deal with diversity of platforms and software products?

7.12. What is the problem of inertia created by legacy systems?

7.13. How do legacy systems cause inertia in information systems?

7.14. What is a just-in-time information system?

7.15. What are the principles of just-in-time information systems?

7.16. What are the sources of diversity in information systems in decentralized organizations?

7.17. What are unstructured information systems?

7.18. What are unstructured databases?

7.19. What is groupware?

7.20. Why is groupware needed?

7.21. What is the role of Internet in information systems?

7.22. Why is knowledge collection and dissemination important in unstructured information systems?

7.23. What is the agent software?

7.24. What is a meta-knowledge base system and its role in the organization?

7.25. What are the approaches related to the operation of an information system in a learning organization?

7.26. What are the ways to deal with errors and faults in information systems?

7.27. Why should we care about learning customer needs and creating enlightened customers?

7.28. How can we create information-systems infrastructure for a learning organization?

7.29. What are the supplier types in information systems?

7.30. Why are supplier relationships important in quality information systems?

7.31. What is the importance of having a close relationship with the data, information, and knowledge suppliers of information systems?

7.32. Who are the suppliers of data, information, and knowledge in information systems?

7.33. Discuss the issue of dependence versus independence in information-systems supplier relationships.

7.34. What is the importance of the recovery plan in information systems?

◆ Problems

7.1. Discuss the pros and cons of customers being the performance evaluators of information-systems workers.

7.2. What are the implications of having a flexible information system?

7.3. Give an example in which a meta-information system could create added value for an organization.

7.4. Give an example of a meta-database system.

7.5. Give two examples of unstructured database systems.

7.6. Discuss possible enhancements of Internet services in the future and the methods of incorporating them into corporate information systems.

7.7. Do you believe that information systems should have an active role in changing the culture of an organization? Why?

7.8. Give an example of the contents of a meta-knowledge-base system for a bank-loan application process.

7.9. Do you agree that we should and could create enlightened customers in information systems? If yes, how can we do it?

7.10. Consider the case of ACCU-INFO discussed throughout this book. Discuss the method for dealing with a report that the evaluation of the credit-worthiness of an individual has been erroneous.

7.11. Consider the case of ACCU-INFO discussed throughout this book. Develop a brief recovery plan for the complaint from an organizational customer that an evaluation of the credit-worthiness of an individual has been erroneous.

Case Questions for the IBM Plan Case

Refer to the case, **IBM Plan** in this chapter and answer the following questions:

1. What are the distinguishing factors in the IBM plan that foster customer focus?
2. Discuss the pros and cons of the IBM plan.
3. Discuss the possible area of information systems where the IBM compensation scheme could be successfully implemented.

Case Questions for the Agent Systems and Software Case

Refer to the case, **Agent Systems and Software** in this chapter and answer the following questions:

1. What are the expectations from agent software and systems?
2. Do you agree with the conclusion of the case that one day people will use their agent software to perform their chores, such as shopping or library searches?
3. Discuss the pros and cons of a world in which robo software and systems perform routine tasks.

O mighty Caesar! dost thou lie so low?
Are all thy conquests, glories, triumphs, spoils,
Shrunk to this little measure?

— Shakespeare, *Julius Caesar*

Without data, all you have is an opinion.

— Anonymous

◆ Chapter Objectives

The objectives of this chapter are:
- To define quality metrics and identify the characteristics of good metrics
- To discuss the types and categories of quality metrics for information systems
- To describe quality metrics for the implementation phase of information systems
- To discuss quality metrics for the operation phase of information systems
- To define and identify metrics for cross-functional teams in information systems
- To describe the organizational prerequisites for the successful use of quality metrics
- To identify possible organizational abuses of quality metrics and the ways to avoid them

◆ Key Words

Metrics definition, metrics types, metrics categories, IS quality metrics, IS implementation metrics, IS operation metrics, software reliability metrics, team-management quality metrics, team-cohesiveness metrics, team-communication metrics, team-output metrics, team-innovation metrics, organizational prerequisites of quality metrics, abuses of quality metrics.

Quality Metrics in
Information Systems

8.1 Information-Systems Quality Metrics
    8.1.1 Components of Quality Metrics
    8.1.2 Nature of Information-Systems Quality Matrices
    8.1.3 Types of Information-Systems Quality Metrics

8.2 Implementation and Operation Metrics for Information Systems
    8.2.1 Zero-Defect Information Systems
    8.2.2 Systems-Implementation Metrics (Optional)
    8.2.3 Software-Reliability Metrics
    8.2.4 Systems-Operation Metrics (Optional)

8.3 Team-Management Quality Metrics for Information Systems (Optional)
    8.3.1 Team-Cohesiveness Metrics
    8.3.2 Team-Communication Metrics
    8.3.3 Team-Effectiveness Metrics
    8.3.4 Team-Output Metrics
    8.3.5 Team-Innovation Metrics

8.4 Organizational Aspects of Quality Metrics
    8.4.1 Organizational Prerequisites of Quality Metrics
    8.4.2 Organizational Abuse of Quality Metrics

◆ Introduction

System improvement requires measurement and analysis. To see the importance of metrics in quality information systems, we need to compare and contrast quality information systems with traditional information systems, introduced in Chapter 1.

In an organization with a quality focus, decision making regarding the quality of various functions, including information systems, is based on facts, while traditional organizations decide based on perceptions and emotions. In quality information systems, performance is judged against the extent of improvement from a previous period, while traditional information systems use a set standard, or worse, the loudness of customer complaints in gauging the performance of the system. In a quality information system, the performance measures are designed specifically for evaluating the system, while a traditional information system uses available data when and if it decides to analyze the system's performance quantitatively. Therefore, measures in quality information systems are designed for prevention, while traditional information systems use them for correction and fire-fighting, if at all. Quality information systems use facts to measure customer satisfaction, while traditional information systems rely on anecdotal cases for evaluating the customers' satisfaction with the system.

Quality metrics are the integral part of the Shewhart-Deming cycle, which, as discussed in Chapter 3, has four phases: plan, do, check, and act. The "planning" of an information system is derived from the vision of the organization and the information-system function. Planning requires increasingly more detailed analysis leading to the design, as discussed in Chapters 5 and 6. "Doing" means translating the plan into working systems, as discussed in Chapter 7. "Checking" requires objective measures, hence the need for quality metrics. It is through the analysis of facts provided by quality metrics that one can evaluate the information system and continuously improve it or put it through a thorough reengineering process. This and the next chapter undertake the development of metrics for information systems to this end. Chapter 10 discusses the analysis of metrics to complete the "checking" phase and delves into the "acting" part of the Shewhart-Deming cycle.

In this chapter, we explore the nature and categories of quality metrics for information systems in Section 8.1, where we define metrics and their desirable characteristics, and categorize them based on various views and phases of the system.

One way to categorize quality metrics for information systems is by stages of system life cycle. Section 8.2 discusses the quality metrics for the implementation and operation stages of information systems. The quality metrics for the design stage are discussed in Chapter 9.

The quality metrics helpful in the management of the information-systems development project could be divided into:

- Team Metrics
- Project-Management Metrics

Although team and project-management metrics are closely related, they have different goals. The first category emphasizes the team and its processes, whereas the second category has its focus on the project and its completion within a specified time and budget. Section 8.3 discusses team-management metrics. The development of project-management metrics is postponed to Chapter 9 because many of these metrics are based on design and design metrics.

The successful use of quality metrics has organizational prerequisites. Otherwise, metrics could lead to organizational abuse and torpedo the entire quality effort. Section 8.4 discusses the organizational prerequisites, possible abuses of quality metrics, and the ways to prevent them.

The coverage of quality metrics continues in Chapter 9, in which design, project management, and reliability quality metrics for information systems are discussed.

Undergraduate students with minimal quantitative background and professionals with little interest in the details of quality metrics can skip the sections identified as "optional." Scanning these sections without regard to the details of mathematical formulas will give the reader some idea about the computation of quality metrics.

8.1 ◆ Information-Systems Quality Metrics

Chapter 1 provided a number of perspectives for the nature of quality. All have, in one way or another, the customer as the focal point in their definition of quality. Therefore, quality metrics, by nature, must focus on customers of information systems.

Chapter 5 argued that the customers of an information system are not limited to the end-users. They include all who are directly affected by the system, such as system developers, system analysts, database administrators, data-entry clerks, programmers, and system maintainers. The indirect customers, such as the impacted public and managers indirectly using the output of the information system, are also considered customers of the information system.

Given the diverse group of individuals who form the customer basis of information systems, quality metrics should reflect their appraisal of the system.

8.1.1 Components of Quality Metrics

According to Fortuna [1988], industrial quality assurance has gone through three eras:

- Product inspection (started in the 1920s), in which end products and sometimes the intermediate products were inspected for faults and defects; we discussed this aspect of quality in Chapter 1
- Process control (started in the 1960s), in which defect data were analyzed for identifying out-of-control process parameters and elements; the enhancement of this concept is process improvement, as discussed in Chapter 3
- Design improvement (started in the 1980s), in which the focus is the improvement in design engineering in order to minimize the defects downstream at the production stage; we discussed this approach to design in Chapter 6

In this and the next chapter, we devise quality metrics that reflect all of the above three approaches.

Measure vs. Metric.   To move beyond abstract and vague ideas of quality to a more objective analysis of quality, we need to define metrics that formalize and quantify quality. The handbook on metrics published by the U.S. Air Force [1991] differentiates between metric and measure in the following way: A metric is a combination of measures designed for depicting an attribute of a system or entity.

The handbook identifies the basic characteristics of a good quality metric as:

- Meaningful to customers
- Containing organizational goals
- Simple, understandable, logical, and repeatable
- Unambiguously defined
- Capable of showing a trend
- Economical in data collection
- Driving appropriate action
- Timely

Focus on Customers and Organizational Goals.   One of the important aspects of a quality metric is that it should be meaningful to customers, that is, the metric has a customer focus. At the same time, it should embody the organization's vision and goals. This latter requirement puts the focus on measuring attributes and features that are crucial to the vision of the organization and its goals.

For example, in the ACCU-INFO case, one may measure the number of times a customer has made inquiry into the same individual's credit history. The inquiry has a customer focus, but is not oriented toward any one of the organization's goals. On the other hand, if one of the organization's goals is the fast and reliable supply of information to its customers, then counting the number of times customers have not received a satisfactory response to their system queries within a reasonable time will be an appropriate quality metric.

Simple, Repeatable, and Unambiguous.   Quality metrics should be simple, understandable, logical, and repeatable. Otherwise, the complexity of data collection and the effort to understand the metric once it is computed could defeat the purpose of using metrics.

Since quality metrics are collected and analyzed more than once, and normally through time, the repeatability of metrics is important. In order to compare a quality metric through time or across similar tasks, one needs to define the metrics in a clear and unambiguous term. Otherwise, the comparison of metrics would be misleading and harmful.

Trend Indicator and Economical.   The metrics should have the capability of showing a trend, such as the increasing or decreasing reliability or responsiveness of the system. The metric should be economical in data collection, preferably automatic whenever possible. Otherwise, the cost of data collection may prevent the regular and effective use of quality metrics.

Action Oriented and Timely.   It is pointless to collect data for quality metrics that do not trigger actions at certain levels. The action could be to continue with the existing system, investigate the existence of a problem, act on improving a component of the system, or change a process. For this reason, the metric should be timely because it should track the performance of the system and provide an early warning signal about system problems.

8.1.2   Nature of Information-Systems Quality Matrices

Little work has been done on the quality metrics for information systems. The traditional approach in quality has been that if the system works, do not fix it. If a customer complains because he or she is not satisfied, and the customer has adequate clout, then the system should be fixed to make the customer quiet. If there is an adequate number of customers complaining, or there is a new technology that may make the system work better, then the old system may be scrapped and a new system created.

Those involved in the day-to-day operation of information systems, as well as the top management that funds information-system projects, find this approach quite costly and inefficient. Ineffective information systems lead to major opportunity loss even if the customers do not complain. Maintaining systems based on customers' loud complaints leads to piecemeal corrections of minor faults, while major faults may go unnoticed, or receive a lower priority because sufficiently loud complaints are lacking. Furthermore, some customers may not complain at all. Dissatisfied external customers may take their business somewhere else, and unhappy internal customers may decide to create their own independent systems, leading to a scattered and fragmented structure in the corporate information system. There is no question that information-systems workers must take a proactive role in monitoring and improving the quality of information systems.

The only quality tradition in areas related to information systems is in software quality. However, almost all models of software quality are traditionally based on the quality assurance concept, in that quality metrics and tests are defined and performed at the end of the software production. This approach is based on the old manufacturing-quality assurance concept that products must be checked after they are produced.

The new approach is to push quality assurance up the production stream into design, and down the operation stream toward customers. Thus, quality metrics should be defined to capture the design as well as the use of information systems.

Guiding Forces in Metrics Definition.   The choice of the appropriate metrics depends on the vision of the information system, the nature of the business processes, and the type and needs of its customers. Information-systems quality metrics should be decided based on the following criteria:

- The corporate vision
- The information-systems vision
- The nature of business processes
- The type and needs of customers

These four components form the guiding light for the definition and implementation of quality metrics.

Information-Systems Attributes Critical to Quality Metrics.   Quality metrics should be able to capture the following attributes of information systems:

- Responsiveness
- Performance
- Service
- Value

Responsiveness of an information system relates to the system's ability to respond to the immediate information needs of its customers. The performance attribute is the indicator of the quality of system operation. The service attribute of the system shows the quality of service delivery, including that of the workers associated with the system. The value attribute of an information system is the extent to which the system adds value to its customers' operations.

In the ACCU-INFO case, for example, when a corporate customer asks for the credit rating of Mr. Smith, a responsive system has information about Mr. Smith; a high-performance system allows the customer to access the information about Mr. Smith within an expected time interval; a system with high quality service makes it easy for the customer to get the information about Mr. Smith; and finally, a system that adds value to the customer's operation provides the type of information about Mr. Smith that makes the customer's decision about him more accurate and less risky.

In defining various metrics for information systems, the metric developer must justify the use of metrics with the appropriate criteria and relevant attributes of the system.

8.1.3   Types of Information-Systems Quality Metrics

Information systems have many aspects and impact the organization and its customers in a variety of ways. One can design metrics to focus on one or more dimensions of the information system. We can break down the focus of information-system metrics into the organization and its customers, as well as into processes and results, as shown in Figure 8.1. Such a breakdown gives us four primary categories:

- Organization-process focus
- Customer-process focus
- Organization-result focus
- Customer-result focus

Organization-Process Focus.   The goal of this type of metrics is the evaluation of the information system's processes from the organization's internal view. Ideally, this internal view is driven by the organization's vision and goals. Since it is process-based, this metric

	Processes	Results
Organization	• Internal view • Design based • Leads to change and improvement • Vision oriented	• Internal view • Implementation and operations based • Early warning signal • Value to the organization
Customers	• External view • Design based • Leads to change and improvement • Customer oriented	• External view • Implementation and operations based • Early warning signal • Value to the customers

Figure 8.1   The Focus of Information-System Metrics

type focuses on the design of the system and its operation procedures. Process metrics are helpful in identifying the areas of improvement and change, and are important tools in continuous improvement efforts, discussed in Chapter 3.

An example of this type of metrics for the ACCU-INFO case is one that measures the length of time, starting with an actual change in an individual's credit status and ending when this change is reflected in the system. This metric measures the efficiency of the data-supply process to the system. It is associated with the part of the vision statement that states: We provide the most up-to-date information to our customers. This metric is part of ACCU-INFO's Shewhart-Deming cycle plan-do-check-act (discussed in Chapter 3). The "planning" for the information system was triggered by the vision statement and its derivative goals. The "doing" was the creation of the information system. Quality metrics provide tools for the "checking" phase. The analysis of metrics (discussed in Chapter 10) helps the continuous-improvement team identify areas in which "acting" is needed.

Customer-Process Focus.   The customer-process focus in information-system metrics provides an external view of the system's design and its operating procedures. The goal of this metric type is to evaluate the processes that affect the customers. It provides input for change and continuous improvement.

An example of this type of metrics is collecting data on the customers' reaction to the delivery processes of information-system services. In the ACCU-INFO case, an example of this type of metric is the response time, defined as the time interval starting with an individual's complaint about his or her credit rating and ending when a satisfactory answer is given to the individual. This metric measures the process of dealing with one category of the system's indirect customers—persons whose credit is being rated by the system.

Organization-Result Focus.   This type of metrics provides an internal view of the system's implementation and operations. The goal of such metrics is to provide signals warning about possible system problems and opportunities for improvement.

An example for the ACCU-INFO case is the faults metric, defined as the number of system failures in a given interval at the implementation-test stage.

Customer-Result Focus.   This type of metrics provides a warning signal about possible system problems from the external point of view. They reflect the system's quality at the implementation or field-operation stages of the system-life cycle. These metrics are used to monitor the system for possible malfunctions. Such malfunctions include physical, design, or behavioral aspects of the system, and workers associated with its service delivery. The design of such metrics is guided by the value the system provides to its customers.

In the ACCU-INFO case, metrics of this type include: the number of customers' monthly complaints about the performance of the system, the number of customers' system queries that remain unanswered in a week, and the number of times the system is inaccessible to customers in a month.

Hybrid Metrics.   While it is important to be aware of the primary focus of a metric, a more desirable metric type is the one that combines these primary aspects into an integrated metric; thus providing a hybrid measure for the system's quality. Many of the metrics defined in this and the next chapter have a hybrid nature, especially designed to merge the organization and customers' views into one metric.

Life-Cycle metrics.   Another way of categorizing information systems metrics is the stages of the system life cycle:

- Design Metrics
- Reliability Metrics
- Implementation Metrics
- Operation Metrics

Design metrics gauge the quality of the system design. Reliability metrics show the reliability of the system from the customers' perspective. Implementation metrics test the system at the implementation phase. Operation metrics measure various aspects of the responsiveness and performance of the system in action. This chapter discusses the implementation and operation metrics, while Chapter 9 covers the design and reliability metrics that have a more technical nature.

Metrics as Tools for Improvement and Change.   In this and the next chapter, we discuss a number of metrics of various types, and many more could be devised using the guidelines given in these two chapters. However, it must be emphasized that each organization should pick and choose the quality metrics that suit its plan-do-check-act cycle and continuous improvement process the best. Quality metrics are tools for realizing the vision through the continuous improvement process and reengineering.

It is not cost-effective to collect quality data when they are not used for taking corrective actions. Furthermore, collecting quality data that does not serve the major vision, missions, and goals of the corporation could discredit the quality effort and portray it as a useless practice. In other words, no quality metric should ever become an end in itself; it should be designed and evaluated as the agent of change and improvement.

8.2 ◆ Implementation and Operation Metrics for Information Systems

This section begins with a discussion of zero defects. The continuous-improvement and quality metrics serve the goal of achieving zero defects; that is, when the system goes on line, no defect is acceptable.

The implementation and field operation of an information system constitute the stages that follow the system design. Implementation in this context refers both to manufacturing and testing the system. It also includes the conversion of the old system to the new system, if an old system exists.

The successful implementation of a system means creating a high-quality system and managing the project effectively. We discuss the quality of the system being implemented in this section, and Chapter 9 discusses quality metrics for project management.

The implementation of information systems sometimes requires software development. In such cases, the reliability of software becomes an implementation issue. In this section, we briefly review the existing approaches to software reliability.

Field operation is the day-to-day working of the system, once it is implemented and is on line. This section explores quality metrics for the operation of information systems in this section.

8.2.1 Zero-Defect Information Systems

Motorola, with its 1987 six-sigma initiative, focused its quality effort on reducing defects to zero. This could be accomplished with a relentless pursuit of designing processes, and finding methods and approaches that move the quality metrics close to zero defects. It means that quality metrics at all levels, especially at the implementation stage of the information system, should have a close tie to quality efforts, including continuous improvement, benchmarking, teamwork, and leadership in the organization.

Quality concepts include the Taguchi approach in reducing variability, as discussed in Chapter 6. This means that the mean (or expected value) and standard deviation of quality metrics are important in tracking the system quality. Each metric value should be computed as the number of standard deviations that it is above or below the mean (or expected value). In a normal probability distribution, three standard deviations above and below the expected value contains more than 99.73 percent (or .9973 out of 1) of all cases. Therefore, we expect to see only .27 percent (or 27 out of 10,000) of metric values to fall outside three sigmas each side of the mean, if the assumption of normality is justifiable. Even if the assumption of normality is not justifiable, according to the Chebychev theorem, *at least* 89 percent of all metric values fall in the three-sigma region.

Furthermore, an organization may set target values for the expected value and standard deviations, hence identifying the target region in which all values of a metric should fall. As the improvement continues, the region will tighten, moving the system toward zero defect, where the region has zero length, as shown in Figure 8.2.

Motorola's six-sigma initiative has the goal of six standard deviations (six sigmas) above and below the mean, which makes the output practically error free (two per billion). The intermediate goal of the initiative is to have 3.4 defective parts per million (PPM). This initiative resulted in a 40 percent increase in productivity and winning the Malcolm Baldridge Award in 1988. It is reported that Motorola saved $1.5 billion in reduced cost [I/S Analyzer, 1994]. From 1987 to 1991, Motorola reduced its average defect rate from 6000 PPM to 30 PPM [Smith, 1993].

When the mean and standard deviation are computed from sample values of a metric, we can use the formulas from elementary statistics to compute them as:

$$\bar{x} = \frac{\sum_{i=1}^{n} x_i}{n}$$

$$s = \frac{\sum_{i=1}^{n} (x_i - \bar{x})^2}{n - 1}$$

where $\bar{x}$ is the sample average, s is the sample standard deviation, x_i is observation i, and n is the number of observations in the sample. For a given population, $\bar{x}$ and s are the estimation of the expected value and standard deviation (sigma) of the population.

The value of all metrics should be translated into the number of standard deviations from the expected value or average to make the value meaningful. For example, in the ACCU-INFO case, assume that the fault metric for the first month of the system implementation of an information system is 5. This value by itself conveys little information. Now assume that the target value of this metric is 3 and its standard deviation is .5. The six-sigma region is $(3 \pm .5)$ or 1.5 to 4.5. The value of metric (5) is four standard deviations above the target value—it is out of six-sigma range and unacceptable. This value could trigger an action, such as a search for the cause of the unacceptable number of faults in the project.

8.2.2   Systems-Implementation Metrics (Optional)

Implementation of the information system design requires the production of the system components—buying or making them. At this stage, errors, faults, failures, defects, and rework are of great importance and should be tracked by implementation metrics.

We can distinguish between errors, defects, faults, and failures, although there is no standard definition for these terms. Here we adopt the definition used in Motorola's quality efforts. In metrics development at Motorola [Daskalantonakis 1992], these terms are defined as:

- *Error:* the fault that is discovered when the component is being produced
- *Defect:* the fault that is discovered after the production phase of the component has ended
- *Fault:* an error or defect
- *Failure:* the inability of the system to function as intended because of an error or defect; failure triggers the search for finding the fault that causes the failure

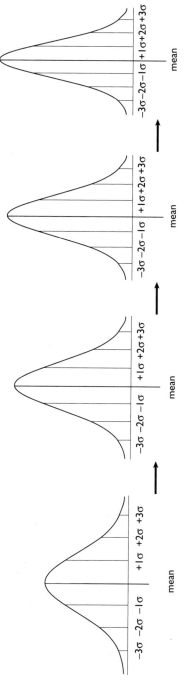

Figure 8.2   Moving Toward Zero Defect

One can define fault metrics based on:

- Error and fault categorization
- Time between two failures
- Number of failures in a test period
- Number of errors in an implementation phase
- Number of defects in an implementation phase
- Number of newly discovered errors or defects
- Weighted average of newly discovered errors or defects
- Average time interval for fixing an error or defect, once it is discovered

Error and Defect Categorization.   One way to identify the major causes of problems in the implementation phase is to categorize the discovered errors and defects and draw the Pareto chart (discussed in Chapter 3) for these categories. The category that shows the highest frequency should be investigated for the identification of the cause of the recurring error or fault.

For example, in the ACCU-INFO case, as new objects are added to the system, the errors are categorized as:

- Coding errors
- Exception-handling errors
- Interface errors
- Missing methods
- Message-processing errors

The defects are categorized as:

- Coding defects
- Exception-handling defects
- Interface defects
- Missing-methods defects
- Message-processing defects
- Design defects
- Requirement defects

As Figures 8.3 and 8.4 show, the Pareto charts for the error and defect categories reveal that interface errors and design defects are the most frequently encountered errors and defects. They indicate that there is a problem in the creation of interfaces among the modules and that there are design defects in the modules. Both are indicators of serious problems at the design stage of the system. (Design metrics are discussed in Chapter 9.)

Time Between Two Failures.   The implementation of an information system goes through a number of phases. At each implementation phase, the time between two

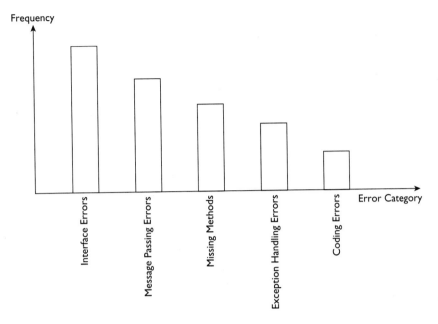

Figure 8.3   Pareto Chart for ACCU-INFO's Error Categories

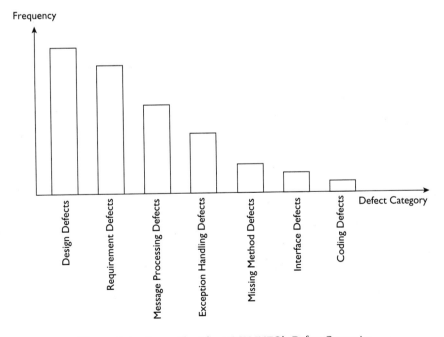

Figure 8.4   Pareto Chart for ACCU-INFO's Defect Categories

consecutive failures is short at the start. As new errors are discovered and fixed, the time between two failures should increase and gradually become very large. Large fluctuations of the time between two failures for a given phase may be the indicator of major problems in the component or system.

Number of Failures in a Test Period.   The flip side of the time between two failures is the number of failures in a time interval within a test period. For example, on the first day of the test of a component or partially assembled system, one may expect (or target) to see 10 percent failures with the standard deviation of 2 percent. That is, the experience has shown that the first day of the component or system test, one should expect to see that 4 to 16 percent (three standard deviations above or below the mean, or six sigmas) of attempts to use the component or system should generate a failure. Now if the first-day test of a component generates 20 percent failures, it gives a signal that the component should be carefully reviewed before it is incorporated into the system.

Number of Errors in an Implementation Phase.   The problem with using failure data in the above example is that many failures may be caused by one error. Another way of keeping track of the quality of the implementation is to track the number of errors in each phase of the implementation interval.

For example, in the ACCU-INFO case, we can define each phase of implementation as adding a module (or an object, as described in Chapter 9) to the system. Experience with benchmarking has shown that when one module is added to the system, one should expect an average of four errors with the standard deviation of one (six-sigma interval is one to seven errors). As new modules are added to the system, the discovered errors are counted. A module with errors above the six-sigma interval signals a serious problem.

Number of Defects in an Implementation Phase.   As the implementation proceeds, defects are discovered for pieces that were thought to be error-free. The data on the defects should be collected and charted as well. Too many defects may signal a possible problem in the error-detection process.

One can also analyze the ratio of errors and defects, as defined by the Motorola experience [Daskalantonakis 1992]:

$$ED_i = \frac{E_i}{E_i + D_i}$$

where ED_i is the ratio of errors in phase i, E_i is the number of errors in phase i, and D_i is the number of defects in phase i.

Alternatively, one can define the ratio for defects (DE_i) as:

$$DE_i = \frac{D_i}{E_i + D_i}$$

This metric is used for making sure that a low number of errors in a phase is not caused by inadequate testing that later becomes a defect problem in subsequent phases of the implementation.

Number of Newly Discovered Errors or Defects.   In some cases, one has to distinguish between new errors and already discovered errors that have not been completely resolved and continue to cause system failure. Keeping track of newly discovered errors could be another measure of the quality of the implementation process. As in the case of failures, errors, and faults, newly discovered errors and defects could be counted within a given interval, or for the duration of an implementation phase.

Weighted Average of Newly Discovered Errors or Defects.   The problem with a simple count of errors or defects is that the metric fails to consider the severity of errors or defects. The weighted-average metric takes into account the severity aspect.

The procedure for computing this metric is the following:

1. Categorize errors or defects into c categories. Error and defect categories should have a standard that is valid for all information-systems projects.
2. Assign a severity rating to each category; call it W_i for all $i = 1, 2, \ldots, c$. The severity ratings should be standard across all information-systems projects.
3. For each time interval, collect data on the occurrences of errors or defects in each category, call it x_i, for all $i = 1, 2, \ldots, c$.
4. Compute the weighted average of the newly discovered errors or defects in one of two ways.

First, the metric is computed as the average newly discovered errors or defects per unit of time:

$$ANT = \frac{\sum_{i=1}^{c} W_i \cdot x_i}{t}$$

where ANT is the average newly discovered errors or defects per time, x_i is the number of the newly discovered errors or defects in category i, c is the number of errors or defects categories, and t is the time interval.

Second, the metric is computed as the average newly discovered errors or defects per module:

$$ANU = \frac{\sum_{i=1}^{c} W_i \cdot x_i}{m}$$

where ANU is the weighted average of the newly discovered errors or defects and m is the number of newly added modules. (In Chapter 9, we will see that we can use objects as practical units for information systems.)

Average Severity of Errors or Defects.   One may measure the average severity of errors and defects discovered in a time interval with the following metric:

$$AS = \frac{\sum_{i=1}^{c} W_i \cdot x_i}{\sum_{i=1}^{c} x_i}$$

where *AS* is the average severity metric, *c* is the number of errors or defects categories, W_i is the severity rating of category *i*, and x_i is the number of discovered errors or defects in category *i*.

Average Time Interval for Fixing an Error or Defect.   Once an error or fault is discovered, the question is how long it takes the implementation team to fix it. This metric is computed as:

$$ATF = \frac{\sum_{i=1}^{n} t_i}{n}$$

where *ATF* is the average time interval for fixing errors or defects, and *n* is the number of discovered errors or defects. We can compute the average and standard deviation of fixing faults to gauge the effectiveness of the implementation process and methods in removing faults from the system.

8.2.3   Software Reliability Metrics

The implementation stage of an information system may involve partial or full software development. Therefore, it is important to be aware of software quality metrics.

Software quality and reliability have been a major concern of software developers and users alike. In the last two decades, numerous theoretical models have been developed to formalize the data collection and testing of software. Research on software reliability has produced more than 20 types of software-reliability models and an extensive body of literature.

Software-reliability metrics could be categorized into two major types: those that are designed for counting the number of errors in a test interval and those that measure the length of time between the occurrence of two errors.

The sheer number, as well as the complexity of these models, prohibit even a rudimentary presentation of them here. These models have been reviewed and categorized by Musa [1971], Jelinski and Moranda [1972], Shooman [1972], Myers [1976], Basili [1980], Brooks and Motley [1980], Ramamoorthy and Bastani [1982], Iannino, Musa, and Littlewood [1983], Goel [1983] and [1985], Malaiya and Srimani [1990], and Zahedi and Ashrafi [1993].

Almost all software-reliability models are concerned with testing the software reliability after the design and coding, rather than focusing on designing reliability into the system. The exceptions are the measures that formalize the complexity of software, such as McCabe's cyclomatic complexity metric and Albrecht's function points. We will use a simplified version of McCabe's metric for the information-system complexity metric in Chapter 9.

A function point is a metric that is the weighted sum of five different factors in a software product [Jones 1991]:

- Inputs
- Outputs

- Logical files
- Inquiries
- Interfaces

Function points are defined as units that the end-user benefits from in a software product. The complexity of a software program depends on how many function points it contains. There have been studies to estimate the number of function points in software products used in various types of enterprises. One analysis estimated that the number of function points owned by a small local bank was 125,000, while the same study estimated the number of function points owned by a large computer manufacturer as 1,650,000 [Jones 1991]. While these figures may have a large degree of inaccuracy and be out-of-date, they show that the concept of function point as a metric for the size and complexity of software has been accepted as a practical metric.

Software Design Metrics. The two major developments that directly impact software reliability are:

- Object-Oriented Design
- Fault-Tolerant and Parallel Modules

Object-oriented design in software is based on the concept that real-world objects should be directly modeled into the design of the software. Object-oriented programming languages, most notably C++ and Smalltalk, make it possible to translate the designed objects into software objects. The object-oriented approach is intended to provide reusability and independence for software modules. We will use the object-oriented concept in the design of information systems in Chapter 9.

The fault-tolerant and parallel modules in software are intended to provide backups for the modules that are critical in running software. In this approach, the software design involves redundant modules, and allows for the possibility of failure in software modules. This is an area that is still in its infancy in software science.

8.2.4 Systems-Operation Metrics (Optional)

The operation of an information system has more than one dimension. We can divide them into two broad categories: performance and reliability. Systems-operation metrics could be categorized along the same two dimensions. Although these two types of metrics are closely related, we discuss the simpler metrics for performance quality in this section, and present a more complicated reliability metric in Chapter 9.

The performance of a system has the following dimensions:

- Timeliness
- Efficiency
- Consistency

- Continuity
- Correctness

Timeliness.   The timeliness of the system reflects the delivery of the information to the system's customers when they need it. Timeliness is defined by customers. Since customers' needs are dynamic and change through time, so does the definition of system timeliness. In the ACCU-INFO case, a weekly update of data might have been timely five years ago. However, because of the change in the market, only a daily and in some cases hourly update of data could be considered timely at present.

In the definition of the timeliness metric, one has to be cognizant of the difference between the availability of information in the system, and the availability of information to the customer. The timeliness metric should reflect the availability of information to customers. For example, in the ACCU-INFO case, the data may be updated on the system on an hourly basis. If it is not processed on time, or, because of the distributed nature of the database system, the information is not integrated until the end of the day when the communication cost is the cheapest. Under those circumstances, the update is not hourly as far as the customer is concerned; it is a daily update and will not be considered as timely by the customer.

We can define a number of metrics for timeliness, such as:

- The time interval between two consecutive updates
- The time it takes for information to become available to users between two consecutive updates
- Access time

The vision of the information system, the nature of the business processes, and the type of customers determine business-dependent metrics of timeliness. For example, in the ACCU-INFO case, the delivery time is when the commercial customers receive credit reports by mail or by e-mail, or when their data files are updated directly. Therefore, the timeliness metric in this case is the interval between the time that a customer makes a credit-evaluation query and the time he or she receives the credit report (by mail, e-mail, or direct update). Obviously, in this case, different types of requests will have different timeliness metrics.

Efficiency.   The performance of the information system is partly measured by the efficiency of the access to information. One can measure the efficiency in a number of ways:

- The time it takes for a customer to access a particular piece of information
- The number of commands, menus, or icons the user must know or access in order to get the needed information
- The ease of updating and manipulating the system
- The time it takes for a novice user to learn to use the system

The choice of the efficiency metric depends on the information-systems vision and its related goals. For example, ACCU-INFO's goal of developing the most up-to-date and readily available information system prompts the use of the first metric in the above list.

Consistency.   Another dimension of system performance is the consistency of information-systems services. The consistency metric shows whether the system performance is predictable for customers. A system that normally takes one minute to access is preferable to a system that may take any time from ten seconds to five minutes to access. A system that normally takes 10 hours for a novice to learn is preferable to a system that takes up to 36 hours for a novice to learn. In both cases, the unpredictability of the system's performance makes it less desirable for customers.

One metric for information-systems consistency is the standard deviation of other performance metrics. For example, assume "time it takes for a customer to access a particular piece of information" is our metric for efficiency. The system is observed over a period of time as various customers try to access different parts of the information system. Therefore, there is a set of data for system-access time. Computing the average of this data set gives us a metric value for the efficiency of the system. The standard deviation of data shows the consistency of the system's efficiency. That is:

$$\bar{a} = \sum_{i=1}^{n} \frac{a_i}{n}$$

where $\bar{a}$ is the average access time, a_i is the observed access time, and n is the number of sampled access times. $\bar{a}$ is a metric for efficiency of the system.

On the other hand, the consistency of the system's efficiency is:

$$s = \left(\sum_{i=1}^{n} \frac{(a_i - \bar{a})^2}{n-1} \right)^{.5}$$

where s is the standard deviation of the access time and is the measure of system consistency in access time.

For example, assume that in the ACCU-INFO case, the following data is sampled from the access time of the system in two months (in seconds):

Month 1: 10, 5, 6, 9, 5, 4, 7, 20, 15, 2

Month 2: 13, 12, 10, 8, 9, 13, 12, 10, 11, 12

The efficiency metric as the average access time of the system for the two months has the values:

$$\bar{x}_1 = 8.3$$
$$\bar{x}_2 = 11$$

The efficiency of the system in Month 1 was better than that of Month 2.

The consistency metrics as the standard deviation of the performance in the two months are:

$$s_1 = 5.5$$
$$s_2 = 1.7$$

The consistency of the system in Month 1 was worse than that of Month 2.

In other words, while the efficiency metric for the performance of the information system declined in the second month, the consistency of its performance improved—the efficiency in Month 2 did not fluctuate as much as Month 1.

Continuity. The continuity of system service is the uninterrupted nature of its service delivery. One metric for this dimension of performance is the percentage of time the system has been unavailable to its customers. One may decide to include or exclude the system unavailability due to the regular update or backup. The continuity metric C is defined as:

$$C = \frac{\sum_{i=1}^{u} t_i}{T}$$

where u is the number of times the system has been unavailable in time period T, and t_i is the length of system unavailability at the ith time the system was unavailable. The zero-defect goal pushes this metric and its standard deviation as close to zero as possible. Continuity as an ingredient of system reliability is discussed in Chapter 9.

Correctness. The correctness of the system's service is to ensure that it delivers the correct information to the customer. The correctness is defined beyond the narrow definition of correct data or processed information. It entails completeness of information as well.

The metrics for correctness include:

- Number of defects discovered after the system has gone into operation
- Number of defects discovered and reported by customers
- Length of time it has taken to fix a reported defect
- Number of defects remaining to be fixed
- Number of defects caused by fixing other defects

As in other metrics, this type of metrics should be defined for an interval of time or should be normalized. Computation of the average and standard deviation of these metrics over the life of information systems gauges the extent of improvement in the system and could provide guidelines for setting improvement targets. These metrics are useful in information-system project management, specifically in fault management. This topic is covered in Chapter 9.

The correctness metrics can be categorized into:

- The average number of wrong data input into the system (over the total number of input data entries) in a given time interval

- The average number of pieces of information that are incorrectly computed (over all the processed pieces of information)
- The average number of times a piece of information has been out-of-date and not updated on time (over all information updates in the system) in a given time interval
- The average number of customers' system queries for which the system has been unable to provide an answer (over all system queries) in a given time interval
- The average number of times the information was erroneously transmitted over communication lines (over all transmitted pieces of information) in a given time interval

While the correctness is computed as an average number over a time interval, the consistency of these correctness metrics is computed as the standard deviation of the same metric in that time interval. The computation is similar to that of the average and standard deviation of the access time discussed in the previous subsection.

Using Pareto charts to analyze the frequency of various categories of the correctness metric could be helpful in improving the system and the processes involved in its creation and operation.

The major problem with performance metrics is that they are computed for various components of the system. None provides an overall metric for how a system is viewed by its customers. In Chapter 9, we will see how these performance metrics could be combined with customers' perceptions in order to provide a single metric for the reliability of information systems.

8.3 ◆ Team-Management Quality Metrics for Information Systems (Optional)

The quality of the cross-functional development team is of critical importance to the successful design and implementation of an information system. Furthermore, the continuous improvement of the system and, ideally, its operation involves cross-functional teams that include information-systems workers with various technical and organizational skills, as well as representatives of the different customer groups and marketing staff.

In Chapter 2, we discussed the desirability of rewarding employees as teams rather than individuals. This means that teams should be given tools for development, checking, and improvement. One set of such tools consists of team-management metrics.

One can measure the performance of a team from two aspects: processes and results. The metrics for team processes show whether a team has the right approach in its problem solving. The metrics that indicate the team-process quality could be categorized into:

- Team-cohesiveness metrics
- Team-communication metrics

The result metrics show the quality of a team's achievement. The metrics that indicate the quality of results are:

- Team-effectiveness metrics
- Team-output metrics
- Team-innovation metrics

In all the team metrics that are discussed here, one has to be sensitive to the difference in size and complexity of the teams' tasks. Comparing teams that differ drastically in size and in the nature of their tasks is like comparing apples and oranges. Furthermore, the team-quality metrics should be used as tools for improvement and change, not for disciplining and punishment.

8.3.1   Team-Cohesiveness Metrics

The quality metrics for team cohesiveness gauge how far the team has evolved into a working group—whether the team has traversed through the team-development stages: forming, storming, performing, and norming, as discussed in Chapter 2. One can use a number of metrics as proxies for team cohesiveness, including:

- Age of the team
- Member-Time Metric
- Team absenteeism
- Team turnover
- Member response

Age of the Team.   One measure of cohesiveness is the length of time a team has worked together. The higher the age of a team, the higher is the probability that the team has completed the maturity stages of team development.

Member-Time Metric.   An objection to using the simple length of time as a metric for team cohesiveness is that a newly formed team may have subgroups of members who have worked together before, and therefore may have already achieved a reasonable cohesiveness faster. For such cases, the member-time metric could be computed as the weighted average of the time that the present team members have worked together. This metric is defined as:

$$MT = \sum_{i=1}^{s} W_i \cdot t_i$$

where MT is the member-time metric, s is the number of subgroups in the team, t_i is the length of time subgroup i has worked together, and W_i is the proportion of the subgroup with respect to the total number of members in the group. Note that one person could be a member of more than one subgroup.

For example, the development team in ACCU-INFO has 6 members: 2 members have worked together for 3 years, two 3-member subgroups have worked together for 1 year, and the entire team has been working together for 3 months. The age of the group is:

$$MT = \left(\frac{2}{6} \times 36\right) + \left(2 \times \frac{3}{6} \times 12\right) + \left(\frac{6}{6} \times 3\right) = 15$$

That is, the member-time metric is 15 months.

As with other metrics, we should use average and standard deviation within the organization to evaluate the age or member-time of a team. Everything being equal, the higher the value of a team's member-time metric, the higher is the team cohesiveness. This assumes that a high member-time value does not create strong factions that negatively impact the team cohesiveness.

The choice of the appropriate metric depends on the culture of the organization and the degree of conflict of interests within the cross-functional team. Information-systems development teams lack the extreme conflict of interests. In most cases, the member-time is a reasonable metric for the cohesiveness of the cross-functional teams for information systems.

Team-Absenteeism Metric.   If many are absent from discussions, the team will have a more difficult time achieving cohesiveness and working together closely. In this context, a *discussion* could be a formal meeting, long-distance conferencing, or electronic get-togethers. The criterion is that the participation of the absent member was expected.

The team-absenteeism metric counts the number of times members have been absent from a meeting. A high value of this metric indicates a low degree of team cohesiveness.

This metric, as with others, should not be used to penalize absent members. Instead, it should serve as a warning signal to the management that the team structure may prevent the team from achieving a desirable degree of cohesiveness and cause the team to fail to achieve its objectives.

Team-Turnover Metric.   Another metric for cohesiveness is the amount of member turnover in a given time interval. If a team has turnovers that are many standard deviations above the average number of turnovers in the organization, then they are an indicator that the team may not achieve a reasonable degree of cohesiveness.

Member Response.   One way to judge whether a team has achieved a comfortable level of cohesiveness is to survey team members periodically about their level of comfort in working together. The organization could devise standard questions that are administered to teams on a regular basis for keeping track of the quality of team cohesiveness.

8.3.2   Team-Communication Metrics

Team communication is an important process. Too little communication among team members may indicate the lack of sufficient input by all team members into the process. Although some may believe that there can never be too much communication, it could indicate the existence of serious issues that may lengthen the development process, and may require management intervention.

The team-communication metrics are helpful tools for the team leader to use in judging the effectiveness of the team, compared to the norm in successful teams within the organization or in the field. The metrics in this category include:

- Number of meetings
- Weighted-meeting-time metric
- Weighted number of discussions

Number of Meetings.   One simple metric for quantifying the extent of communication among team members is the number of meetings they hold in a given time interval. This metric is appropriate when the meetings have a standard length of time, such as one or two hours. The advantage of this metric is that it is simple, and any team leader has the data. As the system moves from one stage of development to another, the number of meetings of various development teams varies. Keeping track of meetings at various stages could be used to uncover possible problems before they lead to low quality output or failure of a team.

For example, in the ACCU-INFO case, assume that the average number of meetings for requirement analysis of the information system is 12 meetings with a standard deviation of 2. The team performing requirement analysis completes its task in two meetings. This should raise the flag: Was there adequate analysis in this case? What was so unique about this particular requirement analysis that needed so few meetings?

There could be simple answers, such as: the customer representatives were well-informed, the analysis methodology was well developed, or the team had such cohesiveness that it could finish its job in two meetings. In such cases, the work of this team should be analyzed and become the model for improving the process in other teams.

On the other hand, one may discover that the customers were not represented in the team, and the requirements analysis went on smoothly because there were no customary objections raised by customer representatives. In this case, the team should be augmented by the appropriate customer representatives, and the analysis should be repeated. Furthermore, there should be an investigation into why the team lacked the appropriate customer representatives.

Weighted-Meeting-Time Metric.   If the organization's meetings do not have a standard length, then counting the number of meetings will not reflect the extent of communication in each team. Furthermore, there might be meetings that are attended by a subgroup of the team.

We define weighted-meeting-time as a metric that reflects the meeting time and member participation:

$$WMT = \sum_{i=1}^{m} W_i \cdot t_i$$

where WMT is the weighted-meeting-time metric, m is the number of meetings, W_i is the proportion of the team members present in meeting i, and t_i is the length of meeting i.

Again, the effective use of this metric is to keep track of various teams of similar size and task complexity, and to develop a sense of the average and standard deviation of this metric for various stages of the information-system development. The metric will help the team leader in monitoring the extent of communication in the team.

Weighted Number of Discussions.   One can take issue with using formal meetings as the measure of team communication. Team members may discuss issues in many ways outside formal meetings. Group and subgroup discussions may take many forms, such as electronic notes, e-mail, or conference calls.

In an organizational culture where these methods of communication are the prevalent mode, the team leader can redefine "meeting" in the weighted-meeting-time metric to mean any discussion that is directed toward reaching the team's objective. Obviously, the more informal discussions are included in this metric, the harder data collection becomes. Here, as in any other metric, one needs to strike a balance between the accuracy of the metric and the cost of collecting data and tracking the metric values.

8.3.3   Team-Effectiveness Metrics

Team effectiveness is the ability of the team to accomplish its goals and objectives within a reasonable time, and with high quality. Therefore, one can divide the dimensions of effectiveness into:

- Goal accomplishment
- Time
- Quality of output

The quality of output is the subject of the next two subsections. Here, we cover timely accomplishment of goals. The metrics for team effectiveness are:

- Goals-accomplished ratio
- Overtime ratio
- Weighted-timely-goals metrics

Goals-Accomplished Ratio.   This metric computes the ratio of goals that are accomplished with respect to the expected completion of goals in a given period of time. More specifically, it is defined as:

$$GA = \sum_{i=1}^{t} \frac{g_i}{G_i}$$

where t is the number of time periods within which a team should complete a given set of goals, g_i is the number of goals completed in time period i, and G_i is the number of goals the team was expected to complete. This metric tracks the time effectiveness of a team through several time periods.

Overtime Ratio.   This metric shows how much the team has run overtime in completing a goal. It is defined as:

$$OT = \sum_{i+1}^{g} \frac{t_i}{T_i}$$

where g is the number of team goals, t_i is the length of time it has taken a team to complete goal i, and T_i is the length of time in which the team was expected to complete goal i.

Weighted-Timely-Goals Metrics.   The above two metrics for team effectiveness are simple, but they fail to take into account the relative importance of various goals. This problem is addressed in the weighted version of goals and overtime metrics, defined according to the following procedure:

1. Categorize goals into c categories.
2. Assign an importance rating of WG_j to the goal category j.
3. Assign an importance rating of WT_i to the on-time completion of goal category i.

Compute the weighted-goals-accomplished as:

$$WGA = \sum_{i=1}^{c} WG_i \cdot \frac{g_i}{G_i}$$

where g_i is the number of goals accomplished in category i, G_i is the expected number of category i goals that are expected to be completed, c and WG_i are defined above. This metric is computed for a given interval.

Compute the weighted-overtime metric as:

$$WOT = \sum_{i+1}^{g} WT_i \cdot \frac{t_i}{T_i}$$

where g, t_i, and T_i are the same as those in overtime-ratio metric and WT_i is the relative importance of the on-time completion of goal i, which is determined by the category in which goal i belongs.

8.3.4   Team-Output Metrics

The ultimate indicator of a team's quality is the quality of its output. The metrics for the team output should reflect the tangible results obtained in a given interval. Among such metrics are:

- Number of problems discovered or solutions found
- Weighted-problem/solution metric

Number of Problems Discovered.   A team's output is the number of problems and solutions it has been able to identify in a given time interval. This is a simple metric, for which the team leader and top managers could provide data. However, as with many simple metrics, it does not reflect the relative importance of discovered problems or solutions to the system and the organization.

Weighted-Problem/Solution Metric.   A more complicated, but representative, metric to measure the number of problems and solutions discovered by a team is the following procedure:

- Categorize problems and solutions into homogeneous types
- Assign a relative importance weight to each category
- Compute the weighted sum of problems and solutions that the team has found in a given interval

Following this procedure, the weighted-problem/solution metric is computed as:

$$WPS = \sum_{i=1}^{p} WP_i \cdot P_i + \sum_{i=1}^{s} WS_i \cdot S_i$$

where WPS is the metric, p is the number of problem categories, P_i is the number of discovered problems in category i, WP_i is the relative weight of category i problems, s is the number of solution categories, S_i is the number of discovered solutions in category i, and WS_i is the relative-importance rating of category i solutions.

For example, in the ACCU-INFO case, the problems have been categorized as:

1. Minor system-interface problems, relative importance = .20
2. Major system-interface problems, relative importance = .70
3. Minor omission of customer requirements, relative importance = .70
4. Major omission of customer requirements, relative importance = 1
5. Minor system error, relative importance = .40
6. Major system error, relative importance = 1

The solutions for this example are categorized as:

1. Minor, routine solution, relative importance = .10
2. Minor, non-routine solution, relative importance = .30
3. Major, routine solution, relative importance = .60
4. Major, non-routine solution, relative importance = 1

In one month, an improvement team has been able to identify 5 category-1 problems, 3 category-2 problems, and 3 category-4 problems. It has been able to offer 2 category-1 solutions, 6 category-2 solutions, and 1 category-4 solution.

The weighted-problem/solution metric for this team is:

$$WPS = (5 \times .20) + (3 \times .70) + (3 \times 1) + (2 \times .10) + (6 \times .30) + (1 \times 1) = 9.1$$

This metric becomes more meaningful when it is compared with the averages and standard deviations of *WPS* of similar teams, or the past performance of the team itself.

8.3.5 Team-Innovation Metrics

Yet another dimension of a team's output is its creativity in finding problems or discovering innovative solutions. It is through innovation and radical rethinking of ways to design and operate a system that a company can capture major markets. The metrics for innovation include:

- Uniqueness of solutions
- Impact on the organization
- Impact on customers

The solutions that a team provides may have unique features that give the company a competitive edge. The impact of the solutions on the organization's financial and market standing may be dramatic. A solution may impact a customer's work and business drastically. Since uniqueness and innovation are qualitative concepts, metrics that quantify them have to involve subjective data.

Team-Innovation Metric.   One metric that combines the innovative nature of team output is the following:

1. Identify the relative importance that the organization assigns to the uniqueness of a solution, the impact on the organization, and the impact on customers. Call them W_u, W_o, and W_c, respectively.
2. Assign a uniqueness rating between zero and one to each solution the team has generated, and call it U_i, for all $= 1, 2, \ldots, n$ solutions.
3. Assign an organizational-impact rating between zero and one to each solution the team has generated, and call it O_i, for all $= 1, 2, \ldots, n$ solutions.
4. Assign a customer-impact rating between zero and one to each solution the team has generated, and call it C_i, for all $= 1, 2, \ldots, n$ solutions.
5. Compute the team-innovation metric *TI* as:

$$TI = \sum_{i=1}^{n} (W_u \cdot U_i + W_o \cdot O_i + W_c \cdot C_i)$$

For example, in the ACCU-INFO case, assume that the organization has assigned the relative importance values of .7, .8, and 1 to uniqueness, organizational impact, and customer impact respectively. The team has generated three solutions, with the following ratings:

	Uniqueness	Organizational Impact	Customer Impact
Solution 1	.7	.8	.8
Solution 2	.2	.4	.9
Solution 3	.9	.7	.1

The team-innovation metric for this team is:

$$TI = .7(.7 + .2 + .9) + .8(.8 + .4 + .7) + 1(.8 + .9 + .1) = 5.28$$

The maximum value of this metric is when all solutions of a team receive a rating of 1. In this case, we have:

$$Max(TI) = \sum_{i=1}^{n}(W_u \times 1 + W_o \times 1 + W_c \times 1)$$

$$= n(W_u + W_o + W_c)$$

which is $3(.7 + .8 + 1) = 7.5$ for the above example.

This metric can be easily expanded to cases where there are more than three dimensions to the innovation. For organizations where innovation is essential, the list of innovation attributes would be more lengthy and detailed. For instance, organizational impact could be broken down into financial impact, market impact, and employee impact. The customer impact may be expanded to include ease of use, more functionality, increased effectiveness, financial gain, and saving time.

Average Team-Innovation Metric.   One may wish to compare teams purely based on their innovations regardless of the number of solutions they have developed. The metric for this case is the average team innovation, defined as:

$$ATI = \frac{TI}{n}$$

$$= \frac{\sum_{i=1}^{n}(W_u \cdot U_i + W_o \cdot O_i + W_c \cdot C_i)}{n}$$

where ATI is the average team-innovation metric, TI is the team-innovation metric defined above, and n is the number of solutions.

The average team-innovation metric can be compared to the organizational average and standard deviation. Furthermore, the most ideal case is when a team receives a rating of 1 for the three dimensions of innovation for all its solutions. In that case, the maximum value for the average team-innovation metric would be equal to:

$$Max(ATI) = \frac{\sum_{i=1}^{n}(W_u \times 1 + W_o \times 1 + W_c \times 1)}{n}$$

$$= W_u + W_o + W_c$$

In the above ACCU-INFO example, the average team-innovation metric for the team is:

$$ATI = \frac{5.28}{3} = 1.76$$

If the three solutions had a rating of 1, with the present rating of innovation dimensions, the average team-innovation value would be:

$$Max(ATI) = W_u + W_o + W_c = .8 + .7 + 1 = 2.5$$

8.4 ◆ Organizational Aspects of Quality Metrics

The successful application of quality metrics requires organizational prerequisites that make them effective tools for change and improvement. Furthermore, the inappropriate use of metrics could render them useless and, worse, could have an adverse impact on the organization and its customers. This section addresses the organizational prerequisites of quality metrics, possible abuses of them, and the ways to prevent abuses.

8.4.1   Organizational Prerequisites of Quality Metrics

Quality metrics can not stand on their own. They should be implemented as a piece of a plan for adding quality to information systems. Quality metrics come with other aspects of quality information systems, including vision, leadership, employee empowerment, commitment to quality and continuous improvement.

Daskalantonakis [1992] reports on the Motorola experience of software metrics that: "There are several cultural and human issues that need to be addressed up front in order to assure the success of such an initiative." He recommends focusing on processes and continuous improvement, and setting quantitative goals and metrics acceptable by all who are involved in the process. The philosophy of using metrics should be articulated by top management. At Motorola, this philosophy was stated as: "The goal is improvement through measurement, analysis, and feedback," [Daskalantonakis 1992].

Furthermore, in managing quality metrics:

- The metrics should be defined for measuring the movement toward the vision and corresponding goals of the organization
- The data collection process and analysis guideline of metric values should be clearly defined
- The focus should be on the use of metrics for actions that lead to continuous improvement
- Management and workers impacted by the quality metrics should have an active role in the process and accept metrics as tools for improvement
- Corporate training programs should include training on metrics, their goals, computations, and analysis, as well as the actions they trigger

In sum, quality metrics should be part of the Shewhart-Deming cycle of plan-do-check-act. For this cycle to be effective, the organization should make a long-term commitment to quality programs and to quality information systems prior to embarking on the design and use of quality metrics.

8.4.2   Organizational Abuse of Quality Metrics

The inappropriate use of metrics may not only lead to project failure, but could create a defensive and consequently destructive culture. Jeffrey Robinson [1993] reports that quality metrics could be misused in a number of ways:

- Using quality metrics to compare projects of different sizes and complexities
- Using quality metrics to compare teams of different sizes and tasks
- Using quality metrics to punish individuals and groups or find guilty parties

Such abuses create a defensive culture, in which people try to:

- Hide defects
- Resist data collection and observation
- Operate in such a way that nobody can blame them if something goes wrong
- Cover up problems
- Blame others for problems
- Fight against quality efforts

This culture goes against the intent for which quality metrics are developed. As Robinson [1993] has observed, the inappropriate use of metrics could be destructive, and gradually the organization builds a defensive attitude with respect to metrics.

To counter the problems associated with the abuse of metrics, Jeffrey Robinson [1993] suggests that:

- Management must actively pursue policies and reward people who identify problems
- Use metrics to evaluate the process: how many errors are new and how many are recurring problems, how the correction process works
- The success of the process should be measured by the percentage of problem types that do not recur (as discussed in Chapter 9)
- Individuals and teams are rewarded for finding new problems and effectively solving them, and establishing procedures for avoiding the recurrence of the same problem

Quality metrics that are process-based and counter the misuse of metrics are:

- Measures of complexity, which show the difference in complexity of the tasks being compared
- Levels of use and reuse, which show the customer's interest in the system
- Measures that show the defect-detection rate during testing and operation, and can be used to reward problem identification and systems improvement

Another ingredient in the successful use of quality metrics is training information-systems workers on the nature and purpose of quality metrics and the ways these metrics are used for improving systems.

◆ Conclusion

In this chapter, we introduced information-systems quality metrics. We defined the components, nature, and type of quality metrics in Section 8.1. In this section, we identified a number of areas for which quality metrics should be devised.

Implementation and operations are two areas for which we discussed quality metrics at the system implementation stage. The system errors and defects should be removed before the system becomes operational. In Section 8.2, we discussed metrics for tracking fault removal from the system. The systems-implementation stage may involve the partial or full development of software. This section briefly reviewed software-reliability metrics.

At the operation stage of the system life cycle, system performance is of great importance. Metrics for tracking various dimensions of system performance were described in this section, including those for timeliness, efficiency, consistency, continuity, and correctness of the information-system services.

Section 8.3 addressed team-management quality metrics. These metrics were categorized into team processes and team outputs. For team processes, we developed team cohesiveness and communication metrics. For results generated by the team, we presented metrics for measuring team effectiveness, team outputs, and team innovation.

The successful implementation of quality metrics requires organizational prerequisites. Without them there would be abuse and waste of resources. These prerequisites, possible abuses, and ways to prevent them were discussed in Section 8.4.

The discussion of this chapter will continue in Chapter 9, which focuses on the design, project-management, and reliability metrics for information systems.

◆ CASE: Automating Quality

Reuters is the world's information clearing house, supplying news, graphics, pictures, television news, and prices to major financial organizations around the globe. Customers make multimillion-dollar decisions on the basis of the prices that Reuters supplies. Yet Reuters has no control over the original input of price information by market makers and traders, which is inevitably subject to human error.

Reuters' solution to this problem has been to develop the Intelligent Quality Toolkit (IQT), a sophisticated computer system that checks every price in real time, using a set of rules that reflects the knowledge and experience of market experts The IQT provides proof of the quality of the data that customers receive, giving Reuters an important commercial advantage over its competitors.

Use of object-oriented software development meant that the time from specification to implementation was much shorter than otherwise would have been the case. It also resulted in a system that can be quickly altered by the end user to reflect changes in a highly complex and rapidly changing financial market.

The Haystack. Many people know Reuters as the world's leading independent news agency, with a reputation for reliability and accuracy stretching back over 140 years.

However, over 90% of Reuters' revenue is now earned from the supply and processing of financial information: news, prices, and other information about or relevant to the financial markets.

The price of information is made up of quotes and trade prices for instruments such as shares, bonds, currencies, and commodities. Reuters' customers watch these prices on some 200,000 screens in more than 140 countries and, on the basis of what they see, carry out deals worth thousands or even millions of dollars. Accuracy is everything for these customers, and they rely on Reuters to provide them with correct information.

The dramatic growth achieved by Reuters over the last decade has been in large part due to customers' confidence in the accuracy of Reuters' information.

The financial markets, and Reuters' coverage of those markets, are continually expanding. At the same time, clients are becoming more demanding, increasingly using computer systems supplied by Reuters and other vendors to monitor and analyze prices and assist in decision making.

The challenge for Reuters is to combine increasing breadth of coverage with increasing quality so as to keep one step ahead of its customers' requirements and expectations.

The Needles. Prices are supplied to Reuters electronically by the exchanges where the transactions take place. The original entry of information is in most cases by the market makers and traders who set the quotes or make the deals—tens of thousands of people working throughout the world. In these circumstances it is inevitable that there will be errors in data entry—and not only after lunch on Friday!

Every exchange and information vendor has procedures for processing and checking the quality of data, usually involving the use of simple computer systems operating relatively crude algorithms. But the complexity and variety of financial trading mean that these systems can carry out only elementary checking.

Detailed checking for bad prices must be carried out by people, so quality assurance is a highly labor-intensive operation. Moreover, effective checking cannot be carried out by just anyone but requires detailed knowledge of the operation of the markets.

The result is that, as the financial markets have grown in scope and complexity, it has become increasingly difficult for vendors to keep pace using traditional ways of monitoring data and checking quality.

In 1992 Reuters UKI (UK and Ireland) decided it was necessary to anticipate customers' demands for even higher levels of quality assurance. The result of this was the development of the Intelligent Quality Toolkit.

The IQT in Operation. The IQT operates on Sun workstations linked to the central Reuters' prices database by a Marketfeed 2000 datafeed. Every item of data from a monitored exchange is analyzed in real time by the IQT as it is released to customers via the Reuters Integrated Data Network (IDN).

The IQT is a rule-based system. Its rules encompass financial knowledge that has been built up over years by leading experts. A rule can be as simple as "the bid price (the price at which an institution will buy shares or other instruments) must be less than the ask price (the price at which the institution will sell.)" Rules also can be highly complex. For example, "night trade"—bargains struck after the official close of trading on an exchange—are not reported until the opening of trading for the following day; but for statistical reasons they are regarded by the exchange as part of the previous day's trading. This can produce results that are apparently erroneous but are in fact correct, and the IQT needs to be able to distinguish these from genuine errors.

In live operation, the exchange data published on IDN is checked by the IQT using the knowledge it has been taught. If it spots a potential problem, the IQT displays full details of the rogue item including the rule (or rules) that has been broken. The operator then checks out the data item, often by contacting the exchange for clarification. If there genuinely was an error, the operator corrects it immediately on IDN and the correction is automatically broadcast to all Reuters subscribers.

IQT System Architecture. The Intelligent Quality Toolkit consists of a DataCache and one or more knowlegebases. The DataCache is responsible for:

- Acquiring data from the Reuters datafeed
- Maintaining an in-memory database of current values
- Maintaining a history of all values received
- Passing data to the appropriate knowledgebase(s)
- Handling requests for data from knowledgebases

The DataCache was developed in C. The knowledgebase component was developed using the Kappa system from IntelliCorp, and is responsible for the analysis of data received from the DataCache.

The knowledgebase component contains an object hierarchy representing the financial instruments under analysis. This hierarchy can be modified by the user to incorporate new fields and new instrument classes while the system is running.

The knowledgebase also contains a model of expected behavior against which data is tested, and knowledge about how to gather evidence for and against the correctness of any data that does not fit the model. The knowledgebase stores the results of analysis in a Sybase database to allow trends to be analyzed and specific data queries to be answered.

The behavior model and evidence-gathering knowledge also can be modified by the user while the system is running.

Multiple knowledgebases can be attached to a single DataCache, either to provide multiple users with individually tailored views of market data or to act as computer servers to cope with large quantities of data. Each knowledgebase can view analyses performed on any other knowledgebase, but (currently) only one knowledgebase is allowed to update the knowledge contained in the system. Any changes made on this master knowledgebase are broadcast to all other knowledgebases to ensure consistency.

How the Knowledgebase Works. Messages (or *updates*) received from the Data-Cache are assigned to instances of the appropriate instrument type. User-defined derivations are performed on the update to calculate extra values or determine related instruments.

Each update of an instrument is tested against a model of expected behavior defined by a set of *constraint rules*. These rules can be defined for any level of the instrument-class hierarchy and are inherited down the hierarchy. If an update arrives that does not match the expected behavior, the data mentioned in the rule is considered suspect.

Suspect data items are examined by *analysis rules* that define how to gather evidence about the correctness of the data. Analysis rules are typically more complex than constraint rules and, in principle, can examine data from any other instrument to corroborate the suspected item. Analysis rules also tend to be more specific to instrument type than constraint rules.

For example, suppose that an equity (stock) price has been flagged as suspect. To verify it, an analysis rule might examine the current price of an option on the equity to see if the theoretical option price based on the suspect equity price is close to the actual option price. Details of how to calculate the theoretical price of an option are entered by the user and the calculation is executed whenever an input data item is updated.

Data items that the IQT cannot show to be correct are displayed to the user as a one-line summary of the problem. If the user decides to examine the data problem, he or she will be shown a display that shows the rules used to suspect and analyze the data and the values used in the running of the rules. Related data items are also displayed, and the user can choose to examine the analysis of these data items as well.

All suspect data items and the results of the analysis on those items are stored in the database. The user can perform a variety of queries on the database or retrieve past analyses for detailed examination.

Benefits of the IQT. For Reuters clients, the IQT means that they receive accurate data or proven quality—data that they can use with confidence in their trading operations. As a measure of the scale of additional checking made possible by the IQT, it is estimated that one IQT is equivalent to between one and two thousand people checking prices by the old methods, with each of these people operating two Pbs.

Reuters benefits from the increased satisfaction of its clients, and from the marketing advantages of checking data more thoroughly and extensively than any of its competitors. The IQT not only enables Reuters to detect incorrect data but to demonstrate why possibly suspect data was correct. Using the IQT, Reuters frequently spots data problems before they have been recognized by exchange supervisory personnel operating with the older, manual systems. Although many of the problems are input errors, the IQT has identified a number of problems with the exchanges' own systems.

Reuters works closely with the exchanges to pin down and resolve these problems, to the benefit of the exchange and all those who receive exchange data.

The Future of the IQT. At present, the IQT is being used by Reuters UKI Exchange Data Group to check quotes and trade prices for virtually all instruments traded on exchanges in the UK and Ireland. Now that the effectiveness and value of IQT have been demonstrated, other IQTs will be installed in Reuters centers around the world with the eventual aim of checking every item of exchange data published by Reuters.

The flexibility of the IQT, and the ease with which rules can be entered and amended, open up further possibilities for use of the system beyond simple price checking. Trading organizations could use the IQT as a trader's aid by entering rules that identify and report trading opportunities. For example, the IQT's ability to scan all incoming trade data could be used to spot unusually large movements in the options market, alerting traders if a competitor is building up a position.

Alternatively, the IQT could identify arbitrage opportunities between an underlying instrument and a derivative, e.g., spotting that the prices of options on a share are undervalued compared with the actual share price itself.

Traders also could add rules to the system as trading progresses, refining and focusing their areas of interest in response to developments in the market. The flexibility of the IQT, due to its object-oriented development, means that rules can be added incrementally as required, unlike conventional systems where the full picture must be specified in advance and can be altered afterwards only with difficulty.

Source: Excerpt from "Automating Quality," Herbert L. Skeet and Peter Clay, *Object Magazine*, March–April 1994, pp. 59–62, reprinted with permission from *Object Magazine*.

◆ References

1. Air Force, HQ AFSC/FMC, 1991. *The Metrics Handbook*, Andrews AFB, D. C.

2. Bailey, J. B. and Pearson, S. W. 1983. "Development of a Tool for Measuring and Analyzing Computer Use Satisfaction," *Management Science*, Vol. 29, No. 5, pp. 530-545.

3. Basili, V. R. 1980. *Tutorial on Models and Metrics for Software Management and Engineering*, IEEE Computing Society Press, Washington, D.C.

4. Basili, V. R. 1985. "Quantitative Evaluation of Software Methodology," *Proceedings of First Pan-Pacific Computer Conference*, September 1985.

5. Brooks, W. D. and Motley, R. W. 1980. "Analysis of Discrete Software Reliability Models," Rep. RADC-TR-80-84, April.

6. Daskalantonakis, Michael K. 1992, "A Practical View of Software Measurement and Implementation Experiences Within Motorola," *IEEE Transactions for Software Engineering*, Vol. 18, No. 11, November, pp. 998–1010.

7. Fortuna, R. M. 1988. "Beyond Quality: Taking SPC Upstream," *Quality Progress*, June 1988.

8. Goel, A. L. 1983. "A Guidebook for Software Reliability Assessment," Rep. RADC-TR-83-176, August.

9. Goel, A. L. 1985. "Software Reliability Models: Assumptions, Limitations, and Applicability," *IEEE Transactions on Software Engineering*, Vol. SE-11, No. 12, pp. 1411-1423.

10. Iannino, A.; Musa, J. D.; and Littlewood, B. 1983. "Criteria for Software Reliability Model Comparison," *ACM Sigsoft Software Engineering Notes*, Vol. 8, No. 3, pp. 12-18

11. I/S Analyzer. 1994. "Software Engineering Productivity and Quality," *I/S Analyzer*, February, Vol. 32, No. 2, pp. 1–18.

12. Jelinski, Z. and Moranda, P. 1972. "Software Reliability Research," in *Statistical Computer Performance Evaluation*, W. Freiberger, Ed. Academic Press, New York, NY, pp. 465-484.

13. Jones, Capers. 1991. *Applied Software Measurement: Assuring Productivity and Quality*, McGraw-Hill, Inc., New York, NY.

14. Malaiya, Y. K. and Srimani, P. K. (Eds). *Software Reliability Models*, IEEE Computer Society Press, Los Alamitos, CA, 1990.

15. McCabe, T. J. 1976. "A Complexity Measure," *IEEE Transactions on Software Engineering*, Vol. 2, pp. 308–320.

16. Musa, J. D. 1971. "A Theory of Software Reliability and its Application," *IEEE Transactions on Software Engineering*, Vol. SE-1, pp. 312-327.

17. Myers, G. J. 1976. *Software Reliability Principles and Practices*, John Wiley & Sons, NY.

18. Page-Jones, Meilir. 1988. *The Practical Guide to Structured Systems Design*, Yourdon Press, Englewood Cliffs, NJ.

19. Ramamoorthy C. V. and Bastani, F. B. 1982. "Software Reliability: Status and Perspectives," *IEEE Transactions on Software Engineering*, Vol. SE-8, pp. 359-371.

20. Robinson, Jeffrey. 1993. "The Dark Side of Software Metrics," *Information Strategy: The Executive's Journal*, Winter, pp. 44–47.

21. Shooman, M. L. 1972. "Probabilistic Models for Software Reliability Prediction," in *Statistical Computer Performance Evaluation*, W. Freiberger, Ed., Academic Press, New York, NY, pp. 485-502.

22. Smith, Bill. 1993. "Six Sigma Quality: A Must Not a Myth," *Machine Design*, February, Vol. 65, No. 3, pp. 63–66.

23. Zahedi, F. and Ashrafi, N. "Software Reliability Allocation Based on Structure, Utility, Price, and Cost," *IEEE Transactions on Software Engineering*, Vol. 17, No. 4, April 1991, pp. 345–356.

24. Zahedi, F. and Ashrafi, N. 1993. "A Decision Framework for Selecting Software Reliability Models," working paper.

◆ Questions

8.1. Describe the three eras of quality assurance.

8.2. What is the difference between measure and metrics?

8.3. Discuss the characteristics of a good quality metric.

8.4. What are the guiding forces in devising quality metrics?

8.5. What is the role of the vision statement in quality metrics?

8.6. What are the information-system attributes that are critical in designing quality metrics?

8.7. Discuss the four dimensions of focus in designing information-system quality metrics—organizational-process, customer-process, organizational-result, and customer-result.

8.8. What are the primary goals of using quality metrics?

8.9. Describe the concept of zero-defect information systems.

8.10. What is the concept of six-sigma?

8.11. What are the differences between error, defect, and fault?

8.12. List some of the systems-implementation metrics.

8.13. Describe the implementation metric: time between two failures.

8.14. What is the significance of counting the number of newly discovered errors and defects?

8.15. Why is "weighted average of newly discovered errors and defects" a better metric than just counting the number of errors and defects?

8.16. Why are software quality metrics important in information systems?

8.17. What is a function point?

8.18. Describe the concept of fault-tolerant and parallel modules.

8.19. List the dimensions of information-system performance.

8.20. List the metrics that measure the efficiency of a system.

8.21. What is consistency in the performance of an information system?

8.22. Describe a metric for consistency of information systems.

8.23. List the metrics for the correctness of a system.

8.24. What are the metric categories that gauge the quality of team processes?

8.25. What are the metric categories that gauge the quality results generated by a team?

8.26. What is team cohesiveness?

8.27. List the metrics for team cohesiveness.

8.28. Compare and contrast the cohesiveness metrics: age of the team and member-time metric.

8.29. List the metrics for team communication.

8.30. What are the team-effectiveness metrics?

8.31. What are the team-output metrics?

8.32. Discuss the importance and dimensions of team innovation.

8.33. What are the team-innovation metrics?

8.34. Discuss the organizational prerequisites for the success of using quality metrics.

8.35. Discuss the abuses of quality metrics and their impacts on the organization.

8.36. Discuss the ways for avoiding abuses of quality metrics.

◆ Problems

8.1. Give an example of error and defect categorization of the network module of the information system.

8.2. For Problem 8.1, give an example of the weighted average of the newly discovered errors.

8.3. For Problem 8.1, assign severity ratings to error and defect categories. What does a severity rating signify? How would you use the average severity metric?

8.4. You are in charge of the implementation stage of a complex and relatively lengthy information-system project. Suggest metrics that you will choose to measure the quality of the implementation.

8.5. A part of the information-system vision statement of an organization is: "to create information systems that even a child can use." List and discuss the efficiency metrics that you think are appropriate for this organization.

8.6. You are given the following data on the efficiency of a system in the last three months (in minutes):

month-1: 5, 2, 4, 8, 10, 23, 12, 5, 3, 7

month-2: 3, 5, 2, 4, 6, 7, 6, 4, 7, 7

month-3: 12, 13, 11, 12, 14, 15, 12, 8, 7, 9

Analyze the efficiency and consistency of the system in the last three months.

8.7. Assume the figures given in Problem 8.6 are for the times that the system was un-available to its customers. Assuming that the system is expected to be operational at all times, compute and analyze the continuity and consistency metrics in each month.

8.8. Give an example of a member-time metric value for a 10-member team.

8.9. Can you compare the member-time metric of a 10-member team with that of 3-member team? Why?

8.10. You are the team leader for a team with the goal of designing a complex system. What metrics would you use in order to track the team processes and results? Justify your answer.

8.11. What is the use of categorizing and assigning ratings to a team's goals, problems, and solutions?

8.12. Give an example of the weighted-problem/solution metric for a distributed-information system.

8.13. Can you compare the weighted-problem/solution metric of two teams with differ-ent sizes? Why?

8.14. In the organization where you work, the uniqueness of solutions generated by teams is of great importance. Suggest a breakdown for the uniqueness attribute of team outputs.

8.15. You have two teams, with the average team-innovation metrics of .75 and 2.5. What do you do?

8.16. In the above question, do you reward the second team twice as much as the first? Justify your answer.

8.17. You are in charge of developing a system, and one of your teams has shown a high degree of absenteeism in the first month of its formation. What do you do? Does your plan include punishing the absent members? Justify your answer.

Observe due measure, for right timing is in all things the most important factor.

— Hesoid, 700 B.C.

Sometimes the more measurable drives out the most important.

— Rene Dobus

◆ Chapter Objectives

The objectives of this chapter are:
- To identify principles of good design
- To define and use objects as component units of information systems
- To develop design-quality metrics for information systems based on the design principles
- To discuss types of quality metrics for information-system project management
- To develop quality metrics for cost analysis in information-systems projects
- To develop quality metrics for the value analysis in information-systems projects
- To develop quality metrics for fault management in information-systems projects
- To develop quality metrics for time management in information-systems projects
- To develop a system-reliability metric that combines customers' preferences with the performance of system components

◆ Key Words

Design principles, design metrics for information systems, uncoupling metrics for information systems, complexity metrics for information systems, cohesion metrics for information systems, cost metrics for information systems, value metrics for information systems, fault-management metrics, time-management metrics for information systems, reliability metrics for information systems, requirements-objects hierarchy, AHP

Quality Metrics for Design, Reliability, and Project Management

9.1 Information-Systems Design Metrics
    9.1.1 Design Principles
    9.1.2 An Object-Oriented Approach to Information-Systems Modules
    9.1.3 Object-Independence Metrics for Information Systems (Optional)
    9.1.4 Uncoupling Guidelines for Information Systems
    9.1.5 Object-Cohesion Metrics for Information Systems
    9.1.6 Object-Complexity Metrics for Information Systems (Optional)

9.2 Project Management Quality Metrics for Information Systems
    9.2.1 Cost-Management Metrics
    9.2.2 Value-Management Metrics
    9.2.3 Fault-Management Metrics
    9.2.4 Time-Management Metrics

9.3 Information-Systems Reliability Metrics (Optional)
    9.3.1 Requirements-Object Hierarchy
    9.3.2 Customers-Requirements Utility Values
    9.3.3 Global Relative Weights of Objects
    9.3.4 Global Relative Weights of Input Objects
    9.3.5 System-Reliability Metric for Information Systems
    9.3.6 Customers with Different Preferences

◆ Introduction

In quality information systems, quality control is pushed up the production stream into design and down the operation stream into customers' added value. In chapter 8, we discussed quality control in the mid-stream of systems development and use—implementation and operation. In this chapter, we move up the stream to design and design metrics and move down to system reliability as customers perceive it. This chapter discusses project management metrics for information systems that are based on the design and design metrics.

In Section 9.1, we introduce the principles of good design, and apply them to developing design-quality metrics for information systems. This section introduces the object-oriented approach and uses it to develop design metrics. It also presents uncoupling, cohesion, and complexity design metrics that are derived from applying the axioms of good design to the object-oriented approach.

Since most information systems are created as projects, it is important to have metrics that help in managing the project quality. We develop project-management metrics that are closely coupled with the design of the system. Section 9.2 describes information-system project-management metrics—cost-analysis, value-management, fault-management, and time-management metrics. These metrics have a close connection to the design elements of the information system.

In Section 9.3, we develop an information-system metric that measures the reliability of the entire system, and combines customer perception and needs with the design structure and performance metrics of system components. This section describes methods for combining views and preferences of different groups of system customers in developing reliability metrics for the system.

Undergraduate students with minimal quantitative background and professionals with little interest in the details of quality metrics can skip the sections identified as "optional." Scanning these sections without regard to the details of mathematical formulas will give the reader some idea about the computation of quality metrics.

9.1 ◆ Information-Systems Design Metrics

Taguchi has focused our attention on the importance of incorporating quality into the design of a product or system. In the quality information systems, design is the most critical stage of system development. It has been shown that a defect in design is hundreds of times more expensive to fix than defects in the production stage. Applied to information systems, this means that every dollar spent in increasing the quality of design has at least a hundred-fold payoff downstream in the implementation and operation stages.

A quality design increases the system's:

- Manufacturability
- Maintainability
- Extendibility

- Openness
- Ease of system migration

Manufacturability refers to the ease and cost associated with the implementation of the information-system design; maintainability is the ease and cost of maintaining the system; extendibility refers to the ease of extending and enhancing the system; openness means whether the system can operate on more than one hardware type or operating software, and is able to connect and communicate with other systems; and ease of system migration refers to the ease of upgrading the system's underlying technology.

One of the basic principles of quality is that one should be able to measure it. Therefore, to ensure the quality of design, we must develop quality metrics for the design of information systems.

Design principles and design metrics are difficult to define and implement. This difficulty exists because design, including the design of information systems, involves creativity and art as well as the knowledge of technology and customers' requirements. Every design is unique, and the process of design is not repeated under identical circumstances. This uniqueness does not lend itself easily to the development of design principles and metrics. That may be why there is very little literature on the design metrics of information systems. In this section, we develop the guidelines that can help us devise metrics for the design of information systems, and apply them in developing design-quality metrics.

9.1.1   Design Principles

The first step in design is to specify functional requirements, starting with customers' functional requirements, then translating them into systems' functional requirements, as discussed in Chapters 5 and 6. Although the identification of functional requirements depends on the customers' needs and the system being designed, the requirements should be independent from each other. Two functional requirements that are dependent on one another are actually one function.

For example, in the ACCU-INFO case, the functional requirements could include credit data that is up-to-date within two days of a credit event (such as a credit-card charge or payment) and the resolution of discrepancies in multiple-source data within one day. These two functional requirements are dependent, and both are part of the same functional requirement: up-to-date credit data.

Suh [1990], in his study of the principles of design, concludes that there could be only two design axioms:

- Independence axiom
- Minimum information axiom

Independence Axiom.   The independence axiom posits that the customer's functional requirements should be translated into design components (or parameters) such that the independence of the functional requirements remain intact. Applied to information systems, this axiom requires that information-systems modules should be designed to preserve the independence of customer requirements.

For example, in designing ACCU-INFO's information systems, the customer requirements include a real-time update of credit data by the data suppliers and the on-line customers' credit inquiries. According to the independence axiom, two independent information-system modules should deal with these two requirements. In this case, these two modules are called *uncoupled*. That is, the task of the module for real-time updating of data is not combined with that of the module for customer query.

Suh [1990] makes an important distinction between *functional uncoupling* and *physical uncoupling*. In functional uncoupling, the functions of modules are independent, but both may be physically located in the same software, hardware, or other physical units. In other words, it is legitimate and desirable to *integrate* or combine uncoupled modules into physical units to create larger modules of the system.

Minimum-Information Axiom.   In this axiom, Suh posits that if we have a choice between two uncoupled modules, each mapping the same functional requirement into a system module, the one that contains minimum information is a better design. This is the principle of simple design. It also applies to system design as a whole—one should also strive to reduce the number of modules.

For example, in the ACCU-INFO case, the module that provides the credit rating may take three pieces of data and use a neural-network subsystem to rate credits, whereas another module may require eight pieces of data to produce a rating with the same reliability. The module that requires less information is a better module, given that both modules satisfy the independence axioms.

Minimization of information is not limited to data requirements. It also includes the complexity of the module, methods used in the module, and modes of its output. For example, of two alternative modules for credit rating in the ACCU-INFO case, the one that has a simpler computational algorithm (given the same accuracy) and requires less interaction with other modules is a better design.

Another interpretation of Suh's minimum-information principle is that a module should have cohesion. Cohesion means that the internal processing of a module should be related and directed towards accomplishing a single objective. For example, a module that performs both updating as well as report-generation tasks does not have cohesion, because it is performing two unrelated tasks.

We will use these design principles in developing design metrics in this chapter.

9.1.2   An Object-Oriented Approach to Information-Systems Modules

In designing products, software, or manufacturing processes, the identification of modules or design parameters looks straightforward in that they mostly have single goals or objectives, such as opening a can (for the design of a product—can opener), processing words (for the design of a wordprocessor software), or making cars (for the design of a car manufacturing process). Information systems may look less straightforward in their design in that they normally have to satisfy multiple, and sometimes divergent, objectives. However, if we model the design of information systems in the object-oriented paradigm, the design concepts apply to the information-systems objects in the same fashion as to the other areas.

The object-oriented paradigm identifies information-systems objects as models of real objects. Here, we use classes and objects interchangeably. Objects refer to the abstract models of the real objects in the information system. In doing so, we have tried to avoid the important, but for present purposes irrelevant, distinction between classes and objects as the instances of classes.

Objects have a hierarchy, similar to what was discussed in Chapter 6. However, in this case, objects are more precisely defined, because they have attributes and behaviors, and the objects on the lower level of the hierarchy inherit the attributes and behaviors of their parents.

For example, in the ACCU-INFO case, the high-level objects of the system may include database, spreadsheet, network, hardware, data, and supplier links. These objects have attributes, such as relational structure type for database, or LAN connection type for network.

There is a hierarchy of objects in that each object has children. For example, the children of database may include: user interface, update, security, report generation, and schema. The lowest level of the hierarchy contains objects that would be created by actions such as purchasing, programming, installing, or populating with data. These actions may lead objects such as query interface, update interface, update authorization, access authorization, and security protocol, as shown in Figure 9.1.

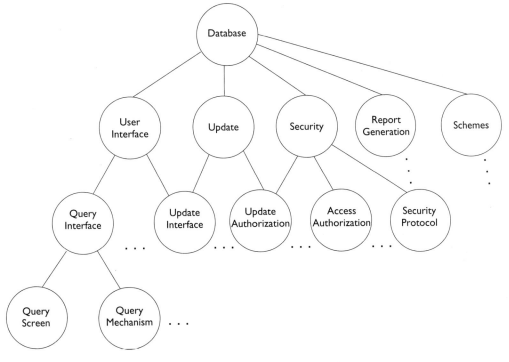

Figure 9.1   An Example of Class-Object Hierarchy

Each object has attributes and methods. The attributes of the object are the parameters that contain data about the object. They can be quantitative or qualitative. For example, query screen as an object may have a number of variables attached to it, such as window, menu, and error messages.

An object has methods. For example, the query screen object has methods or functions: open a window, close a window, request for data, and display data.

The object has a behavior—it sends messages back and forth to other objects in order to perform its tasks. For example, the query screen object sends a message to the query mechanism object and requests the value of a database item. The query mechanism, in turn, identifies the file and the record to be fetched, and requests data from the data file object. In other words, each object has a number of methods, within which they can send and receive messages from other objects in order to perform their desired tasks.

Object-oriented design is a new and promising approach in software development and can be extended to designing information systems. The use of objects in place of modules allows us to have a more concrete structure for the components of information systems.

9.1.3   Object-Independence Metrics for Information Systems (Optional)

In this section, we discuss two metrics that deal with the first design axiom—independence:

- Object-uncoupling metric
- Object-correlation metric

In the object-uncoupling metric, we focus on the definition and design of system objects that have a one-to-one correspondence with the real objects with which the information system deals. The object-correlation metric quantifies the correlation among objects, once they are defined as system objects. Together, these two metrics indicate whether the independence axiom of design is satisfied.

Object-Uncoupling Metric.   Uncoupling in the object-oriented paradigm means that objects at any level should independently model the functional requirements of the information system. For example, the system-functional requirement searching for a record is mapped into one object of the database. The object has children that in turn satisfy the details of the functional requirement.

Following Suh's uncoupling metric, the object-uncoupling information-systems design could be defined as:

$$FR = A \cdot O$$

where FR is the column or vector of functional requirements, A is the design matrix (or table), and O is the vector or column of information systems objects that are the mapping or models of the functional requirements.

For example, the information-systems objects of search object, update object, and network object are the mapping of the functional requirements search and update. The equation for the coupling metric has the following form:

$$\begin{pmatrix} search \\ update \end{pmatrix} = \begin{pmatrix} a_{11} & a_{12} & a_{13} \\ a_{21} & a_{22} & a_{23} \end{pmatrix} \cdot \begin{pmatrix} search\ object \\ update\ object \\ network\ object \end{pmatrix}$$

Matrix A maps system objects to functional requirements. If one can quantify functional requirements and objects, then matrix A contains information about how much a change in one functional requirement would lead to the change in the corresponding system object. However, this is rarely the case in the design of information systems. In information systems, the element a_{ij} of A matrix is the strength of the relationship between the functional requirement i and the system object j.

For the above example, matrix A could have the following values:

$$A = \begin{pmatrix} a_{11} & a_{12} & a_{13} \\ a_{21} & a_{22} & a_{23} \end{pmatrix}$$

$$= \begin{pmatrix} 1 & 0 & .7 \\ 0 & 1 & .4 \end{pmatrix}$$

where $a_{11} = 1$ indicates that the first functional requirement, search, and the first object, search object, are strongly related. $a_{12} = 0$ shows that the search functional requirement and update object are not related. $a_{13} = .7$ indicates that the search functional requirement and network object are moderately related. Similarly, the elements of the second row show that the update functional requirement is not related to search object, strongly related to update object, and somewhat related to network object.

In a completely uncoupled design, matrix A should be a square matrix and have 1 or values close to 1 as its main diagonal and zero or near zero for off-diagonal elements. In other words, the closer A is to a diagonal matrix, the closer the design is to an ideal, uncoupled design.

The interesting feature of the uncoupling metric is that the elements of A are naturally generated by the use of quality function deployment (QFD), discussed in Chapters 5 and 6. The values inside the house of quality show the relationships of requirements (on the left column) and modules (on the top row) of the house. If we divide values in each row by 9, the strength of relations will have values between zero and one. We can use these values as the entries in matrix A.

For example, in the ACCU-INFO case, consider a simplified version of Figure 5.6 in Chapter 5, shown in Figure 9.2 here. Strengths of relations are translated to ordinal values: 9, 3, and 1 for strong, moderate, and weak relations, respectively. Strengths of relations between pairs of requirements and objects are multiplied by the customer ratings of the relative importance of each requirement, generating object ratings of 1.5, 5.5, .6, .9, 5.4, 2.7, 2.7, and 2.7 for the eight system objects in Figure 9.2. Dividing these ratings by their sum (22), gives us normalized relative ratings of objects as .07, .25, .03, .04, .25, .12, .12, and .12 that sum to 1.

To get the elements of matrix A from the house of quality, we can divide the elements by 9 before the computation of the object ratings. Figure 9.3 is similar to Figure 9.2, with the difference that elements in the house are divided by 9. As Figure 9.3 shows, dividing the elements by 9 does not affect the ratings of objects in the last row.

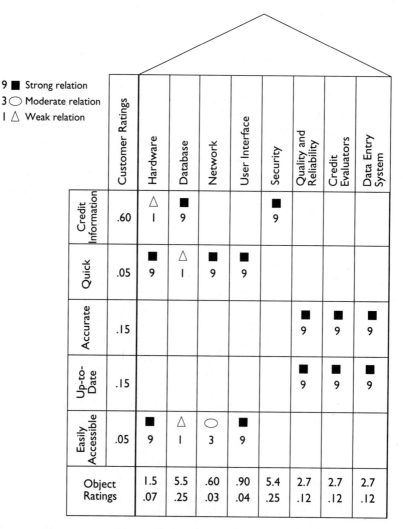

Figure 9.2   An Example of the House of Quality

We can use the table entries in Figure 9.3 as the elements of the design matrix A as:

$$
A = \begin{array}{c} \\ CrIn \\ Quck \\ Accu \\ UpDa \\ EsAc \end{array}
\begin{array}{c} Hdwr \quad Dtbs \quad Ntwk \quad UsIn \quad Scrt \quad QlRl \quad CrEv \quad DtEn \end{array}
\left(
\begin{array}{cccccccc}
\frac{1}{9} & 1 & & & \frac{1}{9} & & & \\
1 & \frac{1}{9} & 1 & 1 & 1 & & & \\
 & & & & & 1 & 1 & 1 \\
 & & & & & 1 & 1 & 1 \\
1 & \frac{1}{9} & \frac{3}{9} & 1 & & & & \\
\end{array}
\right)
$$

In the above metric, one can see that there is a strong coupling among objects: quality and reliability, credit evaluation, and data-entry system, because all three have a

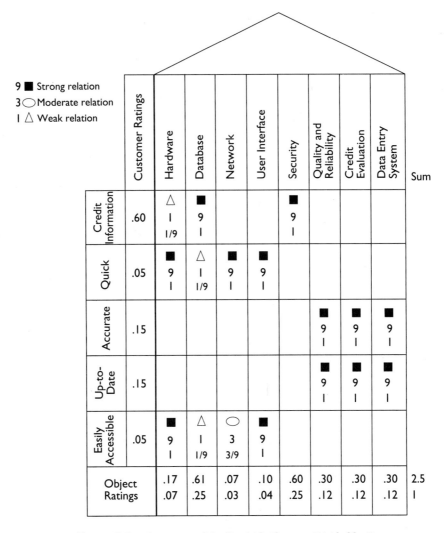

Figure 9.3 The House of Quality with Elements Divided by 9

strong relation with two requirements: accurate and up-to-date. These two requirements are basically the same in that the customer wants reliable data that is accurate and up-to-date. On the other hand, the three objects are pieces of a good data-entry process object that should be of high quality, and have reliable credit evaluators and data-entry system.

Therefore, at this stage of the design, when we are identifying the more macro and abstract objects, a better design is shown in Figure 9.4, with the design matrix A as:

$$
A = \begin{array}{c} \\ CrIn \\ Quck \\ Reli \\ EsAc \end{array}
\begin{array}{cccccc}
Hdwr & Dtbs & Ntwk & UsIn & Scrt & DtEnPro \\
\frac{1}{9} & 1 & & & \frac{1}{9} & \\
1 & \frac{1}{9} & 1 & 1 & 1 & \\
 & & & & & 1 \\
1 & \frac{1}{9} & \frac{3}{9} & 1 & &
\end{array}
$$

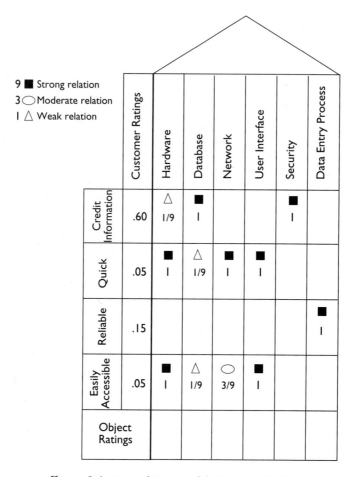

Figure 9.4   Revised Version of the House of Quality

This design matrix is closer to the ideal diagonal matrix than the previous one. The design matrix helps the designers analyze the mapping of requirements to objects such that the requirements map only to one object in the system.

As one develops the subsequent houses of quality in which more detailed objects are developed, the objects of the previous house of quality become the system requirement for the next house of quality. In each house, design matrix A should be as close as possible to a diagonal matrix with diagonal elements equal to 1. That is, the principle of mapping one requirement to an object remains the same in all subsequent designs of the houses of quality.

This way, when system designers use QFD in system design, they can immediately identify the uncoupling metric for the design. This feature gives a great advantage to the metric in that it guides system designers at the time of design to develop modules and objects that have the best uncoupling metric and require little data collection or computation.

Object-Correlation Metric.   The object-correlation metric quantifies the extent of correlation among the modules of objects in the information system. In Chapters 5 and 6, we discussed the house of quality, in which the roof of the house shows the correlation among the modules or objects. If we identify the correlation among the system objects as the extent of functional uncoupling among the objects, we can form a correlation matrix directly using the data from the roof of the house of quality (discussed in Chapter 6.)

For example, in the ACCU-INFO case, assume that in the hierarchy of houses of quality for the design of the information system (Chapter 6), we have identified the following system objects:

- Database
- Quality
- Training
- Hardware
- Network
- Data suppliers

From the roof of the house of quality, we can form a normalized correlation matrix for the above system objects as:

$$
C = \begin{array}{c} \\ \textit{database} \\ \textit{quality} \\ \textit{training} \\ \textit{hardware} \\ \textit{network} \\ \textit{suppliers} \end{array} \begin{array}{cccccc} \textit{database} & \textit{quality} & \textit{training} & \textit{hardware} & \textit{network} & \textit{suppliers} \\ \left(\begin{array}{cccccc} 1 & .9 & .5 & .1 & .1 & 0 \\ .9 & 1 & .8 & .7 & .9 & .9 \\ .5 & .8 & 1 & .5 & .5 & .3 \\ .1 & .7 & .5 & 1 & .1 & 0 \\ .1 & .9 & .5 & .1 & 1 & .2 \\ 0 & .9 & .3 & 0 & .2 & 1 \end{array}\right) \end{array}
$$

In this matrix (or table), each entry shows the correlation between the object on the row with the object on the corresponding column. For example, the correlation between database and quality is .9. This is the element on the first row (database) and the second column (quality). Obviously, the elements on the diagonal of the matrix are equal to one—each object is fully coupled with itself. The matrix is symmetric with respect to its diagonal, in that the elements on the lower half of the matrix are equal to the elements on the upper half of the matrix.

Note that in the above correlation matrix, the entries are the subjective evaluation of the system designers and are normalized to be in the interval of zero to one. Since no computation is performed on the present form of the matrix, one can use ordinal values as the entries in this matrix, such as very high, high, moderate, low, and none. However, setting diagonal-element values to 1—the highest correlation value—simplifies the correlation matrix. The goal of the design should be to define objects such that the off-diagonal entries of the correlation matrix are as close to zero as possible. Moreover, since the matrix is symmetric, we need only to enter and examine the elements on the upper triangle in the matrix.

High values in the correlation matrix indicate strong coupling between the pairs of objects. The ideal design is where there is little correlation or dependency among the objects. Hence, the ideal design has a correlation matrix that has diagonal values equal to 1 and zero or near zero for the off-diagonal elements. High values in the correlation matrix should prompt action to reduce coupling in the design. That is, we need to investigate how the object definitions could be changed in order to reduce the coupling.

In the above example, quality has a high correlation with other objects. We can raise the question: What is the nature of the quality object? Do we have a clear understanding of the role of this object? For this case, quality could be interpreted two ways. One way is to define it as forming a quality group for defining, collecting, and analyzing the quality information about the performance of the information system. Alternatively, one may interpret quality as the quality of the database, hardware, or network objects.

If the first definition of quality is true in this design, then the functioning of the quality team does not have a strong correlation with the other objects in the system. Since the correlation matrix shows a strong correlation between quality and other objects, this definition does not apply here.

In the second definition, quality is an attribute of other objects. Since it is an attribute, it is not an independent object. It should be part of the object itself. Thus, we should drop quality as a separate object, and include it as an attribute of database, hardware, and network.

Another object that has relatively high correlation with other system objects is training. For this object, we should separate the content of training from the organization, scheduling, and setup of the training process. It is obvious that the training process is not correlated with the system objects. However, the content of training is partly correlated with the design of the other objects.

For example, a complex network or database design may increase the training requirements and contents. An extensive training requirement is an indicator that the design is too complex and should be simplified. Otherwise, the cost of system maintenance and use will increase disproportionately. That is, we want to have the training requirement closely attached to the design of each object to monitor its complexity. This logic leads us to the conclusion that the training requirement of each object is one of its attributes, not a separate object of its own.

Thus, with the understanding that the quality and training requirements of each object are the attributes of the object, we can eliminate quality and training as two independent objects. Thus, the correlation matrix will have the following form:

$$
C = \begin{array}{c} \\ \begin{array}{c} database \\ hardware \\ network \\ suppliers \end{array} \end{array}
\begin{array}{cccc}
database & hardware & network & suppliers \\
\left(\begin{array}{cccc}
1 & .1 & .1 & 0 \\
.1 & 1 & .1 & 0 \\
.1 & .1 & 1 & .2 \\
0 & 0 & .2 & 1
\end{array} \right)
\end{array}
$$

This correlation matrix is closer to the ideal identity matrix (matrix with 1 on the diagonal and zero everywhere else). Furthermore, the process of examining the objects provides a better understanding of the nature of system objects.

Assuming that correlation values between .05 to .25 indicate a low level of correlation, the above example with ordinal entries will have the following form:

$$C = \begin{array}{c} \\ database \\ hardware \\ network \\ suppliers \end{array} \begin{array}{cccc} database & hardware & network & suppliers \\ \left(\begin{array}{cccc} 1 & low & low & none \\ & 1 & low & none \\ & & 1 & low \\ & & & 1 \end{array} \right) \end{array}$$

which is relatively close to the ideal form of the correlation matrix.

9.1.4   Uncoupling Guidelines for Information Systems

One can categorize coupling among objects as:

- Data coupling
- Content coupling
- Stamp coupling
- Control coupling
- Hybrid coupling

Data coupling exists when two objects are functionally dependent because they share the same data. *Content coupling* is present when one object knows the internal functions of another object. *Stamp coupling* is present when an object has to know the internal structure of another object in order to send it a message. *Control coupling* exists when one object has control over the internal function of another object. *Hybrid coupling* is present when the message from an object has different meanings, depending the content of the information.

In the design of information-systems objects, one can benefit from some experiences that have been applied to software design. Yourdon and Constantine [1978] and Page-Jones [1988] have made recommendations regarding software design that are valuable in reducing the coupling and functional dependencies among information-system objects:

- Eliminate unnecessary relationships
- Reduce the necessary relationships
- Increase the flexibility of connections
- Examine the nature of connections

Eliminating Unnecessary Relationships.   In the design of information systems, there should be a concerted effort to eliminate unnecessary relationships. The relationships could be among various objects of the information systems or among objects and human workers.

For example, in the ACCU-INFO case, there are two objects: data supplier and error checking. The error checking object checks data based on the type of data supplier. This creates a relationship between the two objects.

One can eliminate this relationship in a number of ways. One way is to perform all error checking for all types of data. In this case, there is no need to distinguish between the suppliers of data in error checking, especially when the error checking is fast and there are some overlaps among various types of suppliers. Another way to eliminate the relationship between the data supplier and error checking objects is to code the supplier type into the data itself. In this case, the error checking object does not need to know which data supplier object has provided the data because the data itself contains the information.

The elimination of the relationship between the two objects makes the error checking object immune to any possible changes that can take place in the data supplier object, such as adding or deleting a supplier type.

Reducing the Necessary Relationships.   Another recommendation for dealing with coupling is the reduction of necessary relationships among modules or objects of information systems. For example, in the ACCU-INFO case, the data for credit ratings should be checked by the error checking object. Since data is collected from various geographical areas and sent to the central office for processing, the error checking object is highly dependent on the network object over which the data travels. When the error checking object discovers an error, it has to send a message over the network to the locality where the data originated for correction and another round of updates over the network. This means that every data item travels through the network object a number of times when the error checking object identifies an error. Thus, there is a strong relationship between the two objects.

To reduce the extent of this dependency, one can break down the error checking object into two: local-error checking and global-error checking. The errors that can be found and corrected at the local level are contained in the local-error checking object. This object is distributed to all local areas that originate data into the system, including the data suppliers' systems. The errors that are global and should be investigated beyond the local level will be checked centrally when the data is assembled from various local areas, such as discrepancies of reporting about the same person from various locations. The global-error checking object still has a relation with the network object. However, the extent of this relationship is reduced by the alternative design, in which part of the error-checking task is delegated to the locations where the data originates.

Increase the Flexibility of Connections.   Another way to reduce the coupling among objects is to separate the external views from the internal views of the objects and to standardize external views of objects. This approach gives flexibility to the connections among objects such that a change in one object will affect the other objects that have relationships with it.

The idea of external and internal views of objects is inherent to the object-oriented approach. Each object has two views: internal and external. The internal view of the object is the way it functions. The external view is the way other objects see and interact with the object. In other words, the external views of system objects are publicly known to all other objects and are used for communication with that object.

In order to increase the flexibility of connections among the information-systems objects, the other objects (except the children of an object in the hierarchical design of objects) should have no access or knowledge of the internal functions of an object. The external views of an object should be standardized such that when the internal functions of an object change, its external view does not alter. This way, when a change takes place in an object, other objects that communicate with it will not be affected.

For example, in the ACCU-INFO case, the internal view of the database object should not be accessible to the network object. Therefore, when we make changes in the database, the network function is not affected. Inversely, the changes in the network object's internal functions should not affect the database object. On the other hand, database and network objects communicate because the locally collected and stored data travel over the network object, which in turn has to deliver data from one database to another. Therefore, the two objects need to know and access each other through their external views.

In a good design, the external views are standardized to the point that no matter how much the internal view changes, the external view is not affected. For example, although the network can be set up to get and receive all types of data and various files of the database, the external view of the database should be standardized such that the network does not have to know what types of files or data are being used in the database or in what format the data is stored. One simple way is that all database files are transformed into ASCII or binary type, and all files are compressed according to a standard compression protocol used for all types of communications. In other words, the interface among objects should have a standard that is rarely affected by changes in the internal functions of the object. This idea is the principle of *encapsulation*, which is one of the important aspects of the object-oriented approach.

Although the idea of encapsulation at the more macro level (such as database or network objects) is natural and understandable, enforcing encapsulation at a more detailed level could easily be ignored or dismissed, leading to an inflexible design.

In the ACCU-INFO case, the database object has children, which are the local databases distributed across the geographical area over which the company operates (see Figure 9.5). The local database objects are siblings and should be completely encapsulated. This means that the communication among local database objects should be independent of the internal functions of each object, and the interface of these objects should be standardized. To accomplish this requires the design of a standard external view for local database objects, regardless of the technology and software used at the local level. The system designer needs to be vigilant about the standardization of the external views and encapsulation of the internal views of these objects. Otherwise, with the assumption that the local databases are independently created, one may overlook the issue of standardization. Furthermore, due to short-term exigencies, some local databases may be linked together in such a way that the principle of encapsulation is compromised.

Separating the internal and external views of objects and encapsulating the internal functions of objects help avoid many types of coupling, such as data, content, stamp, control, and hybrid couplings.

Examine the Nature of Connections.   In designing system objects that are decoupled, one needs to explore the nature of connections among the objects. Interpreting Yourdon and Constantine's recommendation for system objects, in examining the connection among objects, we should:

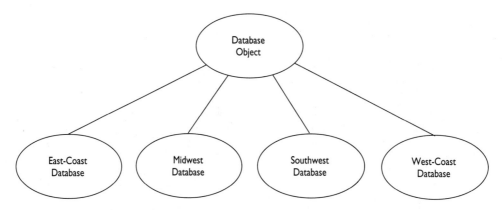

Figure 9.5   The Hierarchy of Databases in the ACCU-INFO Case

- Create narrow (vs. broad) connections
- Create direct (vs. indirect) connection
- Create local (vs. remote) connections
- Make obvious (as opposed to obscure) connections

Narrow vs. Broad Connections.   Narrow connections among objects reduce the probability of coupling among them. Compare the design of two system objects, A and B. In one design, A sends a message to object B, communicating five data items in that message. In the second design, A sends only two data items in its message to B. The second design is better because it has a narrower connection between the two objects. In the case of ACCU-INFO, a local database object may need the credit rating of an individual located in another local database object. One way is to get all raw input from the object, which may be ten data items. Another design is to have the rating computed by the local object and sent to the inquiring object. The design that has less connection is a better design. A narrow connection reduces the chance of control and hybrid coupling.

The problem that the reduced connection poses is that the computation of ratings in one local object may not be the same as in the other. This problem highlights the need for standardization. There should be standards at the regional, national, or international level for the computation of credit ratings. The inquiring object should just request ratings for a given region. It would be the local object's task to know the standard for various regions and respond accordingly. Interfaces and messages regarding the inquiry of the credit rating will not change when a new region is added to the system, the computation of a credit rating is changed, or a new data item is added for the computation of the credit ratings. Only the objects that compute credit ratings will change their internal functions.

Direct vs. Indirect Connections.   The connections among objects should be direct. In the ACCU-INFO case, assume that the local information is collected and summarized by a central database. If a local database needs data from another local database, there is no need to access it through the central database. The local database object should be able to access the information directly from the other local database. Accessing the central database requires that both local and central database objects be operational, while in the local-to-local connection, it is enough to have one local object operating. The problem with this direct connection is that every local database object should be knowledgeable about the other local objects. This issue can be resolved by designing standard interfaces and a central system working as a repository of knowledge about the external views of other local systems (as was discussed in Chapter 7).

Local vs. Remote Connections.   In a design in which two objects communicate locally, as opposed to a design in which the objects communicate remotely, the one with the local connection is superior, everything else being equal. This point is obvious because remote connection involves at least one more object, and that is the network. Therefore, the local connection is more direct and has less coupling.

Obvious vs. Obscure Connections.   The foundation of designing systems based on the object-oriented approach is that system objects are abstract models of real objects. Therefore, the communication of objects should follow the natural and therefore obvious connections. For example, in the case of ACCU-INFO, the supplier object has data and the database object needs data. The obvious connection is that the database object should send a message to the supplier object and get the needed data. An obscure, indirect, and complex connection exists when the request for data is sent by another object, such as credit officer, and entered into the system by the data-entry clerk.

In other words, starting the design without a preconceived notion based on the historical mode of operations, one can design connections that follow the natural flow of information. This method avoids creating artificial connections restricted by past constraints that do not exist anymore. The creation of obvious connections reduces the chance of hybrid and control couplings.

9.1.5 Object-Cohesion Metrics For Information Systems

Using uncoupling metrics as the only guide measure for good design may lead the system designer to create large objects. Taking the uncoupling concept to the extreme, one can design the information system to consist of a single object. Since there is no other object, there is no coupling problem. There is another side to the uncoupling coin, which is cohesion.

The idea of cohesion was suggested by Larry Constantine in the 1960s. Yourdon and Constantine [1979], and Pages-Jones [1988] define cohesion as "the measure of the strength of functional relatedness of elements within a module."

Applied to information-systems objects, cohesion means that an object should have one single abstract task. An *abstract task* is a single task relevant to the level of the object's abstraction.

In the ACCU-INFO case, a database object is defined at a higher level of abstraction than the query-interface object. The task of a database object is to provide data for the information-systems customers, whereas the task of a query-interface object is to allow the direct user of the system to query the database on an ad hoc and on-line basis. The first task is much more global and at a higher level of abstraction than the second task. Each task is appropriate for the level of the object's abstraction.

As the design goes down the object hierarchy, moving from more abstract and global objects to more concrete and a lower level of abstraction, so does the single task associated with the object. In a cohesive object, there is a single task associated with every object at each level. If there is more than one abstract task for each object, then the object lacks adequate cohesion.

In the ACCU-INFO case, if the query interface object also has the task of updating the system or maintaining the security of the database, then the object has less cohesiveness than the object whose only task is to allow the user to query the database. A more cohesive design defines separate objects for updating and system security. In this way, if there is a change or improvement in the security procedure of the system, the updating and query interface objects are not affected. This, of course, is contingent upon the existence of a standard interface (or external view) for each object that does not easily change as its functions are altered.

When the query interface object is called, it sends a message to the security object to issue the access permission. The external view of the security object should be such that the nature of the message from query interface does not change when there are changes in the internal functions of the security object. This means that system designers should design external views that do not change. There are a number of alternatives for the security object's external view. For example, it may require that the query interface object send the name, position, and password of the user for verification and access permission. This interface could easily change if the new security procedure replaces the password with the user's social security number and mother's maiden name. Furthermore, if the query interface object changes its function to allow some users to have security clearance for some data items, such as credit ratings, but not for all, the security interface may require change. This change will affect all objects that need security clearance. In this case, by separating the query interface from the security object to increase cohesiveness, we have introduced a strong coupling to the design.

The appropriate design of external view for the security object increases cohesiveness without introducing the problem of object coupling. One such design of the external view is that whenever a user starts the query, the query interface object sends a message to the security object requesting clearance without passing any information about the user. Then, the security object takes over the process of security clearance and will ask for security data from the query interface or directly from the user in order to issue the access permission. Since the message for requesting access permission from the security object does not assume, a priori, any particular data requirements, the security object can change all its functions with no effect on either its external view or other objects that send messages to it for security clearance.

The point to emphasize is that a good design does not create cohesion at the expense of uncoupling. The appropriate definition of system objects and their tasks, and the standardization of objects' external views provide the cohesiveness and uncoupling simultaneously.

Scales of Cohesion as an Object-Cohesion Metric.   There are times that absolute cohesion may not be possible or desirable among objects. One can divide cohesion into different scales or degrees. Scales of cohesion are defined by Meyers [1975], Stevens et al. [1974], and Yourdon and Constantine [1979] in the content of software design. If we define cohesion of objects as the number of abstract tasks performed by an object, we can use the cohesion scales as one of the cohesion metrics for information-systems design. The cohesion scales are categorized into:

- Functional
- Sequential
- Communicational
- Procedural
- Temporal
- Logical
- Coincidental

Functional.   The best object-cohesion category is *functional* because the object has one task and is encapsulated like a black box, whose internal workings are unknown to other objects. In the ACCU-INFO case, the validation object, which has the sole task of checking the validity of data received from the data suppliers, has a functional level of cohesiveness.

Sequential.   The second-best level of cohesiveness is *sequential*, in that an object carries a sequence of tasks, mostly to accomplish the same goal. In the ACCU-INFO case, an object that checks both the validity of the supplier and the validity of data received from the data supplier, has a sequential level of cohesiveness because it is performing more than one task for the goal of establishing the legitimacy of data.

Communicational.   The third level of cohesiveness is *communicational*, where an object has more than one task that uses the same set of attribute values of the object. In the ACCU-INFO case, an object may establish the validity of data and match the ID of the individual for whom the data is reported, with the list of IDs in ACCU-INFO's database to establish if a prior history existed. Since both tasks use the same data, the level of cohesiveness is communicational.

Procedural.   In the *procedural* level of cohesiveness, an object performs a procedure that may consist of several unrelated tasks. In the ACCU-INFO case, a communication object should go through a procedure for transmitting data. This procedure includes confirming the identity of the sender, compressing the file, encoding the data contained in the file, determining the route over which the data should be transmitted, and sending the data over the communication path. These are a combination of tasks that have to be performed in the communication procedure. The cohesiveness of the object has decreased because there are more than one task and they are unrelated. A more cohesive design would break this object into multiple objects, each of which perform one well-defined task, such as the data compressor, encoder, path finder, and origin verifier objects.

Temporal.   The *temporal* level of cohesiveness exits when tasks that are related in time are bundled into one object. In the ACCU-INFO case, a first day object performs all tasks that should be accomplished in the first day of receiving a complaint about a credit rating. This object has a temporal level of cohesiveness.

Logical.   The *logical* level of cohesiveness exits when the object contains a number of tasks that are logically connected. In the ACCU-INFO case, the resolution object is the object that tries to resolve a complaint about a credit-rating error by trying various strategies. Such strategies include checking the input data, recomputing the credit rating and matching it with the reported rating, verifying the legitimacy of the data supplier, matching the identity of the complainant with the reported rating's ID, and calling the supervisor for human intervention.

Coincidental.   The lowest level of cohesiveness is *coincidental*. At this level, there is no meaningful relationship among the functions an object performs. The object lacks cohesion.

Although these scales form an ordinal metric for examining the extent of cohesiveness, they are not mutually exclusive. An object may be categorized in more than one level of cohesiveness. As in the case of most design metrics, the scales are developed to raise the designers' awareness of about a given aspect of the design, in this case the cohesiveness, rather than the exact measurement of the design attributes.

9.1.6   Object-Complexity Metrics for Information Systems (Optional)

Another type of design metric for information systems is the object-complexity metric. The complexity concept was developed for software design, such as McCabe's cyclomatic complexity metric [McCabe 1976]. However, the complexity of objects in information systems is a relatively new and unexplored territory.

In this section, we develop four complexity metrics for objects:

- Object response
- System-average response and its standard deviation
- Response deviation
- Decision complexity

Object-Response Complexity Metric.   Chidamber and Kemerer [1991], and Li and Henry [1993] define *response* of a class of objects as the number of local functions (or methods) of an object plus the number of methods called by the local methods of an object i:

$$R_i = M_i + OM_i$$

where R_i is the response of an object, M_i is the number of local methods in object i, and OM_i is the number of other objects' methods that object i calls. Since the methods of an object determine the response of a class, Li and Henry [1993] argue that the larger the number of methods for an object, the higher is its complexity.

The problem with the R_i is that it is affected by the way objects are designed. System designer A may include twice as many methods as system designer B for the same object. This could be that system designer A is careful to include the appropriate methods for various routine operations in an object, such as error handling, input, output, ways to construct an object, and ways the object performs regular operations such as addition and assignment. If we go purely by the count of an object's methods, we may conclude that designer A has designed an object twice as complex as that created by designer B.

We will deal with this shortcoming in the response-deviation metric, after defining the system-average response metric.

System-Average Response and its Standard Deviation.   The complexity of the entire system is defined as the average and standard deviation of objects' responses in the system. We define system-average response $\bar{R}$:

$$\bar{R} = \frac{\sum_{i=1}^{n} R_i}{n}$$

where $\bar{R}$ is the average of object responses in the system, n is the number of all objects in the system, and R_i is the response of object i.

We also define the standard deviation (s) of response of system objects as:

$$s = \left(\frac{\sum_{i=1}^{n} (R_i - \bar{R})^2}{n - 1} \right)^{.5}$$

$\bar{R}$ and s together form a metric for the object complexity in the design of an information system. The system that has higher values for $\bar{R}$ and s is a more complex system.

A company that is regularly involved in the development of information systems can gradually develop the accepted or standard level of complexity metrics for the design of an information system. Such inter-project complexity metrics are helpful in evaluating and comparing information-systems projects.

The companies that undertake to design an information system on a one-time basis can use the standards developed in the field by other companies to gauge the object complexity of its design and the variability of complexity across system objects.

Response-Deviation Complexity Metric.   One metric for the complexity of an object in the information system is the distance of the object's response from the average in the system. To gauge the complexity of a given object in the design of an information system, one can define the metric as:

$$RD_i = R_i - \bar{R}$$

where RD_i is the deviation of object i's response from the average (or standard) response in the information system, R_i is object i's response, and $\bar{R}$ is the average (or standard) response in the information system.

Positive values of RD_i show that the object has more complexity than the average (or standard) objects in the system. A very high value for this metric could be an indicator of possible problems of inadequate cohesiveness or uncoupling. Negative values indicate that an object has low complexity. A very low complexity value could be the signal that an object lacks the needed methods for communicating with other objects.

The question then is: How do we define a very high value or a very low value? One way to answer this question is to use the inter-project standard deviation of response s— the standard deviation computed across various information-systems projects. If RD_i is three standard deviations above $\bar{R}$, the object may need redesign. Two standard deviations above $\bar{R}$ is a signal that the design of object i should be reviewed for a possible complexity problem.

Similarly, a RD_i value that is three standard deviations below $\bar{R}$ indicates that the object either lacks adequate methods for communicating with other objects, or its design is too fragmented and should be combined with other objects. A RD_i value that is two standard deviations below $\bar{R}$ should send review warning for object i.

For example, assume that the query interface object in the ACCU-INFO case has $R_i = 38$ methods, whereas $\bar{R}$ and s for the same type of system are 20 and 5 methods respectively. The value of RD_i for this object is:

$$RD_i = 38 - 20 = 18$$

which is more than three standard deviations ($5 \times 3 = 15$) above $\bar{R}$. It shows that this object has a serious complexity problem and should be redesigned.

In another example, assume that the data update object in the ACCU-INFO case has 11 methods, which means that:

$$RD_i = 11 - 20 = -9$$

which is about two standard deviations below the average response $\bar{R}$. The design of this object should be reviewed for possible insufficiency of methods for communication or too much fragmentation of objects in the design.

Decision-Complexity Metric.   Another way to measure the complexity of an object is to count the number of times an object has to make a decision about a particular task. We call this metric the *decision-complexity* metric.

For example, the validation object in the ACCU-INFO case checks the validity of input data. This object has to decide if each data element:

- Has the right range of values
- Belongs to the correct time interval
- Belongs to a legitimate action of a person
- Belongs to an appropriate action of a person
- Matches with the history of the person, if the data belongs to an existing person in the database

Assume that there are 20 different types of input data; each needs a different set of the above 5 decisions. Therefore, this object has 100 decisions. Furthermore, at the arrival of each data element, the object should check if the data element:

- Belongs to a real person in the database, if the individual is already in the database
- Belongs to a real person, if the individual is new

With these two decisions, the decision-complexity metric of this object amounts to 102.

As with the response-complexity metric, we can define the average and standard deviation of the decision-complexity metric for the entire system. The decision-complexity metric of an object is defined as the deviation of the object's decision-complexity metric from that of the system's average. Metric values that are more than two standard deviations above the system average send signals for review and redesign of the object.

9.2 ♦ Project-Management Quality Metrics for Information Systems

Metrics for quality information systems could have different scopes as:

- A single unit of the system
- A stage of the system
- A team working on the system
- All the teams working on one or more systems
- The entire system
- The management of a project

We have covered the first four types in Chapter 8 and in this chapter's design metrics. Metrics for the entire system and the project management are related in that they embody the attributes related to the system as a whole. The difference between the two types of metrics is that the entire-system metrics gauge the technical quality of the system, whereas the project-management metrics are designed for managerial aspects of the development and operation of the system.

Managing an information-system project has four dimensions:

- Cost management
- Value management
- Fault management
- Time management

Information systems as a functional unit and as service-providing products have long been criticized for the lack of quantifiable metrics for cost analysis. This criticism has some validity because no two systems are the same. Therefore, we need to have some unit of measurement to gauge the cost per unit of the system, and compare systems based on their costs.

Value management in an information-system project provides tools for ensuring that the project's output is of value to its customers. Cost-benefit analysis of systems depends on the unit cost as well as the value a system generates for its customers.

Fault management in an information-system project provides opportunity for improving the quality of the project by analyzing the nature of faults and creating safeguards against their recurrence. Time management is one of the critical aspects of information systems that aids project managers in keeping a project within its allocated budget. Together, cost-, value-, fault-, and time-management metrics equip a project manager with tools for detecting problem sources that, if unchecked, could turn into painful and paralyzing cost overruns—a common occurrence in information-system projects.

9.2.1   Cost-Management Metrics

In analyzing the cost of information systems, one needs metrics for measuring the system size and comparing systems based on their unit costs.

In cost analysis of software, it has been suggested to use the number of lines of code (excluding the comment lines) or the function points (discussed in Chapter 8) as the metrics for the size of a software product. The issue in information systems is that software is only one part of the system. Defining information-systems size metrics purely based on the size of the software ignores other components of the system, such as hardware, data, knowledgebase, network, and human inputs. Acceptable sized metrics should include all components of the system. Using the design metrics addresses this issue.

Number of Objects as the Size Metric.   In Section 9.1, we defined objects as the unit of design. A system object could be an encapsulated component of software, independent pieces of hardware, type of data, connection lines in a network, or the skill of the information-system worker needed to operate the system. Therefore, a design object in an information system could represent an information-system unit.

In using objects as information-system units, we need to make a distinction between classes and specific objects. So far, we have used an object to represent both a type of object (class) and an actual object (instance of a class). However, when using objects to represent the size, we should be consistent as to which definition we use. If we use objects to represent classes, in counting objects, we only count the types. Otherwise, we can include all actual objects in the determination of size.

For example, in the ACCU-INFO case, there are 100 PCs, 200 workstations, and 20 mainframes used in the information system. Using classes as the unit of size, there are three classes of objects: PC class, workstation class, and mainframe class. On the other hand, if we use actual objects as the unit, then the hardware represents 320 objects in the system.

One can use either classes or specific objects to represent component units in an information system. However, one must be consistent and clear about which definition is selected.

Object Hierarchy.   Chapters 5 and 6 demonstrated that there is correspondence between the stages of planning and design of the information systems and the levels of the object hierarchy, in that as the plan moves to design and details of design, the objects move from a few abstract objects to more numerous, specific objects. Since we will use size in designing metrics for various stages of system development, objects will have different degrees of abstraction at various levels of the object hierarchy. At the start of a project, all we may know is the number of highly global and abstract objects on the first level of the object hierarchy. As the project proceeds and more specific objects on the object hierarchy are developed, we can use abstract objects on the lower levels of the hierarchy. At the implementation stage, where the objects have become instances of the abstract objects, we can use actual objects in the computation of the size metrics. Since the specificity of the object changes, as the project progresses, the appropriate use of metrics using objects as size requires a careful design of the object-hierarchy standard.

Figure 9.6 shows an example of the object-hierarchy standard. It has five levels:

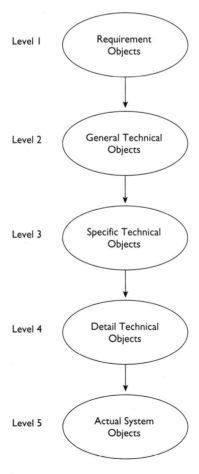

Figure 9.6   An Example of the Levels of Object Hierarchy

- Level 1: requirement objects
- Level 2: general technical objects
- Level 3: specific technical objects
- Level 4: detail technical objects
- Level 5: Actual system objects

At Level 1, the objects are highly abstract and are the translation of customer requirements to general components of the system. This level matches with the first house of quality for information-systems planning, discussed in Chapter 5.

At Level 2, the planned requirement objects are translated to general technical objects. For example, the database object is now translated into relational database with given capacities and specifications. This level corresponds to the second house of quality that launches the logical design of the system, discussed in Chapter 6.

At Level 3, the objects take on a specific technical nature. For example, the relational database object becomes Paradox database. This level matches with the third house of quality, which translates the logical design of the system into the physical design.

At Level 4, details of technical objects are specified. For example, the Paradox database at Level 3 has children: query, input, security, update, and report generation objects at Level 4. This is the detailed physical design of the system and corresponds with the fourth house of quality.

At Level 5, specific objects to be created are specified. For example, the query object at Level 4 has children: query screen, record access, and error messages at Level 5. This level corresponds with the implementation objects of the system. The last house of quality should contain these objects.

We can use objects at each level of the object hierarchy for the determination of size. However, we should make sure that the objects of different levels are not mixed. Otherwise the size metrics would become meaningless.

As discussed in Chapter 8, the successful use of metrics requires careful definition of terms and standards. The standard for the hierarchy is one of the important components of planning for quality metrics.

Size-Complexity Metric.   When the definition of an object or class of objects is a direct mapping of a physical and well-defined real object to the design, using them as units of comparison does not pose major a comparability problem. However, when objects are abstract models that could be defined in more than one way, then we have the issue of comparability. For example, in the ACCU-INFO case, a user query object in one system may be quite different in complexity from that in another system.

In order to take into account the complexity of objects, we can define the size-complexity metric as the unit of the information-systems component.

We can combine the number of objects with the complexity metric of each object in order to define the component unit for the entire system. This metric is defined as:

$$SC = \sum_{i=1}^{n} C_i$$

where SC is the size-complexity metric of a system, n is the number of objects in the design, and C_i is the complexity metric of object i in the design. C_i is one of the complexity metrics defined in Section 9.1.6 that is deemed suitable for a given information system.

We can define a different unit of complexity for each class object or specific object in a system. For example, for the software and human classes of objects, one can use the decision-complexity metric (discussed in Section 9.1.6) as C_i. For hardware, one can compare and assign complexity units to various classes of hardware. In the ACCU-INFO example above, the organization decides that a workstation and PC have the same complexity, while a mainframe class is four times more complex than PCs and workstations.

In the case of hardware objects, the assignment of a complexity metric looks arbitrary. However, when we consider C_i as the relative importance we assign to creating or operating an object, then it makes sense to use the complexity metric to reflect the difference among objects in an information system.

In order to have a standard interval for complexity, we can assign complexity in the interval from zero to one, where one represents the highest possible level of complexity. For each type of object, the most complex object gets a value of 1 for its complexity, and other objects' complexity values will be less than 1, compared to the most complex object. In the above example, if mainframe is the most complex object type in the hardware, it gets a value of 1 for a complexity metric. PC and workstation, which have one fourth the complexity of the mainframe, will have .25 as a complexity value.

If the objects are classified into categories and their complexity is determined by the class to which they belong, then the size-complexity metric could be defined as:

$$SC = \sum_{i=1}^{c} C_i \cdot O_i$$

where SC is the size-complexity metric, c is the category of objects, C_i is the complexity metric of category i objects, and O_i is the number of objects in category i. This metric could be useful for large or complex projects in which there are numerous objects at the lower levels of the object hierarchy. It is also useful for abstract objects at the top levels of the object hierarchy. Organizations with ongoing information-system projects are able to standardize the complexity value of various object types through experience and observation. Such a standard facilitates the analysis of project-management metrics and budgeting for various information-system projects.

Corporate Standards.   The relative complexity of information-systems objects could, and in many cases does, vary from one organization to another. The experience and expertise within an organization can impact the complexity of information-systems objects.

For example, ACCU-INFO has long experience with mainframes; they have been in use there for 20 years, and are connected to the data suppliers' and customers' mainframes. However, it has very little experience with networked PCs, and limited experience with individual workstations. In its new information systems, ACCU-INFO intends to use mainframes, workstations, and PCs, and will use internal expertise to develop the system. The system designers at ACCU-INFO assign a complexity of .25 to mainframes, .50 to workstations, and 1 to networked PCs. Therefore, some object complexities may reflect the complexity of the design and operation of the system for a given organization.

While the organization-based complexity weights make the information-systems units more meaningful for internal cost analysis, one may argue that organization-dependent complexity makes cross-organization comparison of systems invalid.

To address this objection, one can define two sets of complexity weights for objects: industry-standard and organization-based. Since the computation of units is a simple operation of adding the weighted values of objects, one can easily compute both size-complexity metrics for a system. The benefit of computing the size-complexity metric using both industry-standard and organization-based weights is that the complexity weights show the difference between a system developed and operated internally as opposed to a system that is developed and operated by outsourcing—contracted to outside contractors.

For example, in the ACCU-INFO case, the contractor for outsourcing has asked for $800,000, whereas the estimate for doing the job internally is $400,000. It appears that developing the system internally is more cost effective.

To compare the two options, we can compute the size complexity of the system using both the industry-standard and organization-based complexity weights. The organization-based complexity weights applied to objects produced a complexity-size value of 200, whereas the industry-standard weights applied to the same objects produced 100. Results show that developing the system internally is twice as complex as what is common industry-wide. That is, there is half as much expertise inside the organization as outside for developing the system. This raises the question about the validity of the cost estimation for developing the system internally. Can ACCU-INFO develop with half the budget a system that is twice as complex internally as that for an outside contractor? It seems that both ACCU-INFO's cost estimation and the contractor's budget need further review and scrutiny.

Average-Complexity Metric.   One can compute the average object-complexity of a system as:

$$AC = \frac{SC}{O}$$

where AC is the average complexity of an object in a system, SC is the size-complexity of the system, and O is the number of objects used in the computation of SC. The average complexity metric is helpful in comparing different systems and in analyzing the cost of information systems, as discussed below.

Cost Analysis Based on Unit-Cost Metric.   We can use objects and their size-complexity metrics as production units. This allows us to perform unit-cost analysis in information systems the same way as in any other production.

The unit-cost of a system is defined as:

$$UC = \frac{cost}{SC}$$

where *UC* is the unit cost of the system per complexity unit and *cost* is either the development cost or, preferably, the system life-cycle cost.

In cases where accurate *SC* is not available, one can use an average complexity metric in the cost analysis of information-system projects. For example, in comparing the cost of two systems, ACCU-INFO's information-system project manager has cost estimates for two relatively similar projects of $250,000 and $500,000. To compare the two systems' costs, the size-complexity metrics of the two systems are estimated by using an estimation of the number of objects (*O*) and the average complexity of objects (*AC*) for each system as:

$$SC_1 = O_1 \times AC_1 = 100 \times 10 = 1000$$
$$SC_2 = O_2 \times AC_2 = 250 \times 20 = 5000$$

Computing the unit cost of the two systems, we get an average cost of $250 and $100 per complexity unit:

$$UC_1 = \frac{250,000}{1000} = 250$$

$$UC_2 = \frac{500,000}{5000} = 100$$

That is, while the first system has half the cost of the second system, the unit cost of the second system is more than twice as much as that of the first system. In other words, the unit cost in information systems gives us the same cost-analysis capability common in product-cost accounting.

9.2.2   Value-Management Metrics

Shillito and De Marle [1992] argue that value does not dwell in products or services—no product is inherently valuable or valueless. They posit that value is an energy or force between the receiving entity and a product (an item or service). Applied to information systems, the value of an information system is the energy between the customer and the system. The value is the ability of the system to satisfy the customer's needs or wants.

As in physics, Shillito and De Marle [1992] point out that value as an energy has four basic attributes:

- Invisibility
- Causality
- Magnitude
- Energy conservation and conversion

Like gravity and magnetic energy, value is invisible. As in energies in physics, value is the cause of motion in life and society—the underlying source of people's behavior. Value, like any other energy, has intensity of varying magnitude; it can be conserved and converted. We convert one value to another through our efforts to create systems that are needed by their customers. The act of creating the system with minimum financial resources is an act of value energy conservation.

Any value-related metric should contain some or all of the following components:

- Customer requirements
- Relative importance of customers' requirements
- System functions
- Relative importance of system functions in satisfying customers' requirements
- Energies spent in creating or acquiring value—cost or price

Given the fact that value is created only when a system satisfies the customers' needs and wants, to measure the system's value or benefit, one must include the customers' requirements. Since customer requirements do not have equal importance, the relative weights of requirements are needed to make the requirements comparable. Customer needs and wants are one side of the value energy creation. The other side is comprised of system functions that satisfy the needs and wants, and their relative importance in satisfying customers' needs. Finally, the principle of value analysis states that "the maximum value is achieved when an essential function is obtained with minimum cost" [Shillito and De Marle 1992]. This is why cost or price is one of the components of value metrics. Based on these ingredients, we define the following metrics for value management:

- Requirement achievement
- Manufacturing value
- Customer value
- System-performance value
- Object value
- Requirement-object value

Requirement-Achievement Metrics.   This metric is designed for keeping track of the number of requirements incorporated into the system as the project progresses. This metric could be used at the design as well as the implementation stages of the system. The simple form of the simple requirement-achievement metric is:

$$RA = \frac{a}{p}$$

where RA is the requirement-achievement rate, a is the actual number of requirements incorporated into the system, and p is the total number of requirements to be satisfied by the system. The numbers in the above metric should be comparable, in that both should belong to the requirements on the same level in the requirement hierarchy (discussed in Chapter 5).

The problem with the simple requirement-achievement metric is that it does not contain the relative importance of requirements. A requirement may be far more important than the others. The above metric treats all requirements equally—the satisfaction of one is as important as the others.

A more representative requirement-achievement metric is one that includes the relative importance of requirements. Thus, we define the weighted requirement-achievement metric as:

$$WRA = \frac{\sum_{i=1}^{a} W_i}{\sum_{i=1}^{p} W_i}$$

where WRA is the requirement-achievement rate, a is the actual number of requirements incorporated in the system, p is the number of requirements the system is planned to satisfy, and W_i is the relative importance of requirement i. The data for this metric could be obtained directly from the house of quality in QFD analysis, covered in Chapters 5 and 6.

Tracing this metric over the life of a project gives the project manager a tool to ensure that components satisfying customer needs and, hence, creating a higher portion of the system value, are installed and tested in the system earlier than the nonessential parts.

Manufacturing-Value Metric.   The manufacturing-value metric allows the project manager to track the functional capability that is produced per dollar of cost. Producing a system means creating system objects. The cost of an object depends on its complexity. Its value to customers depends on its relative rating in satisfying customers' needs and wants. Therefore, we can define the manufacturing-value of the system as:

$$MV = \frac{\sum_{i=1}^{n} W_i \cdot C_i}{\sum_{i=1}^{n} cost_i}$$

where MV is the manufacturing-value metric, W_i is the relative importance of object i in satisfying customers' requirements, n is the number of produced objects, C_i is the complexity of object i, and $cost_i$ is the cost of producing object i. If the unit object cost is not available, the denominator in the above metric could be replaced by the aggregate cost up to the point of measurement.

This metric shows how much value has been manufactured into the system per dollar of cost. As the project advances, the project manager could track this metric to make sure that financial resources are converted into value energy for the system.

Customer-Value Metric.   The customer-value metric measures the value of the system's services for its customers. This metric has the following form:

$$CV = \frac{\sum_{i=1}^{n} W_i \cdot R_i}{price}$$

where CV is the metric for customer value, W_i is the relative importance of requirement i, R_i is the degree to which the system satisfies customer's requirement i, and $price$ is the price that the customer pays, directly or indirectly, to receive the information-system's services. If the system satisfies requirement i perfectly, the value of R_i will be 1. If the system does not satisfy requirement i at all, R_i will be zero.

This metric is useful in comparing various versions of the same system, different systems on design or performance, or different information-systems projects.

System Performance-Value Metric.   This metric measures the performance value of the system to the customer. In chapter 8, we identified the performance dimensions as:

- Timeliness
- Efficiency
- Consistency
- Continuity
- Correctness

We defined metrics for each of the above performance dimensions in Chapter 8. For an information-system project, we can combine these dimensions into a performance-value metric as:

$$PV = \frac{W_1 \cdot T + W_2 \cdot E + W_3 \cdot CS + W_4 \cdot CT + W_5 \cdot CR}{price}$$

where $W_1 \ldots W_5$ are the relative weights that customers assign to the performance dimensions; T, E, CS, CT, and CR are the choice of metrics that were defined for the above five dimensions in Chapter 8; *price* is what the customer pays for receiving the services of the system. For external customers, *price* is relatively well-defined. For internal customers, there should be a mechanism to determine the *price* a customer pays for getting the information-system's services. In some cases, the cost of the system may replace the price in the above metric.

Object-Value Metric.   The object-value metric determines the value of the object with respect to its cost. It is defined as:

$$OV_i = \frac{W_i}{costW_i}$$

where OV_i is the object-value metric for object i, W_i is the relative importance of object i in satisfying customers' requirements, and $costW_i$ is the relative share of object i's cost in the total system cost.

For example, in the ACCU-INFO case in Figure 9.2, the relative weight of the database object is .25. The share of this object in the total cost of the system is 15 percent. The object-value metric for the database object is:

$$OV_{database} = \frac{.25}{.15} = 1.67$$

That is, for every dollar spent on the database object, a value equal to 1.67 will be generated.

This metric is useful for tracking the allocation of money for the development of various objects in the system. Computing the mean and standard deviation of this metric for various objects in the system provides the project manager with a basis for comparing the object-value metrics of various objects and identifying the objects that generate too little value per dollar of cost.

Requirement Object-Value Metric.   The objective of this metric is to track the allocations of resources for satisfying customer requirements. It is defined as:

$$ROV_i = \frac{W_i}{\frac{1}{cost} \sum_{j=1}^{k} cost_j}$$

where ROV_i is the requirement object-value metric for object i, W_i is the relative importance of requirement i, $cost$ is the total cost of the project, $cost_j$ is the cost of object j, and k is the number of objects created to satisfy requirement i.

In some cases, one may divide the cost into types such as manpower, equipment, and other purchases. ROV_i of requirements could be computed for their demands for various types of resources. This provides a better vehicle for costing information-system projects.

The requirement object-value metric is useful for tracking the resources allocation in satisfying customers' requirements. Some requirements with high relative importance may be satisfied at a lower cost, while others may absorb far more resources than their relative importance justifies; fluctuations in this metric are expected. However, when budgetary constraints dictate choices among various options and enhancements, those requirements that have a high value for this metric are better choices. Moreover, requirements that have ROV_i too far below or above the mean should be reviewed for the design of their objects and resource allocation.

9.2.3   Fault-Management Metrics

In Chapter 8, we developed a number of metrics for tracking the system's errors and defects at the implementation stage of information systems. In managing an information-system project, one needs to track the recurrence of similar faults and the extent of rework in the lifetime of the project. In other words, fault management takes a longer view of the reason for the occurrence of a particular fault, the actions needed to prevent its recurrence, and the degree of rework needed in the life of the project.

The metrics for fault management can be categorized into:

- Fault recurrence
- Rework
- Customer-discovered faults

Fault-Recurrence Metrics.   In the recurrence metric, faults are categorized in detail for their type and novelty. The recurrence metric is the number of faults that have recurred within the same category. The higher the number of recurring faults in the same category, the lower is the project's learning capability. Ideally, once a fault occurs in a project, the project members should not only fix it, but establish processes that prevent the fault from recurring. If the number of recurrences is high, then the project lacks the ability to learn from its mistakes—an important aspect in quality information systems.

One can compute the average fault-recurrence metric in a project as:

$$FR = \frac{\sum_{i=1}^{c} f_i}{c}$$

where *FR* is the fault-recurrence metric, *c* is the number of fault categories, and f_i is the number of faults recurring in category *i*. Tracking this metric in the life of the project allows the project manager to gauge the learning capability of the project team.

For project managers who prefer ensuring the nonrecurrence of severe faults, the weighted fault-recurrence metric is a better choice:

$$WFR = \frac{\sum_{i=1}^{c} W_i \cdot f_i}{c}$$

where *WFR* is the weighted fault-recurrence metric and W_i is the relative severity of category-*i* faults.

Fault-Rework Metrics.   The fault-rework metric keeps track of the time spent on reworking discovered faults. This metric may also be computed as simple or weighted. The simple rework metric is the average time spent on reworking a fault and fixing it:

$$FR = \frac{\sum_{i=1}^{n} t_i}{n}$$

where *FR* is the fault-rework metric, *n* is the number of faults, and t_i is the time spent on reworking fault *i*.

The simple rework metric does not take into account the severity of faults. The weighted fault-rework metric remedies this shortcoming as:

$$WFR = \frac{\sum_{i=1}^{n} W_i \cdot t_i}{n}$$

where *WFR* is the weighted fault-rework metric, W_i is the relative severity of the category to which fault *i* belongs, t_i is the rework time of fault *i*, and *n* is the number of faults.

The fault-rework metrics could be used at all development stages of an information-system project. If this metric increases three standard deviations above the mean in any phase of the project, it may indicate problems in the project's rework process or in the system design.

Customer-Discovered-Faults Metrics.   The most severe type of faults is the one that is discovered by customers. Customer discovery of a fault shows that the internal quality processes have failed to catch and correct the fault. Furthermore, it causes customers to lose confidence, incur cost, and be displeased with and inconvenienced by the system. Therefore, the discovery of faults by customers at any stage of the system development, especially at the implementation and operation stages, is of great importance to the value of the system.

For some projects, counting the customer-discovered faults is a simple and important metric. In the case of more complex and lengthier projects, the weighted version of this metric may be more appropriate:

$$WCF = \frac{\sum_{i=1}^{c} W_i \cdot f_i}{n}$$

where WCF is the weighted average of the customer discovered-fault metric, W_i is the relative severity of the category i fault, c is the number of customer-discovered fault categories, f_i is the number of faults discovered by customers in category i, and n is the number of customer-discovered faults.

This metric gauges the average severity of the customer-discovered faults. If possible, one can ask the customer to assign the relative severity value W_i to the fault he or she has discovered. In this case, customers' perception of the system faults will be captured in this metric.

To find out the ratio of customer-discovered faults in the total system faults, we define the following metric:

$$RCF = \frac{\sum_{i=1}^{c} W_i \cdot cf_i}{\sum_{i=1}^{c} W_i \cdot f_i}$$

where RCF is the ratio of customer-discovered faults, c is the number of fault categories, W_i is the relative severity of category i faults, cf_i is the number of category i faults that customers have discovered, and f_i is the total number of category i faults discovered in the project.

RCF is a metric that could be used for comparison of projects of similar size and complexity. Establishing standards for the expected value and standard deviation of customer-discovered-fault metrics is important in the zero-defect efforts of an organization, as described in Chapter 8.

9.2.4 Time-Management Metrics

Another dimension of project management is managing time and making sure that different stages of system development follow their time schedules. There are standard methods for scheduling, such as PERT (Project Evaluation and Review Technique) and CPM (Critical Path Method). PERT was developed in late the 1950s for managing the Polaris missile project. Later, CPM was developed for industrial projects. At present, PERT/CPM are available on software packages, and their descriptions can be found in any good management-science book, such as that by Anderson, Sweeney, and Williams [1991].

The additional metrics for time management in information systems can be categorized as:

- Project-time metric
- Object-based time metrics

Project-Time Metric.   This metric keeps track of the total allocated time for various phases of the project, as:

$$PT_i = \frac{AT_i}{BT_i}$$

where PT_i is the project-time metric for phase i of the project, AT_i is the actual time spent for phase i of the project, and BT_i is the budgeted time for phase i of the project. The information-system literature contains testimonies that a higher allocation of time to the design phase of a project leads to a shorter implementation and overall project time. For organizations that have ongoing information-system projects, keeping track of the time spent on various phases of a project makes it possible to identify the best allocation of time for various types of development projects. Hence, this metric allows the organization to make cross-project comparisons. This metric is helpful in benchmarking to learn what the optimal time allocation for each development phase is in order to create the best information system.

Object-Based Time Metrics.   In this type of metrics, the project time is determined in relation to objects. One can develop a number of metrics. The first is the time per object, which is a simple metric of average time spent per object:

$$TO = \frac{T}{O}$$

where TO is the time-per-object metric, T is the total project time, and O is the number of objects in the project. At the start, the number of objects is determined from the first level of the object hierarchy. For example, in Figure 9.2, there are eight abstract objects. If the duration of the project is 16 months, on average the time allocation for each object is 2 months. (Note that time allocation for each object includes its integration with other objects.) As the design and project progresses, more detailed levels of the object hierarchy are developed, and this metric becomes more precise. At the lowest level, where the objects are the system objects to be created, this metric shows the time allocation for the implementation of the objects in the project.

Since the objects vary in complexity, the time-per-object metric does not reflect the fact that objects vary in their creation time. A metric that takes into account the complex variability of objects is the time-per-size complexity metric, defined as:

$$TSC = \frac{T}{SC}$$

where TSC is the time-per-size complexity metric and SC is the size-complexity metric defined in Section 9.2.1.

We can compare the actual time spent on the development of an object with the average budgeted time for each object as:

$$TOD_i = \frac{t_i}{C_i} - TSC$$

where TOD_i is the time-per-size complexity-deviation metric for object i, t_i is the actual time spent on object i, C_i is the complexity of object i, and TSC is the time-per-size complexity metric for the project, defined above.

In complex projects in which there are numerous objects, the TOD_i metric helps the project manager identify objects that take an unreasonable amount of development time. This, in turn, may lead to providing assistance and improving the processes for the team that is engaged in developing the object. This way, the project manager can prevent possible development bottlenecks before they force the project to miss its deadlines or lower its quality.

The interesting aspect of object-based metrics is that, over a period of time, the organization will be able to develop standards for the average time needed for the development of an object with a given complexity. These standards will facilitate project planning and budgeting for information-system projects.

Object accounting for cost and time budgeting brings information-systems projects at par with unit-cost accounting in production systems and addresses the ongoing criticism of information systems for their lack of budgeting and project-management measures.

9.3 ◆ Information-Systems Reliability Metrics (Optional)

One of the most commonly used definitions of quality is the correspondence of what the product offers with the customer's needs and expectations. The SIM (Society for Information Management) Working Group recommends developing a performance metric for information systems that incorporates customer-satisfaction measures and factual data on the performance of system components.

We have discussed and used ratings of customer requirements in every aspect of system development and its metrics. In this section, too, we develop a reliability metric that uses customer preference ratings.

In order to demonstrate the process of obtaining the customer ratings, we provide an example in which the AHP (discussed in Chapter 5) is used for combining the customers' requirements and preferences with the technical structure of the system to compute the reliability of an information system. The result is a single metric that can be used for tracking the performance of an information system and as an early signal of the system's persistent malfunction and low service quality.

9.3.1 Requirements-Objects Hierarchy

As we discussed in Section 9.2.2, the value of an information system is the utility it provides for its customers. If the system has no utility for its customers, technical elegance and good design will have little relevance. The question is how to combine the utility of an information system to its customers with its structural components. In Chapters 5 and 6, we showed this translation through QFD analysis.

Here, we use the analytic hierarchy process (AHP) (discussed in Chapter 5) to determine the utility of an information system's components for its customer and relate it to the reliability of the system components. We start with the requirements-objects hierarchy from Level 1 and move downward by an example from the ACCU-INFO case.

At Level 1, customers' utility is in its most aggregate form, indicating the overall preference of customers for the system (Figure 9.7).

Level 2 shows that the utility of an information system for its customers is based on the types of information it provides for making decisions in various areas. Customers are not interested in a particular database, technology, or technical object. The customer needs certain types of information for making decisions and taking actions, regardless of their technical media or file contents.

In the ACCU-INFO case, CEOs require three types of information: information on quality, information on profitability, and information on internal and external satisfaction regarding the company, its performance, and its services. The second level of the hierarchy in Figure 9.7 shows the three information requirements: quality, profitability, and satisfaction. At this stage, the customer specifies the needs, not the design of the system.

At Level 3, customers' information requirements are translated into various objects in the system. In Figure 9.7, the information requirements are translated into four objects: customer, sales, employee, and financial. These are four separate databases that

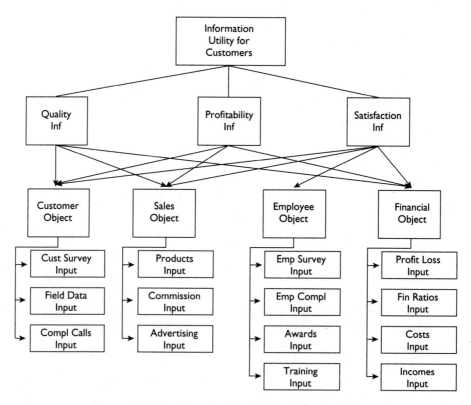

Figure 9.7   The Example of Requirement-Object Hierarchy

are created to satisfy customers' information needs. They may be in the same location or distributed geographically.

At Level 4, we have limited the objects to the greatly simplified input objects, as shown in Figure 9.7. The customer object has three input objects: customer survey, field data, and customer-complaint calls. The sales object also has three input objects: products, sales commissions, and advertising. The employee object has four input objects: employee survey, employee complaints, employee awards, and employee training. The financial object has four input objects: profit and loss (including balance sheet data), financial ratios (across the industry), production costs, and incomes.

9.3.2 Customers-Requirements Utility Values

The requirements-objects hierarchy allows us to get the ratings of different components in the hierarchy at various levels and combine them in order to have a single value for the system. We use the AHP's local and global relative weights obtained from the hierarchy and combine them with the reliability measurements of the components to compute a single reliability metric for the system. These values are available from using the house of quality (discussed in Chapters 5 and 6). Here we discuss how to generate the data independently.

Local Ratings of Elements for Customer Requirements. Customers do not attach the same importance to their information needs. For example, in today's environment of global competition, information on quality may carry a higher weight for customers than information on short-run profitability or satisfaction. Therefore, we need to elicit customers' preference ratings for various information requirements.

To accomplish this, we ask customers to compare the elements of the second level of the hierarchy with respect to the single element on the first level—the utility of the information. This pairwise comparison leads to a matrix of pairwise comparisons A as:

$$A_{Inf,U} = \begin{array}{c} \\ InfQuality \\ InfProfit \\ InfSatis \end{array} \begin{array}{ccc} InfQuality & InfProfit & InfSatis \\ \left(\begin{array}{ccc} 1 & 2 & 4 \\ & 1 & 2 \\ & & 1 \end{array} \right) \end{array}$$

Note that the lower-triangle elements are not shown here because they are the inverse of the upper-triangle elements.

Once the pairwise matrix is completed, the relative weights of the hierarchy's second level can be computed as described in Chapter 5:

$$\hat{W}_{Inf,U} = (.57 \quad .29 \quad .14)$$

$$\hat{\lambda}_{max} = 3$$

Inconsistency ratio $= 0$.

Local Ratings of Elements for System Objects. We can continue the same process for the elements on Level 3 of the hierarchy—information-system objects. The ratings at the third level are the views of system developers or technical workers (with customers' participation) regarding the relative importance of each object in satisfying the customers' requirements.

For the three information requirements, we have:

$$
A_{Obj,InfQuality} =
\begin{array}{c}
\\
ObjCus \\
ObjSal \\
ObjEmp \\
ObjFin
\end{array}
\begin{array}{cccc}
ObjCus & ObjSal & ObjEmp & ObjFin \\
\left(\begin{array}{cccc}
1 & 2 & 2 & 4 \\
 & 1 & 1 & 3 \\
 & & 1 & 2 \\
 & & & 1
\end{array}\right)
\end{array}
$$

$$
A_{Obj,InfProfit} =
\begin{array}{c}
\\
ObjCus \\
ObjSal \\
ObjEmp \\
ObjFin
\end{array}
\begin{array}{cccc}
ObjCus & ObjSal & ObjEmp & ObjFin \\
\left(\begin{array}{cccc}
1 & 1 & 2 & 0.5 \\
 & 1 & 3 & 1 \\
 & & 1 & 0.25 \\
 & & & 1
\end{array}\right)
\end{array}
$$

$$
A_{Obj,InfSatis} =
\begin{array}{c}
\\
ObjCus \\
ObjSal \\
ObjEmp \\
ObjFin
\end{array}
\begin{array}{cccc}
ObjCus & ObjSal & ObjEmp & ObjFin \\
\left(\begin{array}{cccc}
1 & 2 & .5 & 2 \\
 & 1 & .5 & 2 \\
 & & 1 & 4 \\
 & & & 1
\end{array}\right)
\end{array}
$$

Computing the local relative weights for the information objects with respect to each information requirement, we get:

$$\hat{W}_{Obj,InfQuality} = (.44 \quad .24 \quad .22 \quad .10)$$

$$\hat{\lambda}_{max} = 3.97$$

$$inconsistency\ ratio = 0.008$$

$$\hat{W}_{Obj,InfProfit} = (.22 \quad .30 \quad .10 \quad .38)$$

$$inconsistency\ ratio = 0.017$$

$$\hat{W}_{Obj,InfSatis} = (.30 \quad .18 \quad .43 \quad .09)$$

$$inconsistency\ ratio = 0.023$$

9.3.3   Global Relative Weights of Objects

After the computation of the local relative ratings for the elements on the second and third levels, we can combine them to compute the global relative weights of the third-level elements with respect to the customers' utility (the top-level element) as:

$$\hat{W}_{Obj,U} = \hat{W}_{Inf,U} \cdot \begin{pmatrix} \hat{W}_{Obj,InfQuality} \\ \hat{W}_{Obj,InfProfit} \\ \hat{W}_{Obj,InfSatis} \end{pmatrix}$$

$$= (.57 \quad .29 \quad .14) \cdot \begin{pmatrix} .44 & .24 & .22 & .1 \\ .22 & .30 & .10 & .38 \\ .30 & .18 & .43 & .09 \end{pmatrix}$$

$$= (.36 \quad .25 \quad .21 \quad .18)$$

In other words, customers rate the customer object as .36, the sales object as .25, the employee object as .21, and the financial object as .18.

9.3.4 Global Relative Weights of Input Objects

We can continue in the same manner to arrive at the customer utility for the input objects of the system. This provides us with clear ratings for various parts of information systems at the most detailed level.

Since each object has its own inputs that are independent from those of the other objects, the pairwise evaluation of inputs is carried out for one object only—the object to which they belong. Figure 9.7 gives us four matrices of pairwise comparisons of inputs, one for each object.

$$A_{Input,ObjCus} = \begin{matrix} & CusSurvey & FieldData & Calls \\ CusSurvey \\ FieldData \\ Calls \end{matrix} \begin{pmatrix} 1 & \frac{1}{2} & \frac{1}{4} \\ & 1 & \frac{1}{2} \\ & & 1 \end{pmatrix}$$

$$A_{Input,ObjSal} = \begin{matrix} & Products & Commission & Advertising \\ Products \\ Commission \\ Advertising \end{matrix} \begin{pmatrix} 1 & 4 & 2 \\ & 1 & \frac{1}{2} \\ & & 1 \end{pmatrix}$$

$$A_{Input,ObjEmp} = \begin{matrix} & EmpSurvey & EmpCompl & Awards & Training \\ EmpSurvey \\ EmpCompl \\ Awards \\ Training \end{matrix} \begin{pmatrix} 1 & 1 & 2 & 2 \\ & 1 & 1 & 1 \\ & & 1 & 1 \\ & & & 1 \end{pmatrix}$$

$$A_{Input,ObjFin} = \begin{matrix} & ProfitLoss & FinRatios & Costs & Incomes \\ ProfitLoss \\ FinRatios \\ Costs \\ Incomes \end{matrix} \begin{pmatrix} 1 & 1 & 1 & 1 \\ & 1 & 1 & 1 \\ & & 1 & 1 \\ & & & 1 \end{pmatrix}$$

The computation of the local ratings for input objects at level 4 results in:

$$\hat{W}_{Input,ObjCus} = (.14 \quad .29 \quad .57)$$

$$\hat{W}_{Input,ObjSal} = (.57 \quad .14 \quad .29)$$

$$\hat{W}_{Input,ObjEmp} = (.35 \quad .25 \quad .20 \quad .20)$$

$$\hat{W}_{Input,ObjFin} = (.25 \quad .25 \quad .25 \quad .25)$$

The global ratings of the input objects are computed as:

$$\hat{W}_{Input,U} = (.36 \quad .25 \quad .21 \quad .18) \cdot$$

$$\begin{pmatrix} .14 & .29 & .57 & 0 & 0 & 0 & 0 & 0 & 0 & 0 & 0 & 0 & 0 & 0 \\ 0 & 0 & 0 & .57 & .14 & .29 & 0 & 0 & 0 & 0 & 0 & 0 & 0 & 0 \\ 0 & 0 & 0 & 0 & 0 & 0 & .35 & .25 & .20 & .20 & 0 & 0 & 0 & 0 \\ 0 & 0 & 0 & 0 & 0 & 0 & 0 & 0 & 0 & 0 & .25 & .25 & .25 & .25 \end{pmatrix}$$

$$= (.05 \quad .11 \quad .21 \quad .14 \quad .04 \quad .07 \quad .08 \quad .06 \quad .04 \quad .04 \quad .04 \quad .04 \quad .04 \quad .04)$$

Thus, we have identified the ratings of the most detailed objects in the information system in satisfying customers' information requirements.

9.3.5 System-Reliability Metric Information Systems

We can measure the reliability of information systems' objects in a number of ways. The common reliability metrics can be categorized as:

- Number of faults in a fixed time interval
- Time between two faults

Faults in the system, such as wrong information, disconnected line, system crash, or an inappropriate response, represent unreliable responses. The number of faults in a fixed time interval refers to the number of faults with respect to the total number of times the unit has been used in a fixed time interval. The time between two faults is a reliability measure that represents the time it takes for two consecutive faults to occur.

The system-reliability metric developed here is flexible as to how the reliability of objects are measured, as long as it is used consistently. It requires that the object-reliability measure be normalized to a 0-1 interval in order to make it possible to aggregate various reliability measures of objects.

System-Reliability Metric at the Input Level.   We define the index for the reliability of input objects as:

$$SysR_{Input} = \hat{W}_{Input,U} \cdot R'_{input}$$

where $\hat{W}_{Input,U}$ is the vector that represents the customer's relative utility of input objects—the elements at the lowest level of the hierarchy in Figure 9.7. The number of elements in the vector is equal to the number of all input objects in the information system. R'_{input} is the vector of reliability values of input objects. $SysR_{Input}$ is a scaler metric for the reliability of the information system at the input level.

In an expanded form, the system-reliability metric at the input level has the form:

$$SysR_{input} = (input_1, input_2, \ldots, input_T) \cdot \begin{pmatrix} inputR_1 \\ inputR_2 \\ \vdots \\ inputR_T \end{pmatrix}$$

where $input_i$ and $inputR_i$ represent the relative utility and reliability of input object i, for $i = 1, 2, \ldots, T$, and T is the total number of input objects in the system, regardless of which object they belong to.

The system-reliability metric at the input level, therefore, is a combination of the reliability of each input object, weighted by the relative utility that customers assign to each input object in satisfying their global-information needs. This is due to the fact that the relative utility weights for inputs are the global weights that reflect the relative importance of related components on the previous levels.

We computed the relative utility of input objects for ACCU-INFO in the previous section. Assume that we now have the reliability values of each input object for the week. Furthermore, assume that the object-reliability values are computed as a ratio of the number of times the input object has produced reliable data to the total number of times the object has been used. Then, we can compute the system-reliability metric at the input level as:

$$SysR_{input} = \begin{matrix} CusSurvey \\ FieldData \\ Calls \\ Products \\ Commission \\ Advertising \\ EmpSurvey \\ EmpCompl \\ Awards \\ Training \\ ProfitLoss \\ FinRatios \\ Costs \\ Incomes \end{matrix} \begin{pmatrix} .05 \\ .11 \\ .21 \\ .14 \\ .04 \\ .07 \\ .08 \\ .06 \\ .04 \\ .04 \\ .04 \\ .04 \\ .04 \\ .04 \end{pmatrix}' \cdot \begin{pmatrix} .60 \\ .80 \\ .70 \\ .99 \\ .90 \\ .99 \\ .70 \\ .60 \\ .90 \\ .80 \\ .99 \\ .98 \\ .98 \\ .98 \end{pmatrix}$$

$$= .83$$

In other words, the system-reliability metric at the input level for this week is .83, where the desirable level for this metric is 1.

System-Reliability Metric at the Object Level.   There may be applications for which detailed data collection at the input level (fourth level) may not be feasible, desirable, or cost-effective. In such cases, we can limit computation of the information-systems reliability at the object level.

We define the systems-reliability metric at the object level as:

$$SysR_{Object} = \hat{W}_{Object,U} \cdot R'_{Cobject},$$

where $\hat{W}_{Object,U}$ is the vector representing customers' relative utility for the system objects in satisfying their information needs. $R_{Cobject}$ is a vector consisting of the object-reliability values of system objects at Level 3. The size of both vectors is equal to the number of third-level objects in the system. $SysR_{Object}$ is a scaler value for the system-reliability metric at the object level (Level 3).

In its expanded form, the system-reliability metric has the form:

$$SysR_{Object} = (Object_1 \quad Object_2 \quad \dots \quad Object_M) \cdot \begin{pmatrix} CobjectR_1 \\ CobjectR_2 \\ \vdots \\ CobjectR_M \end{pmatrix}$$

where $Object_i$ is the relative utility of object i and $CobjectR_i$ represents the (combined) reliability value of object i. M is the total number of objects in the information system.

Since the objects receive inputs from their input objects, the combined reliability of an object is the product of the object's reliability multiplied by the reliability of input objects. In other words:

$$CobjectR_i = ObjectR_i \cdot \Pi_{\forall j} \; inputR_j$$

where $ObjectR_i$ is the reliability of object i excluding its inputs, $inputR_j$ is the reliability of input object j serving object i, and $CobjectR_i$ is the combined reliability of object i, including its inputs.

In the example, the information-reliability index at the object level can be computed as:

$$SysR_{Object} = \begin{pmatrix} ObjCus & ObjSal & ObjEmp & ObjFin \\ .36 & .25 & .21 & .18 \end{pmatrix} \cdot \begin{pmatrix} .90(.60 \times .80 \times .70) \\ .99(.99 \times .90 \times .99) \\ .90(.70 \times .60 \times .90 \times .80) \\ .99(.99 \times .98 \times .98 \times .98) \end{pmatrix}$$

$$= (.36 \quad .25 \quad .21 \quad .18) \cdot \begin{pmatrix} .30 \\ .87 \\ .27 \\ .92 \end{pmatrix}$$

$$= .55$$

Here, the single value .55 summarizes the system-reliability metric at the object level.

9.3.6   Customers with Different Preferences

So far we have assumed that information-systems customers have similar needs that can be expressed by one representative customer. It is possible to have information-systems customers with different, and, at times, opposing needs and preferences. One can approach the question of multiple customers in three ways:

- Multiple system-reliability metrics
- Group-weighted system-reliability metric
- Multi-criteria system-reliability metric

Multiple System-Reliability Metrics.   If customers (or major groups of customers) have diametrically opposing needs and requirements, the information system is created to satisfy all customers, and each customer (or group of customers) is important, then one can have one system-reliability metric for each group of customers, and measure reliability for each group of customers. This metric would allow the information-system manager to measure the quality of service delivered to each group. If the metric of all groups shows a significant fall, then the system is experiencing a major quality crisis. On the other hand, if the quality metric is stable for some customers and variable for others, the manager can assign priority to the investigation and process improvement based on the importance of the customer group and the extent of variability or drop in the system-reliability metric.

Group-Weighted System-Reliability Metric.   A strategy for generating a single system-reliability metric with multiple groups of customers is to compute a system-reliability metric for each group of customers and combine them using a rating for each group. This metric has the following form:

$$SysR = \sum_{i=1}^{g} W_i \cdot SysR_i$$

where $SysR$ is the overall system-reliability metric, g is the number of customer groups, W_i is the relative importance of customer group i, and $SysR_i$ is the computed system-reliability metric using group i's preference data. The value of W_i is between zero and one, and the W_i's add up to 1.

Multi-Criteria System-Reliability Metric.   Another strategy for designing a single metric to measure system reliability is to combine customers' requirements within the metric itself. This way we generate only one set of preference data and, hence, one value for the system-reliability metric.

For this case, we can use the multicriteria group-decision methods for aggregating preferences of requirements and objects. There are a number of methods for consensus generation [see for example, Zahedi 1987]. Here, we focus on use of the group AHP for the generation of consensus among the information system's customers.

When customers of an information system have different needs and preferences, we have to modify two phases in the computation of the system-reliability metric:

- Hierarchy development phase
- Pairwise comparison phase

When the second level of the requirements-objects hierarchy is being developed, the elements of this level should be generated via a consensus process among all representative customers of the information system. For example, ACCU-INFO's vice president for finance needs only profitability information and cares little about satisfaction information (Figure 9.7), whereas the vice president of quality requires only quality and satisfaction information. In generating the second-level elements, the needs of both customer types should be included in the hierarchy through a consensus process.

Once the requirements-objects hierarchy is created, customers are asked to express their pairwise preferences for various information requirements. Obviously, each customer has his or her own matrix of pairwise comparison. The challenge is to combine customers' preferences in creating a single reliability metric.

The group AHP [Aczel and Saaty 1983] recommends the geometric mean of the corresponding elements of the pairwise matrices. That is, if we have c customers, each with a pairwise matrix of $A^1, A^2, \dots, A^c$, then we can create a single pairwise matrix with a_{ij} element as:

$$a_{ij} = (a_{ij}^1 \cdot a_{ij}^2 \cdots a_{ij}^c)^{\frac{1}{c}}$$

where a_{ij}^1 is the ijth element of customer 1's pairwise matrix, a_{ij}^2 is that of customer 2, ..., and a_{ij}^c is that of customer c's. Once the pairwise matrices are combined, we can apply the same procedure as done for a single customer to compute the reliability metric.

◆ Conclusion

This chapter continued the development of quality metrics for information systems. The metrics discussed in this chapter were for design, project management, and system reliability.

The design metrics were presented in Section 9.1. In this section, we discussed the principles of good design and the use of the object-oriented approach in defining objects of units of information-systems components. Using the principles of design and objects as units of measurement, we developed a number of metrics for object-independence, cohesion, and complexity of information systems.

The project-management metrics were discussed in Section 9.2. In this section, we defined the dimensions of information-system project management as cost, value, fault, and time management. We presented a number of metrics for each dimension of project management.

Section 9.3 developed a reliability metric for the entire system, in which the customers' preferences and views about systems requirements were combined with the reliability metrics of units of the system. This section developed the customer requirements-objects hierarchy, and showed how to elicit and compute the customer-information utility values. Combining the customers' utility values with the relative importance of objects in satisfying the needs of customers led to the computation of the global relative weights for system objects. Combining the global weights with the reliability measures of system objects yielded a single reliability metric for the entire system. This section discussed the methods for dealing with cases in which a system serves heterogeneous groups of customers, who differ in their preferences and views about the system.

◆ References

1. Aczel, J. and Saaty, T. L. 1983. "Procedures for Synthesizing Rational Judgments," *Journal of Mathematical Psychology*, Vol. 27, pp. 93-102.

2. Alavi, M. and Henderson, J. C. 1981. "An Evolutionary Strategy for Implementing a Decision Support System," *Management Science*, Vol. 27, No. 11, pp. 1309-1323.

3. Alexander, Christopher. 1964. *Notes on the Synthesis of Form*, Harvard University Press, London, England.

4. Anderson, David R.; Sweeney, Dennis J.; and Williams, Thomas. 1991. *Management Science: Quantitative Approaches to Decision Making*, Sixth Edition, West Publishing Co., St. Paul, MN.

5. Bailey, J. B. and Pearson, S. W. 1983. "Development of a Tool for Measuring and Analyzing Computer Use Satisfaction," *Management Science*, Vol. 29, No. 5, pp. 530-545.

6. Ballou, D. P. and Pazer, H. L. 1987. "Cost/Quality Tradeoffs for Control Procedures in Information Systems," *Omega*, Vol. 15, No. 6, pp. 509-521.

7. Basili, V. R. 1980. *Tutorial on Models and Metrics for Software Management and Engineering*, IEEE Computing Society Press, Washington, D.C.

8. Brooks, W. D. and Motley, R. W. 1980. "Analysis of Discrete Software Reliability Models," Rep. RADC-TR-80-84, April.

9. Card, David N. and Glass, Robert L. 1990. *Measuring Software Design Quality*, Prentice Hall, Englewood Cliffs, NJ.

10. Chikofsky, E. J. and Rubenstein, B. L. 1988. "CASE: Reliability Engineering for Information Systems," *IEEE Software*, March, pp. 11-16.

11. Chidamber, S. R. and Kemerer. C. F. 1991. "Towards a Metrics Suite for Object-Oriented Design," *Proceedings OOPSLA '91*, pp. 197–211.

12. Daskalantonakis, Michael K. 1992, "A Practical View of Software Measurement and Implementation Experiences Within Motorola," *IEEE Transactions for Software Engineering*, Vol. 18, No. 11, November, pp. 998–1010.

13. DeMarco, T. 1982. *Controlling Software Projects*, Prentice Hall, Englewood Cliffs, NJ.

14. Ives, B. and Olson, M. 1984. "User Involvement and MIS Success: A Review of Research," *Management Science*, Vol. 30, No. 5, pp. 586-603.

15. Ives, B.; Olson, M.; and Baroudi, J. 1983. "The Measurement of User Information Satisfaction," *Communications of ACM*, Vol. 26, No. 10, pp. 785-793.

16. Li, Wei and Henry, Sallie. 1993. "Object-Oriented Metrics that Predict Maintainability," *Journal of Systems Software*, Vol. 23, pp. 111–122.

17. McCabe, T. J. 1976. "A Complexity Measure," *IEEE Transactions on Software Engineering*, Vol. 2, pp. 308–320.

18. Ovio, Markku. 1993. "Incremental Resource Estimation with Real-Time Feedback from Measurement," *Microprocessing and Microprogramming*, Vol. 38, pp. 281–289.

19. Page-Jones, Meilir. 1988. *The Practical Guide to Structured Systems Design*, Yourdon Press, Englewood Cliffs, NJ.

20. Shillito, M. Larry and De Marle, David J. 1992. *Value: Its Measurement, Design, and Management*, John Wiley and Sons, Inc., New York, NY.

21. SIM Working Group. "Focus on Quality: Quality Assessment and Planning Tools for IS," Society for Information Management, Chicago, IL, October 1992.

22. Suh, Nam P. 1990. *The Principles of Design*, Oxford University Press, New York, NY.

23. Yourdon, E. N. and Constantine, L. L. 1979. *Structured Design*, Prentice Hall, Englewood Cliffs, NJ.

24. Zahedi, F. "Group Consensus Function When Preferences Are Uncertain," *Operations Research*, Vol. 34, No. 6, 1986, pp. 883–894.

25. Zahedi, F. "Reliability of Information Systems Based on the Critical Success Factors—Formulation," *MIS Quarterly*, June 1987, pp. 187–203.

26. Zmud, R. W. 1979. "Individual Differences and MIS Success: A Review of the Empirical Literature," *Management Science*, Vol. 25, No. 10, pp. 966-978.

27. Zahedi, F. 1994. "Reliability Metric for Information Systems Based on Customer Requirements," unpublished manuscript, University of Wisconsin, Milwaukee, WI.

◆ Questions

9.1. Discuss the role of design in information systems.

9.2. Describe the principles of design.

9.3. What are the two axioms of good design?

9.4. Discuss objects as units of information-systems modules.

9.5. List the metrics for measuring the independence of objects in information systems.

9.6. Describe the object-uncoupling metric.

9.7. What is the design matrix in the object-uncoupling metric?

9.8. What is the source of data for the design matrix?

9.9. What is the object-correlation metric?

9.10. How can we reduce the correlation among objects?

9.11. List the types of coupling among objects.

9.12. Describe data coupling among objects.

9.13. Describe content coupling among objects.

9.14. Describe stamp coupling among objects.

9.15. Describe control coupling among objects.

9.16. Describe hybrid coupling among objects.

9.17. Discuss the ways for reducing coupling and functional dependence among objects.

9.18. Discuss the difference between narrow and broad connections among objects.

9.19. What is the difference between direct and indirect connections among objects?

9.20. What is the difference between obvious and obscure connections among objects?

9.21. What is the difference between local and remote connections among objects?

9.22. Describe object cohesion in information systems.

9.23. List the scales of cohesion among objects.

9.24. List the types of complexity metrics for information systems.

9.25. Describe the nature of the object-response complexity metric.

9.26. What is the building block in the decision-complexity metric?

9.27. List the scope of quality metrics for information systems.

9.28. List the dimensions of information-system management metrics.

9.29. What is the importance of cost-management metrics for managing information-system projects?

9.30. Discuss the size metrics for information systems.

9.31. Describe the object hierarchy.

9.32. Why is complexity important in identifying the units of information-systems components?

9.33. Describe the size-complexity metrics.

9.34. What is the unit-cost metric?

9.35. Discuss the use of the unit-cost metric in managing information-system projects.

9.36. What is value?

9.37. What are the energy-like attributes of value?

9.38. What are the important components in designing value metrics?

9.39. List four metrics for value.

9.40. Describe the approach used in developing the system performance-value metric.

9.41. Describe a metric that measures the value of an object.

9.42. List the metrics for fault management.

9.43. Why is fault recurrence important in fault management?

9.44. Discuss the time-management metrics specifically designed for information systems.

9.45. Describe the approach used in developing the system-reliability metric.

9.46. Describe the requirements-objects hierarchy.

9.47. Describe the method used in the computation of global weights of objects.

9.48. Describe the way objects' weights are combined with the reliability measures of objects for deriving the system-reliability metric.

9.49. Describe the problem that arises in the computation of the system-reliability metric when there are groups of customers who have divergent preferences.

9.50. Describe ways to deal with conflicts in customers' preferences in the computation of the system-reliability metric.

◆ Problems

9.1. List the possible children of the network object in an information system.

9.2. Describe the methods and behavior for the network object in an information system.

9.3. In a design, the customers' requirements are: remote access and database access. Identify system objects that satisfy these requirements with an acceptable degree of uncoupling.

9.4. In Question 9.3, identify the design matrix A.

9.5. Identify the object-correlation metric for objects in Question 9.3.

9.6. Describe possible ways of reducing off-diagonal correlations in Question 9.5.

9.7. Develop an object hierarchy for a customer-service information system.

9.8. You have the database object that has children: query, update, security, reports, data files, and error checking. Discuss the methods you will use to compute the size-complexity metric of each child object (with a value between 0 and 1) and how you would combine them to compute the size-complexity metric for the database object.

9.9. Discuss the possible use of each size-complexity metric.

9.10. You are given the task of identifying quality metrics that could be helpful in budgeting information-systems projects. Describe the metrics that you will recommend for this purpose.

9.11. You are given the task of devising quality metrics for tracking the value of an information system to its customers. Describe the metrics that you will recommend for this purpose.

9.12. As an information-system manager, you must decide on the type of hardware used in a project. There are two hardware options. One option costs about 20 percent of the total cost of the project and the other costs 15 percent. Assume that the relative importance of the hardware object among all objects is stated to be 10 percent. Which of the two hardware options will you recommend? Justify your answer by using value metric(s).

9.13. You are the project manager of a complex information system that will take two years to complete. In the second year of the project, different parts of this system will be completed and introduced to customers on a gradual basis. Describe the fault-management metrics that you will recommend for this project.

9.14. In the above question, describe the time-management metrics that should be recommended for managing the project.

9.15. You are the project manager of a small information system. For this project, describe the relative importance of the four types of quality metrics—cost, value, fault, and time.

9.16. Give an example of the requirements-objects hierarchy for developing a customer-service information system.

Any idiot can face a crisis—it's this day-to-day living that wears you out.

— Anton Chekhov

We are all controlled by the world in which we live, and part of that world has been and will be constructed by men. The question is this: are we to be controlled by accidents, by tyrants, or by ourselves in effective cultural design?

— Burrhus Frederic Skinner

Mankind will possess incalculable advantages and extraordinary control over human behavior when the scientific investigator will be able to subject his fellow men to the same external analysis he would employ for any natural object, and when the human mind will contemplate itself not from within but from without.

— Ivan Petrovich Pavlov

◆ Chapter Objectives

The objectives of this chapter are:
- To discuss methods for analyzing quality metrics
- To review the underlying theoretical basis for analysis of quality metrics
- To cover the use of control charts in the quality-metric analysis
- To discuss Shewhart-type and non-Shewhart type charts
- To present ways control charts can be used to discover problems in information systems and to improve them
- To review quality tools
- To identify software products for applying quality methods
- To discuss the implementation issues in information-systems quality metrics

◆ Key Words

Statistical quality control, measures of central tendency, measures of variation, control charts, Shewhart-type control charts, non-Shewhart control charts, types of control charts, using control charts in information, quality tools, interrelationship digraph, prioritization matrices, matrix diagrams, process decision program chart, activity network diagram, software for quality methods

Analysis of Quality Metrics

10.1 Statistical Quality Control (SQC)
    10.1.1 Prerequisites of SQC for Information Systems
    10.1.2 Theoretical Basis for SQC
    10.1.3 Measures of Central Tendency
    10.1.4 Measures of Variation
    10.1.5 Probability Distributions Used in SQC

10.2 Control Charts for Quality Metrics
    10.2.1 Underlying Assumptions in Shewhart-Type Control Charts
    10.2.2 Categories of Shewhart-Type Control Charts
    10.2.3 Matching Information-Systems Quality Metrics and Control Charts
    10.2.4 The Estimation of Control-Chart Parameters
    10.2.5 Non-Shewhart Control Charts
    10.2.6 Using Control Charts

10.3 Quality Tools
    10.3.1 Interrelationship Digraph
    10.3.2 Prioritization Matrix
    10.3.3 Matrix Diagrams
    10.3.4 Tree Matrix
    10.3.5 Process-Decision Program Charts
    10.3.6 Activity-Network Diagrams

10.4 Software Products for Quality Methods
    10.4.1 Software for Taguchi Methods
    10.4.2 Software for QFD
    10.4.3 Software for Quality Tools
    10.4.4 Software for AHP

10.5 The Implementation of Quality Metrics
    10.5.1 How to Use Quality Metrics
    10.5.2 When to Use Quality Metrics
    10.5.3 How Much Quality Metrics
    10.5.4 How Often to Use Quality Metrics

◆ Introduction

This chapter discusses methods and tools for the presentation and analysis of quality metrics in information systems. Statistical quality control (SQC) offers techniques for the analysis of quality metrics. However, there are a number of prerequisites that should be satisfied prior to the application of SQC methods. This chapter reviews these prerequisites.

SQC methods have statistics as their theoretical basis, and use measures of central tendency and variations to establish control charts. Control charts are the vehicle for tracking quality metrics and identifying when the metric is out of bound. An out-of-bounds metric indicates that the information system is out of control regarding the attributes that the metric is designed to measure. For example, if the requirement-achievement metric is out of bounds, it is an indicator that the system has failed to meet the requirements of its customer at an acceptable level.

Control charts play an important role in day-to-day monitoring of quality metrics. Shewhart developed control charts in the 1920s, and his type of control charts still are in use for quality control. In this chapter, we briefly review Shewhart control charts and mention some of the non-Shewhart charts that have been developed in recent years. The coverage of control charts in this chapter is not intended to be complete. It intends to provide a general understanding of types of control charts and ways they can be applied in analyzing information-system quality metrics.

In the previous chapters, we have presented a number of quality methods in various stages of strategic planning of information systems and their developments, such as quality function deployment (QFD), Taguchi methods, analytic hierarchy process, affinity diagrams, the decision-tree hierarchy, and the Pareto chart. There are a number of quality tools that have not been discussed so far. They include: interrelationship digraph, prioritization matrices, process-decision program chart, and activity-network diagram. These tools are briefly reviewed in this chapter.

There are a number of software products on the market for applying quality methods. In this chapter, we briefly review available software products for Taguchi methods, QFD, quality tools, and AHP.

The implementation of quality metrics requires answers to questions such as how, when, how much, and how often we should use quality metrics. This chapter poses questions and attempts to offer answers that can be used as starting points in designing quality metrics for a given information system.

◆ CASE: Where Did it Begin?

Sometimes, it sounds as if industry is an offshoot of farming: Startup companies sprout from seed money. Managers plow capital into new plants and cultivate markets to reap profits. But when it comes to quality, agriculture deserves more than a metaphoric nod. In fact, the entire quality movement, and the field of statistics in general, springs from agricultural research, notably the genius of Britain's R. A. Fisher. To speed up development of better crop-growing methods, Fisher perfected scientific shortcuts for sifting through mountains of data to spot key cause-and-effect relationships.

Fisher's work during the first two decades of this century electrified Walter A. Shewhart, a physicist at the AT&T Bell Laboratories. By the 1930s, he had transformed Fisher's methods into a quality-control discipline for factories—and inspired W. Edwards Deming and J. M. Juran to devote their lives to quality. After World War II, Genichi Taguchi, a Japanese engineer, amplified Fisher's insights with some novel twists, and the Taguchi methods soon became a staple of engineering education in Japan. More recent research by statisticians—such as George E. P. Box, a Briton at the University of Wisconsin; Jeff Wu, a Box protégé at Canada's University of Waterloo; and Donald W. Marquardt at Du Pont—has moved beyond those pioneers. But much of this recent work is just starting to be used in industry.

Until Fisher came along, the trouble with crop experiments was that they where agonizingly slow. The main limitation, says A. Blanton Godfrey, chairman of Juran Institute Inc., is that crop researchers "get just one shot a year. They can plan a field experiment all winter long, but they can run it only during the summer." What Fisher devised was a way to organize a series of experiments that, with an incredibly small number of test runs, reveals crucial interactions among a multitude of variable factors—such as various planting times and seed depths, different fertilizer formulations and amounts, and varying amounts of irrigation.

Here's a factory equivalent: Roughly a dozen major variables affect a car's steering performance, from how well the steering column's parts fit together to the stiffness of the shock absorbers and springs. To test what would happen if any one factor were to change, more than 4,000 experiments would have to be run—prohibitive in terms of both time and money. "And you still wouldn't know the effects of interactions," or what happens when two or more factors change at the same time, notes Edward Fuchs, director of Bell Labs' Quality Excellence Center. That would require 479 million tests. Yet Fisher's method would uncover such interactions with just 14 test runs—in much the way that pollsters can divine opinion trends among 250 million Americans by interviewing fewer than 2,000 people.

American manufacturing turned its back on Fisher and Shewhart in the postwar boom, just when Japan was learning the power of statistics from Deming and Taguchi. Today, experts say, American engineers still tend to rely too much on seat-of-the-pants laxity, while Japanese designers use statistical rigor to help please the customer. Only since the 1980s has this begun to change significantly. Eastman Kodak Co., for instance, now puts all managers though a four-month quality course that emphasizes statistics. And Hewlett-Packard Co. is using one of Box's techniques to analyze warranty claims, though as yet only part of the findings are recycled to improve design.

Now, many U.S. companies are taking a look at what the newest statistical tools promise: a way to leapfrog Japan. Taguchi's ideas have become "old hat," says J. Stuart Hunter, professor emeritus of statistics at Princeton University. Even better techniques for modeling processes and improving quality are evolving all the time, many perfected by Wisconsin's Box—who continues to build on the heritage of R. A. Fisher.

Source: Otis Port and John Corney, "Quality: A Field with Roots That Go Back to the Farm," *Business Week,* Quality 1991, p. 15. reprinted from October 25, 1991 issue of Business Week by special permission, copyright © 1991 by McGraw-Hill, Inc.

10.1 ◆ Statistical Quality Control (SQC)

Statistical quality control is the collection of statistical methods for the analysis of quality data. The observations of quality metrics, like any other business data, has a random element. Therefore, deviation of observed values of metrics from its expected target could have two sources:

- Random or chance elements that have the same probability distribution in all observations of a quality metric (common causes)
- A shift in system performance that causes the quality metric to deviate or fluctuate from its target value for a specific reason (special causes)

In analyzing quality metrics, one needs to distinguish between these two sources of fluctuation in metric values, because it is the second source that is the cause of problems and opportunities for system improvement. Statistical analysis allows us to distinguish between random fluctuations and specific shifts.

Statistical quality control for information systems could be used for:

- Measuring system quality
- Identifying signals for changes of condition
- Providing ideas for quality improvements

Measuring System Quality. Using metrics for measuring system quality is one of the fundamental components of any quality program. Statistical quality-control techniques provide objective tools for analyzing system quality. These techniques include methods for collecting metric data, setting up boundaries for acceptable values of metrics, and signaling when the system has gone beyond the acceptable quality region.

For example, in the ACCU-INFO case, the statistical analysis of the fault metric has established that the system is expected to be down between two to five times per month—a number within the acceptable region. If the system has faults outside the acceptable region, then the system is called *out of control.*

Identifying Signals for Changes of Conditions. Statistical quality-control techniques establish acceptability regions. When the system's quality metrics exhibit values that are beyond the acceptable regions, it is a signal to the system managers that the conditions of the system may have changed and, therefore, an investigation regarding possible causes would be in order. That is, the teams responsible for the continuous improvement of the system take as part of their inputs the signals provided by the statistical analysis of the quality-metric values.

In the ACCU-INFO case, if the fault metric for the month shows that the system has been down seven times, then the system may be out of control and the continuous-improvement team should investigate the reasons that have caused the system to be down so often.

In some cases, quality-control methods establish a warning region. When the value of the quality metric falls in this region, it sends a signal that the system should be watched closely for the possibility that the system might be out of control.

Providing Ideas for Improvements.   An out-of-control system is not always low in quality. If the value of a quality metric falls well above what is expected and shows higher-than-expected quality performance, the system is performing above its acceptable level. The investigation of a positive or desirable out-of-control quality metric generates ideas for the ways one can improve the information system.

For example, in the ACCU-INFO case, the system has no faults in a month. The continuous-improvement team should look into the reasons why the system operated with no faults, and try to revise processes and decisions that would bring the system closer to a no-fault condition.

10.1.1   Prerequisites of SQC for Information Systems

Prior to the implementation of statistical quality control, there are a number of prerequisites to be satisfied. These prerequisites include:

- Determine system attributes related to the information-system vision
- Determine variables that quantify attributes
- Determine metrics that measure the quality of system variables
- Determine the data to be observed
- Set up a system for data collection
- Decide on sampling methods
- Prototype and test quality metrics and their control process
- Standardize the quality-control process

Determine System Attributes Related to the Information-System Vision.   Analysis of irrelevant attributes is a useless and costly practice. The first step in an effective analysis of quality metrics is the identification of system attributes that are of importance to the information-system vision.

For example, in the case of ACCU-INFO, the vision statement stated in Chapter 1 was: we provide the most accurate information on credit-worthiness of shoppers within the United States. This statement identifies accuracy as the most critical attribute of the information system.

Determine Variables That Quantify System Attributes.   Once vision-related system attributes are determined, then we should identify the variables that quantify them. For example, in the ACCU-INFO case, the accuracy attribute should be translated to more specific variables, such as: update frequency, data errors, system faults, and system response. Identification of these variables help specify high-priority metrics.

Determine Metrics That Measure the Quality of System Variables.   System variables show the type of metrics that should have a higher priority. For example, in the ACCU-INFO case, update frequency, data errors, system faults, and system response could be combined with customer views in computing the system-reliability metric, described in Chapter 9. In other words, the attributes that are the underlying drivers of the information-system vision are translated into a system metric.

Determine the Data to be Observed.   The implementation of system-quality metrics necessitates the determination of data to be observed. In the ACCU-INFO case, selecting system reliability as a quality metric requires the following data: customer requirements, system objects, AHP preference data, update frequency, data errors, system faults, and system response. Furthermore, the frequency of the observation for each data item should be determined. Data for customer requirements and system objects are collected once. Data for customers' preference in AHP is collected, say, once every six months. System accuracy data, such as update frequency, data errors, system faults, and system response are collected every day.

Set up a System for Data Collection.   A system is needed for collecting data, preferably automatically. The data collection module for quality metrics should be designed into the system. In the ACCU-INFO case, following the object-oriented design, the system could have an object module that keeps track of update frequency. Another object module could be designed to keep track of system faults that cause the system to shut down. An object asks customers about system faults and errors. Yet another object module automatically records system errors and shutdowns. An object module keeps track of system response. The data-collecting objects send the observed data into a quality database, specially designed for the system.

Such a subsystem requires designing data collecting objects into the system. This means that decisions about quality metrics and analysis should be made at the design stage of system development.

Decide on Sampling Methods.   Another decision regarding data collection is the choice of sampling method, such as:

- Random sampling
- 100 percent observation

Random sampling involves the design of data collection in a manner that ensures data is random and represents the underlying population. This means that the design of the data-collection subsystem should contain the sampling method. Sampling can be done in a number of ways, such as simple random sampling, stratified sampling, cluster sampling, and acceptance sampling. The sample size should also be decided using statistical methods.

For example, in the ACCU-INFO case, the types of system customers are divided into: end-users, system maintainer, and data entry personnel. The system asks every tenth customer in each category to express his or her opinion about the accuracy and speed of the system. Categorizing the customer types and asking every tenth customer is an example of stratified sampling design. This design assumes that customer types are evenly distributed in the customer population of the system.

If we know that end-user customers represent 90 percent of system use and others the remaining 10 percent, then the data collection should be designed for the sample to contain 90 percent end-user data and 10 percent other categories. Random sampling topics and related issues are addressed in more detail in statistics textbooks (see, for example, Cryer and Miller 1991).

100 percent observations is when all observed data for quality metrics are stored for analysis. The decision for sampling or full collection depends on the nature of data as well as resources. In the ACCU-INFO case, the update frequency is a data type that requires collecting 100 percent observations. On the other hand, the speed of system response could be sampled or collected fully. Limited storage capacity may limit the amount of data, making sampling a more reasonable method of data collection.

Prototype and Test Quality Metrics and Their Control Process.   Determining suitable quality metrics, the appropriate data collection method and frequency, and the correct method of analysis may require more than one trial. Moreover, the company has to determine the procedures to be followed once a quality metric shows the system to be out of control. In other words, the control process for quality metrics consists of:

- Selecting the quality metrics
- Establishing the data-collection process
- Establishing the analysis process
- Determining the process for dealing with an out-of-control system

The control process should be designed in close relation with the continuous-improvement plans. Therefore, it is important to create a prototype for the quality-control process and test it for a while prior to installing it into the system.

For example, in the ACCU-INFO case, the company chooses a simple fault metric to measure the system's accuracy. After testing the metric, it finds out that faults vary in their severity, and decides that the faults should be categorized in their degree of impact on customers. Furthermore, the length of time the system remains faulty is another aspect that should have been taken into account. The prototyping and testing of metrics allow the company to find the set of quality metrics and data collection and analysis strategies that best suit the vision and missions of the system.

Standardize the Quality-Control Process.   The data collection and analysis of quality metrics should be an integral part of all improvement and resource-allocation decisions.

They should be at par, or even more important than, the financial and sales data that influence major decisions and actions. Giving quality metrics such a critical role requires that the data collection and analysis methods of quality metrics be standardized across the organization (and hopefully across the industry).

For example, in the ACCU-INFO case, the fault categories, the data-collection methods for the fault-recurrence metric, and analysis methods should be standardized and implemented uniformly across all information-system projects. The standardization allows the managers to gauge and compare the quality of information systems and evaluate their performance through time. The analysis of quality data helps the managers identify the opportunities for improvement, select approaches and processes that lead to the highest level of quality, and allocate resources to projects that contribute to the maintenance and improvement of the system's quality.

10.1.2   Theoretical Basis for SQC

Collecting data for quality metrics should follow statistical sampling procedures. This means that the data should be collected at random or should contain 100 percent of observations. The collected data should be the representative of the underlying population or process.

Here, *population* is a set of existing units, in this case, the entire set of values that the quality metric takes in a system. A *process* is a series of actions or operations that takes inputs and produces outputs [McClave and Benson, 1992]. In this application, the information system or its components may constitute a process. A *sample* is a (normally small) proportion of the entire population, or of the outputs of a process. The statistical analysis of sample data reveals the nature of the underlying population of the quality metric or the process it measures.

Analyzing data requires summarizing it in a fashion that will represent the fundamental nature of the population or process. There are two types of measures commonly used for summarizing data:

- Measures of central tendency
- Measures of dispersion or variation

Measures of central tendency indicate where the center of the data is, whereas measures of dispersion show the variability of the data, commonly around the center of data. Both measures of central tendency and dispersion are estimates of the corresponding population (or process) parameters.

In other words, we should distinguish between:

- Population or process parameters
- Sample statistics

Population or process parameters are aspects of the population or process that we are interested in, but cannot observe. For example, we would like to know the true mean of the reliability-metric values in the system, but it is not available to us. We take samples of the metric values and use sample statistics to estimate the parameters that are of interest to us. For example, sample mean $\bar{x}$ is a sample statistic, and we use it in order to estimate the true mean (μ) of the metric values. Similarly, sample standard deviation s is a sample statistic that we use to estimate the true population or process standard deviation (σ) of metric values.

Analyzing quality data is mostly performed by setting up control charts, in which a measure of central tendency of the sample values and a measure of variation are used to define the limits within which the system is considered in control.

Control charts are visual representations of the statistical test of hypothesis. The hypothesis is that the population or process from which the data is sampled indeed has a given expected value.

There are a number of ways that one can test the hypothesis in control charts. One way is to test whether an observation x could have come from the population of metric values with a given mean and standard deviation. For example, if the customer-value metric (discussed in Chapter 9) for a system is .5, one can test it as:

$$H_0: \mu = .9$$
$$H_a: \mu \neq .9$$

Could this project belong to the population of metric values (or the information-system process) that has a mean of .9 and the standard deviation of .1?

One can argue that .5 is so far below .9 that we can tell that the customer-value of this project does not belong to the company's population of projects. However, we have to answer this question by a statistical test, because there are random elements in all projects that make this metric vary from one project to another.

Another type of hypothesis is testing the sample mean. For example, the fault-rework metric is defined as the average time spent on reworking and fixing a fault in the system. We have computed this metric for a project over 5 cases, and found it to be 19. The hypothesis to be tested in this case is:

$$H_0: \mu = 15$$
$$H_a: \mu \neq 15$$

Could this sample average belong to a population of projects whose average of fault-rework has a mean value of 15 and standard deviation of 6? On the face of it, 19 is far above 15. But the statistical analysis may prove that because of the random elements shared by all projects, a fault-rework average of 19 could indeed belong to such a population of projects. ($t = \frac{19-15}{6/\sqrt{5}} = 1.49$.)

If 19 looks unacceptable, it means that the degree of variation of this metric (standard deviation of 6) is at an unacceptable level, and that steps should be taken to reduce the variability of this metric among information-system projects.

Alternatively, if 19 looks unacceptable, one can increase the sample size to make the test more reliable. Since the above test depends on the size of the sample ($s_{\bar{x}} = \frac{s}{\sqrt{n}}$), increasing the sample size from 5 to, say, 36 will tighten the range of acceptable mean values of the metric because the standard deviation of the sample mean drops from $\frac{6}{\sqrt{5}} = 2.7$ to $\frac{6}{\sqrt{36}} = 1$. This alternative, however, is not always possible because of the limited number of cases for which the metric value is available, and does not necessarily preclude seemingly unacceptable values from the acceptable range of mean values for the metric.

The test of hypothesis and the rejection of H_0 depend on Type I and Type II errors. A Type I error is the probability that H_0 hypothesis is true, but we reject it. An example of a Type I error is when the value of the requirement-achievement metric indeed belongs to the population of the successful information-systems projects in the company, but we decide otherwise. In other words, a Type I error is the probability of a false alarm about a working system. Obviously, launching an investigation based on a false alarm is costly and demoralizing.

Normally we want this probability to be zero. However, it is not possible, because by doing so, we increase the Type II probability—the probability that the system is out of control and we fail to recognize it. The common practice is to set the Type I error at 1 percent for upper and lower control limits and at 5 percent for the warning lines.

Note that in some metrics, the distance from only one side of the mean is undesirable. For example, when a fault-rework metric is too far above the mean, there is cause for concern about the quality of fault management in a project. However, in this chapter, we will always look at both sides even if only one side is undesirable, because being out of bounds on the desirable side is an impetus for discovering the causes that have made the system perform at a higher quality level.

Using the theoretical basis of hypothesis testing, control charts establish the acceptable regions for a quality metric. This allows information-system managers to visually track the performance of the system on control charts, without the need to go through the statistical test of hypotheses everytime a new value for the quality metric is observed.

For example, in the ACCU-INFO case, the fault values for a category are expected to be 3 per month plus or minus 1. That is, if the fault values fall in the range of 2 to 4, the system is considered to be in control from the fault-management point of view. The meaning of this range is that we test the sample result each month to see whether the current month's metric value belongs to a population that has an average fault rate of 3 per month. If the metric value falls in the range of 2 to 4, the hypothesis that the current month's value has come from such a population cannot be rejected. On the other hand, if the metric value falls outside the range, we can reject the hypothesis that the metric belongs to such a population. This is an indication that there has been a shift in the population of the metric values.

10.1.3   Measures of Central Tendency

There are three measures that show the center of data:

- Mean
- Median
- Mode

Mean is the most common measure of central tendency, and is used in control charts in most cases. However, when there is the possibility of one extreme value affecting the measure drastically, one may decide to use median as the center of the sampled data. Mode is mostly used to identify the most frequently observed data.

Note that the computation of measures of central tendency is the same whether the data is from a sample or from 100 percent of the observations.

Mean. The computation of mean is:

$$\bar{x} = \frac{\sum_{i=1}^{n} x_i}{n}$$

where x_i is observation i and n is the number of observations.

When there is more than one sample of a quality metric, the average of the sample means, or the grand mean, is:

$$\bar{\bar{x}} = \frac{\sum_{j=1}^{f} f_j \bar{x}_j}{\sum_{j=1}^{f} f_j}$$

where f is the number of samples, f_j is the size of jth sample, and $\bar{x}_j$ is the mean of jth sample. When the sample sizes (f_j) are equal, then the computation of the grand mean reduces to taking the simple average of all sample means [Montgomery 1991].

The grand mean is used in setting the centerline in a control chart, as discussed in a later section.

Median. The median of a quality metric is the value of the observation that lies in the $\frac{n}{2}$th observation—the middle of the sample. When the sample size is even, median is the average of the $\frac{n}{2}$th and $\frac{n+1}{2}$th observations.

To compute the median of a sample, the observations should be arranged in ascending order. For example, the observations in the following sample:

$$2, 4, 8, 2, 7, 3, 7, 7, 9, 3$$

should be arranged in ascending order as:

$$2, 2, 3, 3, 4, 7, 7, 7, 8, 9$$

Since the number of observations is even, then the median is:

$$m = \frac{4 + 7}{2} = 5.5$$

When there is more than one sample, the average median of all samples is:

$$\bar{m} = \frac{\sum_{i=1}^{f} m_j}{f}$$

where f is the number of samples and m_j is the median of sample j. The average median of all samples is used in establishing the centerline of control charts.

Mode. Mode is the observation that has the highest frequency in a sample. In the above example, mode is 7 because it is repeated three times in the sample—the highest among all observations. This measure is rarely used in control charts.

10.1.4   Measures of Variation

There are a number of measures that show the variation in data. They include:

- Standard Deviation
- Range
- Mean absolute deviation

There are less common measures of variation, such as inter-quartile range, that are not discussed here. Of the above three measures, standard deviation and range are commonly used. Mean-absolute deviation is the least-used measure of the three.

Standard Deviation.   As we have discussed in Chapter 9, the most frequently used measure of dispersion in a sample is its standard deviation, defined as:

$$s = \sqrt{\frac{\sum_{i=1}^{n}(x_i - \bar{x})^2}{n - 1}}$$

where n is the size of the sample, $\bar{x}$ is the sample mean, and x_i is the ith observation in the sample.

Since the process involves repeated sampling, the average standard deviation is commonly used in establishing the limits of control charts that use s. This average is defined as:

$$\bar{s} = \frac{\sum_{j=1}^{f} s_j}{f}$$

where $\bar{s}$ is the average standard deviation, s_j is the standard deviation of jth sample, and f is the number of samples. One can use $\bar{s}$ in the control chart by multiplying it by a factor $\frac{1}{c}$. This factor is a constant and depends on the sample size [Montgomery 1991].

The assumption is that all samples have equal size. If the samples do not have equal size, the sample sizes should be used as weights in the computation of the average standard deviation, similar to the computation of the grand mean.

An alternative estimation is to compute the weighted average of all sample variances (s_j^2 values), and take the square root of the result. The weights are the sample sizes, similar to the weights in the computation of the grand mean.

When the standard deviation is computed for the variation of the mean value of a metric, the standard deviation of the metric is divided by the factor $\sqrt{n}$. That is:

$$s_{\bar{x}} = \frac{s}{\sqrt{n}}$$

where $s_{\bar{x}}$ is the standard deviation of the mean, and s is the standard deviation of the sample.

For example, suppose ACCU-INFO's requirement-achievement metric has a standard deviation equal to .5. For a sample size of 9, the sample mean of this metric has a standard deviation equal to $\frac{.5}{\sqrt{9}}$ or .17.

If the metric has a binary value (such as fault or no fault), the computation of the standard deviation of the metric that represents the number of faults would be:

$$s = \sqrt{n\hat{p}(1 - \hat{p})}$$

where n is the sample size and $\hat{p}$ is the proportion of faults in the sample.

If the metric represents the ratio of a binary value, such as the ratio of faults in a sample, then the computation of the sample standard deviation is:

$$s = \sqrt{\frac{\hat{p}(1 - \hat{p})}{n}}$$

This distinction becomes critical when we discuss the type of control charts.

Range.   A simpler measure of dispersion is range, defined as:

$$r = x_{max} - x_{min}$$

where x_{max} is the maximum observed metric value in the sample, and x_{min} is the smallest value in the sample. The average range of many samples is:

$$\bar{r} = \frac{\sum_{j=1}^{f} r_j}{f}$$

where $\bar{r}$ is the average range, r_j is the range of sample j, and f is the number of samples. The average range is used in setting up control charts. It is used to estimate the standard deviation as $s = \frac{\bar{r}}{d}$, where d is a constant factor, defined for various sample sizes [Montgomery 1991].

Mean Absolute Deviation.   Mean absolute deviation is another measure of dispersion that is less frequently used. It is defined as:

$$MAD = \frac{\sum_{i=1}^{n} |x_i - \bar{x}|}{n}$$

Both mean absolute deviation and standard deviation compute the average distance of observations from the mean—the center of data. The difference is that mean absolute deviation avoids the negative values generated in taking the difference between each observation and the mean by taking the absolute value, whereas standard deviation raises the difference to the second power and offsets this squaring by taking the square root of the overall result.

10.1.5   Probability Distributions Used in SQC

In the statistical tests and in establishing the acceptable intervals, one needs to use a probability distribution to represent the underlying distribution of the quality metric. More precisely, the probability distribution provides the alternative method of computing the sample standard deviation, as well as the factor by which the standard deviation should be multiplied in order to establish the acceptable range for a metric value.

In developing control charts, there are a number of probability distributions that are relevant to the quality metric:

- Normal distribution
- Binomial distribution
- Poisson distribution
- Other distributions

Normal Distribution.   The normal distribution is the most frequently used distribution in control charts. The normal distribution has a bell shape and is appropriate when the metric has a continuous value. It can be used as approximation for cases where the metric takes discrete values.

Many quality metrics, described in Chapter 9, are comprised of summing random variables, especially when they are defined as the mean of a number of observations or elements. Using the Central Limit Theorem, one can assume that a metric has a normal distribution. The theorem posits that when a random variable is the sum of a number of components that are also random variables, the probability distribution of the sum tends toward the normal distribution as the number of its components increases.

When the size of a sample is small, student t distribution is substituted for the normal distribution.

Binomial Distribution.   This distribution is appropriate when the metric takes binary values, such as fault and no fault, satisfactory and unsatisfactory, or success and failure. If each observation of the metric is independent of the others and all observations have equal probability of having a given binary value (such as failure), then the use of the binomial distribution is suitable for constructing the control chart of the number of faults or no faults in the sample.

The binomial distribution has the population mean of np and standard deviation of $\sqrt{np(1-p)}$, where n is the number of trials or observations, and p is the probability of success in each trial.

When np and $n(1-p)$ are relatively large so that $np \pm 3\sqrt{np(1-p)}$ is between 0 and n, the binomial distribution could be approximated by the normal distribution.

In cases where proportion, rather than the number of successes, is of interest, the above values are divided by n. That is, the mean of the proportion of successes is p and its standard deviation is $\sqrt{\frac{p(1-p)}{n}}$.

Poisson Distribution.   The Poisson distribution is useful for metrics that count the occurrences of an event in an interval, especially an interval of time or space. This distribution is appropriate when the events are independent from one another and are not a common occurrence, such as the number of system faults per month. If the faults are not caused by the same source, the Poisson distribution is an appropriate distribution for such a metric. This distribution has the population mean of λ—the average rate of events per interval, and the population standard deviation of $\sqrt{\lambda}$.

When λ is large (more than 9), the Poisson distribution can be approximated by a normal distribution.

Other Distributions.   Exponential and hypergeometric distributions are two probability distributions that may be suitable for quality metrics.

When events in a given interval have a Poisson distribution, the time between two events has an exponential distribution. Therefore, if a metric measures the time between two events, such as the interval of time between two faults, then the exponential distribution is a suitable distribution for this metric. The population mean and standard deviation of this distribution is $\frac{1}{\lambda}$.

When the size of the underlying population is limited and the sampling is without replacement, the hypergeometric distribution should replace the binomial distribution. For example, assume that the quality metric represents the number of system modules that are faulty. In a system where there is a limited number of modules and observing the status of the modules makes it ineligible for a second round of observation, the underlying distribution of the metric could be represented by the hypergeometric distribution. Under certain conditions, the hypergeometric distribution, too, can be approximated by either the binomial or normal distribution.

10.2 ◆ Control Charts for Quality Metrics

Control charts have a number of components, as shown in Figure 10.1:

- A fixed centerline
- Fixed lines of upper and lower control limits
- Fixed lines of warning (in most, but not all charts)
- Plot of the sample results

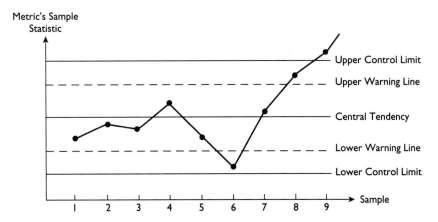

Figure 10.1   Shewhart-Type Control Chart with Two-Sided Control Limits and Warning

The center of the chart is the line representing the expected value of the sample mean (or any other measure of central tendency), as shown in Figure 10.1. There are cases in which the median has been used to represent the central tendency of the population, such as the case where a few extreme values affect the mean disproportionately.

Note that in the control charts that track the variability of the system, the centerline is set at the expected standard deviation (or expected range) of the metric. In such cases, the average standard deviation or the average range (with the constant factor) is used as the centerline in the chart.

The upper control limit (UCL) and lower control limit (LCL) are set by adding and subtracting the measure of variability multiplied by a variability factor from the centerline as:

$$upper\ control\ limit\ =\ centerline\ +\ variability\ factor \times variability$$
$$lower\ control\ limit\ =\ centerline\ -\ variability\ factor \times variability$$

The common practice is to use standard deviation as the measure of variability. The variability factor depends on the variability measure as well as the probability of Type I error, discussed in Section 10.1.2.

If the underlying distribution of the test statistic is normal, and we use standard deviation as the measure of variation, the variability factor of 3 gives less than 1 percent for a Type I error. This is why three-sigma is a popular factor in many cases for establishing the range of acceptability on the two sides of the mean.

If median or range is used in the control chart, the computation of the variability factor becomes more complex. Any textbook on statistical quality control (including the ones listed in this chapter) covers the variability factor in such cases.

The warning upper and lower lines are set by either using 2 as the variability factor, or the value that makes the warning range have a Type I error of 5 percent. If the normal distribution is the underlying distribution of the sample result plotted on the chart, 2 is a close approximation for the variability factor that has a Type I error of 5 percent.

The observed values of the metric or their sample statistics are plotted on the chart. If a value falls above the upper limit or below the lower limit, it is an indication that the system is out of control, as is the case in observation 9 in Figure 10.1.

On the other hand, if an observation falls outside the warning lines, it sends a warning that the system should be monitored more closely for the possibility of being out of control, such as observations 6 and 8 in Figure 10.1. In such cases, more samples should be taken immediately to check if the suspicion is justifiable.

10.2.1   Underlying Assumptions in Shewhart-Type Control Charts

There are two basic assumptions in Shewhart-type control charts:

- Independence of observations
- Normal distribution of the observations plotted on the control chart

The basic assumption in control charts is that metric values are generated independently from one another and are not correlated. Alwan and Roberts [1988] and

Montgomery and Mastrangelo [1991] have designed control charts for autocorrelated forms of dependent data. Furthermore, the non-Shewhart control charts are less sensitive to this assumption.

The control interval has the basis in the metric to have an approximately normal distribution. However, Wheeler and Chambers [1992] argue that control charts are robust with respect to this assumption. They quote from Shewhart [1931] that one does not need to prove that the metric has a normal distribution before using control charts. It has been shown that using three sigmas for establishing the interval of control charts is valid for many shapes and types of distributions [Wheeler and Chambers 1992].

If the normal distribution is not a good approximation for a metric, other distributions, such as binomial, Poisson, exponential, or hypergeometric could be utilized.

10.2.2   Categories of Shewhart-Type Control Charts

Shewhart-type control charts are categorized into:

- x chart, c chart, np chart
- p chart
- u chart
- $\bar{x}$ and m charts
- r chart and s chart
- $\bar{x} - s$ chart, $\bar{x} - r$ chart, $m - s$ chart, and $m - r$ chart
- Extreme value chart

x **Chart, c Chart, np Chart.**   This chart is designed for tracking the cumulative number of failures in a sample of n binary-valued metric, however failure is defined. For example, in the ACCU-INFO case, the x chart is used for tracking the number of unanswered queries in a given sample of customer queries of a system. This chart is also called the c chart and np chart. The probability distribution used for these charts is the binomial distribution, and np is the mean of the binomial distribution. As mentioned in Sections 10.1.4 and 10.1.5, the binomial distribution can be approximated by the normal distribution.

p **Chart.**   This control chart is used for tracking the proportion of failures in a sample, such as the proportion of the number of unanswered queries in a sample of customer queries. The parameters in this chart are divided by the size of the sample, as was discussed in Sections 10.1.4 and 10.1.5.

u **chart.**   This chart is used for tracking metric values that represent events in an interval of time or in a physical unit. One can use the Poisson distribution for this chart. For example, in the ACCU-INFO case, the number of faults per month would be an appropriate candidate for this chart.

$\bar{x}$ **and m Charts.** $\bar{x}$ and m charts are also called *mean* chart and *median*, respectively. These charts are used for metrics with sample means or medians as their values. For example, in the ACCU-INFO case, one of the fault-management metrics used is the fault-rework metric, defined in Chapter 9. This metric is the average time spent on reworking a fault and fixing it.

If there are cases in which a few observations with large fault values inflate the sample mean, the company may use the median chart for this metric.

r Chart and s Chart.   These control charts are designed to keep track of the variability of a metric. In this case, range (in r chart) or standard deviation (in s chart) should be on the control chart.

For example, in the ACCU-INFO case, we want to keep track of the variability of the metric faults per month through time. The variability of the metric could be tracked by the r chart or s chart.

$\bar{x} - s$ chart, $\bar{x} - r$ chart, $m - s$ chart, and $m - r$ chart.   These charts have two tracks. One track is for mean or median ($\bar{x}$ or m), and another track is for standard deviation or range (s or r). They are two charts shown on the same page or screen. For example, ACCU-INFO might decide to use an $\bar{x} - s$ chart to track the average time interval for the fault-rework metric.

Extreme Value Chart.   This control chart contains the single value of the individual observations. That is, each observation is plotted on the chart. The observations with extreme values receive attention in these charts, hence the name. When the number of observations is large, this chart is of little use.

10.2.3   Matching Information-Systems Quality Metrics and Control Charts

Different quality metrics discussed in Chapter 9 vary in nature. The choice of the control chart depends on the nature of the metric.

A quality metric may have discrete or continuous values. The most important case in discrete-value metrics is the binary-value metric. For binary-value metrics, the x chart and the u chart are the appropriate ones.

In the discrete-value metrics, if the normal distribution is used, there is an adjustment (of .5) in the computation of the upper and lower limits by the normal distribution. Most of the elementary statistics books discuss the discrete adjustment for the normal approximation.

If the metric represents the proportion of a binary-value metric, then the p chart is the appropriate control chart.

When the quality metric takes continuous values (other than proportion values), one has to decide on the information expected from the chart. For a single chart, one should decide whether the needed information is central tendency or variation. If central tendency is of interest, the mean chart, median chart, and extreme-value chart are suitable choices. An example of quality metrics that can use these charts is the average-complexity metric, discussed in Chapter 9.

If variation of the metric is of interest, then the s chart or r chart should be used. For a single chart, if both individual location and variation are of interest, then the extreme-value chart is the right choice. The size-complexity metric is a good candidate for the extreme-value chart.

If the choice is a double-track chart, one of the following double-track charts should be used: $\bar{x} - s$, $\bar{x} - r$, $m - s$, or $m - r$. Metrics such as the unit-cost metric or the customer-value metric are good candidates for these charts.

10.2.4   The Estimation of Control-Chart Parameters

In designing a control chart, one needs to establish the centerline, upper and lower control limits, and warning lines. The chart parameters that are needed for this task are:

- Central tendency
- Variation
- Variation factor

The control chart parameters could be set according to the objectives of the system. However, if these objectives are not realistic, tracking metrics with control charts becomes a useless practice. Therefore, if system objectives are used for setting up the control-chart parameters, they should be at a level that are achievable by the existing system.

For example, ACCU-INFO may set the fault-per-month metric at 2 per month plus or minus 1—the acceptable range of 1 to 3. If this is too unrealistic, month after month, the number of faults will fall above the acceptable range because the metric values do not belong to the population with the mean of 2. The chart signals an out-of-control condition month after month with little consequence.

In some cases, the parameters are set by observing the system in action. In other cases, the parameters are set by performance standards and specifications. The most important issues in observing the system for establishing the chart parameters are that:

- The system should be in control—operating under its normal condition
- Samples should represent all possible conditions under which the system works in its normal mode

Observing the system in its normal mode does not mean that data should not contain crisis or unusual conditions if they are a part of the normal working of the system.

When control-chart parameters are decided by sampling, the centerline is the average of sample means (the grand mean) or the average median discussed in Section 10.1.3; and the variation is represented by the average of sample standard deviations or the average of sample ranges discussed in Section 10.1.4. (In s amd r charts, the chart has the average range or average standard deviation (with the constant factor) as the centerline.)

The variation factor depends on the underlying probability distribution and the level of Type I error, as discussed before.

In collecting the information-system quality metrics, we have access to the raw data from which the metric values are computed. This access gives us the option to compute the mean and standard deviation for the control chart either from the raw data or from the computed values of metrics. The decision depends on the metric's nature. This issue is not covered because of the limited statistical background in this chapter.

10.2.5   Non-Shewhart Control Charts

There are a number of control charts that do not follow Shewhart's charts. Non-Shewhart charts are reported to be more sensitive towards shifts in the centerline or its variation. The non-Shewhart charts require more complex methods of establishing control limits and testing for the system's out-of-control status. Here we briefly mention four types of such charts; textbooks on statistical control charts cover these control charts in detail:

- MOSUM charts
- EWMA charts
- CUSUM
- Modified Shewhart charts

MOSUM Charts.   MOSUM is the abbreviation for the moving sum of the sample statistic used in a control chart. For example, in the $\bar{x}$ chart, the sample statistic plotted on the chart is sample mean $\bar{x}$. The MOSUM plots the average of the sample means (the grand mean) for k period. For example, if $k = 5$ days, the statistic plotted on day 11 is the average of sample means taken on days 7, 8, 9, 10, and 11—the most recent five days.

EWMA Chart.   The exponentially weighted moving average (EWMA) chart combines the sample statistic for two consecutive periods with a weight of w and $(1 - w)$, and plots it on the chart. For example, if $\bar{x}$ is the sample statistic, and the weight is set at $w = .80$ for today's sample mean and $(1 - w) = .20$ for yesterday's sample mean, the plotted value for today will be:

$$y_t = .20y_{t-1} + .80\bar{x}_t$$

where y_t is today's plotted value on the chart, and y_{t-1} is yesterday's plotted value. The EWMA chart needs a plot value for time 0 (y_0), which is the target value of the metric. When we apply this method recursively—substituting the value of y_{t-1} for its equivalent of $.20y_{t-2} + .80\bar{x}_{t-1}$, we see that

$$y_t = .20(.20)y_{t-2} + .20(.80)\bar{x}_{t-1} + .80\bar{x}_t$$

or

$$y_t = .20(.20)(.20)y_{t-3} + .20(.20)(.80)\bar{x}_{t-2} + .20(.80)\bar{x}_{t-1} + .80\bar{x}_t$$

and so forth.

In other words, the plotted value for time t is 80 percent of today's sample mean and 20 percent of the sample means from time 0 up to $t - 1$. As the sample mean goes farther back, it receives an exponentially lower weight.

CUSUM Chart.   The cumulative sum (CUSUM) chart subtracts the sample statistic from a target value and computes the sum for the entire period up to time t. For example, for $\bar{x}$ as the sample statistic, we have:

$$y_t = \sum_{i=1}^{t} (\bar{x}_i - target)$$

When the sample mean stays around the target value, y_t does not have an upward or downward trend. However, when there is a shift in the sample mean from the target value, y_t will show a clear movement upward (or downward). It is reported that this chart can identify shifts in the sample mean, even those that are short-lived.

Modified Shewhart Charts.   Shewhart charts are modified to include process capability—the capability of the system to maintain its specifications even in a stable and in-control mode. Mittag and Rinne [1993] and Bissell [1994] provide detailed discussions of these charts.

10.2.6   Using Control Charts

Deming in his forward to the text by Wheeler and Chambers [1992] observes that:

> *Dr. Shewhart perceived two kinds of variations. (1) Variation from constant causes, the same causes from hour to hour, lot to lot, worker to worker. Dr. Shewhart's term was chance causes. (2) Variation from a special cause.*

The purpose of control charts is to discover variation caused by special circumstances and to take appropriate actions. Normally, special causes are identified by the points that are outside the control limits. When a point is out of bounds at an undesirable level, the system is performing poorly and should be investigated for discovering and removing the problem causes. When a point on the control chart is beyond limits in a desirable direction, it provides the opportunity for discovering the causes of such out-of-bounds positive performance and making them a permanent facet of the system.

Another way for analyzing data on control charts is the search for special patterns. Even when a quality metric is not out of bounds, the pattern of points on the control chart could reveal many interesting aspects of the quality metric, and those of the system.

When a variation in metric values is caused purely by chance causes, the plotted data on the control chart do not show any predictable pattern. If one can find a pattern in the control chart, it indicates that predictable and special causes exist in the system that can be discovered.

Figure 10.2 shows examples of possible patterns in the Shewhart-type control charts. Assume that the metric on Figure 10.2-a represents ACCU-INFO's reliability metric on a daily basis. It shows that this metric goes through a five-period cycle. For five days, the reliability of the system improves, then it falls for the subsequent five days, and again goes up on the next five days. The question is: Why should the system reliability have a five-day cycle? Is it because different types of customers use the system in a particular

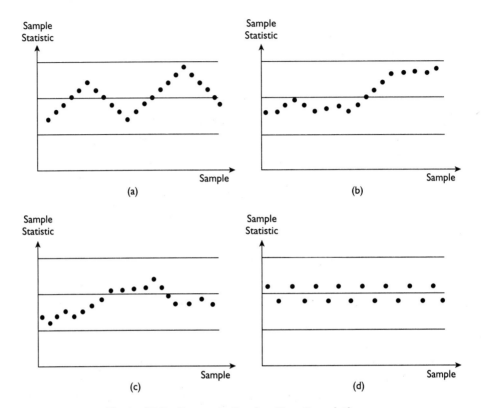

Figure 10.2   Patterns in Shewhart-Type Control Charts

week? If so, the system is working well for some customer types and poorly for others. Is it because of the week of the month? Does the system work better in some weeks than in others? Why? What weeks are the bad weeks, and how can we eliminate poor performance on bad weeks?

Another pattern is shown on Figure 10.2-b. This chart shows a persistent shift of the metric toward the upper limit. Assume that this chart represents the unit-cost metric for ACCU-INFO. What is the reason for this persistent upward shift? Is it inflation? If so, the metric should be adjusted for the inflation rate. In other words, the metric should be adjusted for the uncontrollable factors. Is it a technology change? The new technology is normally cheaper than the old. Is it the erosion of the information-system workers' skills? Is it fat in the bureaucracy?

The pattern in Figure 10.2-c shows clustered points above and below the centerline. Assume that this chart represents the size complexity of information-systems projects. It may indicate that projects developed by certain groups or managers have less complexity than others. The task is to study how the units with lower size complexity have operated and interacted, and to propagate that mode of system development to all projects.

Figure 10.2-d shows a predictable pattern of points alternating above and below the centerline. Assume this control chart represents the customer-discovered fault metric.

There are two customers using the system, and each reports faults on a monthly basis. It could be that the system works with less fault for the first customer than for the second customer. Alternatively, the first customer may be less reluctant to report faults than the other customer. Before this becomes a sore point for the second customer, who reports more faults, an investigation regarding the performance of the system for that customer is in order. On the other hand, we have to make sure that the first customer is well aware of our needs for his or her reporting of system faults and the way to do so.

Note that the system is not out of control in any of the above cases. However, one can extract useful information from the control chart even when the system is in control.

Significant patterns are not always visible to the naked eye. There are statistical tests, called run tests, that identify patterns that are not attributable to pure chance. Wheeler and Chambers [1992] provide an accessible discussion of these tests.

10.3 ◆ Quality Tools

There are a number of quality tools that have been developed by the quality practitioners both in the U.S. and Japan. As Brassard [1989] reports, the origin of quality tools as a set is the result of the work by a committee of Japan's Society for QC Technique Development from 1972 to 1979. This committee published its work in 1979 as *Seven New Quality Tools for Managers and Staff*. The English translation of this book was published by Mizuno in his edited book *Management for Quality Improvement: The Seven New QC Tools* in 1988.

GOAL/QPC and Michael Brassard brought the seven quality tools to the U.S. in *Memory Jogger*^{TM} in 1984. *Memory Jogger Plus +*^{TM}, published in 1989, contains seven new management and planning tools. *Memory Jogger II*^{TM} [1994] contains both sets of tools.

The interesting feature of these tools is that they can be used in conjunction with one another—the output of one tool can be used as the input to another for planning and design. Some of the quality tools are already covered in the previous chapters of this book: Affinity diagram in Chapter 2, Pareto charts, the cause-and-effect diagram, tree and hierarchy diagrams in Chapter 3, and the data-flow diagram in Chapter 4.

Although not in the list of seven tools, the quality function deployment (QFD) (covered in Chapters 5 and 6) and analytic hierarchy process (AHP, covered in Chapter 5 and 9) are also considered to be important quality tools.

The remaining quality tools discussed in the U.S. and Japanese sources include:

- Interrelationship digraph
- Prioritization matrix
- Matrix diagrams
- Process decision program charts
- Activity-network diagrams (or arrow diagrams)

As Brassard [1984] notes, these tools are not new. They are simplified forms of the methods developed in operations research, management science, and decision analysis. However, they are compiled as tools that practitioners can use in their planning and management endeavors. The strengths of the quality tools are their simplicity, graphical nature, and connection to quality efforts.

This section provides a brief review of the remaining tools. Brassard [1989] and Mizuno [1988] provide a detailed discussion of them.

10.3.1   Interrelationship Digraph

The interrelationship digraph [Brassard 1989] or relation diagram [Mizuno 1988] is a diagram for graphically displaying the interrelationships among various factors. In some cases, this diagram may also exhibit the causal relationship. This diagram can be used after identifying the problem components with the affinity diagram (Chapter 2). Each arrow shows the direction of influence or causality in the diagram. This diagram is developed iteratively as the problem components are connected and analyzed. The final diagram may have a problem point, to which all influence or causality arrows lead.

For example, in the ACCU-INFO case, there is a critical problem with customer satisfaction and the quality of the data. After identifying the problem components through the affinity diagram, we can create an interrelationship digraph, shown in Figure 10.3, for identifying the relationships among various contributing factors. (Brassard [1989] shows how the interrelationship digraph can be converted into tabular form.)

Among the advantages of this tool are that it [Mizuno 1989]:

- Simplifies and clarifies the relationships among various components of a question or problem
- Identifies departments that have a role in the process
- Highlights the key issues in a problem or question

The disadvantages of this tool are:

- The diagram may become too big and complex
- If the factors are not identified and communicated clearly, the direction of arrows may be erroneous
- The diagram is difficult to develop for complex problems
- The correct development of the diagram requires repeated redrawing, which demands patience and time

Some of the disadvantages of the relation graph could be overcome by careful analysis of the problem—the intention of using the diagram in the first place.

10.3.2   Prioritization Matrix

The prioritization matrix is similar to the pairwise comparison matrix (or table) in the analytical hierarchy process (AHP) and its use in the house of quality in quality function deployment (QFD). AHP, in conjunction with QFD, is covered in Chapter 5.

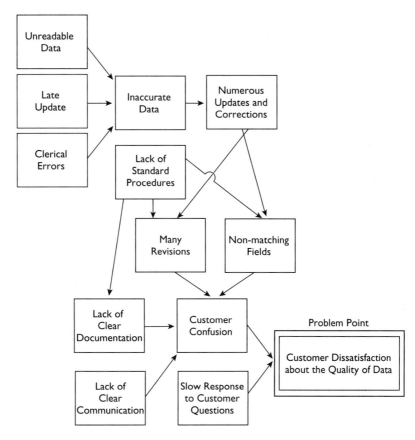

Figure 10.3 An Example of the Interrelationship Digraph for the ACCU-INFO Case

10.3.3 Matrix Diagrams

Matrix diagrams are two—or three—dimensional tables for representing the intersection between two (or three) variables. They include:

- L-shaped matrix
- T-shaped matrix
- X-shaped matrix
- Y-shaped matrix
- C-shaped matrix
- Tree Matrix

Figure 10.4 shows an example of each type of the first four types of matrix diagrams. The C-shaped matrix is similar to the Y-shaped matrix with the difference that the

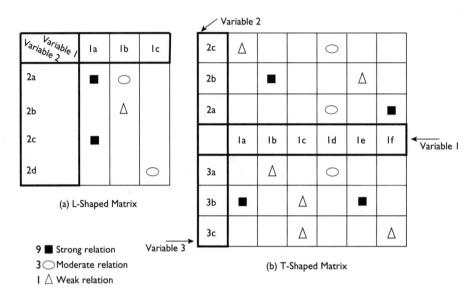

Figure 10.4   Examples of Matrix Diagrams

relations are at the intersection of the three variables. The entries of these matrices are mostly the strength of relations among the row and column values. In the C-matrix, an entry indicates a three-dimensional relationship.

10.3.4   Tree Matrix

The tree matrix is similar to the L-shaped matrix except that the hierarchies upon which columns and rows are built are also displayed on the top and left side of the matrix, as shown in Figure 10.5. The tree matrix is useful in setting up the house of quality.

10.3.5   Process-Decision Program Charts

Process-decision program charts are similar to the decision hierarchy described in Chapter 5. This diagram has a hierarchical structure, and is useful for breaking down a decision or an action into its subcomponents. An example of process-decision program charts is given in Figure 10.6.

10.3.6   Activity-Network Diagrams

Activity-network diagrams are similar to the PERT/CPM method developed for project management in management science. An example of the activity-network diagram is given in Figure 10.7. Mizuno [1988] uses a simpler version of this tool and calls it the arrow diagram. The idea of the arrow diagram is to show the sequence of steps needed for the completion of a project or a job.

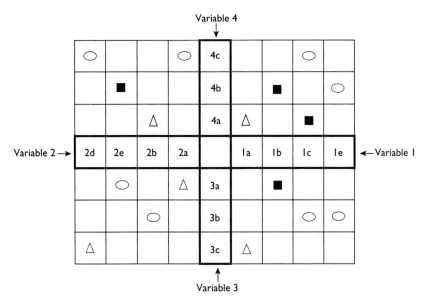

(c) X-Shaped Matrix

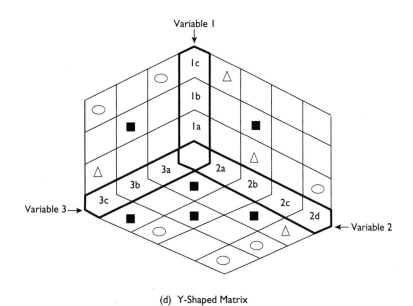

(d) Y-Shaped Matrix

Figure 10.4   Examples of Matrix Diagrams (*continued*)

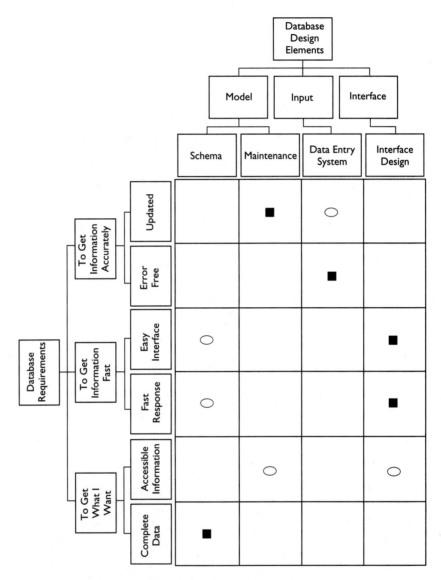

Figure 10.5 An Example of Tree Matrix

The PERT/CPM method breaks down a project or job into tasks that should be finished to complete the job. The input to this method consists of the tasks, their sequence, and estimation of time that it takes to finish a task. The nodes in Figure 10.7 represent completed tasks. An arc in this diagram contains the length of time it takes to finish the task to which the arrow points. This method computes the earliest and latest times that a task could be finished. The difference between the earliest and latest times for finishing a task is called *slack*. The path that has tasks with zero slack is called the

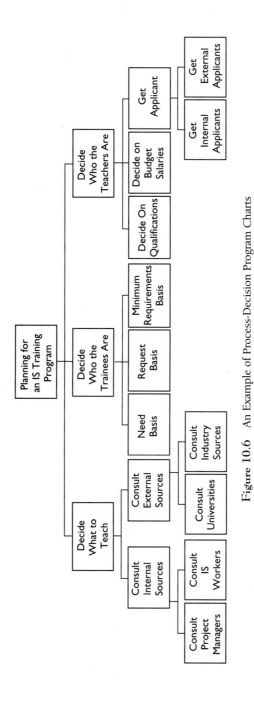

Figure 10.6   An Example of Process-Decision Program Charts

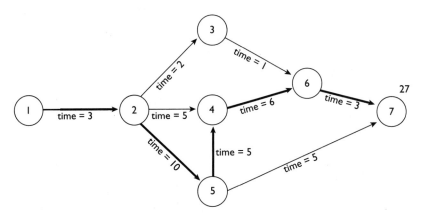

Figure 10.7   An Example of Activity-Network Diagrams

critical path. Tasks on the critical path are critical to the completion time of the project. A delay in finishing any of the tasks on the critical path will delay the completion of the project or job.

This method provides a project manager with the knowledge of critical tasks and their role in completing the project or job on time. As discussed in Chapter 9, this method is one of the common methods in management science and is used for project time management.

10.4 ◆ Software Products for Quality Methods

There are software products on the market that support a number of quality methods discussed in this book. Here, we briefly review examples of software products available for the following methods:

- Taguchi
- QFD
- Quality tools
- AHP

10.4.1   Software for Taguchi Methods

Responsible Management (Durham, NH) has developed a software product for Taguchi's orthogonal arrays, called OATS^{TM}, Orthogonal Arrays Taguchi Style. This package analyzes the designed experiments for developing products or processes that are robust. This software facilitates the use of Taguchi's methods at the design stage.

Another software product for the Taguchi methods is DOE Wisdom (Windows Software for Design of Experiment Methods), developed by Launsby Consulting (Colorado Springs, Colorado). This product is based on the Microsoft Windows^{TM} environment.

10.4.2   Software for QFD

GOAL/QPC (Methuen, MA) has developed QFD/CAPTURE. It captures, organizes, and reports data generated using the QFD (quality function deployment) method. It contains matrices for various parts of the house of quality. Figure 10.8 shows the main screen of QFD/CAPTURE. The main screen shows components of the house of quality and is connected to tables or matrices for each piece of the house of quality.

GOAL/QPC has developed the software with ITI (International TechnicalGroup Incorporated), which provides hotline support for the software.

10.4.3   Software for Quality Tools

Memory Jogger Plus $+^{TM}$ now has a companion software with the same name that is developed by Quality Decision Management. GOAL/QPC (Methuen, MA) holds trademark and markets the software. This software automates the construction of the quality tools (called seven management and planning tools), accelerates the documentation process, and produces presentation quality output. In this software, one can share information among tools. The tools covered in this software are: the affinity diagram, interrelationship digraph, tree diagram, prioritization matrices, matrix diagrams, process-decision program chart, and activity-network diagram.

10.4.4   Software for AHP

There are a number of software products that support the application of the analytic hierarchy process. The oldest and most widely used software for AHP is Expert Choice, developed by Ernst Forman and marketed by Expert Choice Inc. (Pittsburgh, PA).

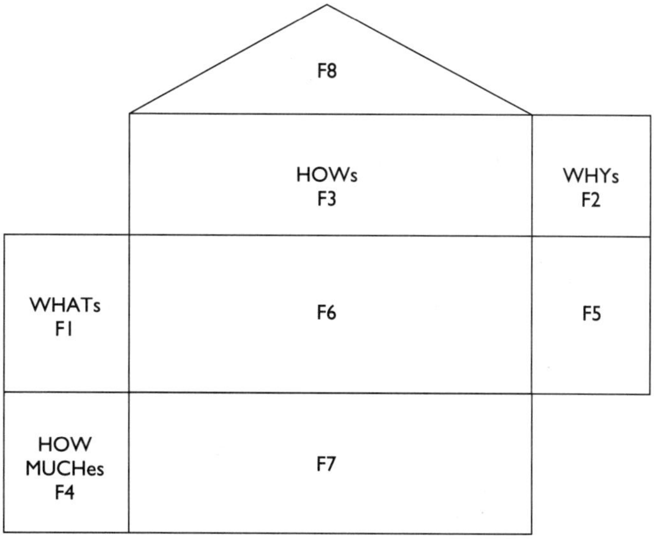

Figure 10.8   The Features of the Main Screen in QFD/CAPTURE

This software helps the user create the decision hierarchy, prompts the user to input elements of the pairwise comparison matrices, and computes the local and global relative weights. It also reports the measure of inconsistency. Figure 10.9 shows a sample print from Expert Choice. This figure shows the application of Figure 5.3 (Chapter 5) in Expert Choice.

A recent extension of this software is Team Expert Choice (TeamEC), developed by Expert Choice Inc. This software is designed to facilitate the use of the AHP for group decision-making and assigning relative weights to alternatives. Team Expert Choice has a three-step process: brainstorming, structuring, and evaluation. This software is useful in facilitating group decision-making for evaluating various alternatives, requirements, or objects. Such decisions are needed at the design stage of information systems.

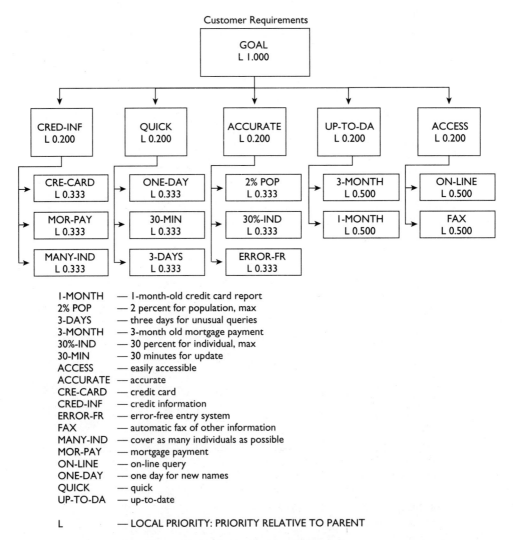

Customer Requirements

I-MONTH	— I-month-old credit card report
2% POP	— 2 percent for population, max
3-DAYS	— three days for unusual queries
3-MONTH	— 3-month old mortgage payment
30%-IND	— 30 percent for individual, max
30-MIN	— 30 minutes for update
ACCESS	— easily accessible
ACCURATE	— accurate
CRE-CARD	— credit card
CRED-INF	— credit information
ERROR-FR	— error-free entry system
FAX	— automatic fax of other information
MANY-IND	— cover as many individuals as possible
MOR-PAY	— mortgage payment
ON-LINE	— on-line query
ONE-DAY	— one day for new names
QUICK	— quick
UP-TO-DA	— up-to-date

L   — LOCAL PRIORITY: PRIORITY RELATIVE TO PARENT

Figure 10.9   A Sample Print of Expert Choice

10.5 ◆ The Implementation of Quality Metrics

After the decision to implement quality metrics is made, the next step is the decision on the extent and scope of implementing quality metrics. The implementation of quality metrics requires a number of answers to questions such as:

- How
- When
- How much
- How often

The purpose of this section is to pose these questions. Answers to these questions are unique to the organization, and the circumstances under which the metrics are implemented. Therefore, the answers to these questions should be considered suggestions, rather than the ultimate solutions.

10.5.1   How to Use Quality Metrics

The analysis of quality metrics can be used for two purposes. The first is for monitoring the quality of the system. When the metric value falls outside the control limits, the system requires inspection.

Secondly, when the inspection identifies a number of causes for the system being out of control, we have to decide whether to improve the system, and if so, which contributing cause to remove first. In the ideal condition of unlimited resources, all causes should be removed immediately. However, such an ideal condition is rarely present. Under normal conditions, we need to prioritize the improvement plans. To do so, we can investigate the sensitivity of the metric to each improvement plan.

For example, consider the reliability metric, discussed in Chapter 9. This metric has a number of components. A sensitivity analysis of the metric may reveal that the complaint calls component has the highest priority for system customers. That is, a 1-percent increase in the reliability of this component of the metric has four times more impact than a 1-percent increase in the reliability of, say, the commission component.

Thus, the analysis of metrics provides a guideline for assigning priorities to various plans in system quality.

10.5.2   When to Use Quality Metrics

Designing quality metrics, collecting data regularly, and tracking the system's quality obviously involve costs. We may have to ask under what circumstances such additional costs are justifiable. Under ideal circumstances, the answer could be that all operational information systems should use metrics as odometers of quality.

We rarely encounter the ideal case. The question then becomes what characteristics of the information system make it a better candidate for the implementation of quality metrics. In other words, if we had to choose one system among a number of information systems to implement quality metrics, what should be the criteria?

There are two dimensions that stand out: the corporate value of the information system and the complexity of the system. As Figure 10.10 indicates, the system with a high value for the corporation and high level of complexity is the most appropriate candidate for regular tracking of quality metrics. On the other hand, the system with a low corporate value and low level of complexity is not a prime candidate for quality tracking. The other two quadrants have medium priority for quality tracking.

Admittedly, complexity itself is a composite dimension. One can use common sense to judge the complexity of a system or apply a more formal measure, such as complexity metrics, to judge the degree of the system's complexity.

10.5.3   How Much Quality Metrics

We can track the quality of information systems at different levels of detail. For example, in the computation of the reliability metric discussed in Chapter 9, one can develop the hierarchy and its required data at different levels of detail. In the first application of the system, one may limit the hierarchy and its required data collection at the modular level (third level in Figure 9.3 in Chapter 9). Later, as the understanding and use of the reliability metric increases, one may expand the metric to include the fourth level as well. In other words, the extent of detail and accuracy in the computation of a quality metric could change from one stage of implementation to another.

Another dimension of this question is: How many quality metrics should we implement in monitoring the system quality? We can choose to implement only one metric or all quality metrics discussed in Chapter 9. Again, this decision depends on the stage of implementation. One can start with a few metrics that are clearly related to the vision of the information system and expand on them as needed.

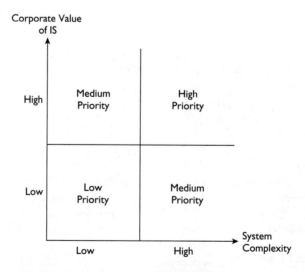

Figure 10.11   The Application Priority of Information-System Metrics

A third dimension of this question is whether quality metrics should be implemented in one ongoing information system or project, or in all corporate systems. The answer to this question depends on the organization and its culture. One can start the implementation on a few trial sites and systems, and expand it as the organizational know-how about the quality-control process increases and the benefits of process control are discovered.

10.5.4   How Often to Use Quality Metrics

The frequency of data collection is another dimension of implementing quality metrics. Frequent data collection allows us to monitor the system more closely. On the other hand, collecting and analyzing frequently collected data are more costly. One needs to balance the cost of more frequent data collection and analysis with the resulting benefits.

A more preferred mode of data collection is to incorporate it into the system so that the data is collected and processed automatically. One could also automate the routine analysis methods inside the system in order to reduce the cost of quality analysis. Incorporating quality metrics and their analysis into the system is in line with Taguchi's approach, which advocates incorporating quality into the design of products and processes.

◆ Conclusion

In this chapter, we discussed the methods for the analysis of information-systems quality metrics. In Section 10.1, we presented statistical quality-control methods, the prerequisites for applying them to information systems, and their theoretical basis. Since statistical quality control depends on sample statistics, an understanding of the measures of central tendency, variation, and probability distribution is critical to such analysis. These topics were discussed in Section 10.1

Control charts are the most important methods in statistical quality control for tracking quality metrics. Section 10.2 discussed these charts, their underlying assumptions, Shewhart-type charts, and non-Shewhart-type charts. Since each type of quality metric matches with a particular control chart, this section discussed how to match information-system quality metrics with different control charts.

Setting control charts requires estimation of chart parameters, an issue that also was reviewed in Section 10.2. Finally, this section discussed how to take advantage of the information revealed in control charts patterns. These patterns aid us in understanding the nature of the system and in discovering the ways we can improve it.

We have discussed a number of quality methods in this book, such as the affinity diagram (Chapter 2), Pareto charts, cause-and-effect diagram, tree and hierarchy diagrams (Chapter 3), data-flow diagram (Chapter 4), quality function deployment (Chapters 5 and 6), and analytic hierarchy process (Chapter 5 and 9). There are a number of quality tools that were not covered in the previous chapters. They include the interrelationship digraph, prioritization matrices, matrix diagrams, process-decision program chart, and activity network diagram. These tools were reviewed briefly in Section 10.3.

There are a number of software products on the market that are designed to facilitate the use of quality methods. Section 10.4 listed and briefly reviewed software products for Taguchi methods, quality function deployment, quality tools, and analytic hierarchy process.

In implementing quality metrics for information systems, there are a number of questions to be answered, such as how, when, how much, and how often one should use quality metrics—rarely discussed questions. In Section 10.5, we posed the questions and attempted to offer suggestions that could be helpful in initiating discussions on these issues.

◆ References

1. Alwan, L. C. and Roberts, H. V. 1988. "Time-Series Modeling for Statistical Quality Control," *Journal of Business and Economic Statistics*, Vol. 6, pp. 87–95.

2. Brassard, Michael. 1984. The Memory Jogger^{TM}, GOAL/QPC, Methuen, MA.

3. Brassard, Michael. 1989. The Memory Jogger Plus $+^{TM}$, GOAL/QPC, Methuen, MA.

4. Brassard, Michael. 1994. The Memory Jogger II ^{TM}, GOAL/QPC, Methuen, MA.

5. Bissell, Derek. 1992. *Statistical Methods for SPC and TQM*, Chapman & Hall, London.

6. Cryer, J. and Miller, R. 1991. *Statistics for Business: Data Analysis and Modelling*, PWS-Kent Publishing, Boston, MA.

7. Farnum, Nicholas R. 1994. *Modern Statistical Quality Control and Improvement*, Duxbury Press, Belmont, CA.

8. McClave, J. and Benson, P. G. 1992. *A First Course in Business Statistics*, fifth edition, Macmillan Publishing, New York, NY.

9. Mittag, H. J. and Rinne, H. 1993. *Statistical Methods of Quality Assurance*, Chapman & Hall, London.

10. Mizuno, Shigeru (Editor). 1988. *Management for Quality Improvement: The Seven New QC Tools*, English Translation by Productivity Press, Cambridge, MA.

11. Montgomery, D. C. 1991. *Introduction to Statistical Quality Control*, second edition, John Wiley and Sons, New York, NY.

12. Montgomery, D. C. and Mastrangelo, C. M. 1991. "Some Statistical Process Control Methods for Autocorrelated Data," *Journal of Quality Technology*, Vol. 23, pp. 179–193.

13. Shewhart, W. A. 1931, *Economic Control of Quality of Manufactured Products*, D. Van Nostrand, Princeton, NJ, reprinted by the American Society for Quality Control, Milwaukee, WI.

14. Shewhart, W. A. 1939. In *Statistical Method from the Viewpoint of Quality Control*, W. E. Deming (Ed.), The Graduate School, Department of Agriculture, Washington D.C.

15. Wheeler, Donald J. and Chambers, David S. 1992. *Understanding Statistical Process Control*, Second Edition, SPC Press, Inc. Knoxville, TN.

◆ Questions

    10.1. What is statistical quality control and how does it relate to quality metrics?

    10.2. What are the prerequisites for using statistical quality control in information systems?

    10.3. What are measures of central tendency?

    10.4. What are measures of variation?

    10.5. Why are probability distributions important in statistical quality control?

    10.6. What are the roles of measures of central tendency and variation in control charts?

    10.7. What are the components of control charts?

    10.8. What are the underlying assumptions in Shewhart-type control charts?

    10.9. What are the categories of Shewhart-type control charts?

    10.10. What are the ways of estimating control-chart parameters?

    10.11. List non-Shewhart control charts. Describe one of them.

    10.12. What is the significance of discovering patterns in control charts?

    10.13. What are quality tools?

    10.14. Describe the interrelationship digraph.

    10.15. Describe prioritization matrices.

    10.16. What are the types of matrix diagrams?

    10.17. Describe the activity-network diagram.

    10.18. What is difference between the activity-network diagram and the arrow diagram?

    10.19. What is the importance of software products for using quality methods?

    10.20. What are the issues related to the implementation of quality metrics in information systems?

    10.21. How should we use quality metrics in information systems?

    10.22. When should we use quality metrics in information systems?

    10.23. How often should data for quality metrics be collected?

◆ Problems

    10.1. Give an example in which median is more appropriate than mean as the measure of central tendency.

    10.2. Give an example in which range is more appropriate than standard deviation as the measure of variation.

    10.3. Compute the mean and standard deviation of the following data for the fault-rework metric that represents the number of hours spent on reworking a fault and fixing it.

        23, 14, 16, 24, 17, 2, 37, 2, 12, 4, 15, 25, 13, 5, 3, 6, 20, 12, 34, 15

10.4. What type of control charts are appropriate for problem 10.3?

10.5. Establish the control chart for Problem 10.3. Use 3 and 2 as the variation factors in establishing the control limits and warning lines, respectively.

10.6. Assume that the quality metric is the number of times the system is down per month. What type of control charts are appropriate for this metric?

10.7. Assume that the quality metric is the number of objects per information system. What type of control charts are appropriate for this metric?

10.8. Give an example of a control chart for a quality metric that has a cyclical pattern. Discuss the nature of the metric and possible causes for the pattern.

10.9. Find an example of a control chart for a quality metric that has an upward trend pattern. Discuss the nature of the metric and possible causes for its pattern.

10.10. Discuss the quality metrics for which a double-track control chart is desirable. Justify your answer.

10.11. When do you recommend the use of the extreme-value control chart?

10.12. Give three examples of quality metrics for which you recommend r or s charts. Justify your answer.

10.13. Assume the target value for the metric in Problem 10.3 is 9. Compute the points to be plotted on the CUSUM control chart for Problem 10.3. (Hint: compute y_t values.)

10.14. Using the discussion of hierarchies in Chapter 5, give an example of the tree matrix for requirements analysis in information systems.

Would it be too bold to imagine, that in the great length of time, since the earth began to exist, perhaps millions of ages before the commencement of the history of mankind, would it be too bold to imagine, that all warm-blooded animals have arisen from one living filament which the Great First Cause endued with animality ... and this possessing the faculty of continuing to improve by its own inherent activity, and of delivering down those improvements by generation to its posterity, world without end!

— Erasmus Darwin

Index

abstract task, 337
abuse minimization, 200
acceptability range, 388
acceptance sampling, 379
access time
  standard deviation, 299
Ackoff, 6
acquisition, 77
activity-network diagrams, 396, 398
Aczel, 366
Advanced Project Group, 201
affinity diagram, 43, 395
  assembling team, 44
  assigning header, 46
  generating ideas, 45
  grouping ideas, 45
  posing question, 45
agent software, 265
AHP, 22, 178, 184, 357, 374
Albrecht, 296
American Society for Quality
    Control, 9, 48
analytic hierarchy process, 22
  eigenvalue method, 181
  Expert Choice, 181
  global ratings, 180
  group preference, 182
  hierarchy structure, 177
  inconsistency measure, 181
  levels, 179
  local relative weights, 181
  normalization, 174
  pairwise comparisons, 180
  rating, 174
  weight assessment, 177
AQAP-1, 14
arrow diagram, 396
artificial intelligence, 265
ASQC, 9, 13, 48

average-complexity metric, 348, 390
average cost, 349
average fault-recurrence metric, 354
average-team-innovation metrics,
    309
awards, 11
  Baldrige, 13
  European Quality, 14
  Fanatic Quality, 11

Baldrige Award, 34, 48, 52
Barrett, 241
benchmarker networks, 141
benchmarking, 7, 56, 86, 112, 261,
    294, 356
  analysis, 121, 129
  comparability analysis, 132
  competitive, 119
  continuous improvement, 143
  data comparability, 131
  data randomness, 130
  data time interval, 132
  data variability, 130
  documentation, 127, 129
  evaluation, 143
  functional, 119
  future goals, 142
  gap determination, 132
  generic, 119
  implementation, 142
  information, 122
  internal, 118
  iteration, 140
  Japan, 113
  metrics, 118, 131
  objectives, 118
  partner, 120, 121
  performance analysis, 129
  plan, 117

policy analysis, 138
process analysis, 133
questionnaire, 128
reasons, 112
relevance, 113
reports, 141
results, 141
setting goals, 142
site visit, 128
sources, 120
steps, 115
structure analysis, 139
survey design, 128
types, 118
U.S., 113
benchmarking analysis, 121
benchmarking information
  analysis, 129
  data collection methods, 128
  performance metrics, 122
  policies, 126
  processes, 125
  structures, 126
  type, 122
benchmarking partner
  consent, 121
benchmarking results
  shared understanding, 141
beyond hierarchy, 248
binomial approximation, 387
binomial distribution, 386
Blackbird project, 201
bottom-up process, 196
brainstorming, 40, 101, 206
  categorization phase, 41
  discussion phase, 41
  generation phase, 40
  selection phase, 41
Brassard, 395

BS 5750, 14
Burger King, 8

c chart, 389
case managers, 201
catch ball, 18, 63
cause-and-effect diagram, 101, 395
cause-effect approach, 89
Central Limit Theorem, 386
centralized structure, 201
certification, 27
Chambers, 389
Champy, 195
change factors, 239
change model, 6
chart parameters, 391
Chase Manhattan, 8
Chebychev theorem, 289
Chidamber, 340
classes, 344
Clausing, 166, 226
client-server, 257
client-server technology, 240
cluster sampling, 379
code maintenance, 75
cohesion, 324, 338
    coincidental, 339, 340
    communicational, 339
    functional, 339
    logical, 339, 340
    procedural, 339, 340
    scales, 339
    sequential, 339
    temporal, 339, 340
coincidental cohesion, 340
commitment, 17
    project-based, 17
    vision-based, 17
communication, 18, 62
    defensive, 63
    listening, 63
    one-way, 18
    open process, 63
    supportive, 63
    two-way, 18
communicational cohesion, 339
competitive benchmarking, 119
    difficulties, 119
complex object, 347
complexity
    organization dependent, 348
complexity metrics, 340
    decision complexity, 340
    object response, 340
    response deviation, 340
    system-average response, 340

complexity weights, 348
    industry-based, 348
    organization-based, 348
concurrent design
    parallel design, 206
concurrent engineering, 201
    design for assembly, 204
    design for delivery, 204
    design for maintainability, 204
    design for manufacturing, 204
    design for reliability, 205
    simultaneous process planning,
        203
Concurrent Engineering Research
    Center, 202
connections, 335
    broad, 335, 336
    direct, 335, 337
    indirect, 335, 337
    local, 335, 337
    narrow, 335, 336
    obscure, 335, 337
    obvious, 335, 337
    remote, 335, 337
connectivity, 262
Constantine, 333
consulting services, 274
contact points, 201
content coupling, 333
continuous improvement, 78, 83,
    86, 90, 197
continuous-improvement team, 377
control, 19
    by others, 19
    by self, 19
control-chart parameters, 391
control charts, 6, 374, 381, 382, 387
    assumptions, 388
    c chart, 389
    categories, 389
    centerline, 388
    CUSUM, 393
    double track, 391
    EWMA, 392
    extreme value chart, 390
    lower limit, 388
    m chart, 390
    $m - r$ chart, 390
    $m - s$ chart, 390
    mean chart, 390
    median chart, 390
    modified Shewhart, 393
    MOSUM, 392
    non-Shewhart type, 392
    np chart, 389
    p chart, 389

r chart, 390
    s chart, 390
    Shewhart-type, 388, 389
    u chart, 389
    upper limit, 388
    using, 393
    x chart, 389
    $\bar{x}$ chart, 390
    $\bar{x} - r$ chart, 390
    $\bar{x} - s$ chart, 390
control coupling, 333
control interval, 389
control process, 379
corporate standards, 347
corporate virtual workspace, 241
corporate vision, 285
correctness metrics, 301
    average number, 301
correlation matrix, 331
correlation roof, 173
correlation values, 333
cost, 22
    direct, 22
    disposal, 218
    environmental, 220
    life cycle, 218
    long run, 220
    lost opportunities, 218
    maintenance, 218
    non-conformance, 218
    obsolescence, 219
    ownership, 22
    public, 220
    quality, 22
    replacement, 218
    social, 220
    software obsolescence, 219
    support, 218
    upgrade, 218
    warranty, 218
cost analysis, 348
cost control, 200
cost estimation, 206
cost management metrics, 344
cost of quality, 7
cost reduction, 200
coupling, 335
    content, 333
    control, 333
    data, 333
    hybrid, 333
    stamp, 333
critical path, 402
Crosby, 4, 11, 65
    fourteen steps, 11
    training, 52

cross-functional teams, 66, 303
customer, 39
  direct, 246
  diverse, 254
  evaluators, 248
  external, 39, 246
  focus, 39
  indirect, 246
  internal, 39, 246
  knowledge, 248
  performance evaluation, 248
  performance evaluators, 244
  relative importance, 247
  relative weights, 247
customer-discovered faults, 353
customer-discovered-faults metrics,
  354
customer focus, 241
customer requirements, 77, 166,
  209
  analysis, 77
  relative importance, 168
customer-requirements hierarchy,
  167
customer-requirements utility,
  359
customer satisfaction, 274
customer-value metric, 351
customer voice, 166, 171
customers preferences, 365
CUSUM charts, 393
CVW, 241
cyberspace, 241

dantotsu, 7
Dantzig, 6
DARPA, 201
Daskalantonakis, 290
data, 254, 255
  accuracy, 255
  diversity, 254
  quick access, 256
  spread, 256
data coupling, 333
data flow diagram, 133
  action, 133
  entity, 134
  external entities, 134
  internal entities, 134
  process, 133
  storage, 134
  symbols, 134
data suppliers, 273
  external, 273
  internal, 273
  internal generators, 273

databases
  unstructured, 263
De Marle, 349
decentralized structure, 201
decision analysis
  preference elicitation, 177
  weight assessment, 177
decision-complexity metric, 342
decoupling, 242
DEF STAN 05-21, 14
defects, 290
  average severity metric, 295
  average time interval for fixing
    metric, 296
  category, 292
Delphi method, 165
demand pull, 20
demand push, 259
Deming, 9, 35
  deadly diseases, 9
  14 points, 9, 48
  training, 52
Deming Prize, 13
deployment, 78
design, 23
  concurrent, 23
  concurrent engineering, 203
  factors, 227
  logical, 346
  maintenance, 76
  new system, 77
  object-oriented, 297
  physical, 77, 346
  sequential, 23
  specificity, 212
  team, 206
design defects, 292
design factors, 227
  signal-to-noise ratio, 227
design for assembly, 204
design for delivery, 204
design for engineering analysis,
  205
design for maintainability, 204
design for manufacturing, 204
design for reliability, 205
design maintenance, 76
design metrics, 322
design principles, 323
design prototype, 38
design-quality metrics, 323
design requirements, 209
detection, 24
Devanna, 3, 8, 35
DICE, 201
direct cost, 22

disposal cost, 218
  hardware, 219
distributed systems, 255
diversity, 262
  complexity, 262
  size, 262
  structure, 262
DOE Wisdom, 402
double-track chart, 391
dynamic information systems, 20

eigenvalue method, 181
Electrical Communication Laboratories,
  216
employee development, 52
employee empowerment, 48, 52,
  199
employee involvement, 52
employment pact, 270
empowerment, 48
encapsulation, 227, 335
end-user involvement, 159
enlightened customers, 270
environmental safety, 220
error-checking modules, 205
errors, 21, 290
  average severity metric, 295
  average time interval for fixing
    metric, 296
  detection, 21
  failure, 21
  prevention, 21
European Foundation for Quality
  Management, 14
European Quality Award, 14
evaluation chart, 42
EWMA charts, 392
Executive College, 11
Expert Choice, 181, 403
exponential distribution, 387
extendibility, 322
external contact points, 200, 201
external-meta systems, 252
external view, 338
extreme value chart, 390

facilitating, 55
failures, 290
fanatic quality award, 11
fault management, 344
fault-management metrics, 353
fault metrics
  customer discovered, 354
fault ratio, 88
fault recurrence, 353
fault-recurrence metrics, 354

fault-rework metrics, 354
fault-tolerant modules, 297
fault-tolerant system, 205
faults, 290
feasibility study, 77
Feigenbaum, 3, 11, 62
    ten benchmarks, 11
fire fighting, 24
Fisher, 6
flat organizations, 246
flow charting, 136
focus, 17
Forman, 403
forming, 302
fractional factorial method, 23
Freeman, 249
freezing, 6
Frisch, 6
Fuji-Xerox, 113, 166
function points, 296
functional-based approach, 204
functional benchmarking, 119
    advantages, 119
functional cohesion, 339
functional-requirement modules,
    206
functional uncoupling, 324

games method, 164
GATT, 240
general systems theory, 7
generic benchmarking, 119
geometric mean, 366
global economy, 240
global relative weights, 181, 360
globalization, 240
GM, 8
goal-accomplished ratio metric, 305
GOAL/QPC, 395
goals, 34
Goldratt, 87
grand mean, 383
group AHP, 366
group pairwise comparisons, 183
group preference analysis, 182
group requirements analysis, 182
group vision, 37, 38
groupware, 264

Hammer, 195
Hannan, 249
Hart, 242
Hawthorne effect, 5
Henry, 340
Heskett, 239, 242
hierarchical organization, 243

hierarchy, 65, 66
    flat, 66
    levels, 179
    rating, 178
    upside-down, 65
hierarchy diagram, 102
hierarchy structure, 177
hin shitsu, 166
Hoshin planning, 87
house of quality, 171, 207, 330,
    351
    borders, 210
    components, 171
    interrelationships, 212
    roof, 210
hybrid coupling, 333
hypergeometric distribution, 387

improvement, 75
    information system, 75
    paradigms, 74
improvement ideas, 377
inconsistency measure, 181
inconsistency ratio, 359
independence axiom, 323, 324
inertia, 258
    investment volume, 258
    partial obsolescence, 259
    type of use, 258
information engineering, 22
information-reliability index, 364
information superhighway, 264
information systems, 2
    active, 263
    added value, 242
    breakthrough services, 239
    complexity, 158
    concurrent engineering, 203
    consistency, 299
    continuity, 300
    correctness, 300
    country-specific, 252
    creating flexibility, 250
    creation, 259
    customer focus, 159
    customer-focused, 239
    customer inputs, 243
    customer investment, 243
    customer payments, 243
    customers, 247
    delivery, 239, 259
    design metrics, 322
    development budget, 217
    disadvantages, 242
    efficiency, 298
    external-meta, 252

    flexible, 249
    implementation, 289
    innovative use, 198
    inter-connected, 261
    just-in-time, 259
    life cost, 217
    loss function, 217
    manufacturing, 260
    metrics, 242
    mixed-meta, 251
    object-oriented paradigm, 325
    operation, 289, 297
    passive, 263
    proactive workers, 285
    project costing, 353
    project management, 343
    projects, 343, 349
    providers, 239
    quality metrics, 283
    rapid deployment, 261
    rapid response, 261
    recovery, 274
    recovery plan, 275
    reliability, 357
    requirements analysis, 156
    responsiveness, 286
    robust, 205, 226
    role, 241
    self-monitoring, 205
    services, 243
    social impacts, 220
    suppliers, 272
    timeliness, 298
    uncoupling guidelines, 333
    unstructured, 263
    utility, 357
    value added, 240
    vision, 298, 377
    workers, 246
    zero defect, 289
innovation, 78
input objects, 361
    global relative weights, 361
intelligent components, 200
intelligent systems, 26, 265
internal benchmarking
    advatages, 118
internal-meta systems, 252
International Standard Organization,
    14
Internet, 264
interrelationship digraph, 396
involvement, 18
    general, 18
    special, 18
ISO, 14

ISO 9000, 14
ISO 9001, 14
ISO 9002, 14
ISO 9003, 14
ISO 9004, 14
iterative benchmarking, 140

Japanese Union of Scientists and
    Engineers, 9, 13
JIT, 21
Juran, 4, 10
    seven steps, 10
    training, 52
JUSE, 9, 13
just-in-time, 21, 198, 259, 262
just-in-time system, 196

K-strategy, 249
kaizen, 78
kanban, 21, 260
Kemerer, 340
ki no, 166
KJ Method, 43
knowledge management, 242
knowledge management structure,
    242

L. L. Bean, 118
leadership, 34
    macro, 17
    micro, 17
learning
    joint, 271
    network, 271
    symbiosis, 271
learning organizations, 248, 268
legacy systems, 254, 258
Lewin, 6
Li, 340
local ratings, 359, 360
local relative weights, 181
Lockheed, 201
logical cohesion, 340
logical design, 346
loss function, 6, 220

m chart, 390
$m - r$ chart, 390
$m - s$ chart, 390
main hoshins, 87
maintainability, 322
maintenance, 75
    cost, 83
    customer requirement, 76
    design, 76
    system, 78

maintenance cost, 218
Malcolm Baldrige Award, 13
management by wandering around,
    63
management science, 6
manufacturability, 322
manufacturing-value metric, 351
matrix diagrams, 396, 397
MBWA, 63
McCabe, 296
mean, 382, 383
mean absolute deviation, 384
mean chart, 390
measures, 284, 380
    central tendency, 380
    definition, 284
    dispersion, 380
    variation, 380
median, 382, 383
median chart, 390
member response metric, 303
memory jogger, 395
    software, 403
mental mapping, 43
meta-database, 253, 255
    advantages, 253
    data access, 256
    data accuracy, 255
    data diversity, 254
    data spread, 256
    data volume, 254
    diverse customers, 254
    response to change, 257
meta-database systems, 250, 253,
    254
    internal, 253
    mixed, 253
meta-information systems, 250, 267
    structure, 258
meta-knowledge base systems, 267
meta organization, 20
meta-systems, 252
metric values, 85
metrics, 85, 284
    access time, 298
    age of team, 302
    average complexity, 348
    average severity, 295
    average-team innovation, 309
    characteristics, 284
    complexity, 297
    components, 283
    consistency, 299
    continuity, 300
    correctness, 300
    cost management, 344

customer-discovered faults, 353,
    354
customer value, 351
cyclomatic complexity, 296
decision-complexity, 342
definition, 284, 285
design, 288, 322
efficiency, 298
fault, 292
fault management, 353
fault recurrence, 353, 354
fault rework, 354
fixing defects, 296
function points, 296
goal-accomplished ratio, 305
guiding forces, 285
hybrid, 288
implementation, 288
improvement tools, 288
information systems, 283
life cycle, 288
manufacturing value, 351
member response, 303
member time, 302
number of defects, 294
number of errors, 294
number of failures, 294
number of meetings, 304
number of newly discovered
    errors, 295
number of problems, 307
object-based time, 356
object cohesion, 337
object complexity, 340
object correlation, 326, 331
object independence, 326
object-response complexity, 340
object uncoupling, 326
object value, 352
operation, 289
operations, 288
organizational abuse, 310
organizational aspects, 310
organizational prerequisites, 310
overtime ratio, 306
performance, 301
project management, 282, 343
project time, 356
reliability, 288
requirement achievement, 350
requirement object value, 353
response-deviation complexity,
    341
rework, 353
size, 297, 344
size complexity, 346

metrics (*cont.*)
  software design, 297
  software quality, 296
  software reliability, 296
  system-average response, 341
  system implementation, 290
  system operation, 297
  system performance, 297
  system performance value, 352
  system reliability, 362
  team, 282
  team absenteeism, 303
  team cohesiveness, 301, 302
  team communication, 301, 303
  team effectiveness, 301, 305
  team innovation, 301, 308
  team management, 301
  team output, 301
  team process, 301
  team quality, 306
  team turnover, 303
  time between failures, 294
  time management, 355
  time-per-size complexity, 356
  timeliness, 298
  unit cost, 348
  update, 298
  value management, 349, 350
  weighted-meeting time, 304
  weighted-number of discussions, 305
  weighted problems, 307
  weighted-timely-goals, 306
Meyers, 339
MIL-Q-9858, 14
MIL-Q-9858A, 14
minimum information axiom, 323, 324
mission, 33
mission statement, 84, 138
  information system, 84
mixed-meta information systems, 251
mixed-meta systems, 252
Mizuno, 396
mode, 382, 383
modified Shewhart control charts, 393
modular coding, 75
modules, 332
  fault tolerant, 297
  parallel, 297
MOSUM charts, 392
Motorola, 8, 290, 310
multi-team approach, 206
multitrack process, 199

NAFTA, 240
needs anticipation, 157
needs elicitation, 156
needs validation, 157
needs verification, 157
neural networks, 265
newly discovered errors, 295
  computation, 295
  weighted average, 295
Nielsen, 215
non-conformance, 218
non-modular coding, 75
non-Shewhart control charts, 392
normal approximation, 386, 387
  binomial, 386
  hypergeometric, 387
  Poisson, 387
normal distribution, 386
norming, 302
np chart, 389

object
  system-reliability metric, 364
object abstraction, 337
object accounting, 357
object-based time metrics, 356
object-cohesion metrics, 337
object-correlation metric, 326, 331
object hierarchy, 338, 345
object-hierarchy standard, 345
object-independence metrics, 326
object-oriented approach, 297, 325
object-oriented method, 164, 204
object-oriented programming, 297
object uncoupling, 326
object-uncoupling metric, 326
object-uncoupling metrics, 326
object value, 353
  metrics, 353
object-value metric, 352
objects, 332, 344
  actual system, 346
  coincidental cohesion, 340
  communicational cohesion, 339
  complexity metrics, 340
  detail technical, 346
  functional cohesion, 339
  general technical, 346
  global relative weights, 360
  hierarchy, 345
  logical cohesion, 340
  procedural cohesion, 340
  requirement, 346
  response complexity metrics, 340
  sequential cohesion, 339
  specific technical, 346

temporal cohesion, 340
  value metric, 352
obsolescence, 219, 273
obsolescence cost
  people, 219
  software, 219
open network structure, 204
open systems theory, 7
openness, 322
operational experiment, 164
operations research, 6
optimal design, 228
optimum control, 200
organization culture, 303
organizational culture, 8, 68
organizational improvement, 90
organizational structure, 65
  flexible, 249
organizations
  flat, 246
  hierarchical, 246
  modes, 249
orthogonal arrays, 228
outsourcing, 348
overtime ratio metric, 306
ownership cost, 22

p chart, 389
Page-Jones, 333, 337
pairwise comparisons, 180, 359
pairwise matrix, 359
parallel design, 206
parallel process, 206
Pareto chart, 99, 292, 301, 374
Parsaei, 203
performance dimensions, 352
  consistency, 352
  continuity, 352
  correctness, 352
  efficiency, 352
  timeliness, 352
performance evaluation process, 246
performance evaluators, 244
performance metrics, 301, 357
performing, 302
PERT/CPM, 402
Peters, 242, 248, 249
physical design, 346
physical uncoupling, 324
pilot approach, 164
plan-do-check-act, 95, 287
planning process, 87
plans, 34
platform, 257
  diversity, 257
Poisson distribution, 386

policy deployment, 83
population, 380
population parameters, 381
prevention, 24
pricing mechanism, 244
principles, 34
prioritization matrix, 396
private vision, 37
problem identification tools, 99
procedural cohesion, 340
process, 90, 380
    continuous improvement, 90
    performance evaluation, 246
process decision program charts,
        396, 398
process design, 198
process parameters, 381
process planning
    simultaneous, 203
product liability, 244
product life cycle, 241
project management, 344
    cost metrics, 344
    customer value metric, 351
    metrics, 351
    size metrics, 344
    time-management metrics, 355
project-management metrics, 282
project-management quality metrics,
        343
project-time metric, 356
projects, 343
    cost management, 343
    fault management, 343
    time management, 343
    value management, 343
protocol analysis, 216
prototype
    manual, 164
prototyping, 164
Pruitt, 241

Q1 Standard, 14
Q90, 14
Q91, 14
Q92, 14
Q93, 14
Q94, 14
QFD, 22, 26, 166, 177, 195, 207,
        330, 351, 357, 374
    design, 212
    general structure, 168
    software, 403
    systems planning, 168
quality
    circles, 7, 79

cost, 7
    definition, 3
    education, 56
    perception, 4
    teams, 95
    techniques, 24
    training, 57
quality circles, 7, 79
quality council, 58
quality deployment function, 22
quality design, 223
    reliability, 288
quality education, 56
quality function deployment, 166
quality graphs, 26
quality gurus, 8
quality information systems, 16
    customers, 160
    developer-users, 161
    end-users, 161
    indirect users, 161
quality management, 55
quality metrics, 85
    100 percent observation, 379
    absolute mean deviation, 385
    action oriented, 285
    age of team, 302
    average complexity, 348
    average severity, 295
    average-team innovation, 309
    binary value, 390
    categories, 286
    characteristics, 284
    components, 283
    consistency, 299
    continuity, 300
    continuous, 390
    correctness, 300
    cost management, 344
    counter misuse, 311
    customer-discovered faults, 353,
        354
    customer-process focus, 286, 287
    customer-result focus, 286, 288
    customer value, 351
    data collection, 378
    decision-complexity, 342
    design, 288, 322
    discrete, 390
    economical, 284
    efficiency, 298
    fault management, 353
    fault recurrence, 353, 354
    fault rework, 354
    faults, 292
    fixing errors, 296

goal-accomplished ratio, 305
    goals, 284
    guiding forces, 285
    how much, 406
    how often, 407
    how to use, 405
    hybrid, 288
    implementation, 288, 405
    improvement tools, 288
    life cycle, 288
    manufacturing value, 351
    mean, 383
    median, 383
    member response, 303
    member time, 302
    mode, 383
    nature, 285, 390
    number of defects, 294
    number of errors, 294
    number of failures, 294
    number of meetings, 304
    number of newly discovered, 295
    number of problems, 307
    object-based time, 356
    object cohesion, 337
    object complexity, 340
    object correlation, 326, 331
    object independence, 326
    object-response complexity, 340
    object uncoupling, 326
    object value, 352
    operation, 288, 289
    organization-process focus, 286,
        287
    organization-result focus, 286,
        287
    organizational abuse, 310
    organizational aspects, 310
    organizational prerequisites, 310
    overtime ratio, 306
    performance, 286
    process-based, 311
    project management, 343
    project time, 356
    prototyping, 379
    random fluctuation, 376
    random sampling, 379
    range, 385
    repeatable, 284
    requirement achievement, 350
    response-deviation complexity,
        341
    responsiveness, 286
    rework, 353
    sampling methods, 378, 379
    service, 286

quality metrics (*cont.*)
    simple, 284
    size, 344
    size complexity, 346
    software design, 297
    software reliability, 296
    specific shifts, 376
    system-average response, 341
    system implementation, 290
    system performance, 297
    system performance value, 352
    system reliability, 362
    team absenteeism, 303
    team cohesiveness, 301, 302
    team communication, 301, 303
    team effectiveness, 301, 305
    team innovation, 301, 308
    team management, 301
    team output, 301, 306
    team process, 301
    team turnover, 303
    testing, 379
    time between failures, 294
    time management, 355
    time-per-size complexity, 356
    timeliness, 298
    timely, 285
    trend indicator, 284
    types, 286
    unambiguous, 284
    unit cost, 348
    value, 286
    value management, 349
    weighted-meeting time, 304
    weighted-number of discussions,
        305
    weighted problems, 307
    weighted-timely-goals, 306
    when to use, 405
quality movement, 6
quality process, 380
    standardization, 380
quality teams, 95
quality techniques, 24
quality tools, 395
    activity-network diagrams, 398
    C-shaped matrix, 398
    interrelationship digraph, 396
    L-shaped matrix, 398
    matrix diagrams, 397
    prioritization matrix, 396
    process-decision program charts,
        398
    software products, 402
    T-shaped matrix, 398
    tree matrix, 398

    X-shaped matrix, 398
    Y-shaped matrix, 398
quality-control process, 379
questioning, 39

r chart, 390
r-strategy, 249
random sampling, 379
range, 384, 385
rating
    aggregation, 180
    attributes, 178
    global, 180
    pre-normalized, 210
    relative, 180
recognition, 18
    sporadic, 18
    systematic, 18
recovery, 274
recovery plan, 24, 275
    implementation, 275
recurrent engineering
    cost estimation, 206
redundant modules, 205
reengineering, 78, 80, 195
    centralized structure, 201
    characteristics, 196
    combining jobs, 199
    contact points, 200, 201
    cost reduction, 200
    decentralized structure, 201
    employee empowerment, 199
    intelligent components, 200
    multitrack process, 199
    process, 196
    process design, 198
    process focus, 197
    requirements, 198
    rule-breaking, 198
    sweeping change, 197
    work placement, 200
reengineering process, 196
relative importance, 247
reliability, 21, 76
    testing, 76
reliability index, 364
reliability metric, 85, 131, 205
reliability metrics
    group weighted, 365
    multicriteria, 365
    multiple systems, 365
repertory grids, 165
replacement cost, 218
requirement hierarchy, 167
requirement object-value metric,
    353

requirements
    investment, 257
    relative importance, 351
requirements analysis, 156, 184
    abstract methods, 164
    concrete methods, 163
    Delphi method, 165
    games method, 164
    methods, 163
    needs elicitation, 156
    operational experiment, 164
    pilot approach, 164
    prototyping method, 164
    quality function deployment, 166
    repertory grids method, 165
    simulation method, 164
    software, 183
    survey method, 165
requirements-objects hierarchy, 357,
    366
resolution process, 64
response time, 223
response-deviation complexity
    metric, 341
rework, 353
Robinson, 311
robo software, 265
robust information systems, 205,
    226
Roy, 228

s chart, 390
Saaty, 366
sample, 380
sample mean, 392
sample statistics, 381
sampling methods, 378, 379
Sasser, 239, 242
Schein, 8
scientific management theory, 5
self-monitoring system, 205
Senge, 268
sequential cohesion, 339
service life cycle, 241
service monitoring, 23
Shewhart, 6, 374
Shewhart-Deming cycle, 95, 287,
    310
    act, 98
    check, 97, 98
    do, 97
    plan, 95
Shillito, 349
signal-to-noise ratio, 226, 228
SIM, 357
simple random sampling, 379

simulation, 23
simulation method, 164
simultaneous process planning, 203
six sigmas, 289
size-complexity metric, 346–348, 391
Skunkworks, 202
slack, 402
Smalltalk, 297
Society for Information Management, 357
Socratic method, 90
software metrics, 310
software quality, 285
software reliability, 289, 296
    models, 296
software requirements analysis, 183
SQC, 374, 376
    prerequisites, 377
    probability distributions, 385
    theoretical basis, 380
stamp coupling, 333
standard design, 261
standard deviation, 290, 299, 341, 384
standards, 26, 201
static information systems, 20
statistical quality control, 374, 376
statistics, 6
steering teams, 58
Stevens, 339
storming, 302
strategic planning, 83
strategy, 86
    just-in-time, 260
    K-strategy, 249
    r-strategy, 249
stratified sampling, 379
structures, 19
    flat, 19
    hierarchy, 19
student t distribution, 386
subsystems, 210
suggestions, 99
    handling, 99
    implementing, 99
    seeking, 99
Suh, 206, 323
Sullivan, 203
suppliers, 273
    communication, 273
    data, 272
    hardware, 273
    network, 273
    relationships, 272, 274
    software, 273

supply push, 20, 259
support cost, 218
survey method, 165
system
    architecture, 261
    design team, 207
    distributed, 255
    external-meta, 252
    fault ratio, 86, 88
    human factors, 89
    inertia, 258
    integration, 257
    integrity, 195
    internal-meta, 252
    just-in-time, 260
    legacy, 258
    manufacturability, 204
    mixed-meta, 252
    out of control, 376
    reengineering, 195
    reliability, 86, 98
    usability, 194
    utility, 194
system architecture, 261
system-average response, 341
system construction, 77
system improvement, 82
    active, 82
    ad hoc, 81
    champion-driven, 82
    complaint-driven, 82
    corrective, 82
    data-driven, 82
    dynamic, 82
    functional-based, 82
    passive, 82
    planned, 81
    preventive, 82
    proactive, 82
    quality-based, 82
    static, 82
system integrity, 195
system life cycle, 76, 81
system migration, 322
system performance-value metric, 352
system planning, 207
system quality, 376
    measuring, 376
system reliability, 357
system-reliability metric, 362
system usability, 194
system utility, 194
systems
    objects, 332
systems attributes, 377

systems efficiency
    consistency, 299
systems planning, 168
systems requirements, 172
    competitor comparison, 175
    correlations, 173
    customers, 173
    ratings, 174
    target values, 174

t distribution, 386
tactics, 86
Taguchi, 12, 216
    loss function, 12, 217, 223
    measure of quality, 222
    minimum variation, 217
    orthogonal arrays, 228
    philosophy, 217
    quality design, 223
    robust design, 217
    signal-to-noise ratio, 226
    variability reduction, 223
Taguchi approach, 289
Taguchi methods, 6, 12, 195, 216
    software, 402
Taylor, 5
team-absenteeism metrics, 303
team cohesiveness, 301
    metrics, 301–303
team-cohesiveness metrics, 302
    age of team, 302
    member response, 303
    member time, 302
    team turnover, 303
team communication, 301
team-communication metrics, 301, 303
    number of meetings, 304
    weighted-meeting time, 304
    weighted-number of discussion, 305
team development, 58
    familiarity, 59
    formation, 58
    performance, 60
    power, 60
    synergy, 60
team effectiveness, 301, 305
team-effectiveness metrics, 301, 305
    goal-accomplished ratio, 305
    overtime ratio, 306
    weighted-timely-goals, 306
Team Expert Choice, 404
team innovation, 301
team-innovation metric, 301, 308
team-management metrics, 301

team metrics, 282
team output, 301
team-output metrics, 301, 306
    average-team innovation, 309
    number of problems, 307
    team innovation, 308
    weighted problems, 307
team-turnover metric, 303
teams, 58, 95, 246, 247
    cross functional, 95, 246–247
    facilitator, 58
    forming, 58
    norming, 58
    performing, 58
    storming, 58
teamwork, 18, 58, 65
    broad-based, 18
    project-based, 18
technical requirements, 207
technology, 240, 241, 258
    change, 258
    client-server, 240
    direction of change, 241
telecommunication, 26
    range, 26
    reach, 26
temporal cohesion, 340
ten kai, 166
Texas Instruments, 241
theory of constraints, 87
    evaporating clouds solution, 89
    steps, 87
throughput, 90
Tichy, 3, 8, 35
time management, 344
time-management metrics, 355
time-per-size complexity metric, 356
Tinbergen, 6
top-down policy, 196
total quality management, 3
traditional information systems, 16
training, 52
    continuous commitment, 55
    custom-made, 56
    evaluation, 57
    functional, 55
    general, 56
    on-the-job, 56
    participants, 54

plan, 57
professional, 56
quality, 55
trainer, 56
U.S. companies, 55
transformational leaders, 8
transparent access, 253
tree diagram, 102
tree matrix, 398
trial and error, 23
Type I error, 382, 388, 391
Type II error, 382

u chart, 389
uncoupled design, 327
uncoupling, 338
    functional, 324
    guidelines, 333
    physical, 324
uncoupling guidelines, 333
unfreezing, 6
unit-cost metric, 348
update interval, 34
upgrade cost, 218
usability
    assessment, 215
    assessment methods, 216
    criteria, 214
    heuristics, 215
    testing, 216
usability assessment
    group analysis, 216
    interview, 216
    logging use, 216
    observation method, 216
    protocol analysis, 216
usability engineering, 195, 212
use-as-is, 23
user interface, 214
    batch, 214
    line-based, 214
    technology, 214
user prototype, 38
user requirements analysis, 22, 38
utility values, 359

value
    causality attribute, 349
    energy-conversion attribute, 349

invisibility attribute, 349
    magnitude attribute, 349
value analysis, 350
value energy conservation, 350
value management, 344, 350
value-management metrics, 349
value metrics, 351, 352
values, 34
virtual organization, 20
vision, 32
    corporate, 285
    creating, 38
    definition, 32
    group, 37, 38
    long-term, 22
    private, 37
    statement, 36
    working, 38
vision statement, 36, 39, 83, 138, 184
    example, 37
    information system, 83
voice of customer, 171

warranty cost, 218
weighted-meeting-time metric, 304
weighted-number of discussions metric, 305
weighted-problem/solution metric, 307
weighted-timely-goals metric, 306
Wheeler, 389
wide-area networks, 240
work placement, 200
working vision, 38

x chart, 389
$\bar{x}$ chart, 390
$\bar{x} - r$ chart, 390
$\bar{x} - s$ chart, 390
Xerox, 9, 113

Yourdon, 333

zero defect, 289, 300
    goals, 300
    moving toward, 290
    six sigmas, 289
zero error, 21